cha Gacha™

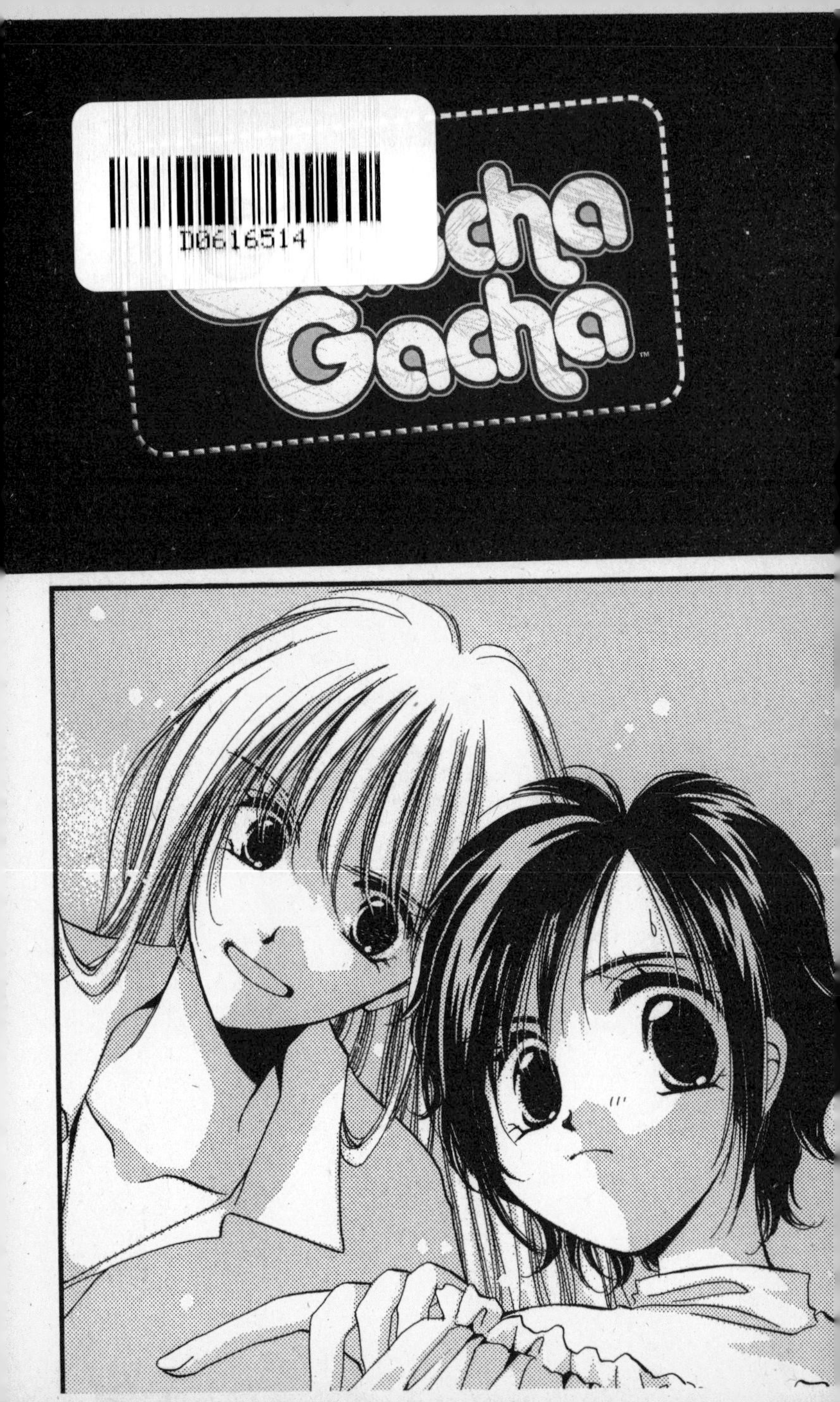

Gatcha Gacha Volume 2
Created by Yutaka Tachibana

Translation - Adrienne Beck
English Adaptation - Jamie S. Rich
Retouch and Lettering - Mike Graniel
Production Artist - Jihye "Sophia" Hong
Cover Design - James Lee

Editor - Rob Valois
Digital Imaging Manager - Chris Buford
Production Manager - Elisabeth Brizzi
Managing Editor - Lindsey Johnston
Editor-in-Chief - Rob Tokar
VP of Production - Ron Klamert
Publisher - Mike Kiley
President and C.O.O. - John Parker
C.E.O. and Chief Creative Officer - Stuart Levy

A **TOKYOPOP** Manga

TOKYOPOP Inc.
5900 Wilshire Blvd. Suite 2000
Los Angeles, CA 90036

E-mail: info@TOKYOPOP.com
Come visit us online at www.TOKYOPOP.com

ISBN: 1-59816-154-7

First TOKYOPOP printing: July 2006
10 9 8 7 6 5 4 3 2 1
Printed in U.S.A

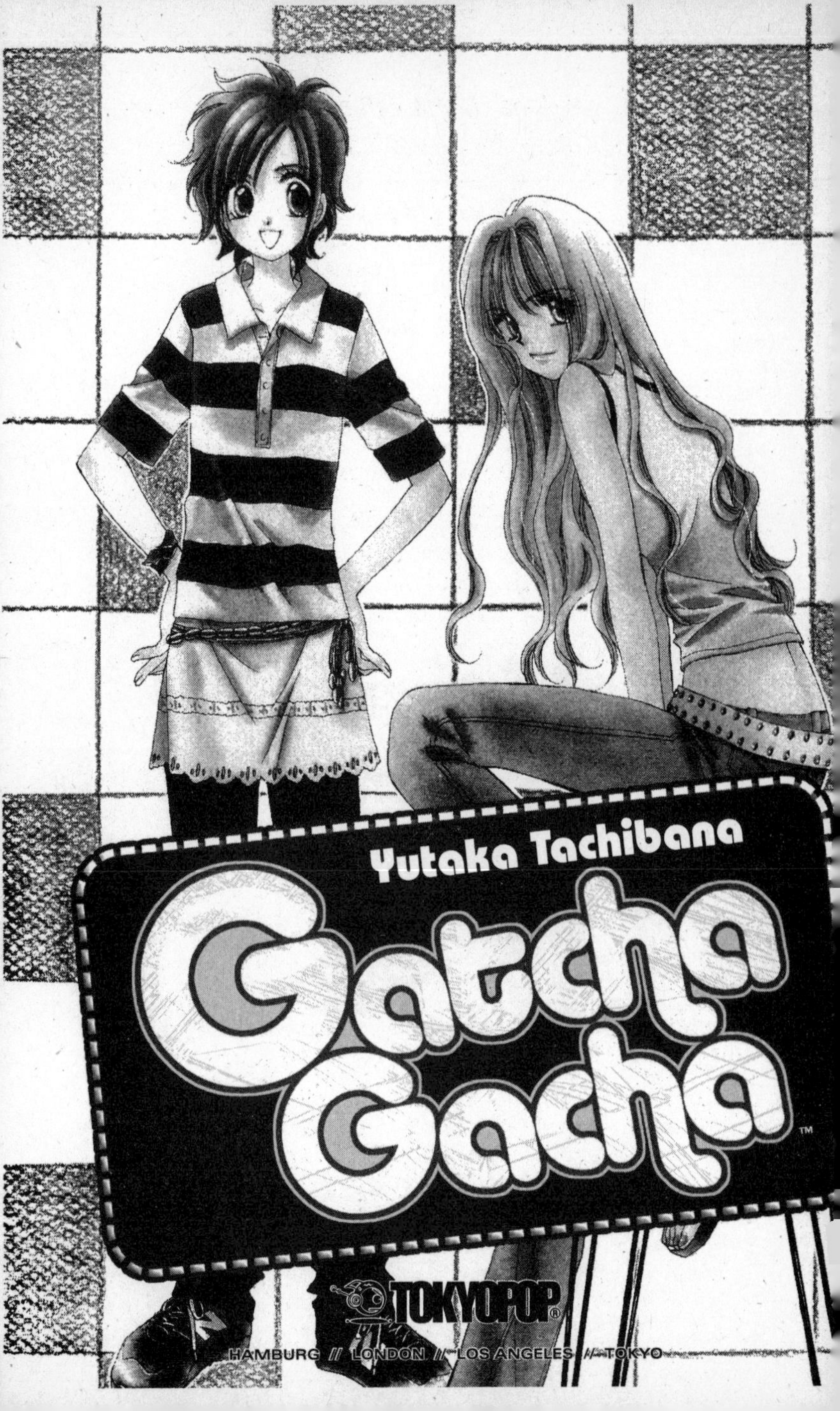
Yutaka Tachibana
Gatcha Gacha™
TOKYOPOP®
HAMBURG // LONDON // LOS ANGELES // TOKYO

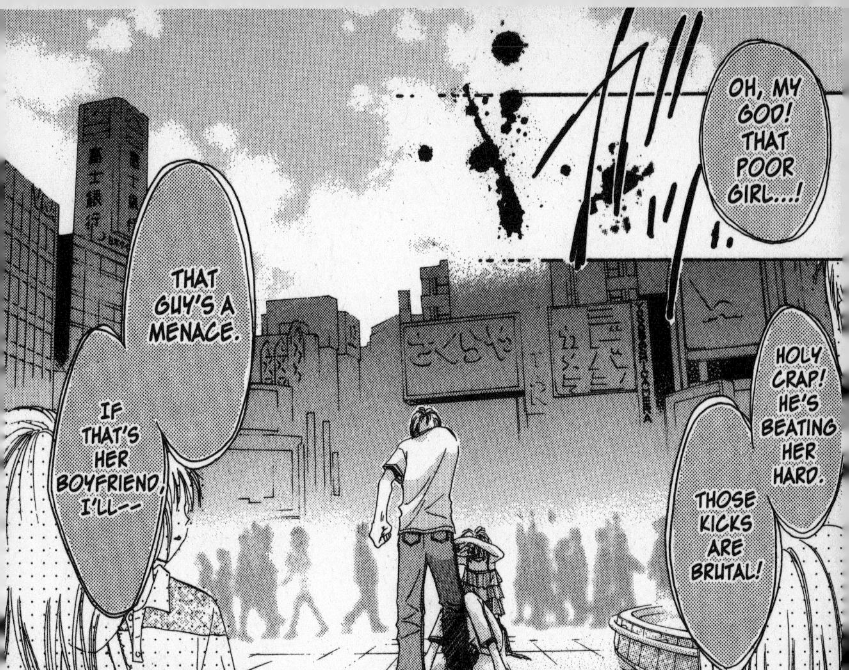
OH, MY GOD! THAT POOR GIRL...!
HOLY CRAP! HE'S BEATING HER HARD.
THOSE KICKS ARE BRUTAL!
THAT GUY'S A MENACE.
IF THAT'S HER BOYFRIEND, I'LL--
THE WER ARGU AND T ALL C SUDD HE--
OW!
KENJI! STOP IT!
Aah!
SHUT UP! THIS IS YOUR FAULT!
THAT DUDE TOTALLY FREAKED OUT ON HER.

This time, instead of a specific movie recommendation, I'm just going to recommend movies in general. There are all sorts of them out there, in theaters and on TV and stuff. You should go watch some. I don't have as much time to watch them as I used to. It's sad.

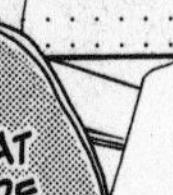

The best actor to dub Ed Harris into Japanese has to be Masane Tsukayama. His voice is so wonderful, it makes me melt!

So I've got some weird hobbies. I don't care.

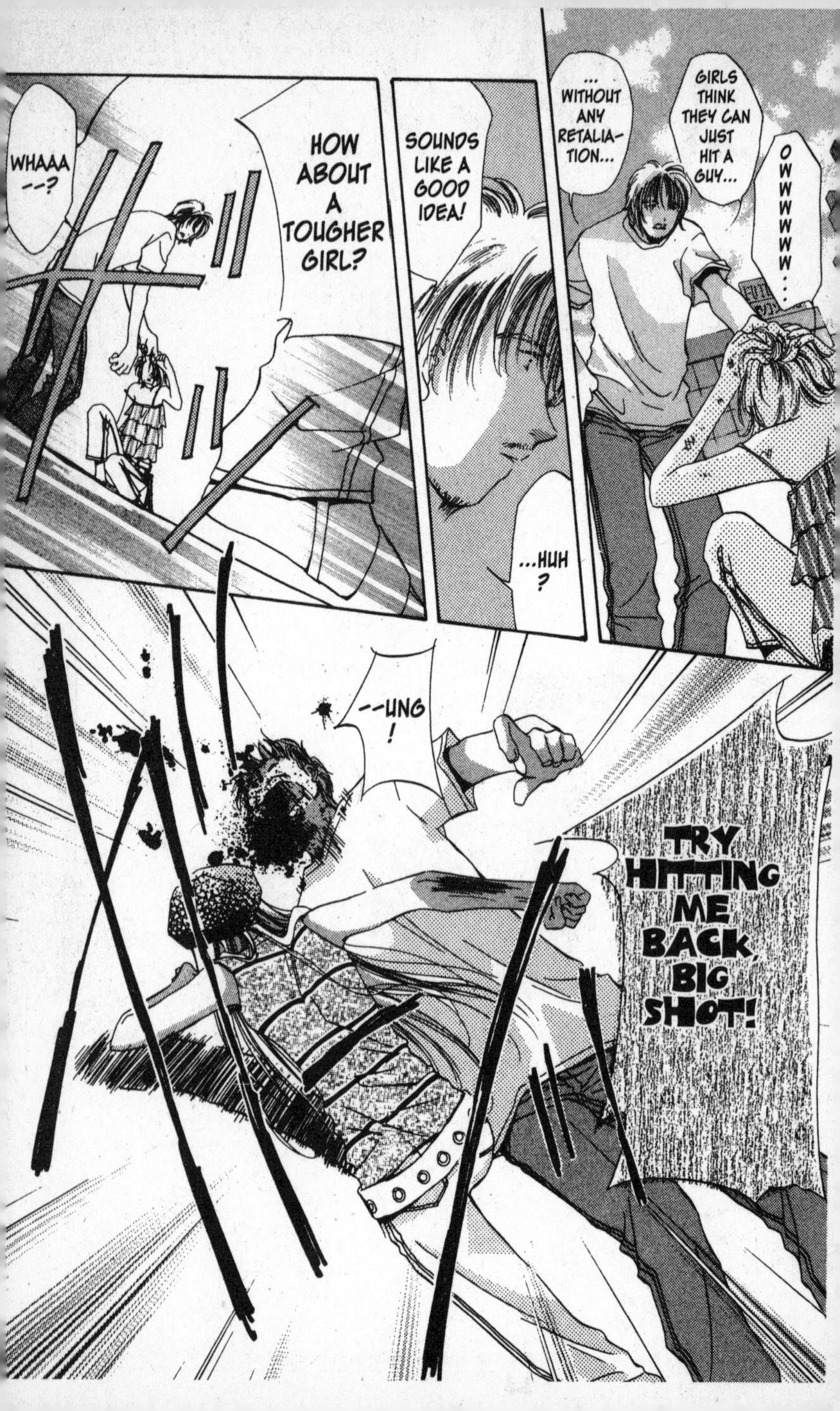
OWWWWWWW...
GIRLS THINK THEY CAN JUST HIT A GUY...
...WITHOUT ANY RETALIATION...
SOUNDS LIKE A GOOD IDEA!
...HUH?
HOW ABOUT A TOUGHER GIRL?
WHAAA--?
TRY HITTING ME BACK BIG SHOT!
--UNG!

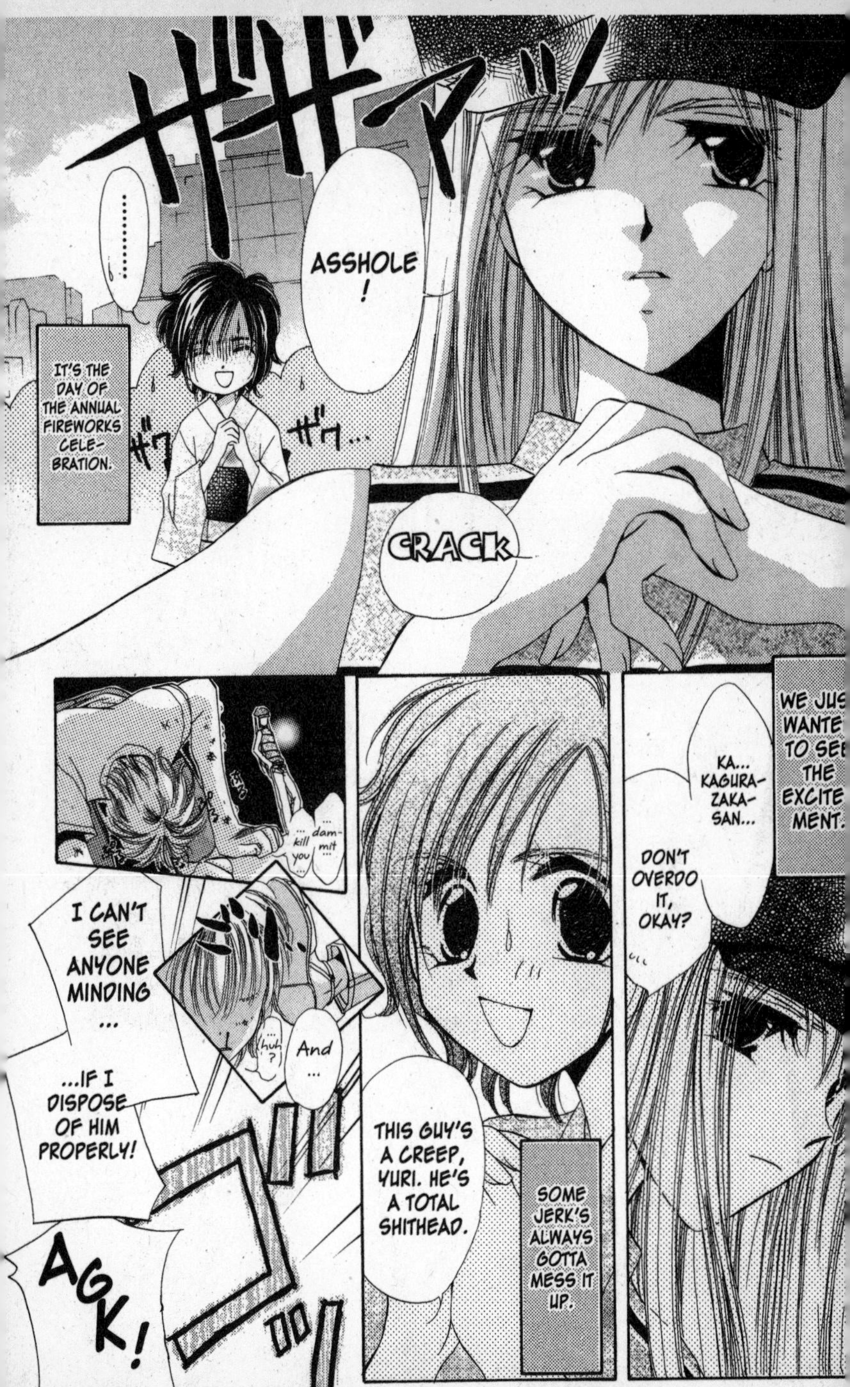

ザザァッ!
ASSHOLE!
......?
IT'S THE DAY OF THE ANNUAL FIREWORKS CELEBRATION.
ザワ ザワ...
CRACK
WE JUS WANTE TO SEE THE EXCITE MENT.
KA... KAGURA-ZAKA-SAN...
DON'T OVERDO IT, OKAY?
SOME JERK'S ALWAYS GOTTA MESS IT UP.
THIS GUY'S A CREEP, YURI. HE'S A TOTAL SHITHEAD.
...dam-mit...
...kill you...
I CAN'T SEE ANYONE MINDING...
...huh?
And...
...IF I DISPOSE OF HIM PROPERLY!
AGK!

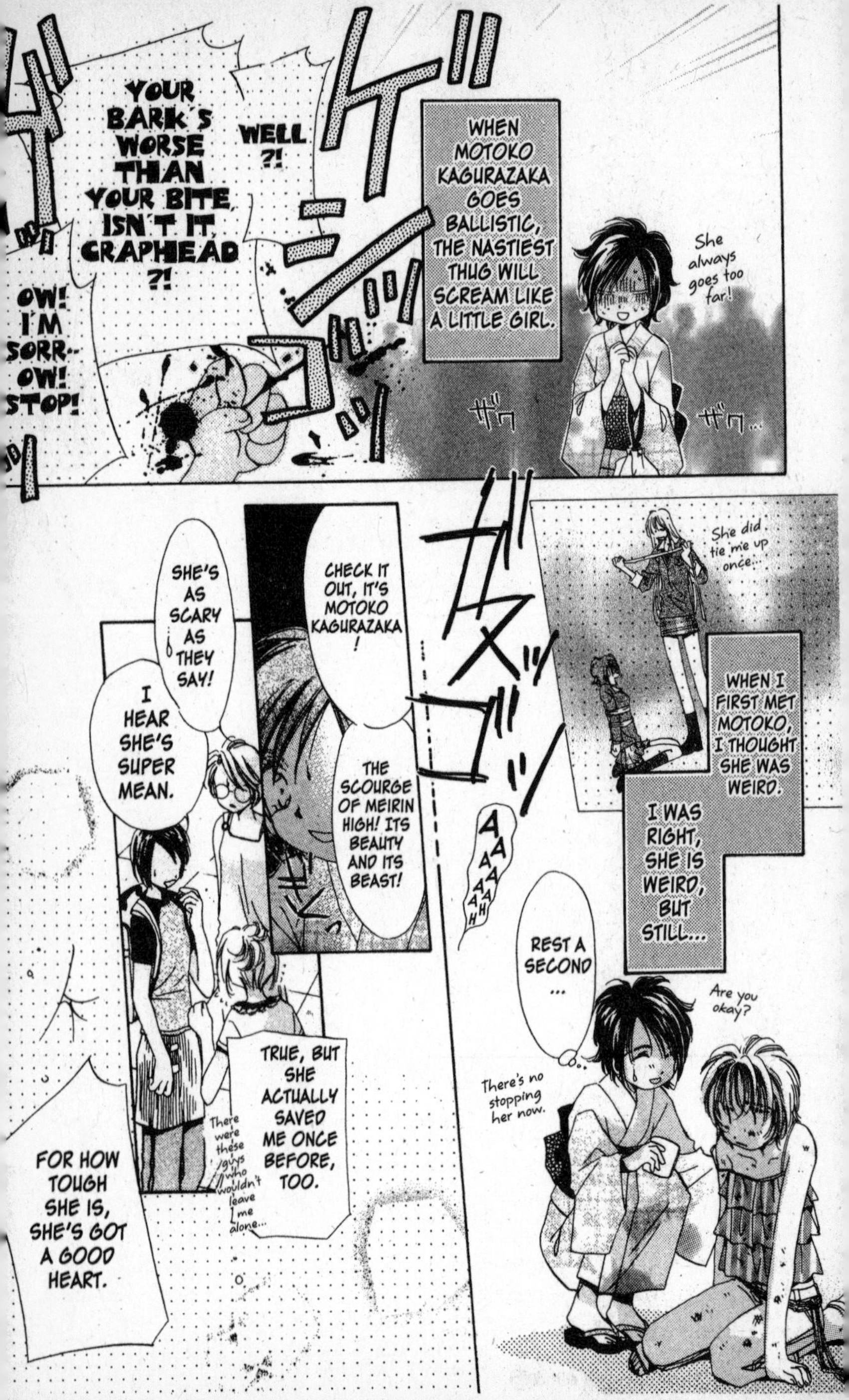
WHEN MOTOKO KAGURAZAKA GOES BALLISTIC, THE NASTIEST THUG WILL SCREAM LIKE A LITTLE GIRL.
She always goes too far!
ザク ザク...
WELL ?!
YOUR BARK'S WORSE THAN YOUR BITE ISN'T IT, CRAPHEAD ?!
OW! I'M SORR-OW! STOP!
She did tie me up once...
WHEN I FIRST MET MOTOKO, I THOUGHT SHE WAS WEIRD.
I WAS RIGHT, SHE IS WEIRD, BUT STILL...
AAAAAAH
REST A SECOND...
Are you okay?
There's no stopping her now.
CHECK IT OUT, IT'S MOTOKO KAGURAZAKA!
THE SCOURGE OF MEIRIN HIGH! ITS BEAUTY AND ITS BEAST!
SHE'S AS SCARY AS THEY SAY!
I HEAR SHE'S SUPER MEAN.
TRUE, BUT SHE ACTUALLY SAVED ME ONCE BEFORE, TOO.
There were these guys who wouldn't leave me alone...
FOR HOW TOUGH SHE IS, SHE'S GOT A GOOD HEART.

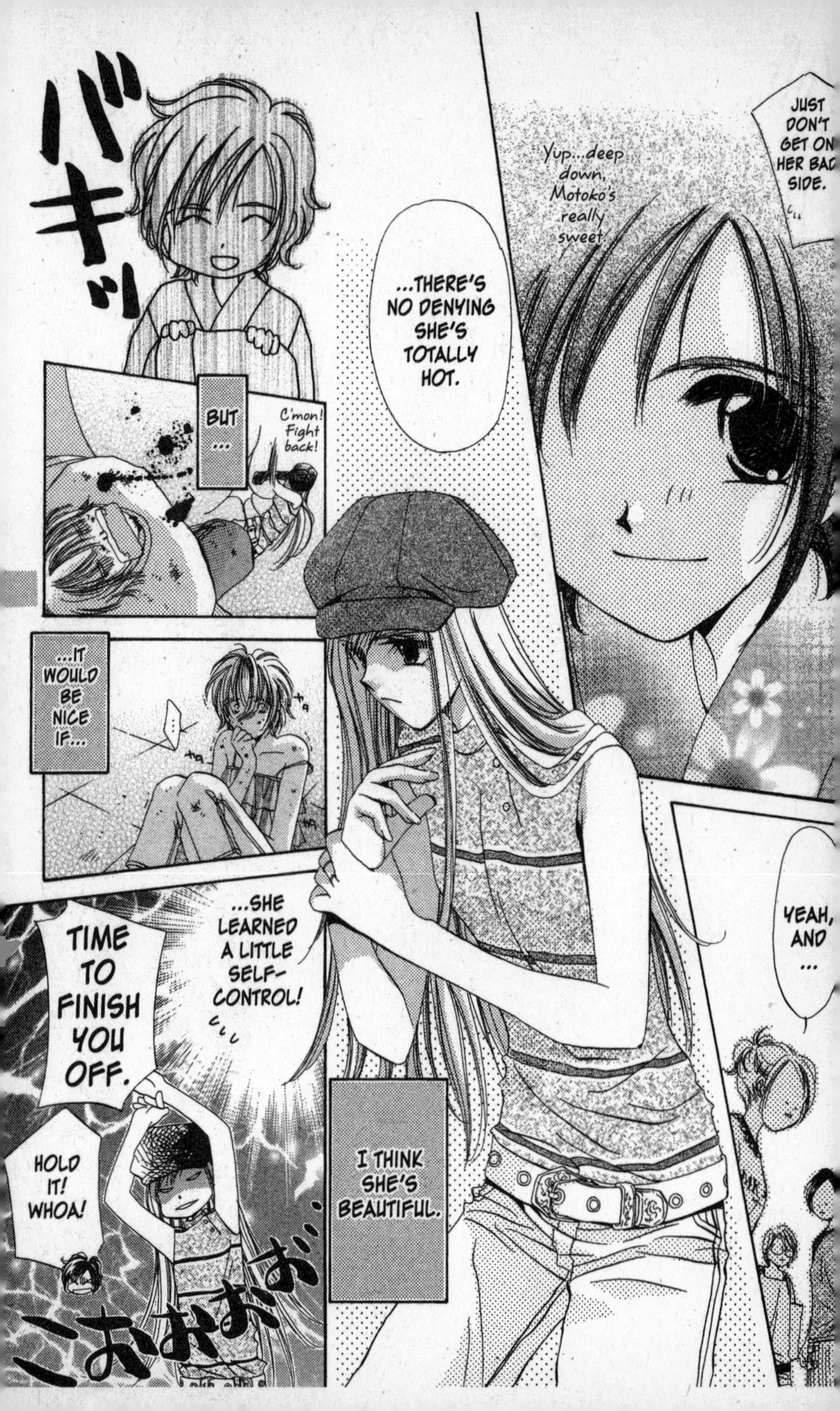
JUST DON'T GET ON HER BA SIDE.
Yup...deep down, Motoko's really sweet.
...THERE'S NO DENYING SHE'S TOTALLY HOT.
バキッ
BUT ...
C'mon! Fight back!
...IT WOULD BE NICE IF...
...SHE LEARNED A LITTLE SELF-CONTROL!
TIME TO FINISH YOU OFF.
HOLD IT! WHOA!
こおおお
YEAH, AND ...
I THINK SHE'S BEAUTIFUL.

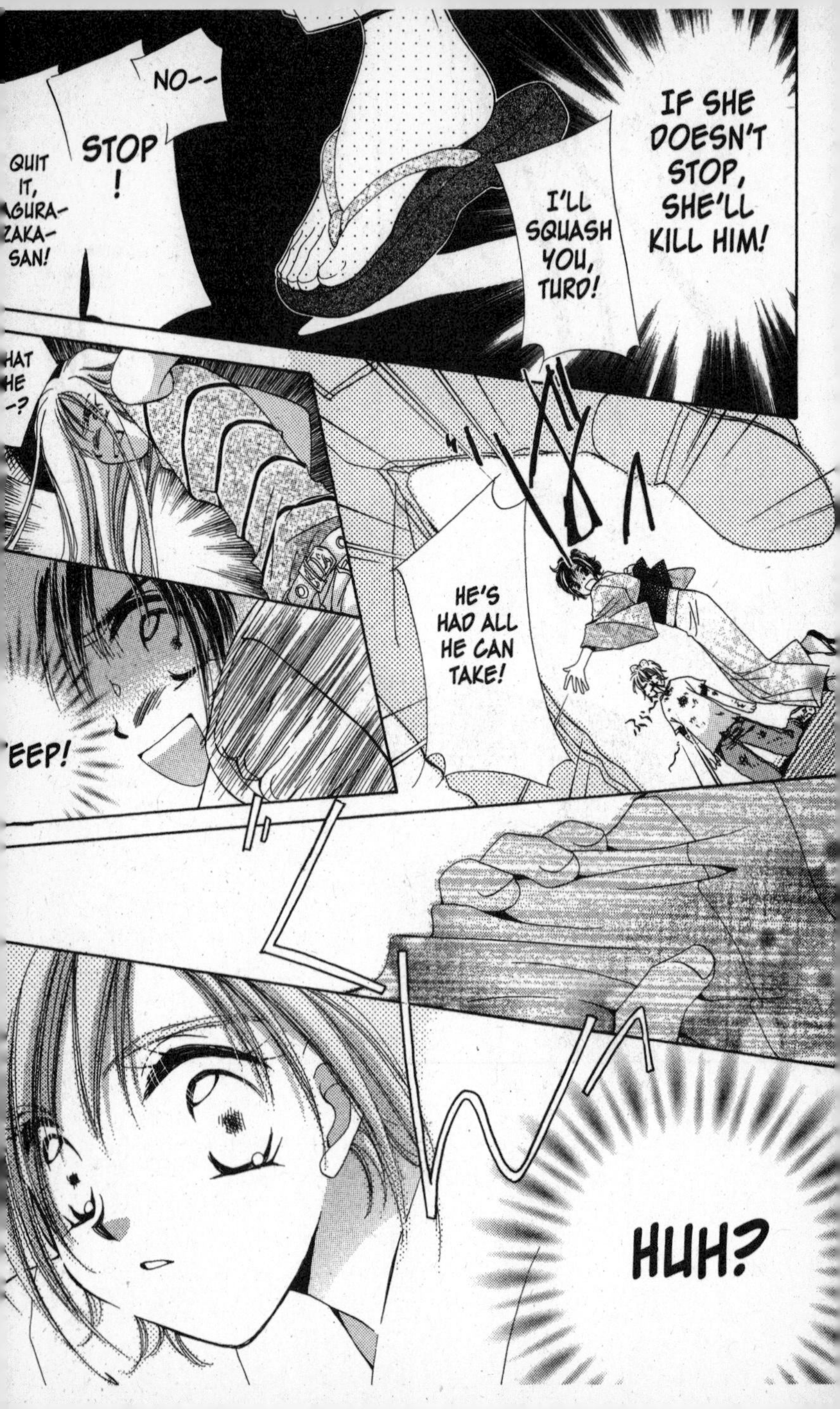
IF SHE DOESN'T STOP, SHE'LL KILL HIM!
I'LL SQUASH YOU, TURD!
NO--
STOP!
QUIT IT, AGURA-ZAKA-SAN!
HE'S HAD ALL HE CAN TAKE!
HAT HE --?
EEP!
HUH?

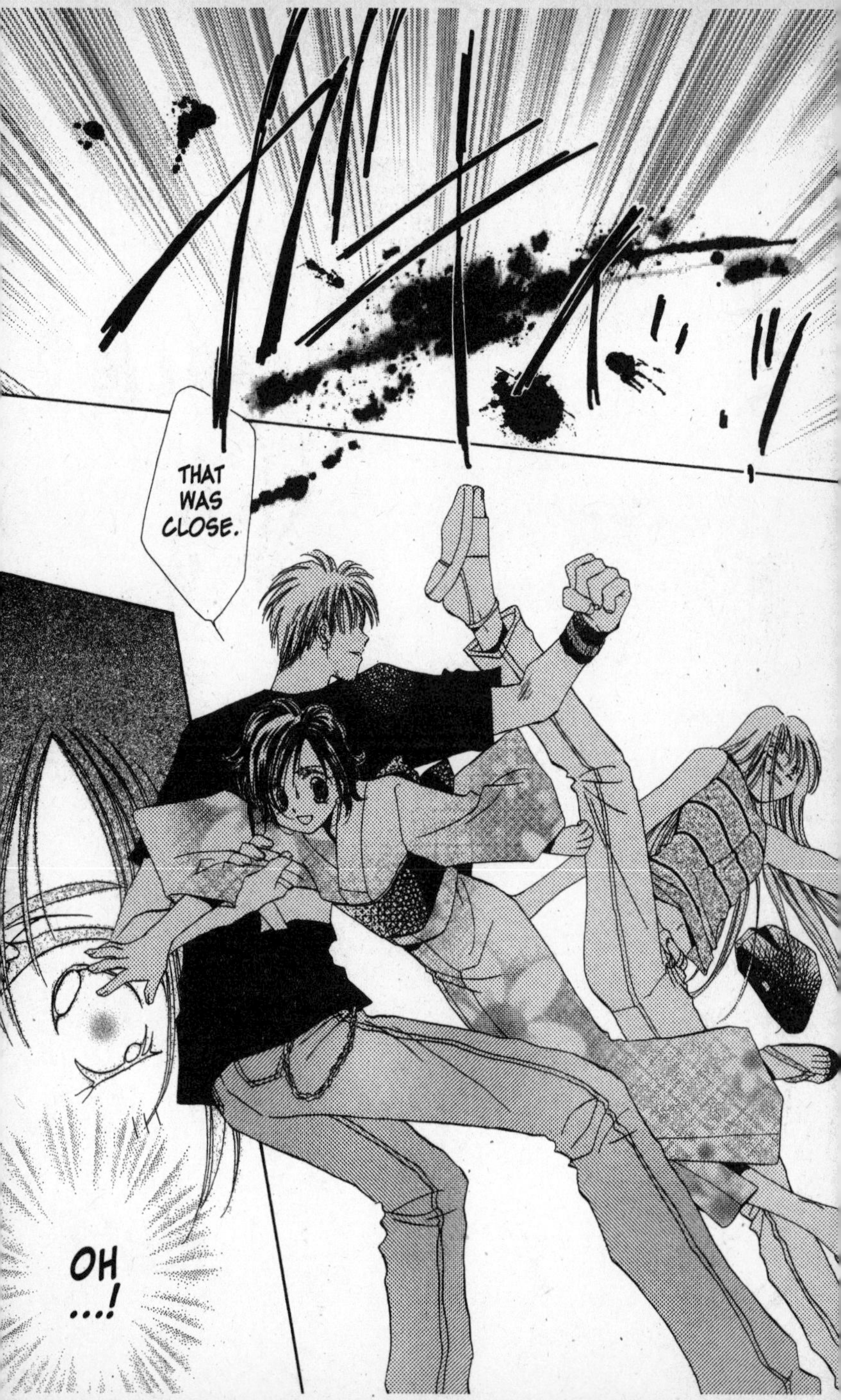
THAT WAS CLOSE.
OH ...!

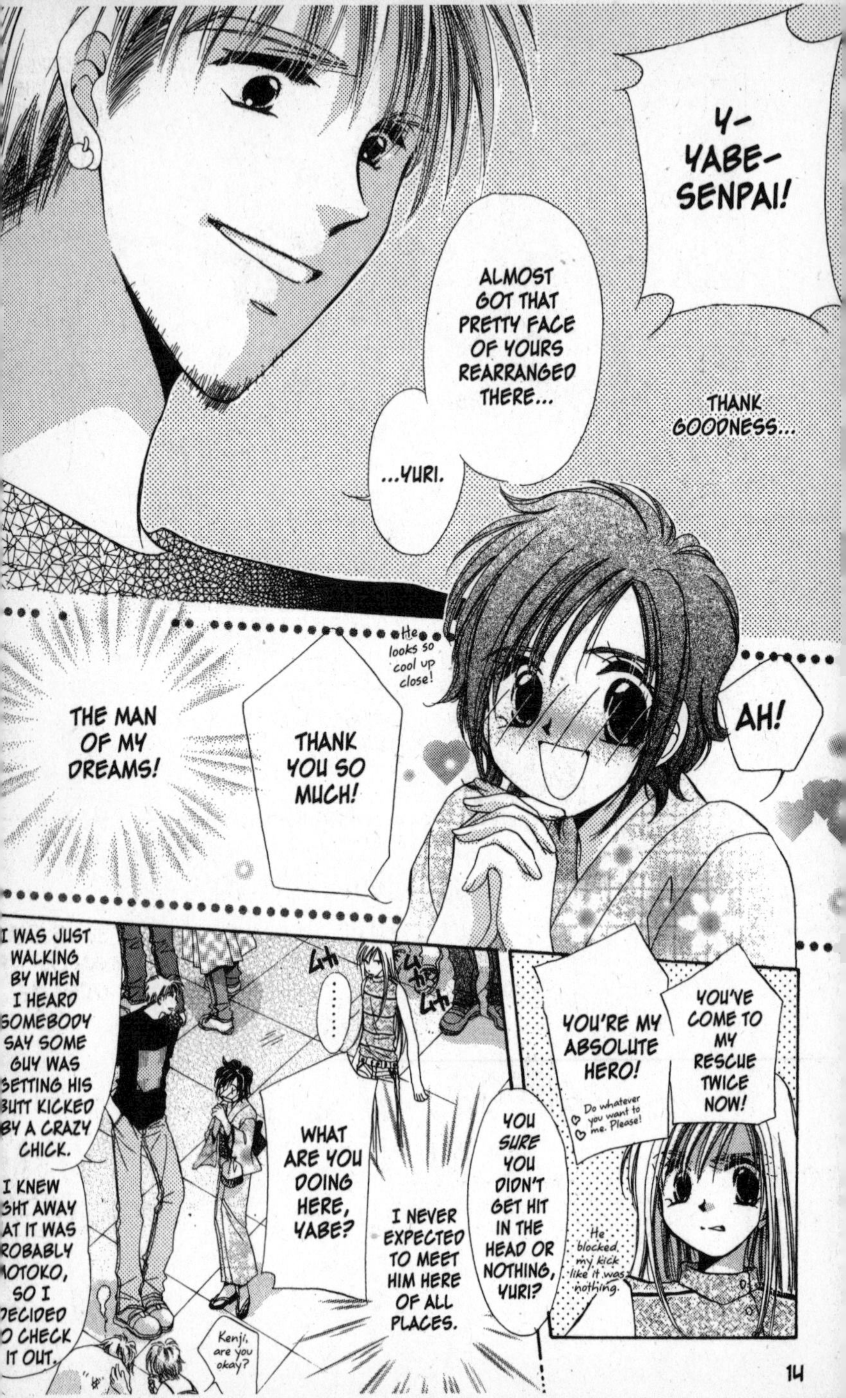

Y-YABE-SENPAI!
ALMOST GOT THAT PRETTY FACE OF YOURS REARRANGED THERE...
...YURI.
THANK GOODNESS...
AH!
He looks so cool up close!
THANK YOU SO MUCH!
THE MAN OF MY DREAMS!
YOU'VE COME TO MY RESCUE TWICE NOW!
YOU'RE MY ABSOLUTE HERO!
Do whatever you want to me. Please!
He blocked my kick like it was nothing.
YOU SURE YOU DIDN'T GET HIT IN THE HEAD OR NOTHING, YURI?
I NEVER EXPECTED TO MEET HIM HERE OF ALL PLACES.
WHAT ARE YOU DOING HERE, YABE?
......
I WAS JUST WALKING BY WHEN I HEARD OMEBODY SAY SOME GUY WAS ETTING HIS UTT KICKED Y A CRAZY CHICK.
I KNEW GHT AWAY AT IT WAS ROBABLY OTOKO, SO I ECIDED O CHECK IT OUT.
Kenji, are you okay?

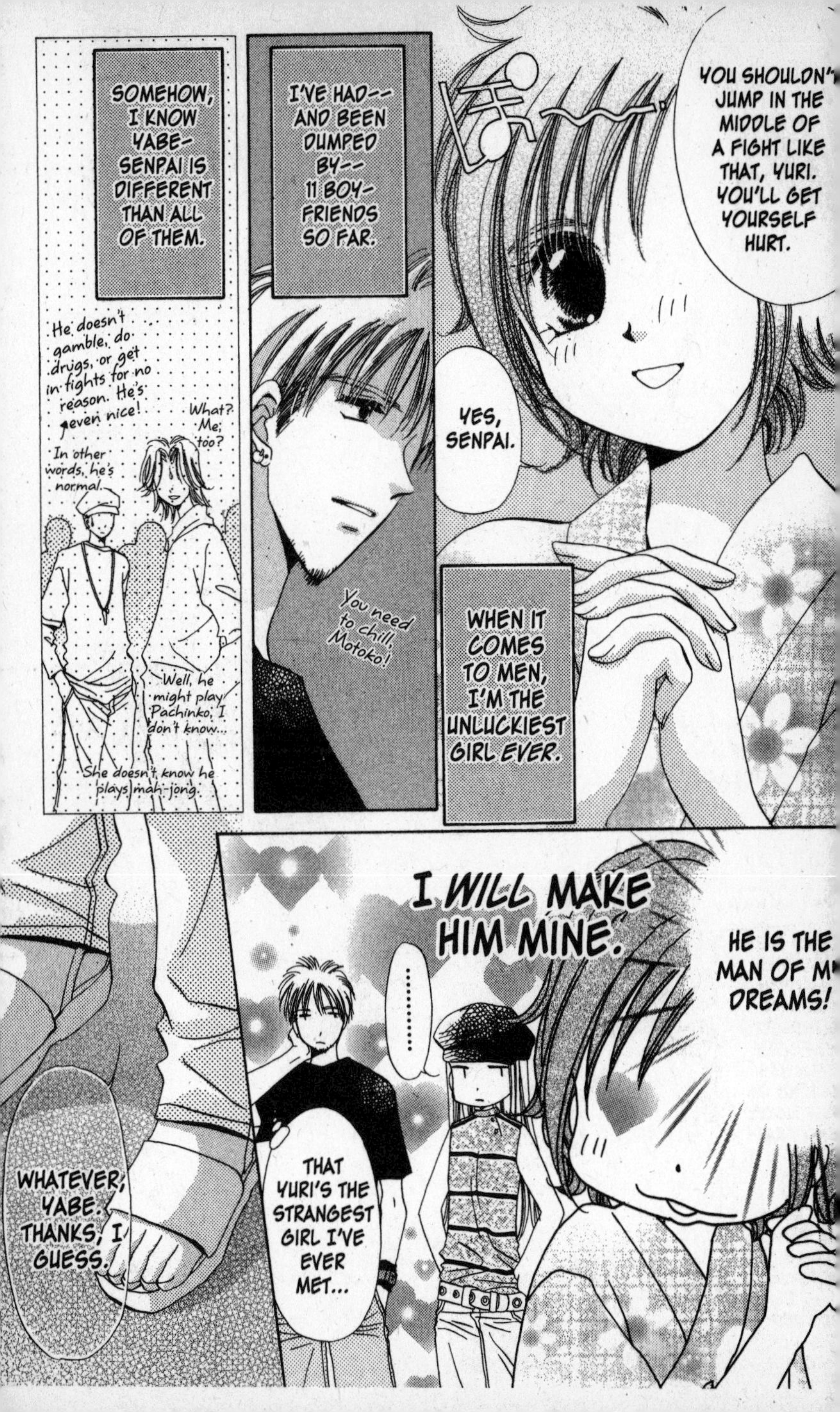
YOU SHOULDN'T JUMP IN THE MIDDLE OF A FIGHT LIKE THAT, YURI. YOU'LL GET YOURSELF HURT.
YES, SENPAI.
WHEN IT COMES TO MEN, I'M THE UNLUCKIEST GIRL EVER.
I'VE HAD-- AND BEEN DUMPED BY-- 11 BOY-FRIENDS SO FAR.
You need to chill, Motoko!
SOMEHOW, I KNOW YABE-SENPAI IS DIFFERENT THAN ALL OF THEM.
He doesn't gamble, do drugs, or get in fights for no reason. He's even nice!
What? Me, too?
In other words, he's normal.
Well, he might play Pachinko, I don't know...
She doesn't know he plays mah-jong.
HE IS THE MAN OF M DREAMS!
I WILL MAKE HIM MINE.
......
THAT YURI'S THE STRANGEST GIRL I'VE EVER MET...
WHATEVER, YABE. THANKS, I GUESS.

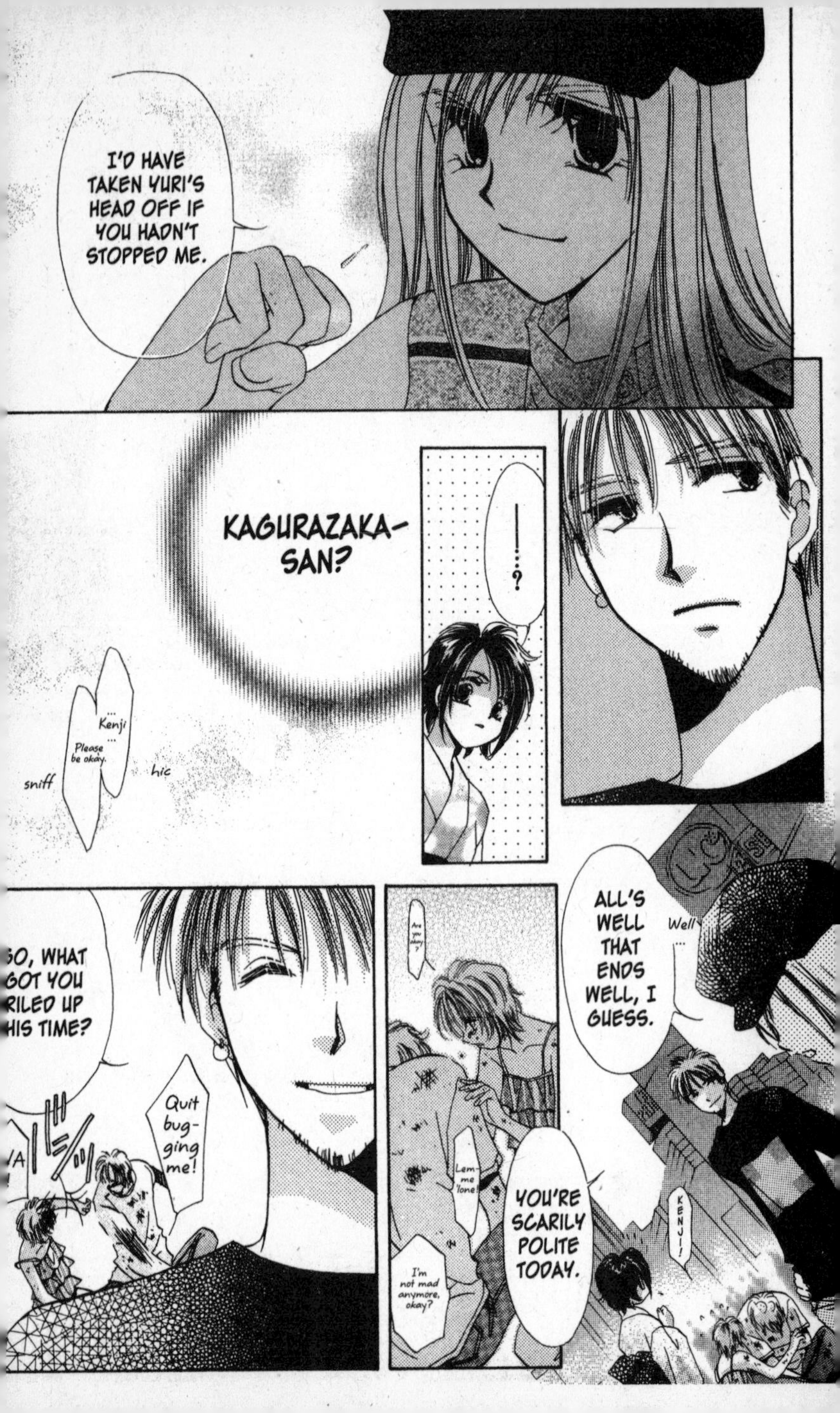
I'D HAVE TAKEN YURI'S HEAD OFF IF YOU HADN'T STOPPED ME.
—...?
KAGURAZAKA-SAN?
...Kenji...
Please be okay.
hic
sniff
Well...
ALL'S WELL THAT ENDS WELL, I GUESS.
KENJI!
Are you okay?
YOU'RE SCARILY POLITE TODAY.
Lem-me 'lone!
I'm not mad anymore, okay?
SO, WHAT GOT YOU RILED UP THIS TIME?
Quit bug-ging me!

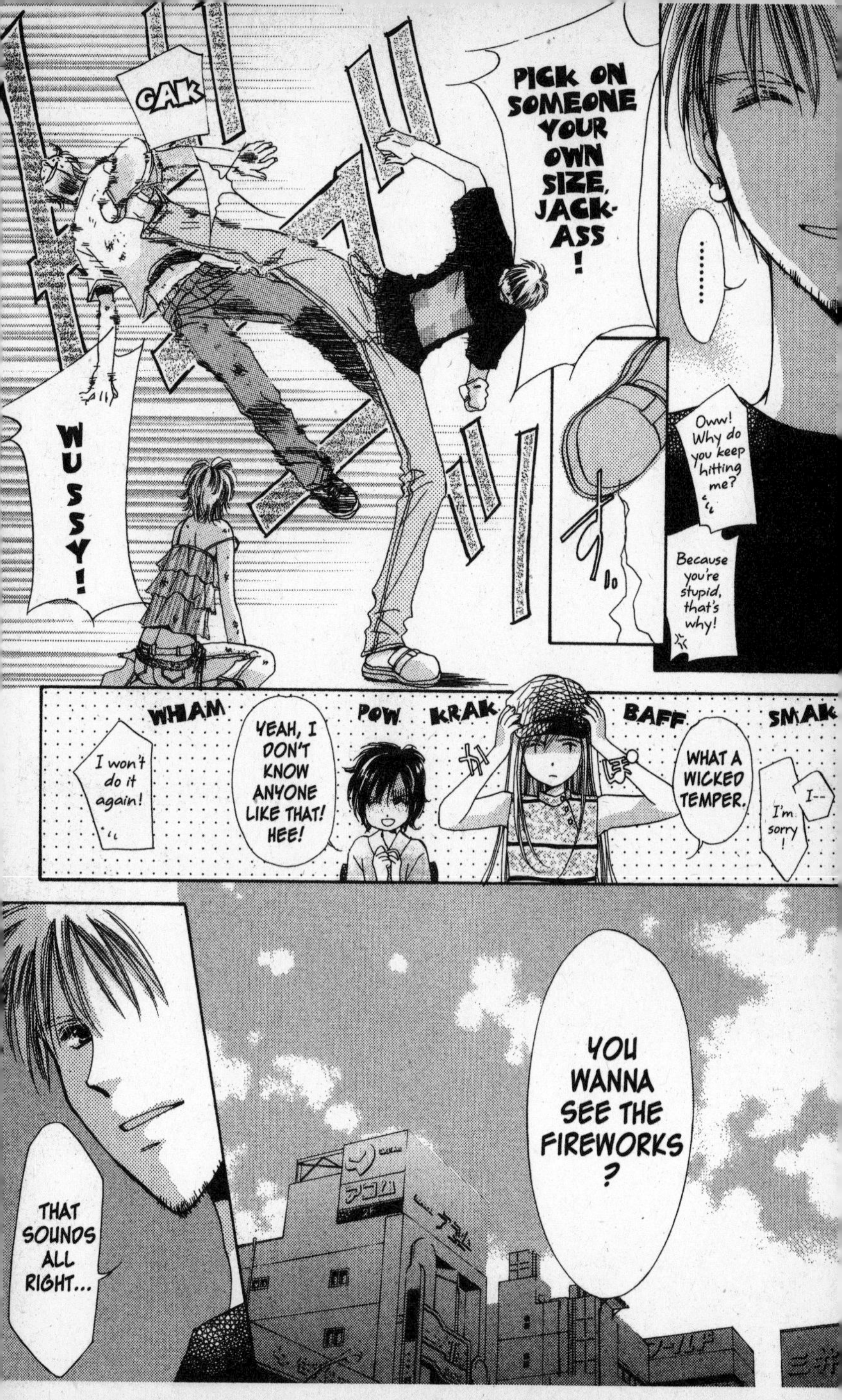

......
Oww! Why do you keep hitting me?
Because you're stupid, that's why!
PICK ON SOMEONE YOUR OWN SIZE, JACK-ASS!
GAK
WUSSY!!
SMAK
I-- I'm sorry!
WHAT A WICKED TEMPER.
BAFF
KRAK
POW
YEAH, I DON'T KNOW ANYONE LIKE THAT! HEE!
WHAM
I won't do it again!
YOU WANNA SEE THE FIREWORKS?
THAT SOUNDS ALL RIGHT...

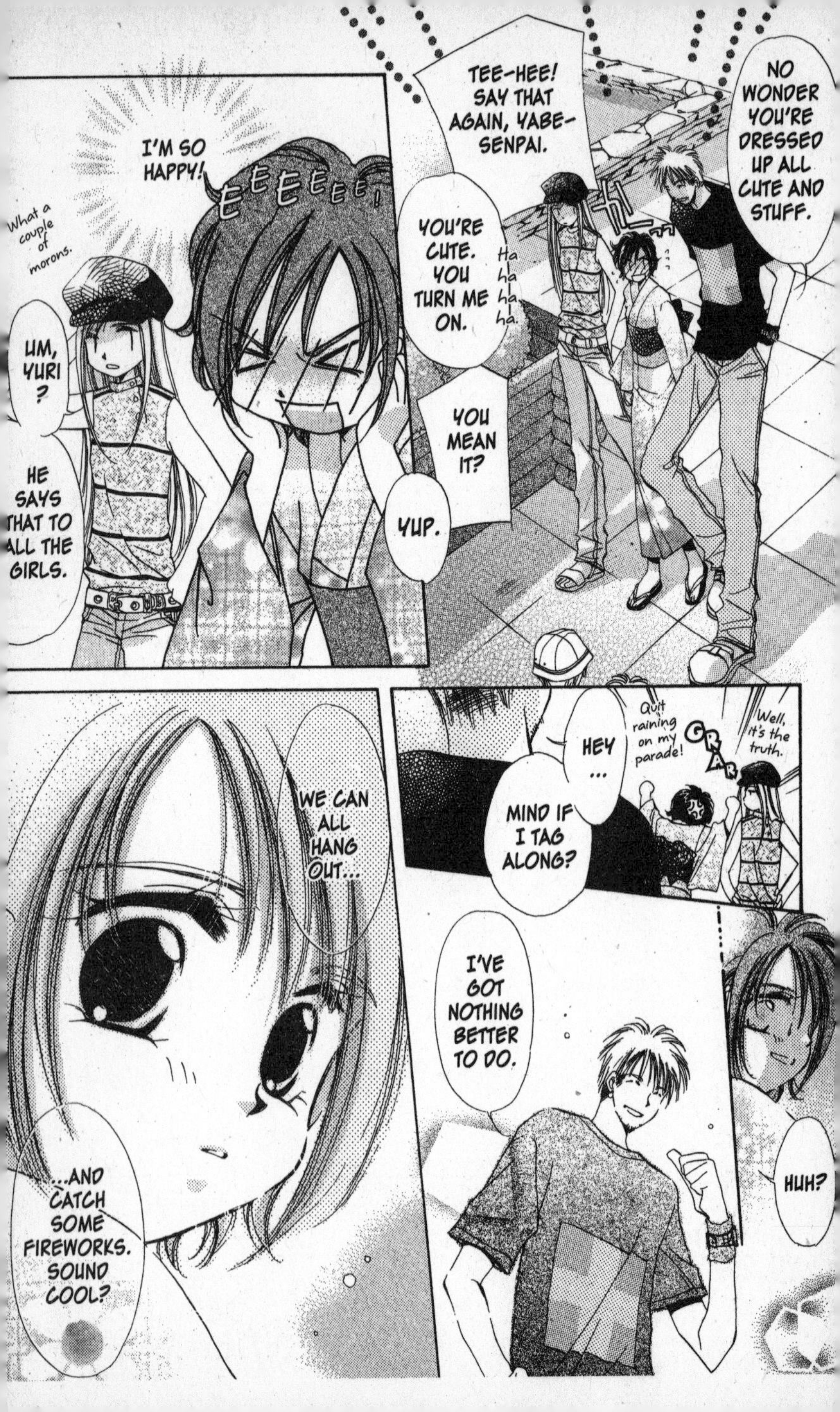
NO WONDER YOU'RE DRESSED UP ALL CUTE AND STUFF.
TEE-HEE! SAY THAT AGAIN, YABE-SENPAI.
YOU'RE CUTE. YOU TURN ME ON.
Ha ha ha ha.
YOU MEAN IT?
YUP.
I'M SO HAPPY!
What a couple of morons.
UM, YURI?
HE SAYS THAT TO ALL THE GIRLS.
Well, it's the truth.
GRAR
Quit raining on my parade!
HEY ...
MIND IF I TAG ALONG?
HUH?
I'VE GOT NOTHING BETTER TO DO.
WE CAN ALL HANG OUT...
...AND CATCH SOME FIREWORKS. SOUND COOL?

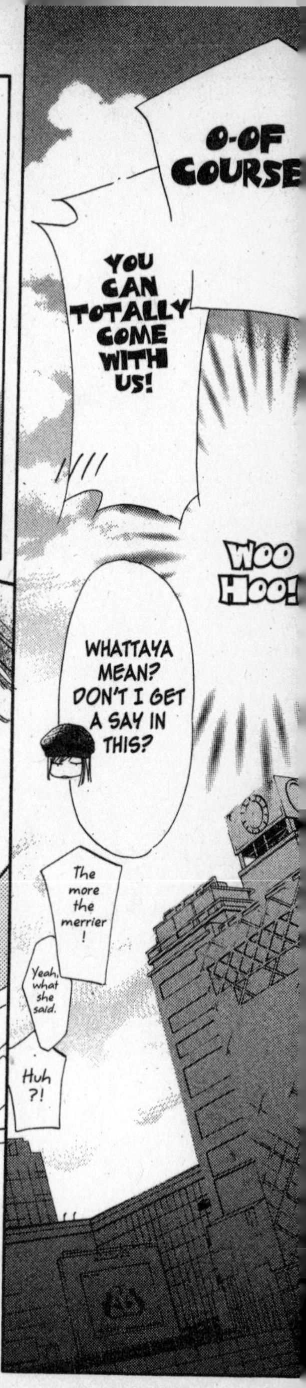
O-OF COURSE
YOU CAN TOTALLY COME WITH US!
WOO HOO!
WHATTAYA MEAN? DON'T I GET A SAY IN THIS?
The more the merrier!
Yeah, what she said.
Huh?!

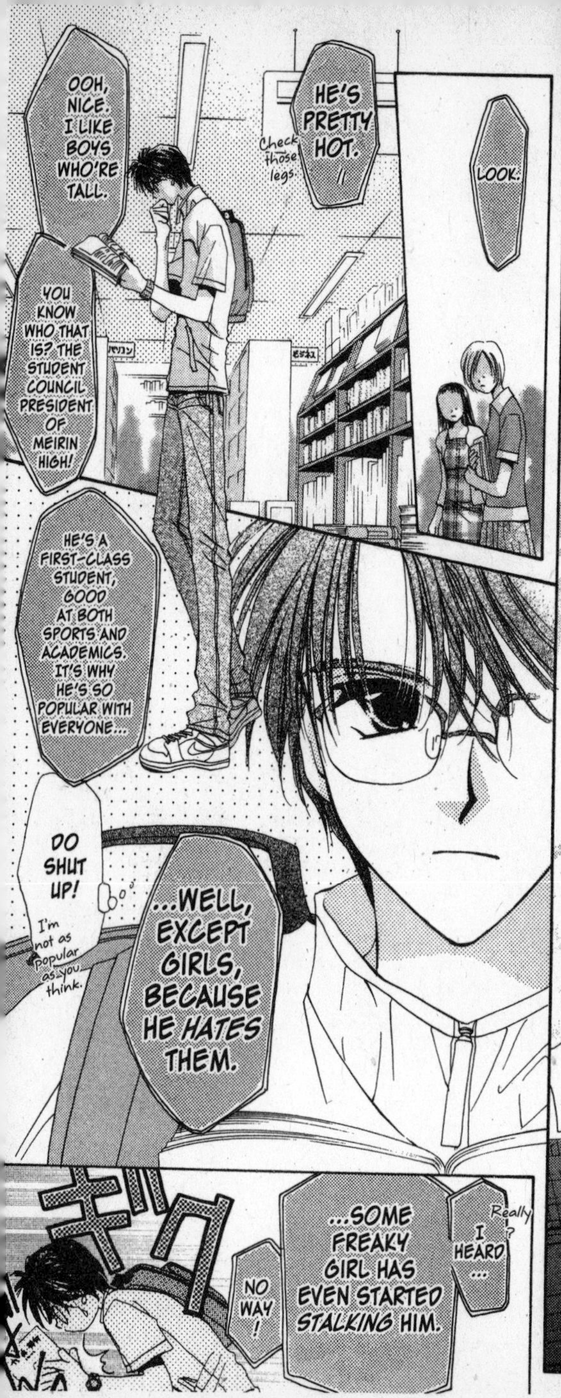
LOOK.
HE'S PRETTY HOT.
Check those legs.
OOH, NICE. I LIKE BOYS WHO'RE TALL.
YOU KNOW WHO THAT IS? THE STUDENT COUNCIL PRESIDENT OF MEIRIN HIGH!
HE'S A FIRST-CLASS STUDENT, GOOD AT BOTH SPORTS AND ACADEMICS. IT'S WHY HE'S SO POPULAR WITH EVERYONE...
...WELL, EXCEPT GIRLS, BECAUSE HE HATES THEM.
DO SHUT UP!
I'm not as popular as you think.
I HEARD...
Really?
...SOME FREAKY GIRL HAS EVEN STARTED STALKING HIM.
NO WAY!

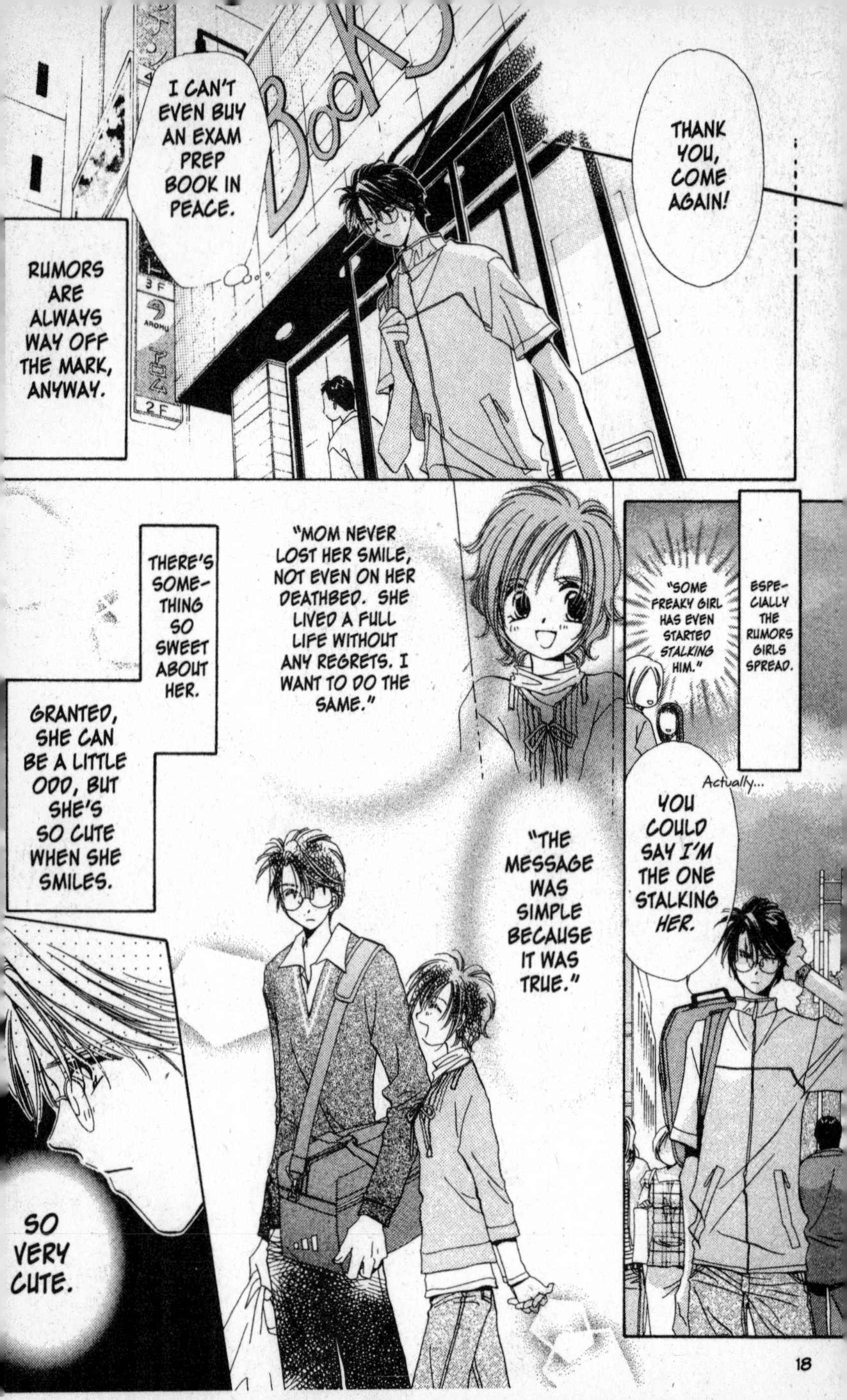
THANK YOU, COME AGAIN!
I CAN'T EVEN BUY AN EXAM PREP BOOK IN PEACE.
RUMORS ARE ALWAYS WAY OFF THE MARK, ANYWAY.
ESPE-CIALLY THE RUMORS GIRLS SPREAD.
"SOME FREAKY GIRL HAS EVEN STARTED STALKING HIM."
Actually...
YOU COULD SAY *I'M* THE ONE STALKING *HER.*
"MOM NEVER LOST HER SMILE, NOT EVEN ON HER DEATHBED. SHE LIVED A FULL LIFE WITHOUT ANY REGRETS. I WANT TO DO THE SAME."
THERE'S SOME-THING SO SWEET ABOUT HER.
GRANTED, SHE CAN BE A LITTLE ODD, BUT SHE'S SO CUTE WHEN SHE SMILES.
"THE MESSAGE WAS SIMPLE BECAUSE IT WAS TRUE."
SO VERY CUTE.

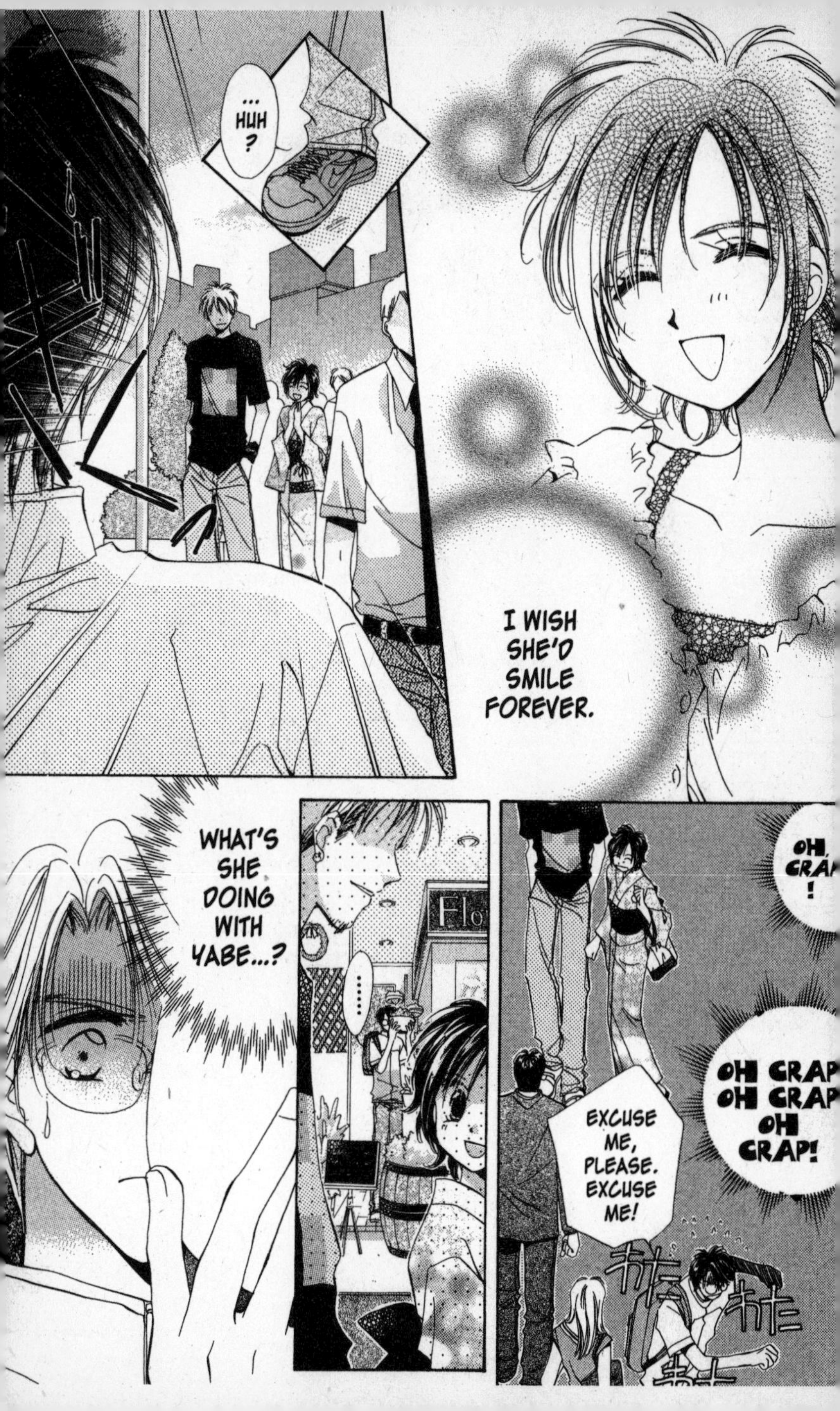
I WISH SHE'D SMILE FOREVER.
... HUH ?
OH, CRA!
OH CRA OH CRA OH CRAP!
EXCUSE ME, PLEASE. EXCUSE ME!
......
WHAT'S SHE DOING WITH YABE...?

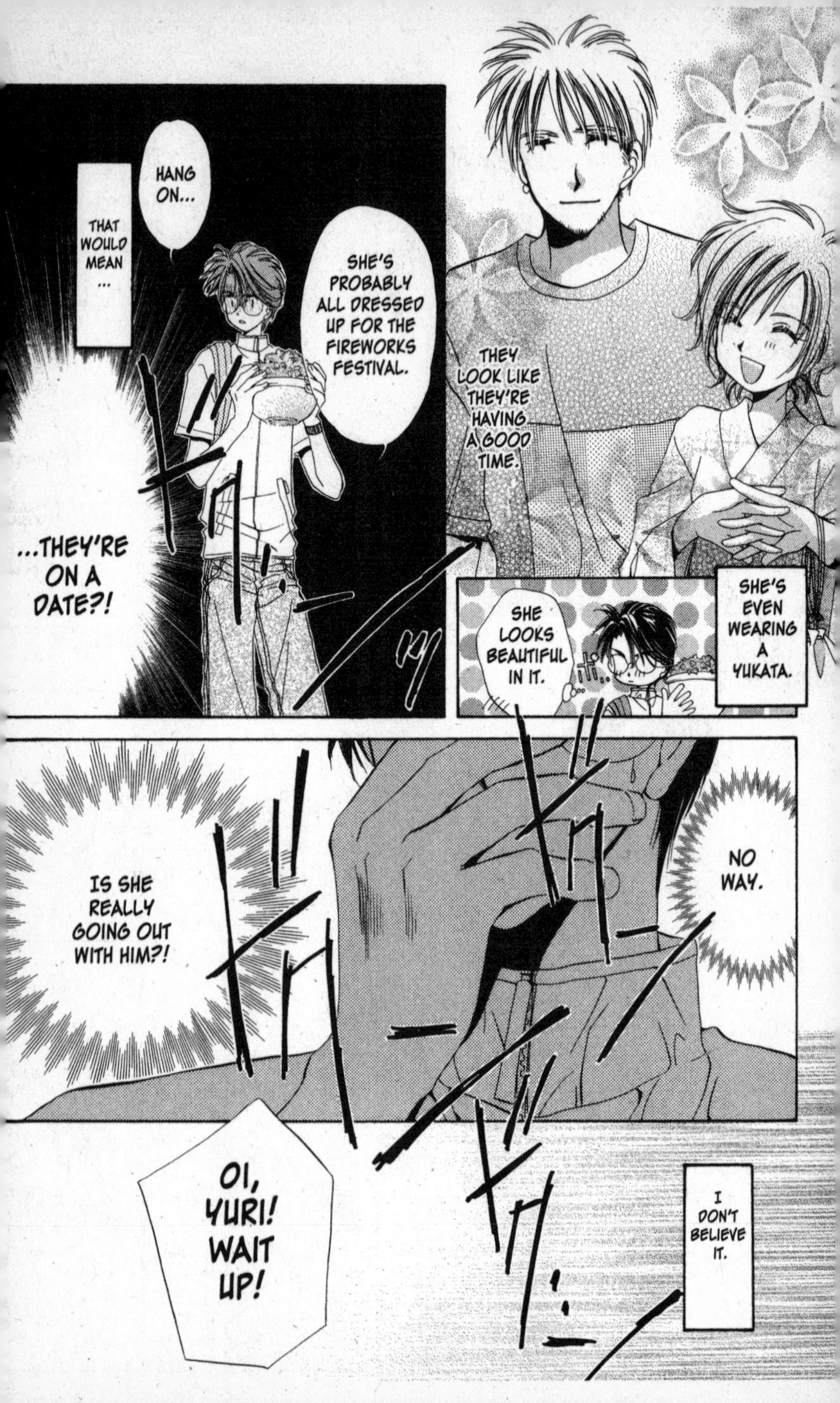

THEY LOOK LIKE THEY'RE HAVING A GOOD TIME.
SHE'S EVEN WEARING A YUKATA.
SHE LOOKS BEAUTIFUL IN IT.
SHE'S PROBABLY ALL DRESSED UP FOR THE FIREWORKS FESTIVAL.
HANG ON...
THAT WOULD MEAN ...
...THEY'RE ON A DATE?!
NO WAY.
IS SHE REALLY GOING OUT WITH HIM?!
I DON'T BELIEVE IT.
OI, YURI! WAIT UP!

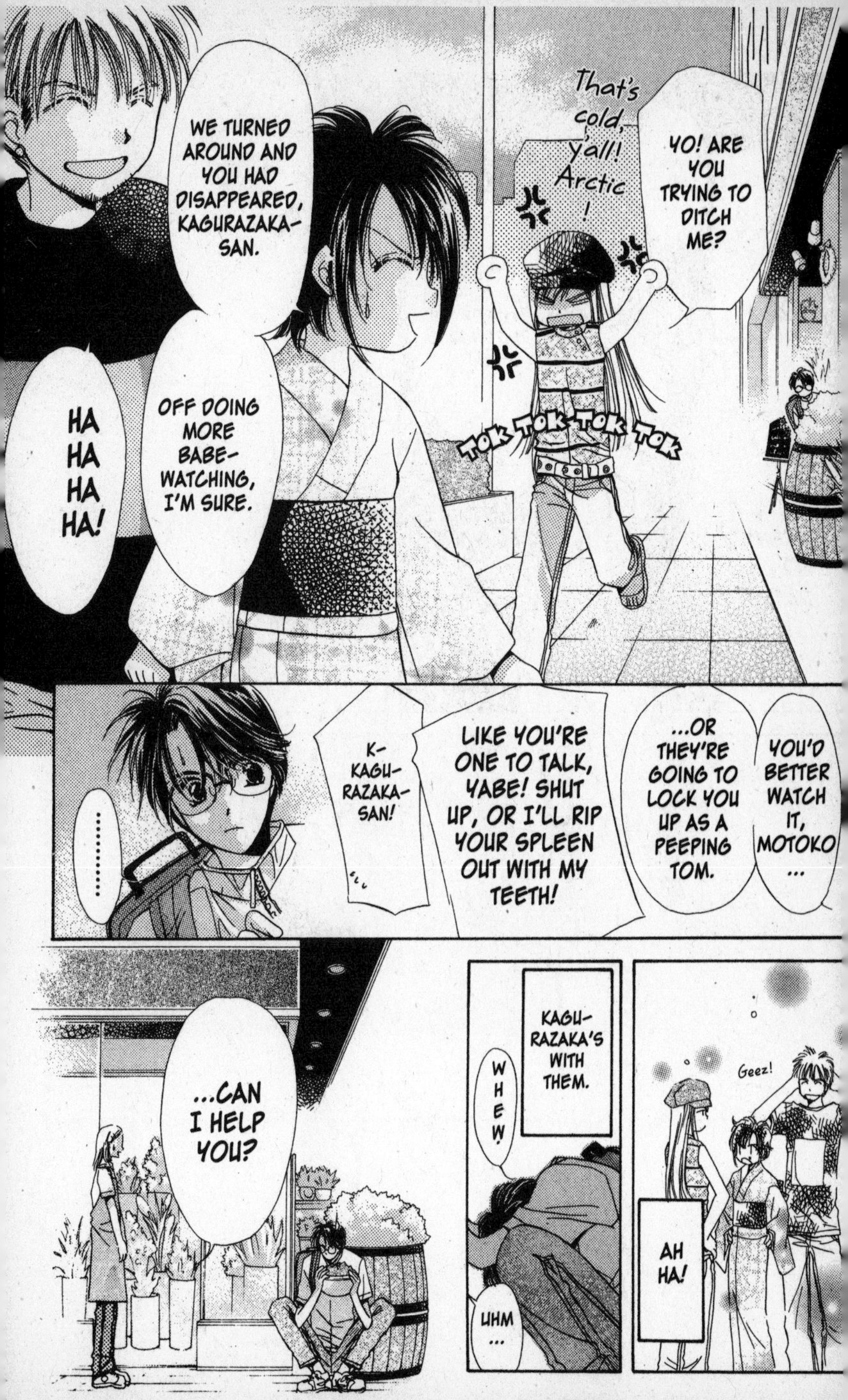
YO! ARE YOU TRYING TO DITCH ME?
That's cold, y'all! Arctic!
TOK TOK TOK TOK
WE TURNED AROUND AND YOU HAD DISAPPEARED, KAGURAZAKA-SAN.
OFF DOING MORE BABE-WATCHING, I'M SURE.
HA HA HA HA!
YOU'D BETTER WATCH IT, MOTOKO...
...OR THEY'RE GOING TO LOCK YOU UP AS A PEEPING TOM.
LIKE YOU'RE ONE TO TALK, YABE! SHUT UP, OR I'LL RIP YOUR SPLEEN OUT WITH MY TEETH!
K-KAGURAZAKA-SAN!
....
Geez!
AH HA!
KAGURAZAKA'S WITH THEM.
WHEW!
UHM...
...CAN I HELP YOU?

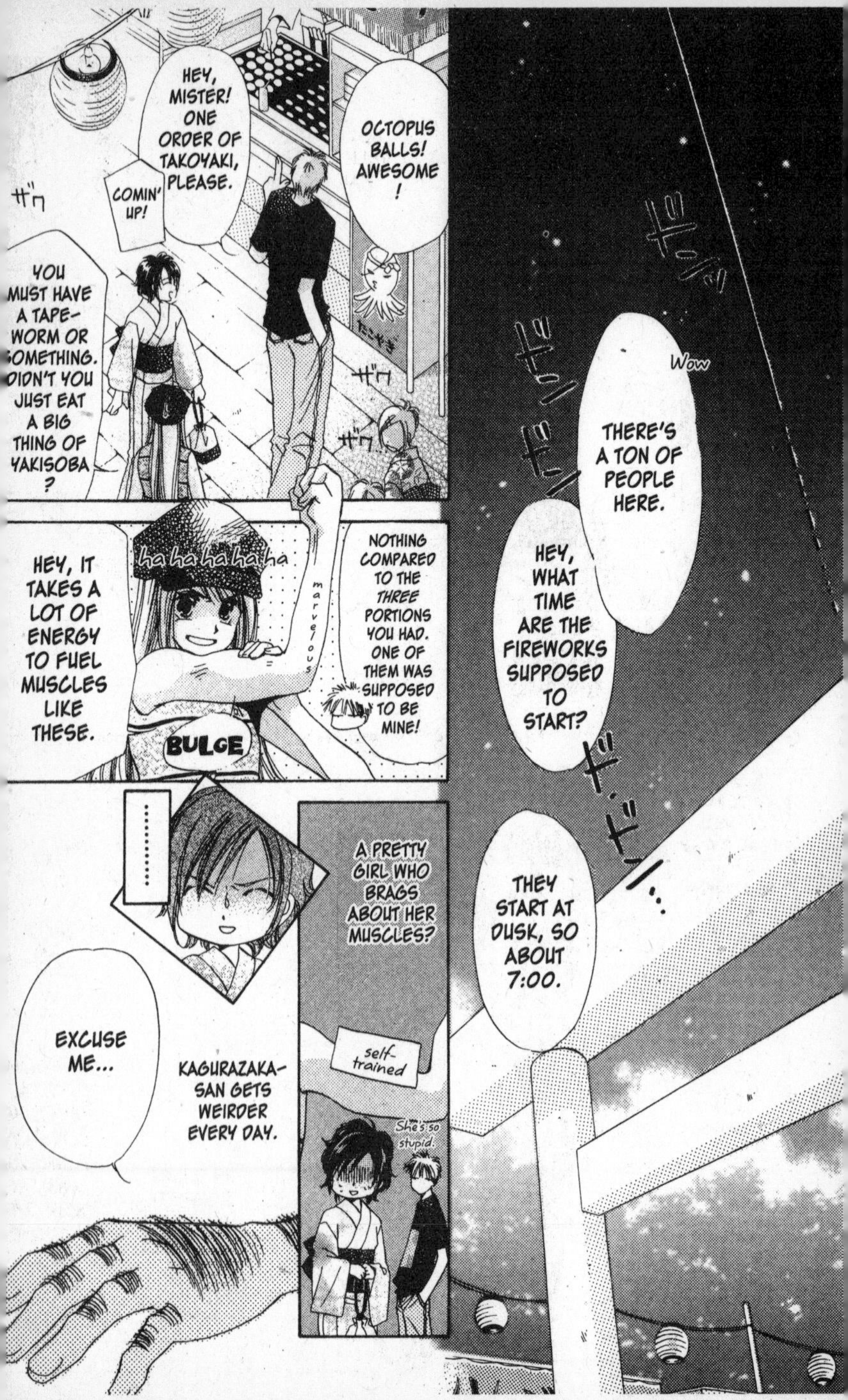
Wow
THERE'S A TON OF PEOPLE HERE.
HEY, WHAT TIME ARE THE FIREWORKS SUPPOSED TO START?
THEY START AT DUSK, SO ABOUT 7:00.
OCTOPUS BALLS! AWESOME!
HEY, MISTER! ONE ORDER OF TAKOYAKI, PLEASE.
COMIN' UP!
YOU MUST HAVE A TAPE-WORM OR SOMETHING. DIDN'T YOU JUST EAT A BIG THING OF YAKISOBA?
NOTHING COMPARED TO THE THREE PORTIONS YOU HAD. ONE OF THEM WAS SUPPOSED TO BE MINE!
marvelous
ha ha ha ha ha ha
HEY, IT TAKES A LOT OF ENERGY TO FUEL MUSCLES LIKE THESE.
BULGE
A PRETTY GIRL WHO BRAGS ABOUT HER MUSCLES?
self-trained
She's so stupid.
....
KAGURAZAKA-SAN GETS WEIRDER EVERY DAY.
EXCUSE ME...

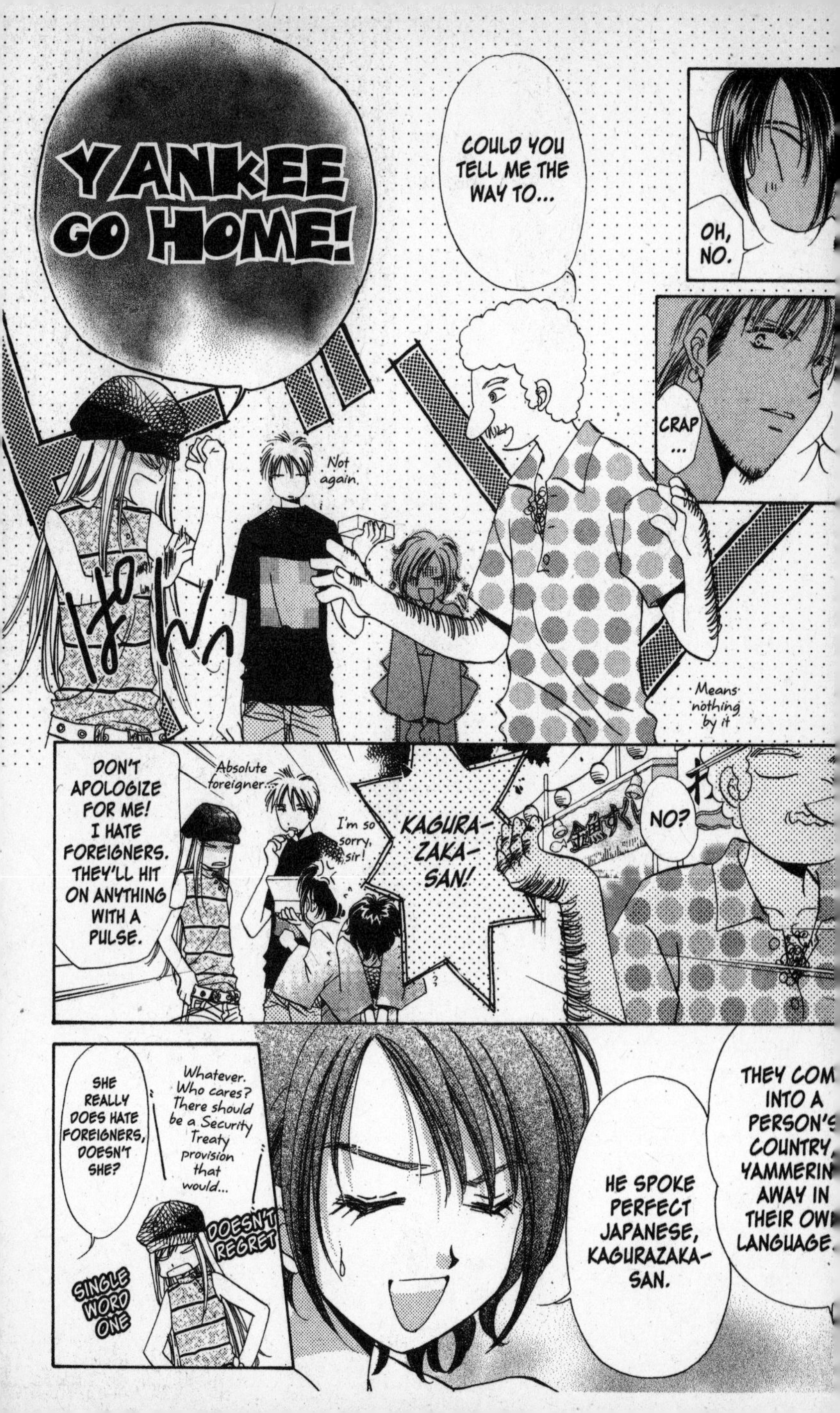
OH, NO.
CRAP...
COULD YOU TELL ME THE WAY TO...
YANKEE GO HOME!
Not again.
Means nothing by it
NO?
KAGURAZAKA-SAN!
I'm so sorry, sir!
Absolute foreigner...
DON'T APOLOGIZE FOR ME! I HATE FOREIGNERS. THEY'LL HIT ON ANYTHING WITH A PULSE.
THEY COM INTO A PERSON'S COUNTRY, YAMMERIN AWAY IN THEIR OW LANGUAGE.
HE SPOKE PERFECT JAPANESE, KAGURAZAKA-SAN.
SHE REALLY DOES HATE FOREIGNERS, DOESN'T SHE?
Whatever. Who cares? There should be a Security Treaty provision that would...
DOESN'T REGRET
SINGLE WORD ONE

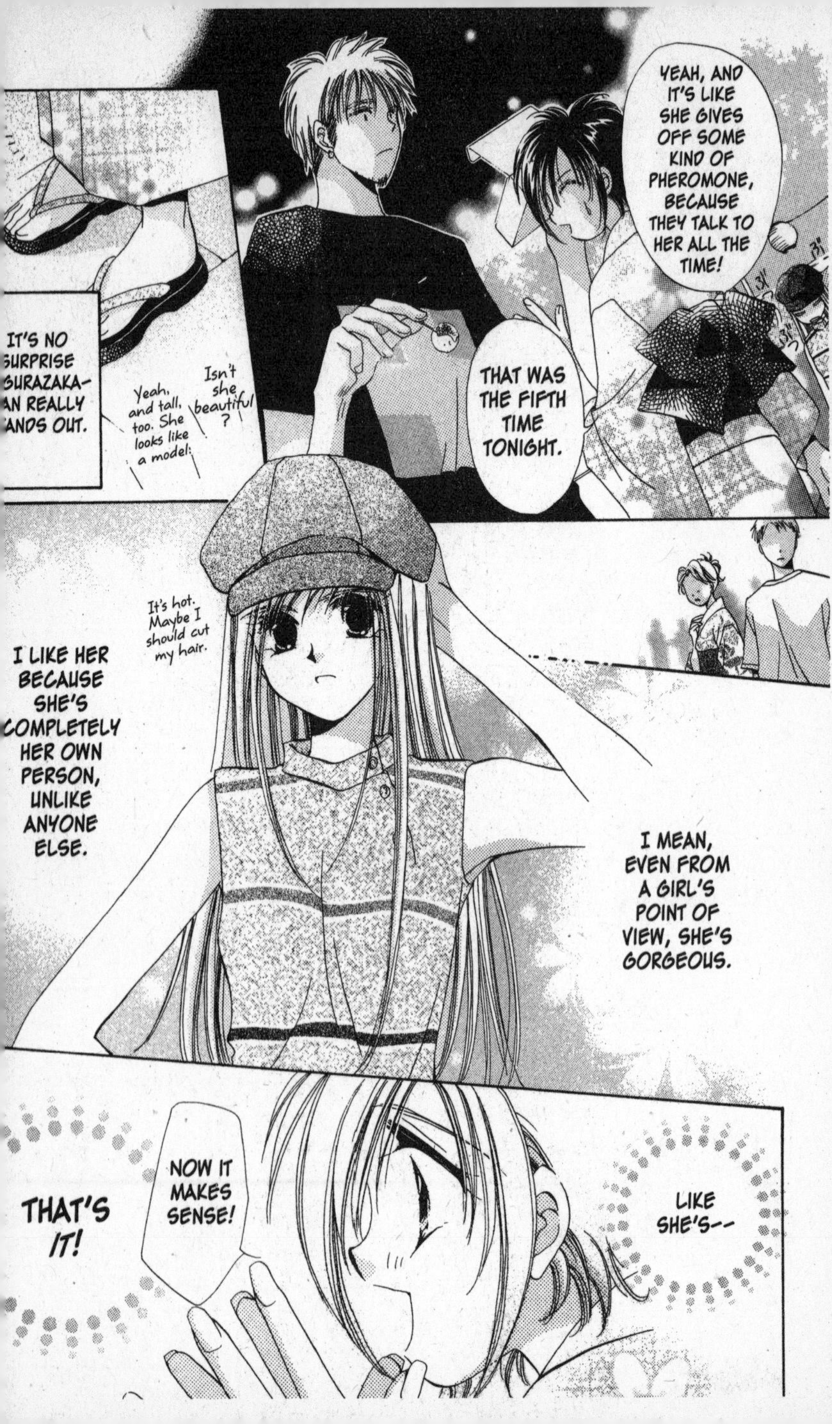
YEAH, AND IT'S LIKE SHE GIVES OFF SOME KIND OF PHEROMONE, BECAUSE THEY TALK TO HER ALL THE TIME!
THAT WAS THE FIFTH TIME TONIGHT.
Isn't she beautiful?
Yeah, and tall, too. She looks like a model.
IT'S NO SURPRISE URAZAKA- AN REALLY ANDS OUT.
I MEAN, EVEN FROM A GIRL'S POINT OF VIEW, SHE'S GORGEOUS.
It's hot. Maybe I should cut my hair.
I LIKE HER BECAUSE SHE'S COMPLETELY HER OWN PERSON, UNLIKE ANYONE ELSE.
LIKE SHE'S--
NOW IT MAKES SENSE!
THAT'S IT!

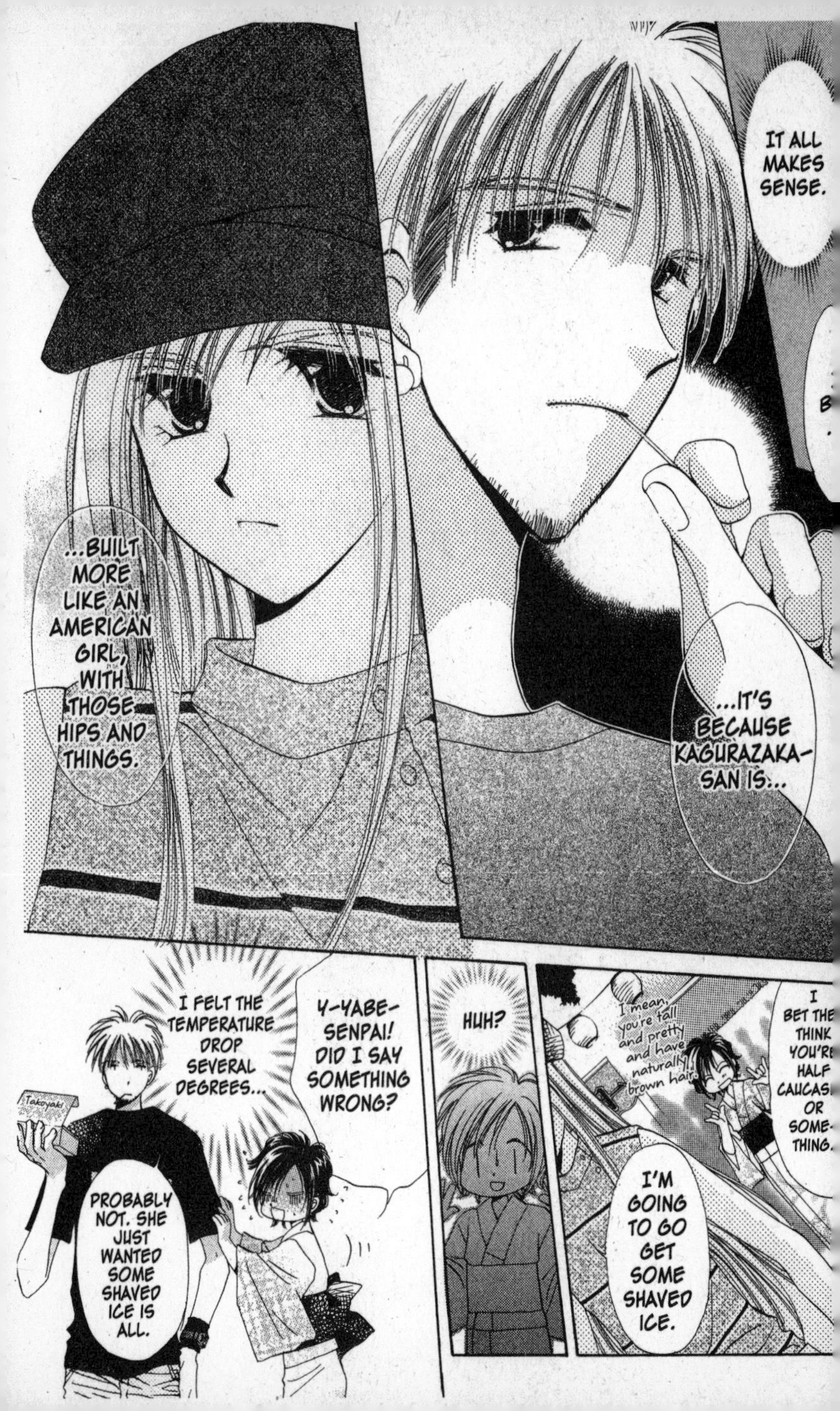
IT ALL MAKES SENSE.
...IT'S BECAUSE KAGURAZAKA-SAN IS...
...BUILT MORE LIKE AN AMERICAN GIRL, WITH THOSE HIPS AND THINGS.
I BET THE THINK YOU'R HALF CAUCAS OR SOME-THING.
I mean, you're tall and pretty and have naturally brown hair.
I'M GOING TO GO GET SOME SHAVED ICE.
HUH?
Y-YABE-SENPAI! DID I SAY SOMETHING WRONG?
I FELT THE TEMPERATURE DROP SEVERAL DEGREES...
Takoyaki
PROBABLY NOT. SHE JUST WANTED SOME SHAVED ICE IS ALL.

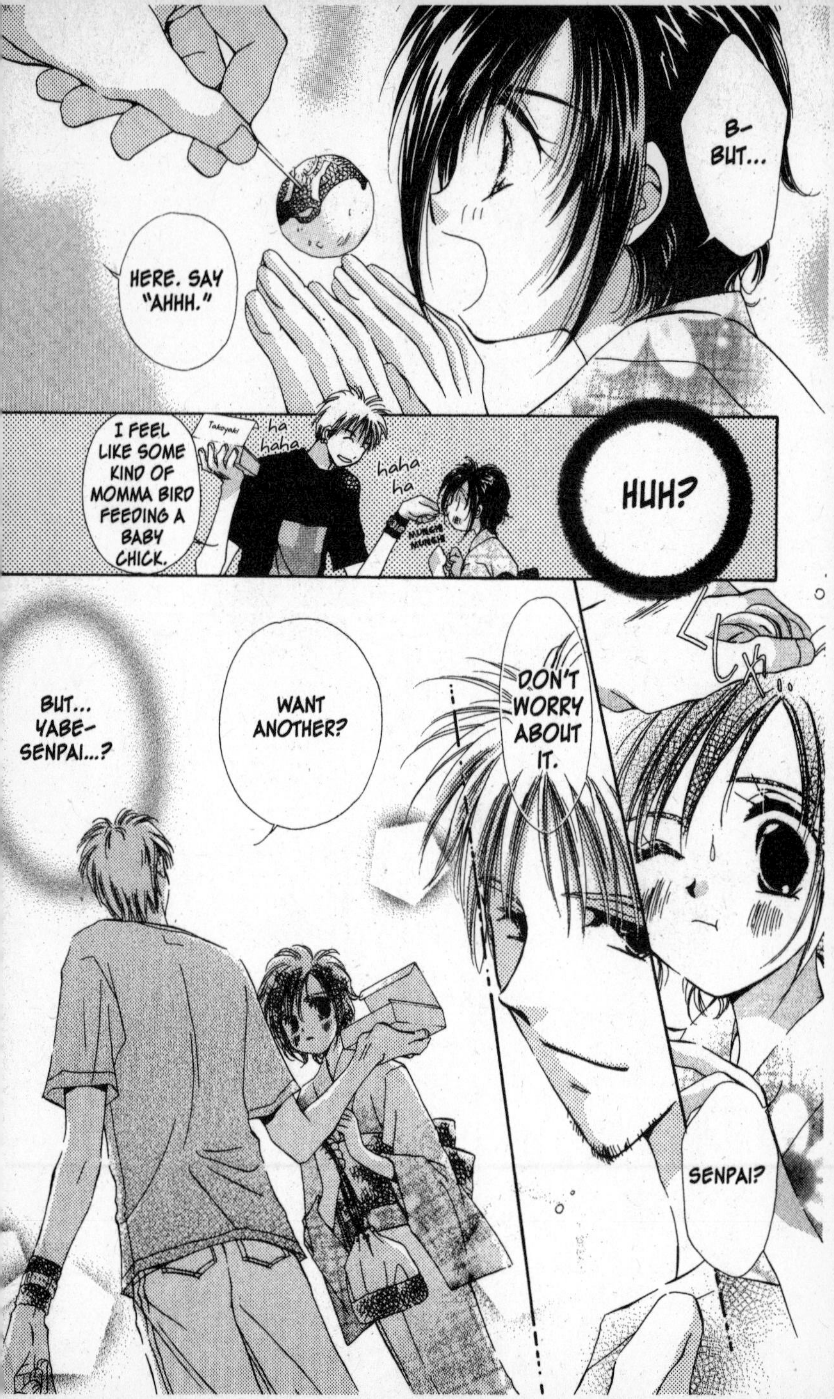
B-BUT...
HERE. SAY "AHHH."
HUH?
I FEEL LIKE SOME KIND OF MOMMA BIRD FEEDING A BABY CHICK.
ha haha
haha ha
DON'T WORRY ABOUT IT.
SENPAI?
WANT ANOTHER?
BUT... YABE-SENPAI...?

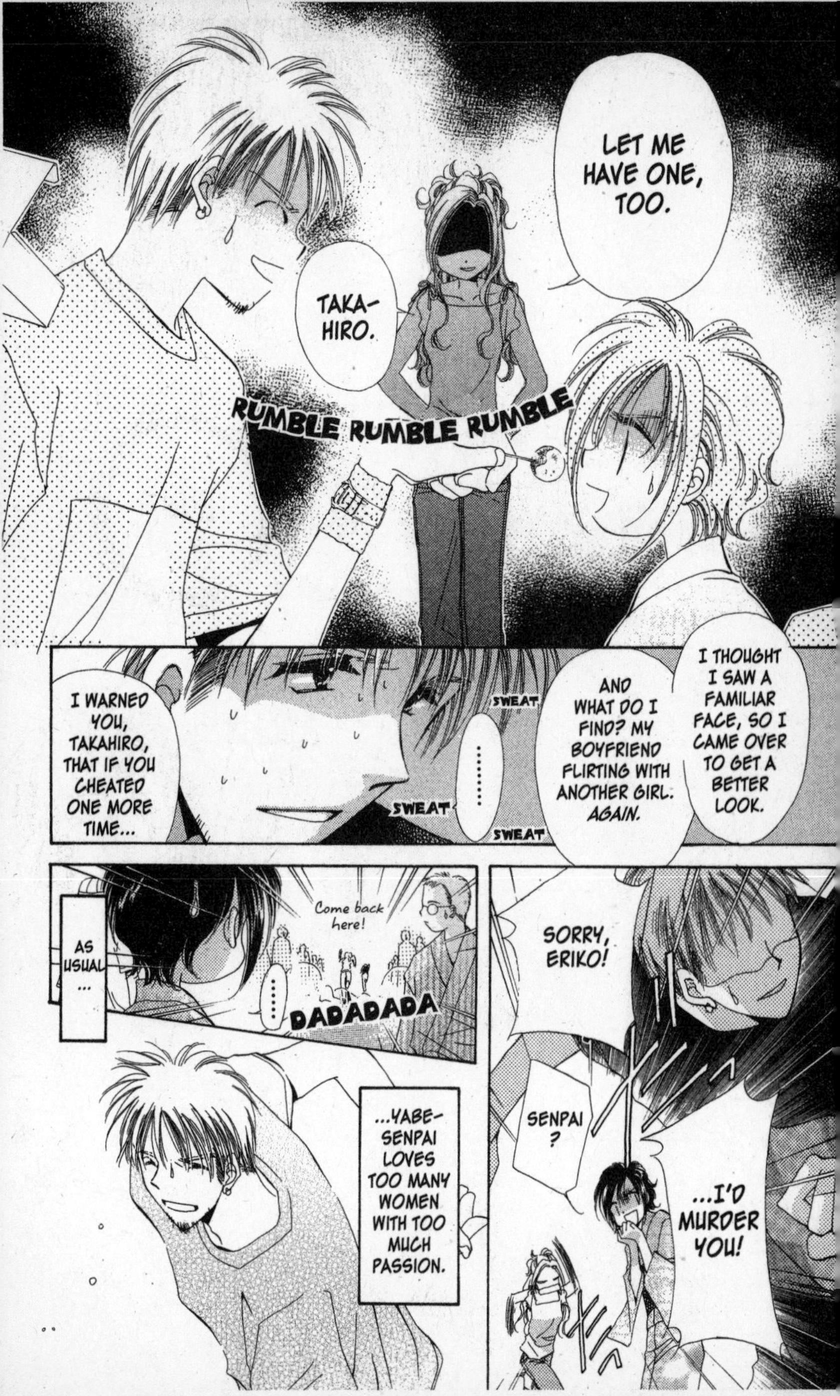
LET ME HAVE ONE, TOO.
TAKA-HIRO.
RUMBLE RUMBLE RUMBLE
I THOUGHT I SAW A FAMILIAR FACE, SO I CAME OVER TO GET A BETTER LOOK.
AND WHAT DO I FIND? MY BOYFRIEND FLIRTING WITH ANOTHER GIRL. AGAIN.
SWEAT
....
SWEAT
SWEAT
I WARNED YOU, TAKAHIRO, THAT IF YOU CHEATED ONE MORE TIME...
...I'D MURDER YOU!
SORRY, ERIKO!
SENPAI ?
Come back here!
......
DADADADA
AS USUAL...
...YABE-SENPAI LOVES TOO MANY WOMEN WITH TOO MUCH PASSION.

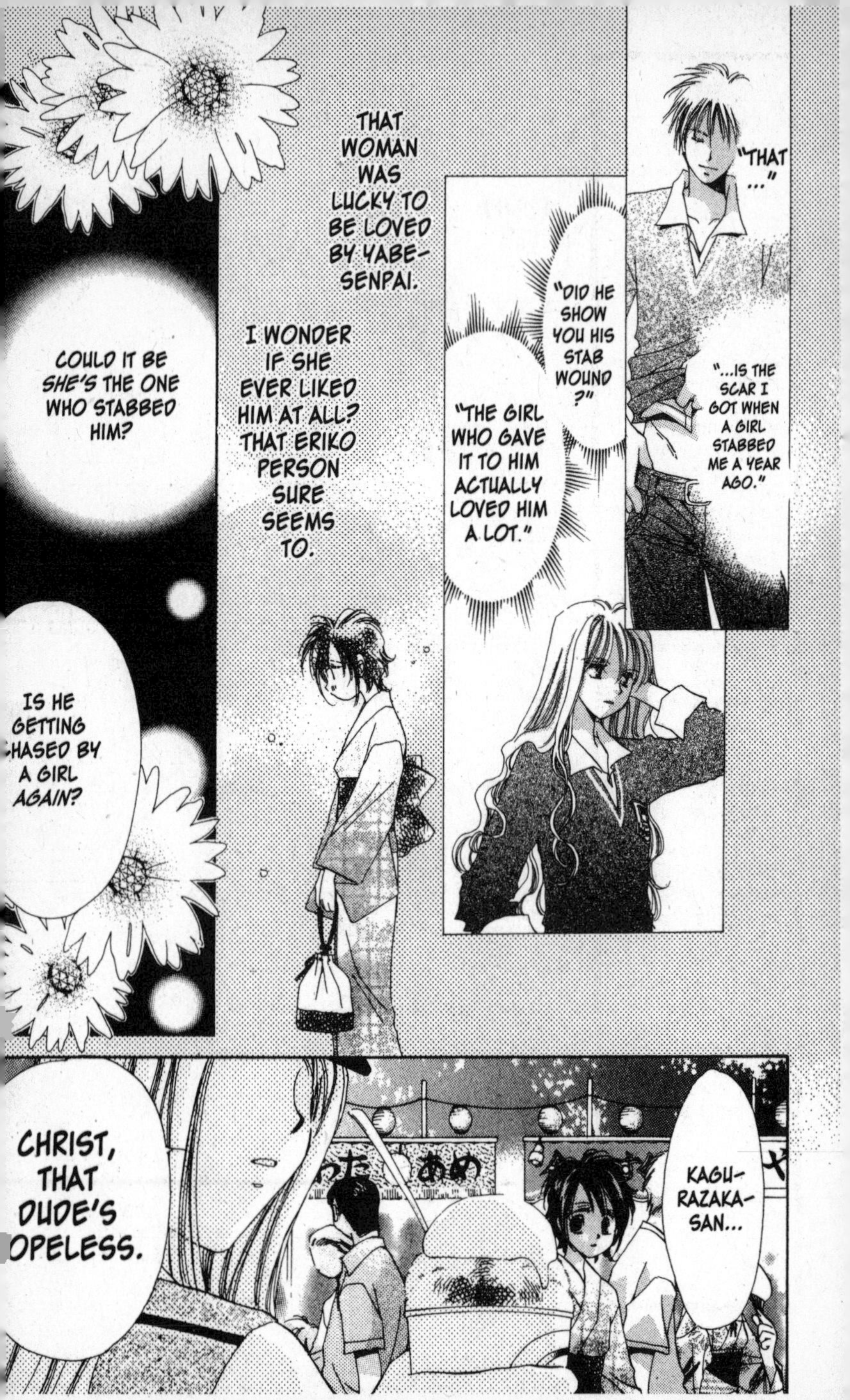
"THAT ..."
"...IS THE SCAR I GOT WHEN A GIRL STABBED ME A YEAR AGO."
"DID HE SHOW YOU HIS STAB WOUND?"
"THE GIRL WHO GAVE IT TO HIM ACTUALLY LOVED HIM A LOT."
THAT WOMAN WAS LUCKY TO BE LOVED BY YABE-SENPAI.
I WONDER IF SHE EVER LIKED HIM AT ALL? THAT ERIKO PERSON SURE SEEMS TO.
COULD IT BE SHE'S THE ONE WHO STABBED HIM?
IS HE GETTING HASED BY A GIRL AGAIN?
KAGU-RAZAKA-SAN...
わた あめ
CHRIST, THAT DUDE'S OPELESS.

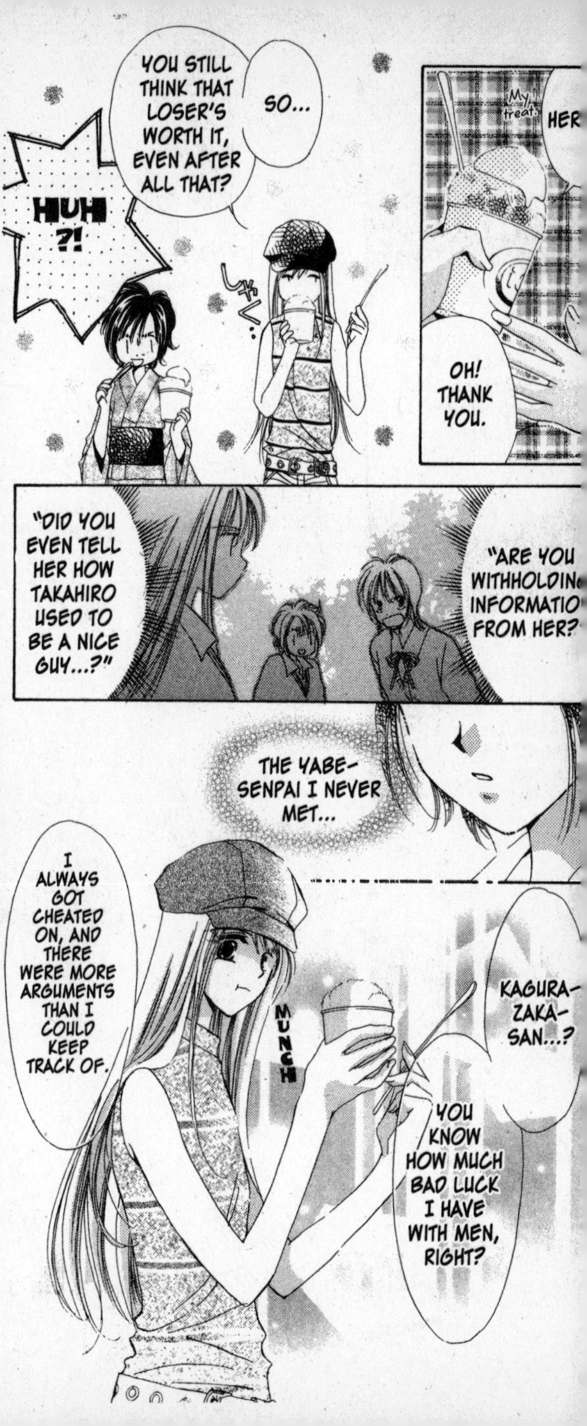

My treat.
HER
OH! THANK YOU.
SO...
YOU STILL THINK THAT LOSER'S WORTH IT, EVEN AFTER ALL THAT?
HUH ?!
しゃく
"ARE YOU WITHHOLDIN INFORMATIO FROM HER?
"DID YOU EVEN TELL HER HOW TAKAHIRO USED TO BE A NICE GUY...?"
THE YABE-SENPAI I NEVER MET...
KAGURA-ZAKA-SAN...?
YOU KNOW HOW MUCH BAD LUCK I HAVE WITH MEN, RIGHT?
MUNCH
I ALWAYS GOT CHEATED ON, AND THERE WERE MORE ARGUMENTS THAN I COULD KEEP TRACK OF.

Hello, everyone! I would just like to say a big THANK YOU to all of you who have purchased this, *my 30th comic book volume!*

30...That's such a nice, round number. I wonder if somebody out there owns all 30 of my graphic novels?

While thoughts like that do flit through my mind on occasion, the one thought occupying my mind right now is: "My tooth hurts." I went to the dentist for the first time in years, and I had to get a root canal. That was three weeks ago, yet my tooth still really, really hurts. (Cries)

I went back to the dentist and all he said was, "That's impossible..." So, I went to a different dentist, and now things are getting a little better. (He found out what the problem was.)

Everyone, take good care of your teeth, 'kay?

Bye-bye, bacteria!

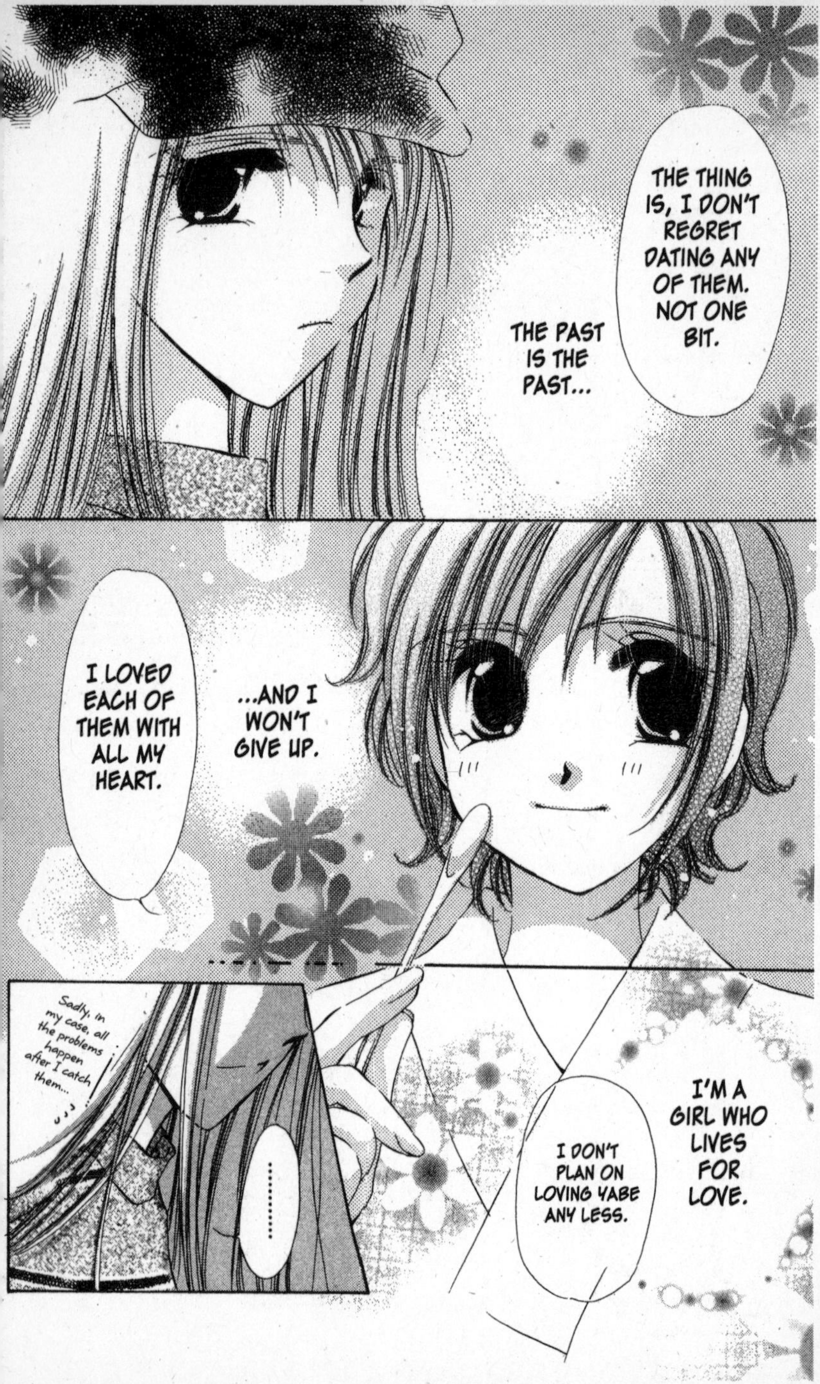
THE THING IS, I DON'T REGRET DATING ANY OF THEM. NOT ONE BIT.
THE PAST IS THE PAST...
...AND I WON'T GIVE UP.
I LOVED EACH OF THEM WITH ALL MY HEART.
I'M A GIRL WHO LIVES FOR LOVE.
I DON'T PLAN ON LOVING YABE ANY LESS.
Sadly, in my case, all the problems happen after I catch them...
......

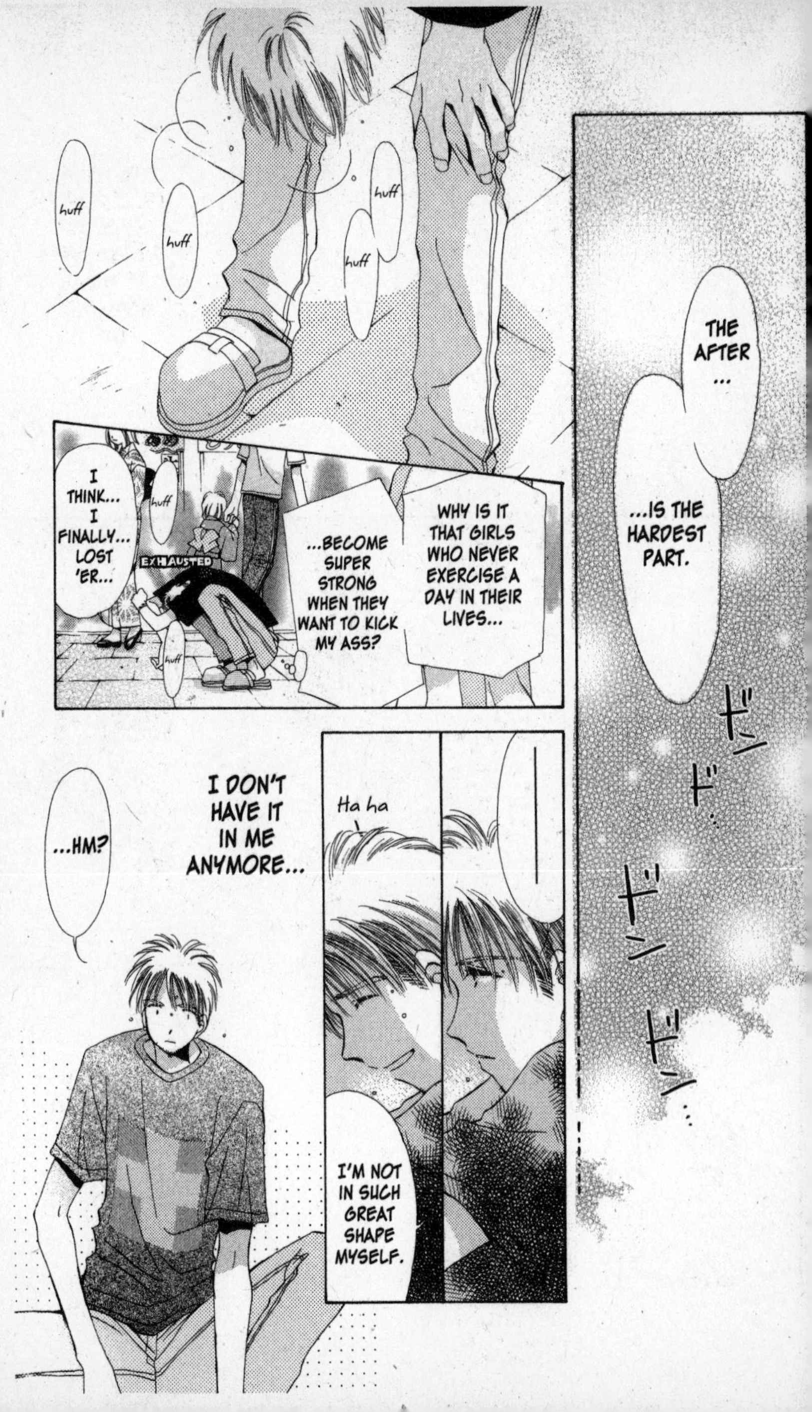

THE AFTER...
...IS THE HARDEST PART.
huff
huff
huff
huff
WHY IS IT THAT GIRLS WHO NEVER EXERCISE A DAY IN THEIR LIVES...
...BECOME SUPER STRONG WHEN THEY WANT TO KICK MY ASS?
huff
I THINK... I FINALLY... LOST 'ER...
EXHAUSTED
huff
—
Ha ha
I'M NOT IN SUCH GREAT SHAPE MYSELF.
I DON'T HAVE IT IN ME ANYMORE...
...HM?

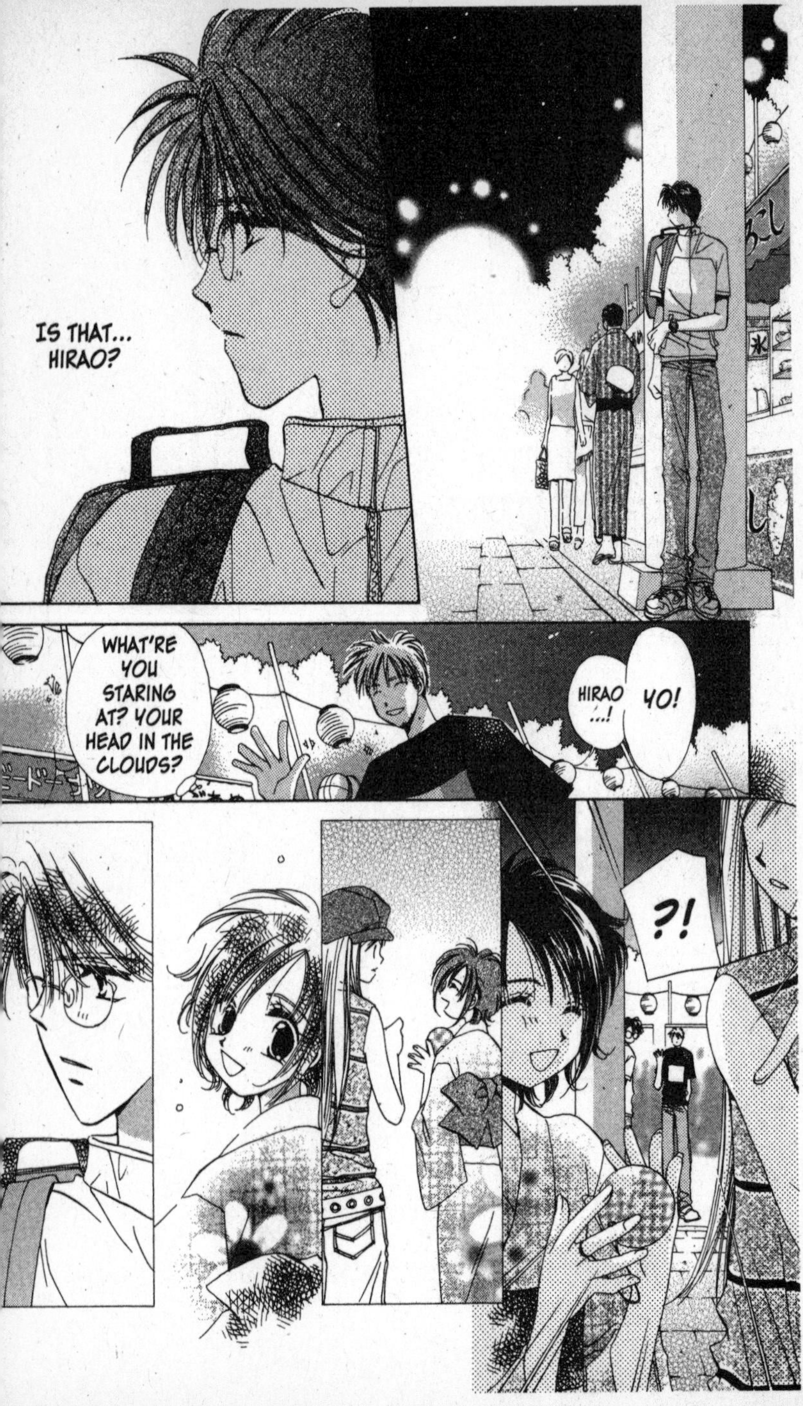
IS THAT... HIRAO?
YO!
HIRAO ...!
WHAT'RE YOU STARING AT? YOUR HEAD IN THE CLOUDS?
?!

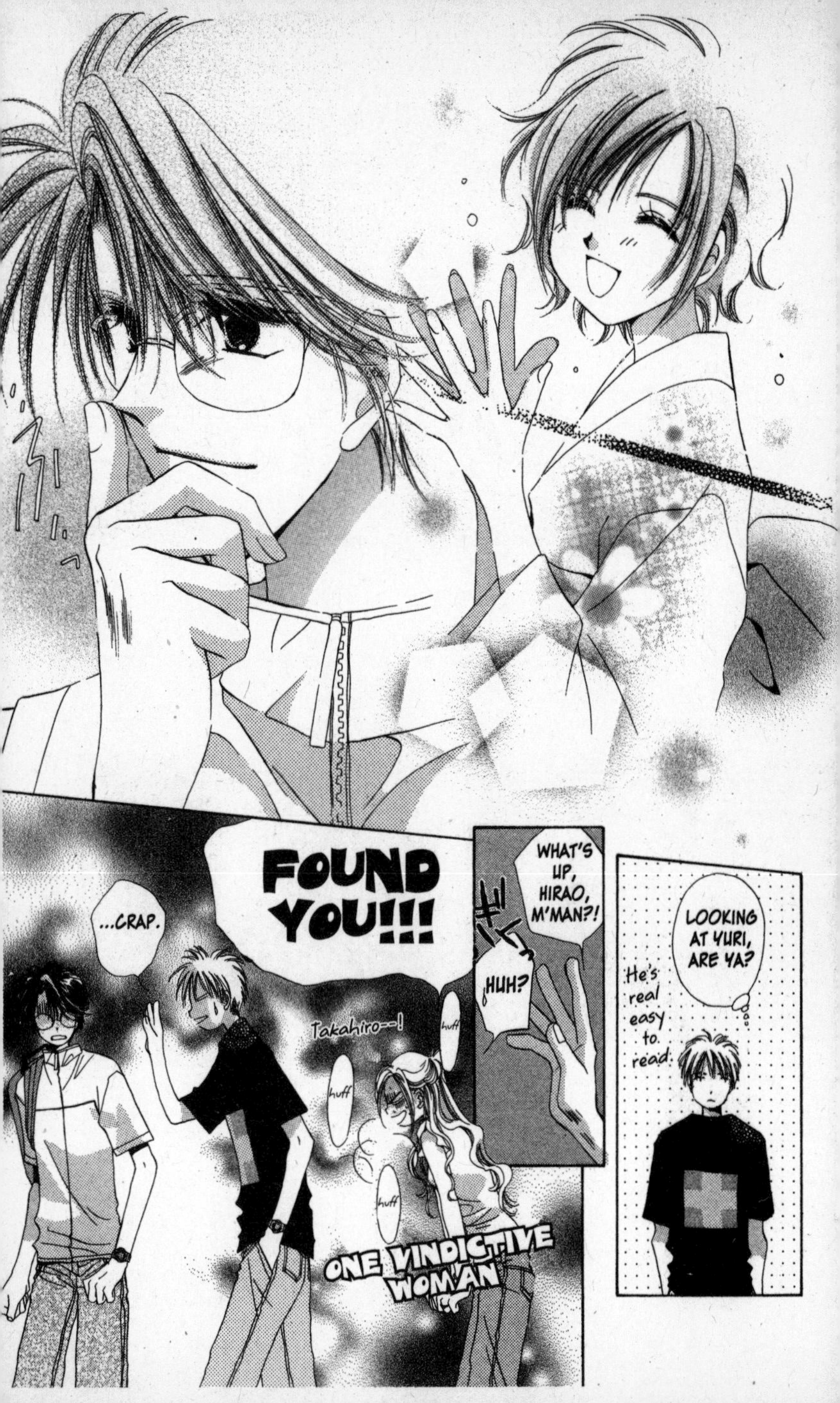
LOOKING AT YURI, ARE YA?
He's real easy to read.
WHAT'S UP, HIRAO, M'MAN?!
HUH?
FOUND YOU!!!
...CRAP.
Takahiro--!
huff
huff
huff
ONE VINDICTIVE WOMAN

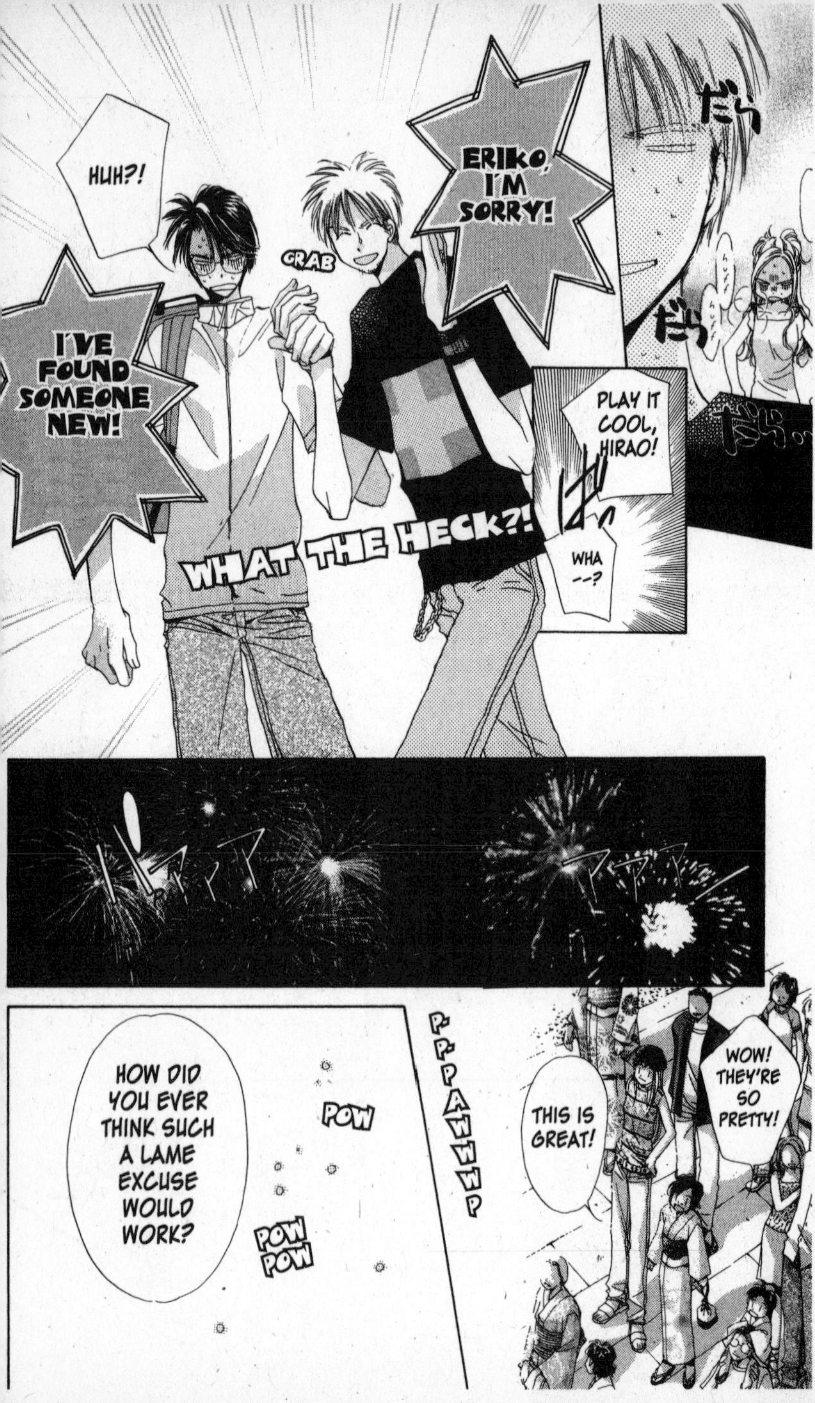

だら
だら
だら…
PLAY IT COOL, HIRAO!
ば
WHA--?
ERIKO, I'M SORRY!
GRAB
HUH?!
I'VE FOUND SOMEONE NEW!
WHAT THE HECK?!
WOW! THEY'RE SO PRETTY!
THIS IS GREAT!
P-P-PAWWWP
POW
POW POW
HOW DID YOU EVER THINK SUCH A LAME EXCUSE WOULD WORK?

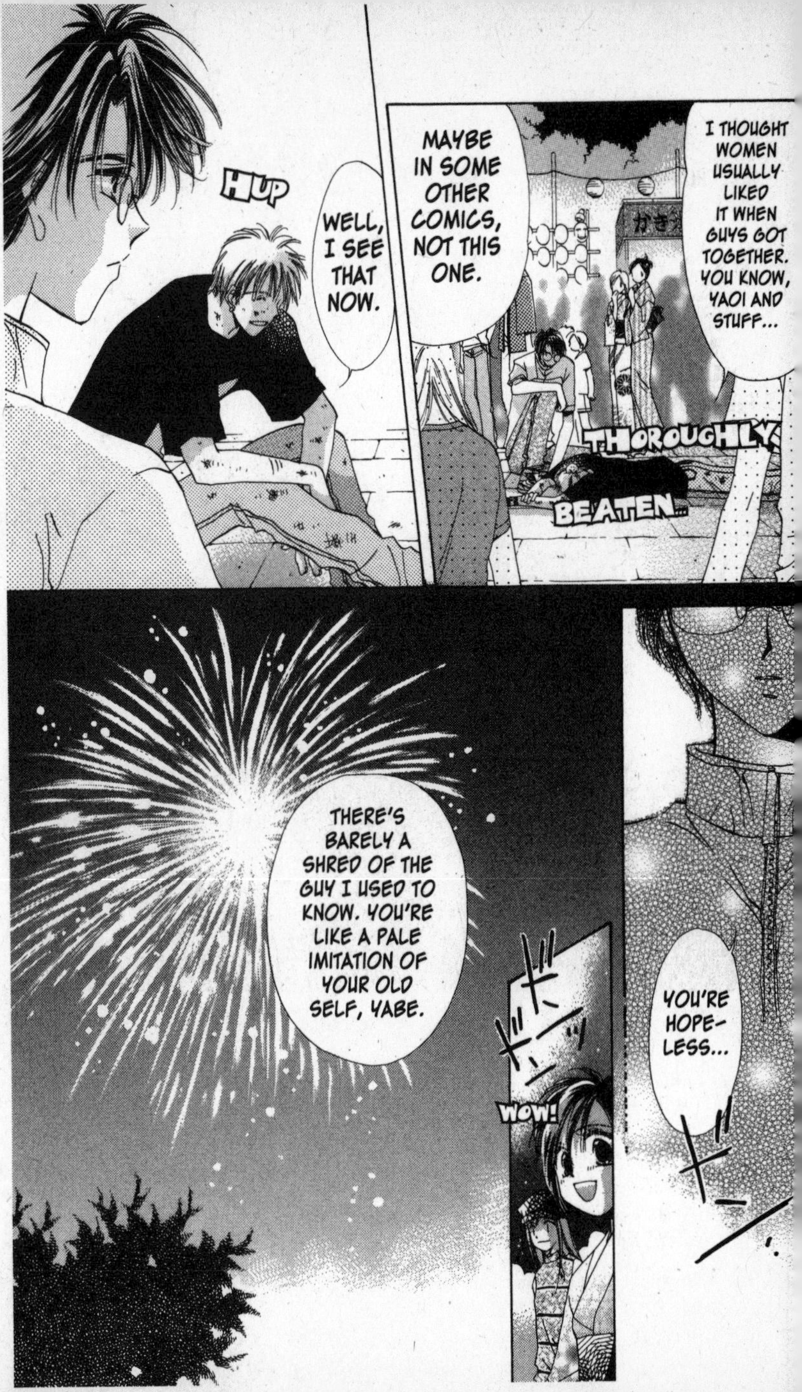
I THOUGHT WOMEN USUALLY LIKED IT WHEN GUYS GOT TOGETHER. YOU KNOW, YAOI AND STUFF...
MAYBE IN SOME OTHER COMICS, NOT THIS ONE.
THOROUGHLY BEATEN...
WELL, I SEE THAT NOW.
HUP
YOU'RE HOPE-LESS...
WOW!
THERE'S BARELY A SHRED OF THE GUY I USED TO KNOW. YOU'RE LIKE A PALE IMITATION OF YOUR OLD SELF, YABE.

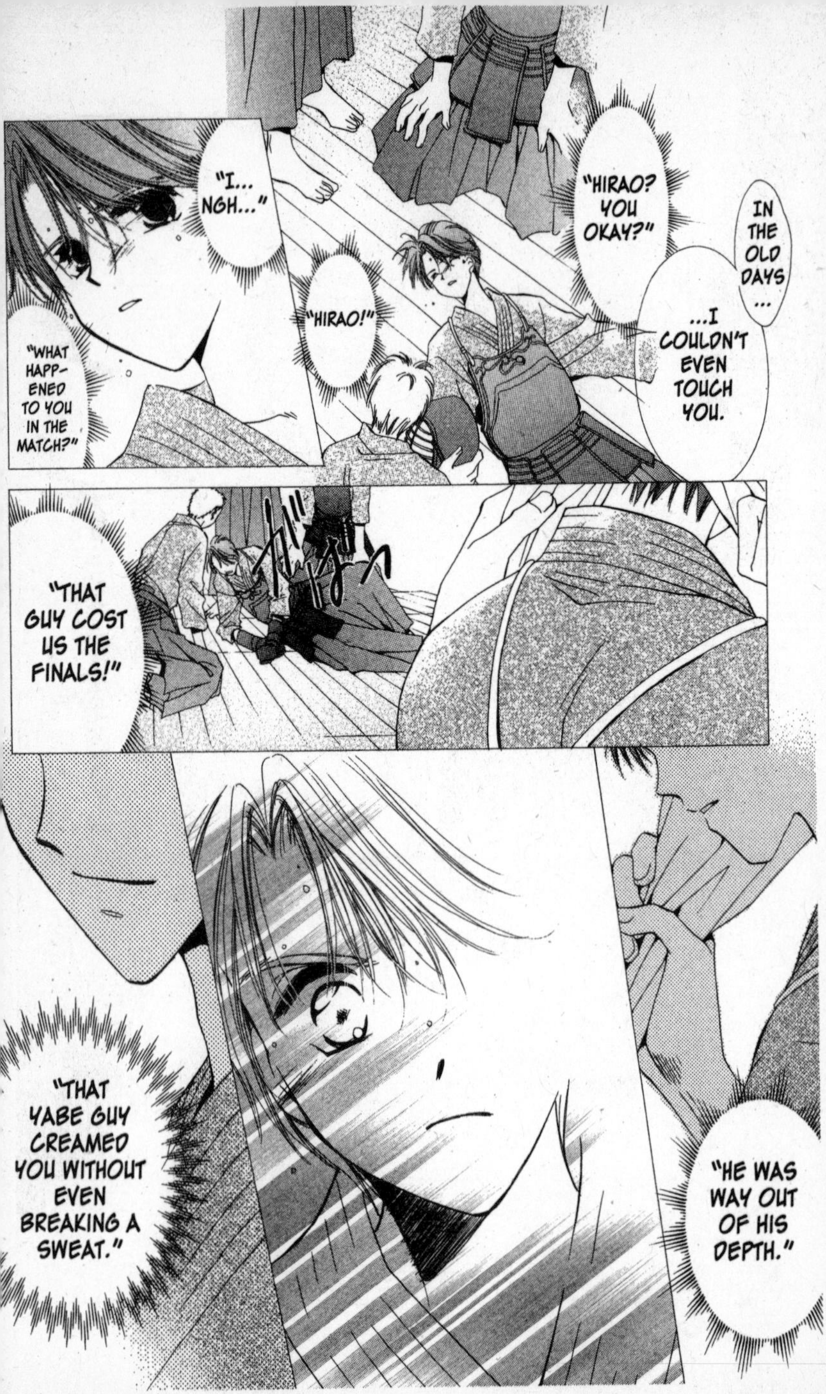
IN THE OLD DAYS...
...I COULDN'T EVEN TOUCH YOU.
"HIRAO? YOU OKAY?"
"HIRAO!"
"I... NGH..."
"WHAT HAPP-ENED TO YOU IN THE MATCH?"
"THAT GUY COST US THE FINALS!"
"HE WAS WAY OUT OF HIS DEPTH."
"THAT YABE GUY CREAMED YOU WITHOUT EVEN BREAKING A SWEAT."

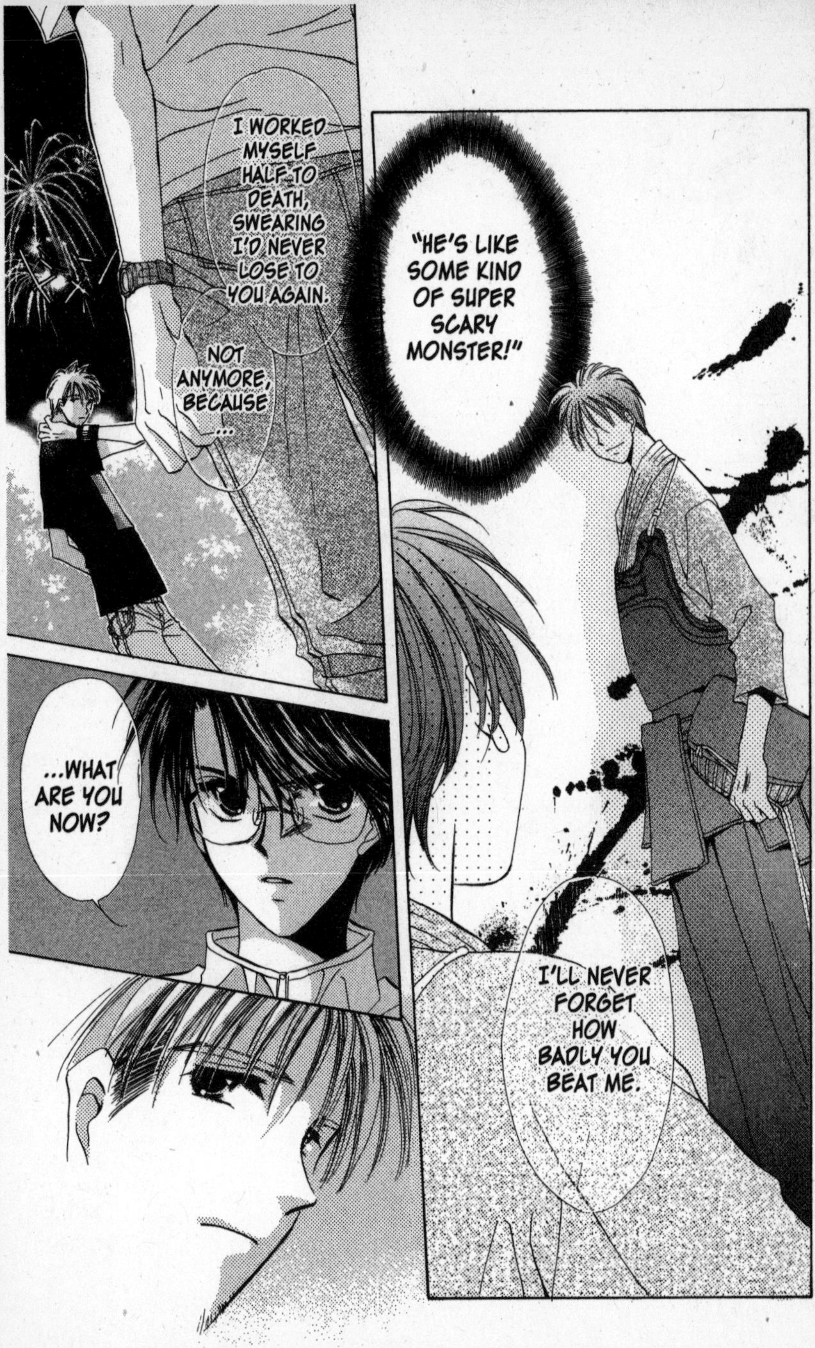
"HE'S LIKE SOME KIND OF SUPER SCARY MONSTER!"
I'LL NEVER FORGET HOW BADLY YOU BEAT ME.
I WORKED MYSELF HALF TO DEATH, SWEARING I'D NEVER LOSE TO YOU AGAIN.
NOT ANYMORE, BECAUSE ...
...WHAT ARE YOU NOW?

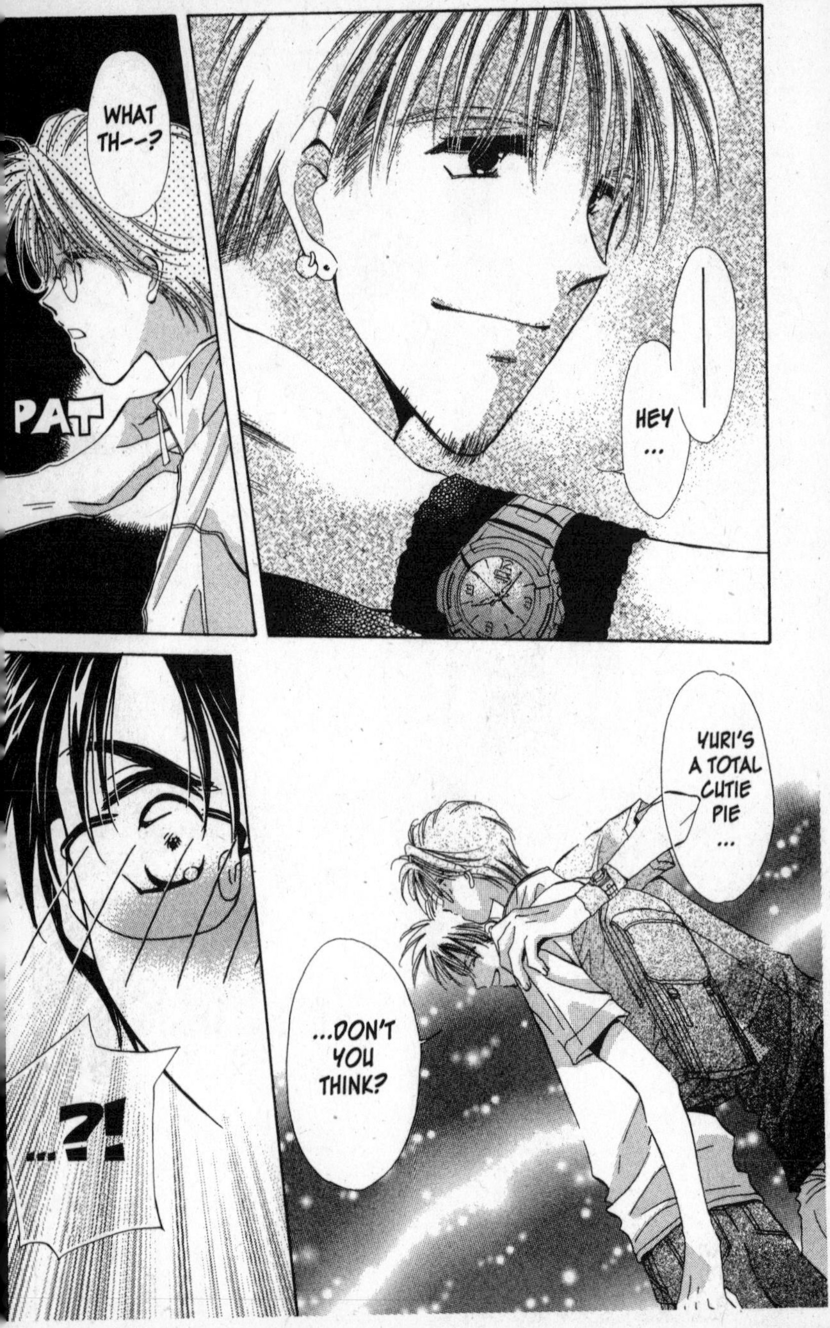
HEY ...
WHAT TH--?
PAT
YURI'S A TOTAL CUTIE PIE ...
...DON'T YOU THINK?
...?!

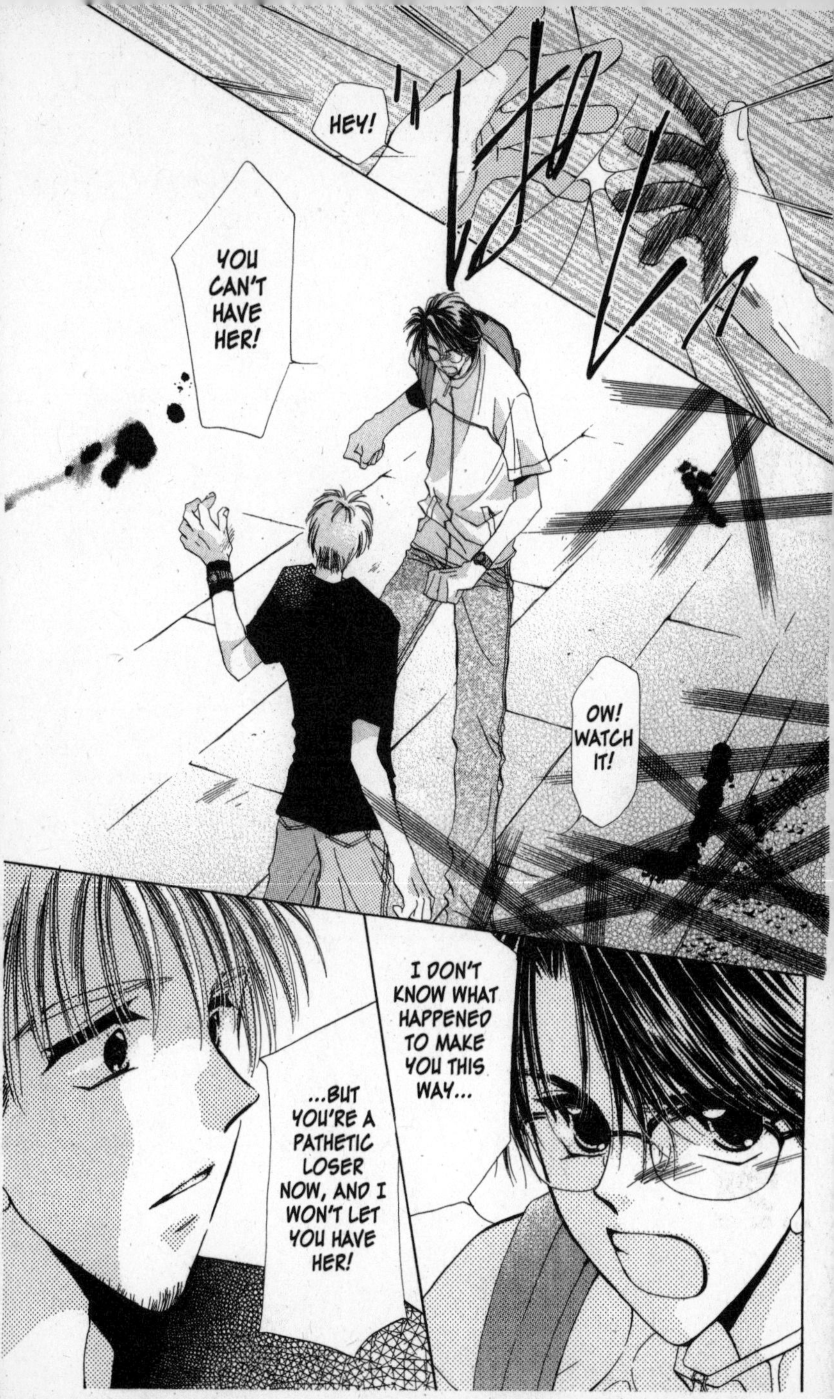
HEY!
YOU CAN'T HAVE HER!
OW! WATCH IT!
I DON'T KNOW WHAT HAPPENED TO MAKE YOU THIS WAY...
...BUT YOU'RE A PATHETIC LOSER NOW, AND I WON'T LET YOU HAVE HER!

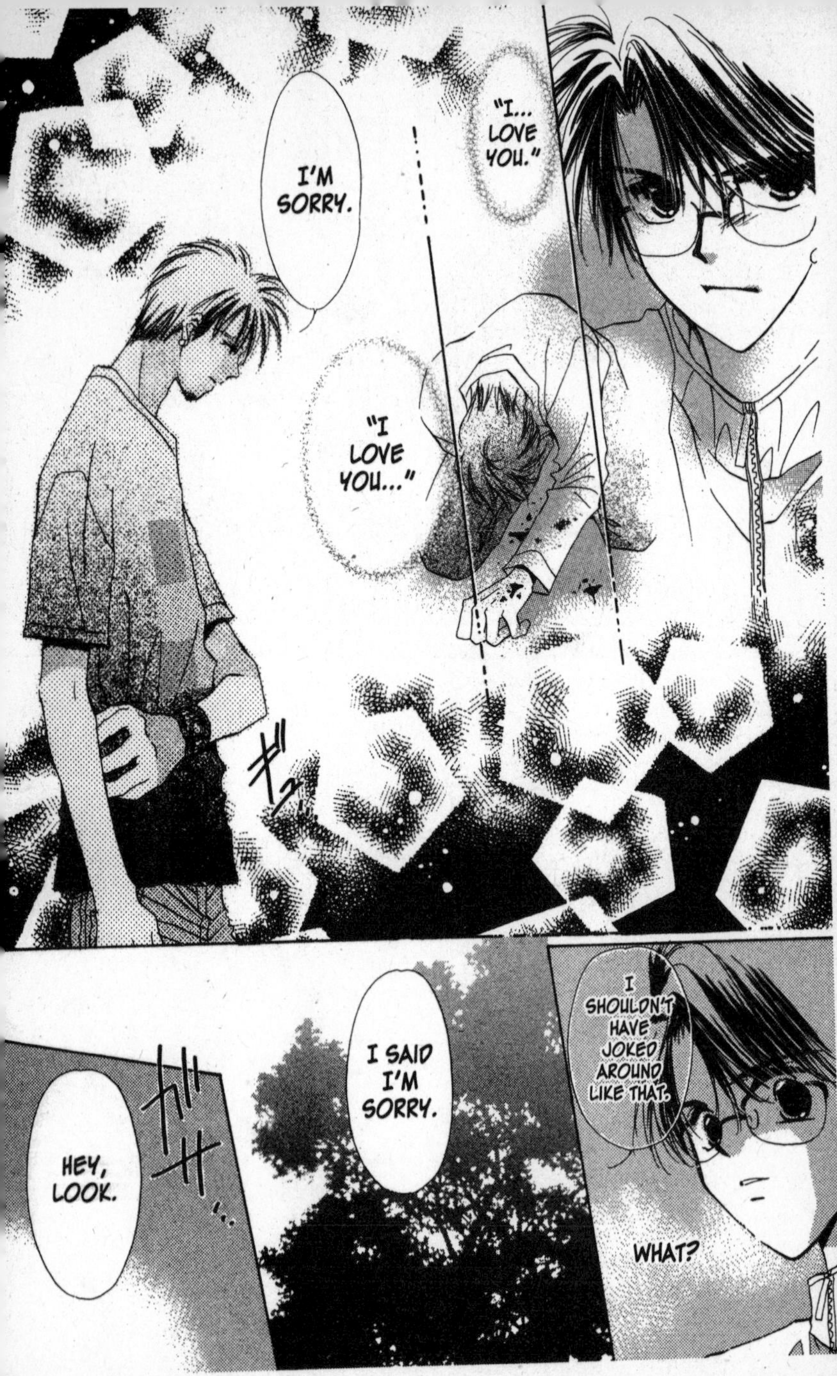
"I... LOVE YOU."
I'M SORRY.
"I LOVE YOU..."
I SHOULDN'T HAVE JOKED AROUND LIKE THAT.
WHAT?
I SAID I'M SORRY.
HEY, LOOK.

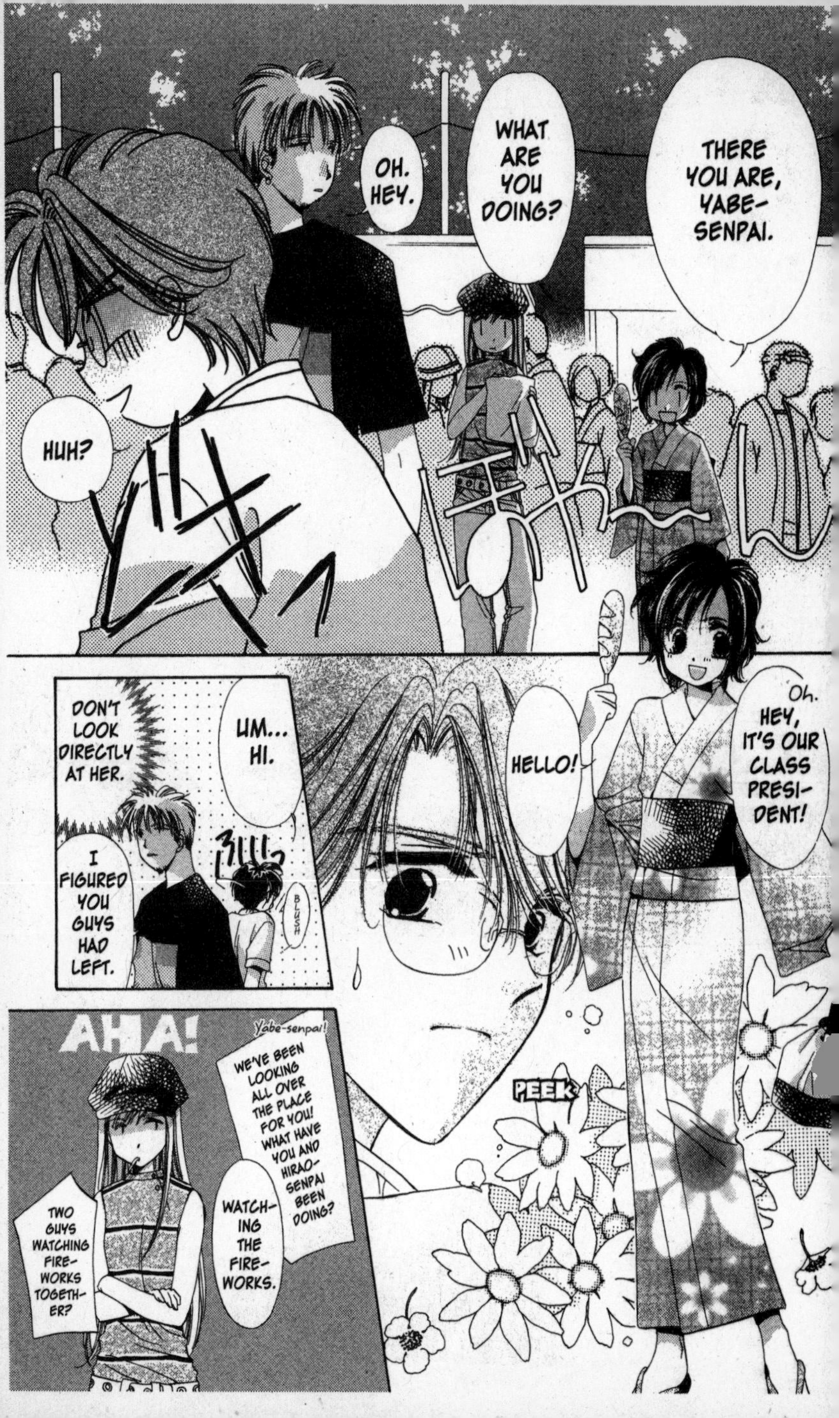

THERE YOU ARE, YABE-SENPAI.
WHAT ARE YOU DOING?
OH. HEY.
HUH?
Oh.
HEY, IT'S OUR CLASS PRESIDENT!
HELLO!
PEEK
UM... HI.
DON'T LOOK DIRECTLY AT HER.
I FIGURED YOU GUYS HAD LEFT.
BLUSH
Yabe-senpai!
AHA!
WE'VE BEEN LOOKING ALL OVER THE PLACE FOR YOU! WHAT HAVE YOU AND HIRAO-SENPAI BEEN DOING?
WATCHING THE FIRE-WORKS.
TWO GUYS WATCHING FIRE-WORKS TOGETHER?

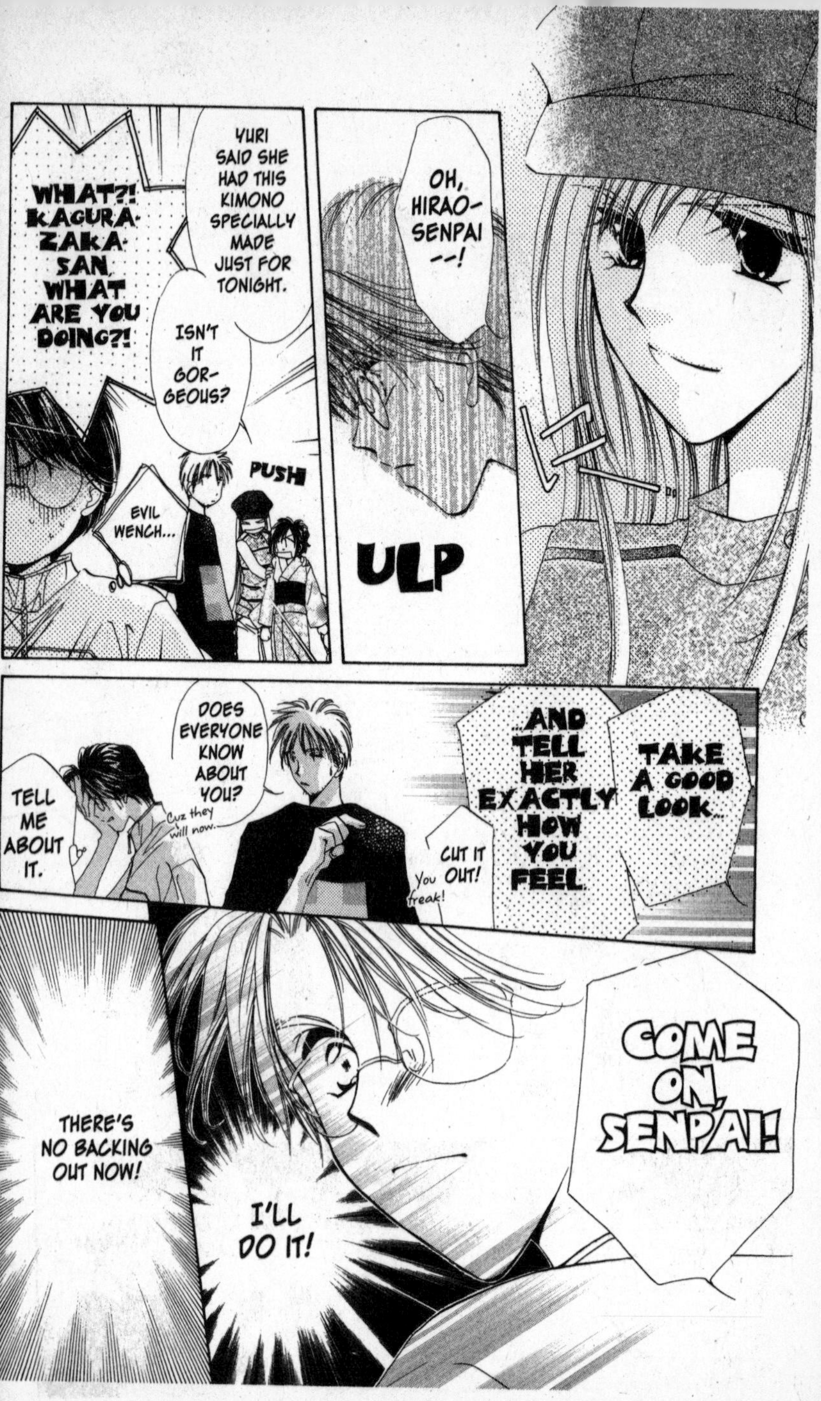
OH, HIRAO-SENPAI--!
ULP
YURI SAID SHE HAD THIS KIMONO SPECIALLY MADE JUST FOR TONIGHT.
WHAT?! KAGURA-ZAKA-SAN, WHAT ARE YOU DOING?!
ISN'T IT GORGEOUS?
PUSH
EVIL WENCH...
TAKE A GOOD LOOK...
...AND TELL HER EXACTLY HOW YOU FEEL
CUT IT OUT!
You freak!
DOES EVERYONE KNOW ABOUT YOU?
Cuz they will now...
TELL ME ABOUT IT.
COME ON, SENPAI!
I'LL DO IT!
THERE'S NO BACKING OUT NOW!

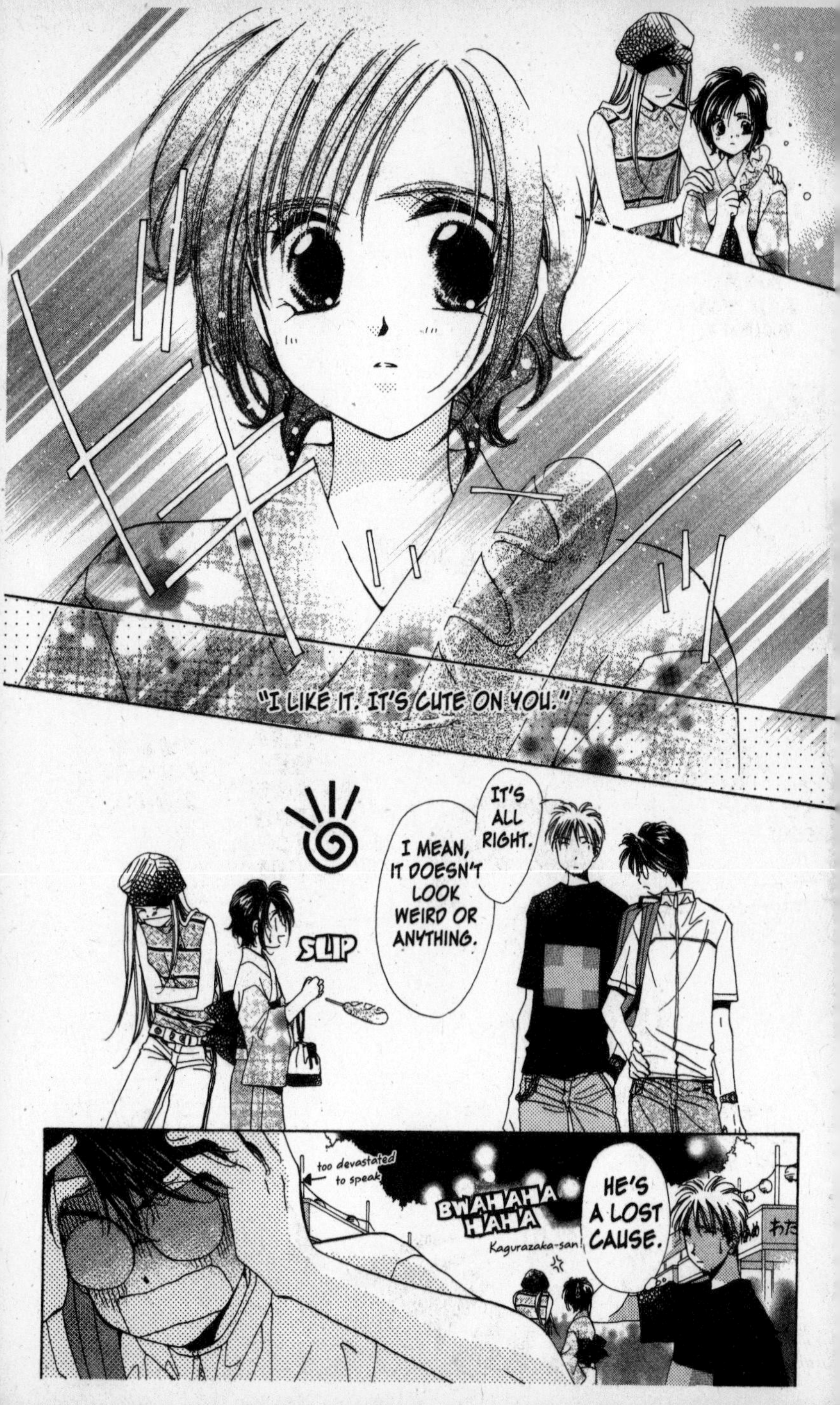
"I LIKE IT. IT'S CUTE ON YOU."
IT'S ALL RIGHT.
I MEAN, IT DOESN'T LOOK WEIRD OR ANYTHING.
SLIP
HE'S A LOST CAUSE.
Kagurazaka-san!
BWAHAHA HAHA
too devastated to speak

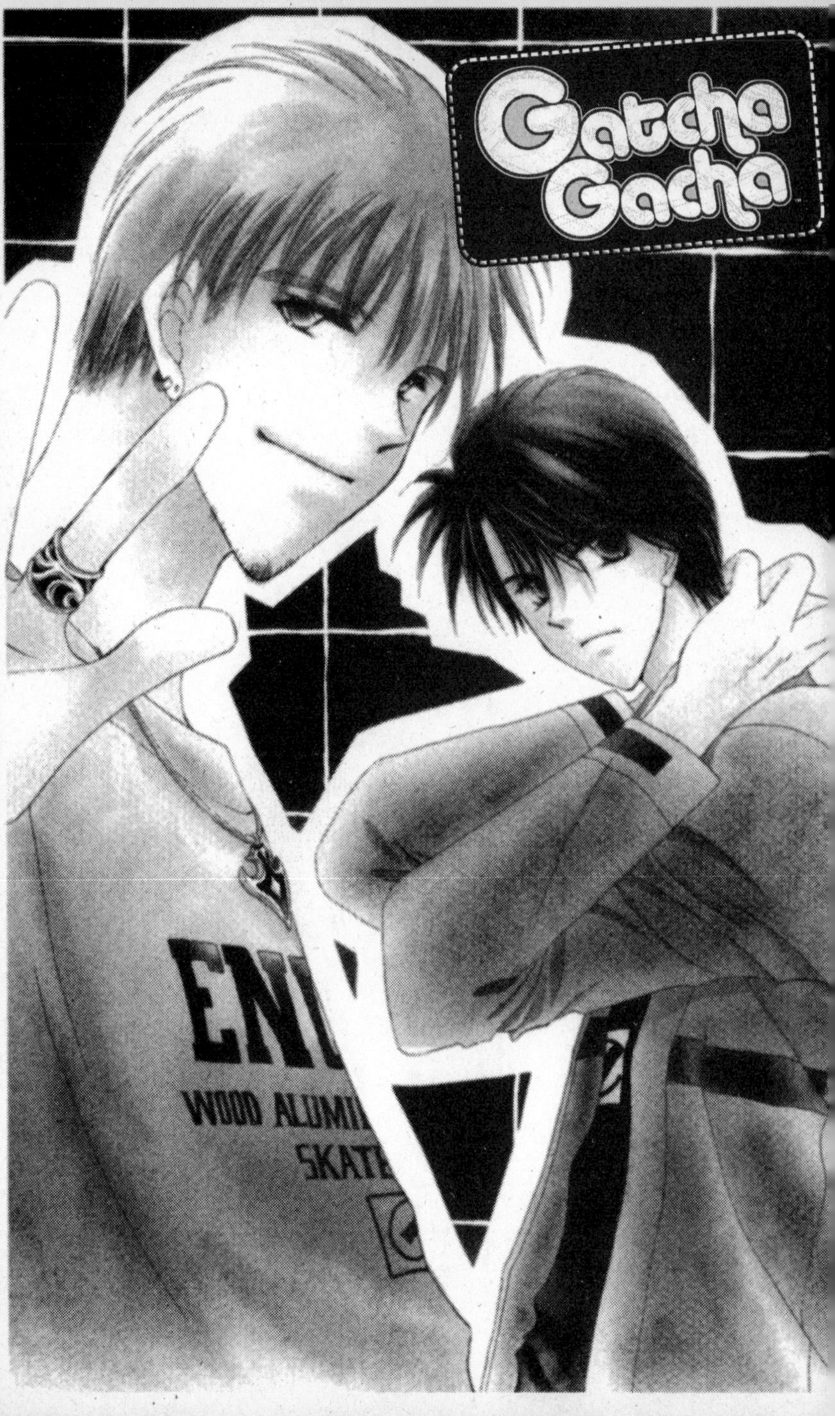
Gatcha Gacha
ENI
WOOD ALUMI
SKATE

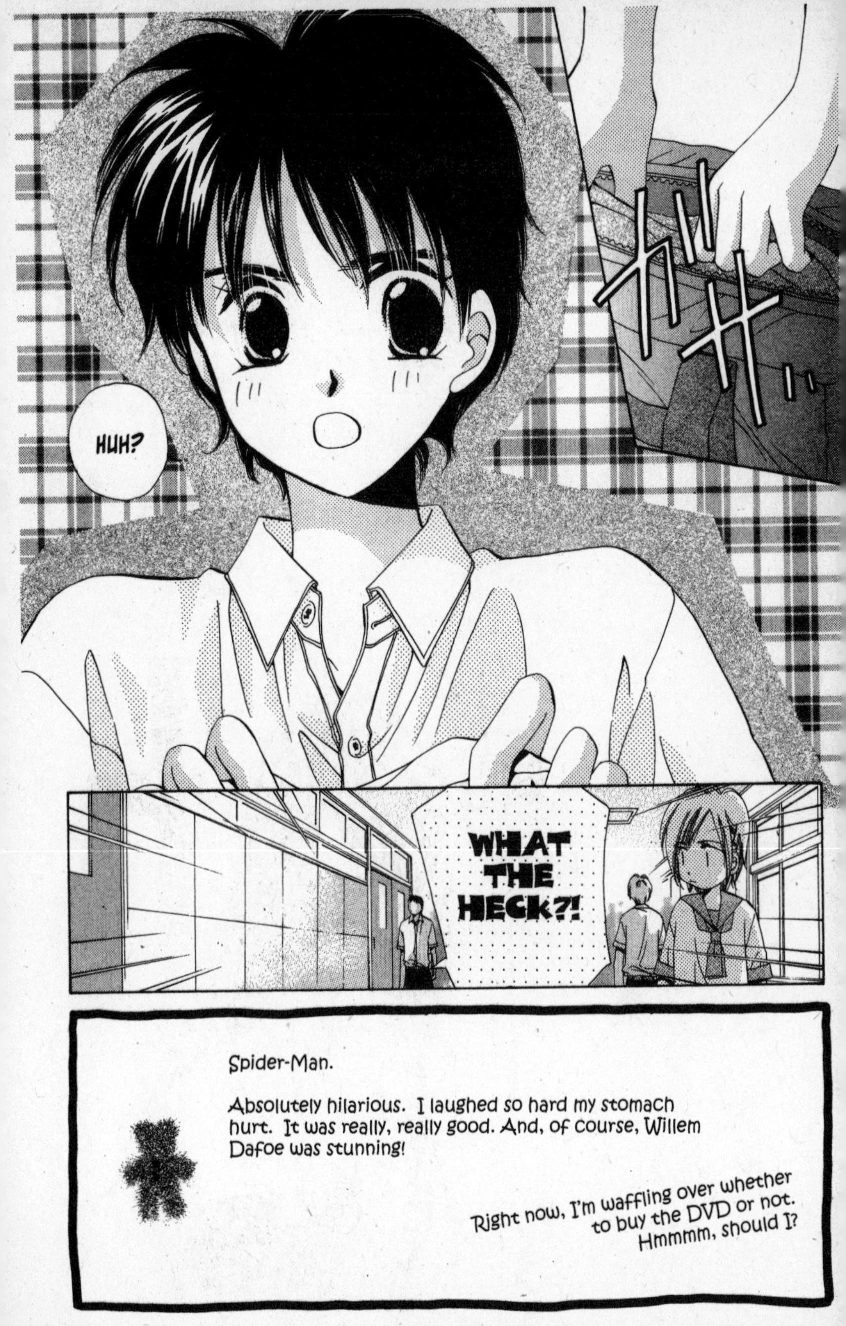
HUH?
WHAT THE HECK?!

Spider-Man.

Absolutely hilarious. I laughed so hard my stomach hurt. It was really, really good. And, of course, Willem Dafoe was stunning!

Right now, I'm waffling over whether to buy the DVD or not. Hmmmm, should I?

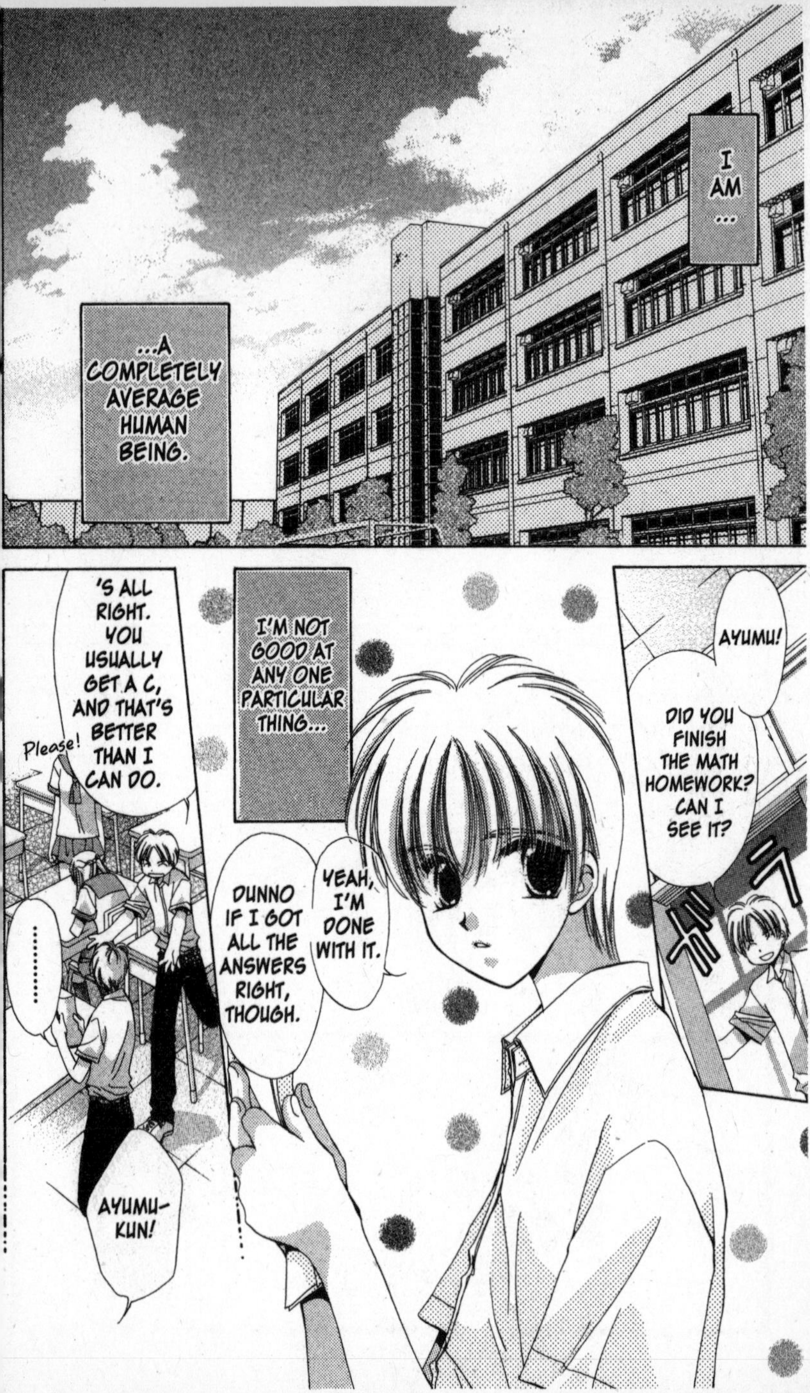
I AM ...
...A COMPLETELY AVERAGE HUMAN BEING.
AYUMU!
DID YOU FINISH THE MATH HOMEWORK? CAN I SEE IT?
I'M NOT GOOD AT ANY ONE PARTICULAR THING...
YEAH, I'M DONE WITH IT.
DUNNO IF I GOT ALL THE ANSWERS RIGHT, THOUGH.
'S ALL RIGHT. YOU USUALLY GET A C, AND THAT'S BETTER THAN I CAN DO.
Please!
......
AYUMU-KUN!

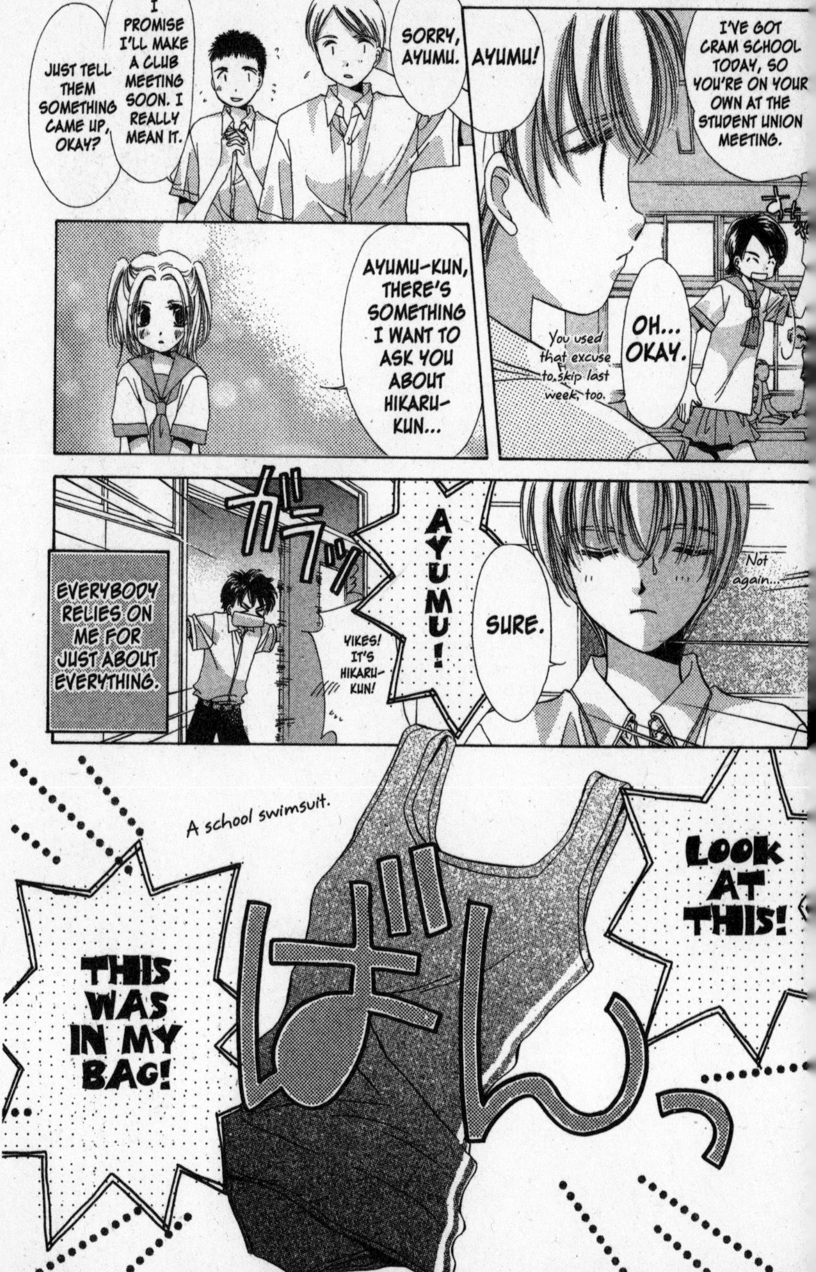

AYUMU!
I'VE GOT CRAM SCHOOL TODAY, SO YOU'RE ON YOUR OWN AT THE STUDENT UNION MEETING.
OH... OKAY.
You used that excuse to skip last week, too.
SORRY, AYUMU.
I PROMISE I'LL MAKE A CLUB MEETING SOON. I REALLY MEAN IT.
JUST TELL THEM SOMETHING CAME UP, OKAY?
AYUMU-KUN, THERE'S SOMETHING I WANT TO ASK YOU ABOUT HIKARU-KUN...
Not again...
SURE.
AYUMU!
YIKES! IT'S HIKARU-KUN!
ガラッ
EVERYBODY RELIES ON ME FOR JUST ABOUT EVERYTHING.
LOOK AT THIS!
A school swimsuit.
ばんっ
THIS WAS IN MY BAG!

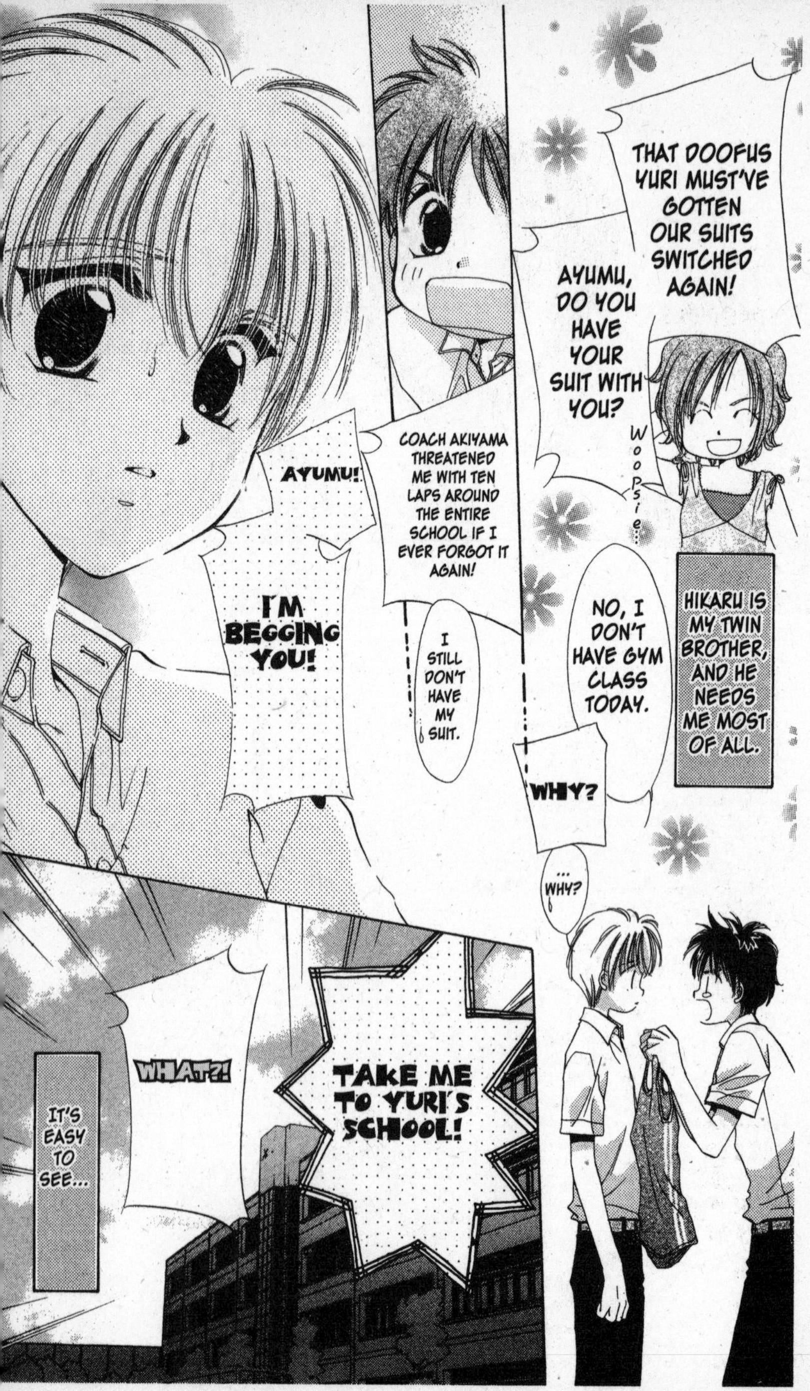
THAT DOOFUS YURI MUST'VE GOTTEN OUR SUITS SWITCHED AGAIN!
AYUMU, DO YOU HAVE YOUR SUIT WITH YOU?
Woopsie...
HIKARU IS MY TWIN BROTHER, AND HE NEEDS ME MOST OF ALL.
NO, I DON'T HAVE GYM CLASS TODAY.
WHY?
...WHY?
COACH AKIYAMA THREATENED ME WITH TEN LAPS AROUND THE ENTIRE SCHOOL IF I EVER FORGOT IT AGAIN!
I STILL DON'T HAVE MY SUIT.
AYUMU!
I'M BEGGING YOU!
TAKE ME TO YURI'S SCHOOL!
WHAT?!
IT'S EASY TO SEE...

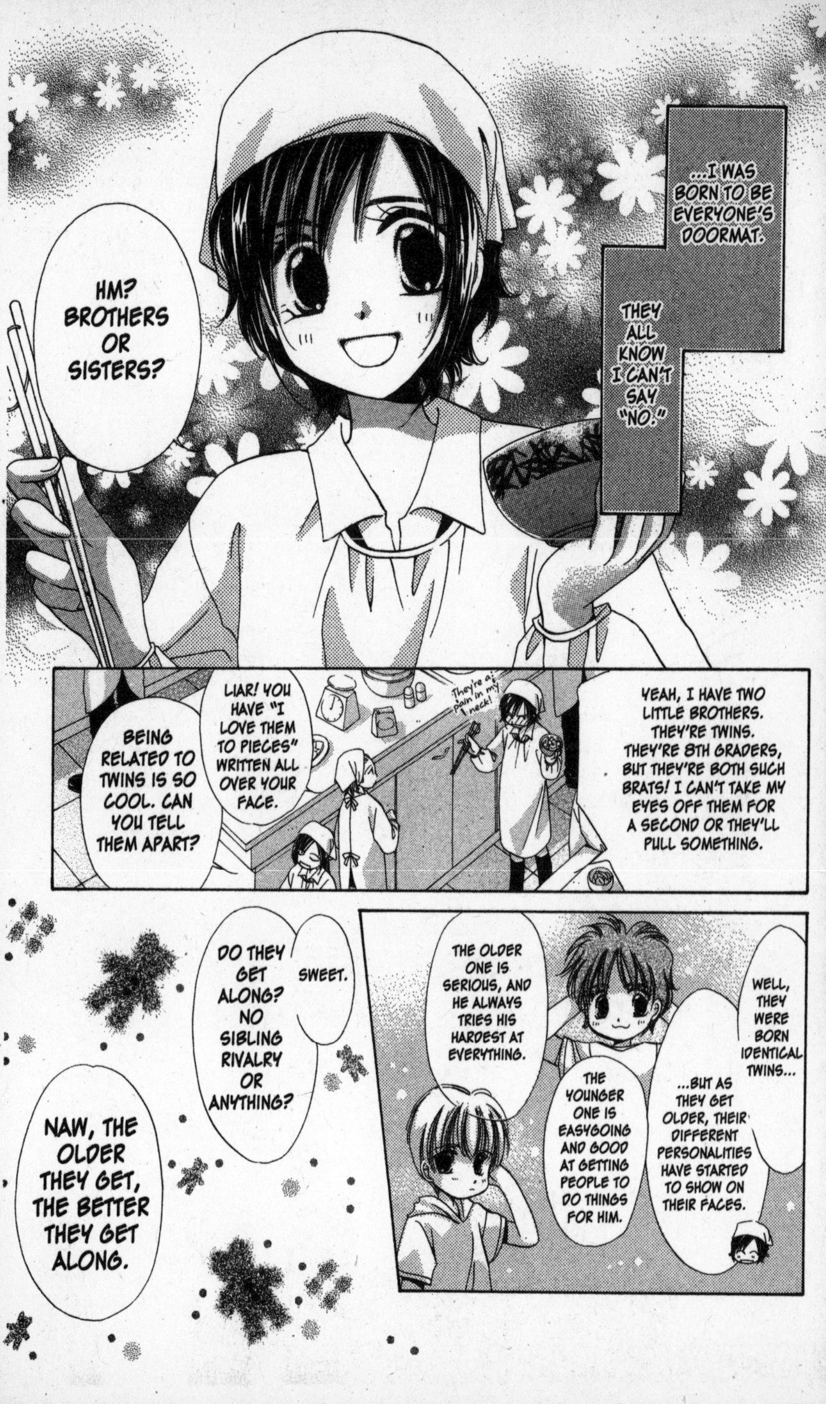
...I WAS BORN TO BE EVERYONE'S DOORMAT.
THEY ALL KNOW I CAN'T SAY "NO."
HM? BROTHERS OR SISTERS?
YEAH, I HAVE TWO LITTLE BROTHERS. THEY'RE TWINS. THEY'RE 8TH GRADERS, BUT THEY'RE BOTH SUCH BRATS! I CAN'T TAKE MY EYES OFF THEM FOR A SECOND OR THEY'LL PULL SOMETHING.
They're a pain in my neck!
LIAR! YOU HAVE "I LOVE THEM TO PIECES" WRITTEN ALL OVER YOUR FACE.
BEING RELATED TO TWINS IS SO COOL. CAN YOU TELL THEM APART?
WELL, THEY WERE BORN IDENTICAL TWINS...
...BUT AS THEY GET OLDER, THEIR DIFFERENT PERSONALITIES HAVE STARTED TO SHOW ON THEIR FACES.
THE OLDER ONE IS SERIOUS, AND HE ALWAYS TRIES HIS HARDEST AT EVERYTHING.
THE YOUNGER ONE IS EASYGOING AND GOOD AT GETTING PEOPLE TO DO THINGS FOR HIM.
SWEET.
DO THEY GET ALONG? NO SIBLING RIVALRY OR ANYTHING?
NAW, THE OLDER THEY GET, THE BETTER THEY GET ALONG.

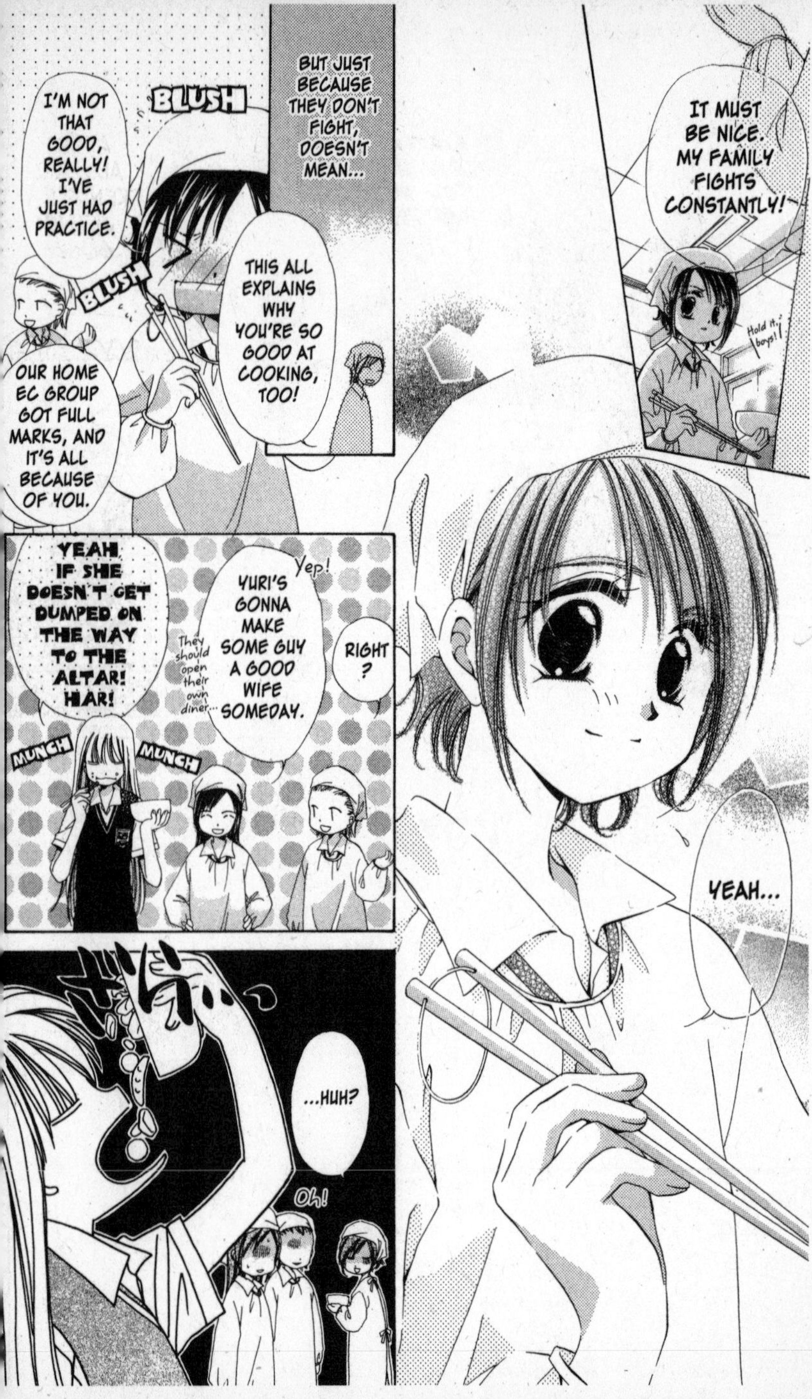
IT MUST BE NICE. MY FAMILY FIGHTS CONSTANTLY!
Hold it, boys!!
YEAH...
BUT JUST BECAUSE THEY DON'T FIGHT, DOESN'T MEAN...
THIS ALL EXPLAINS WHY YOU'RE SO GOOD AT COOKING, TOO!
BLUSH
I'M NOT THAT GOOD, REALLY! I'VE JUST HAD PRACTICE.
BLUSH
OUR HOME EC GROUP GOT FULL MARKS, AND IT'S ALL BECAUSE OF YOU.
RIGHT?
Yep!
YURI'S GONNA MAKE SOME GUY A GOOD WIFE SOMEDAY.
They should open their own diner...
YEAH IF SHE DOESN'T GET DUMPED ON THE WAY TO THE ALTAR! HAR!
MUNCH
MUNCH
...HUH?
Oh!

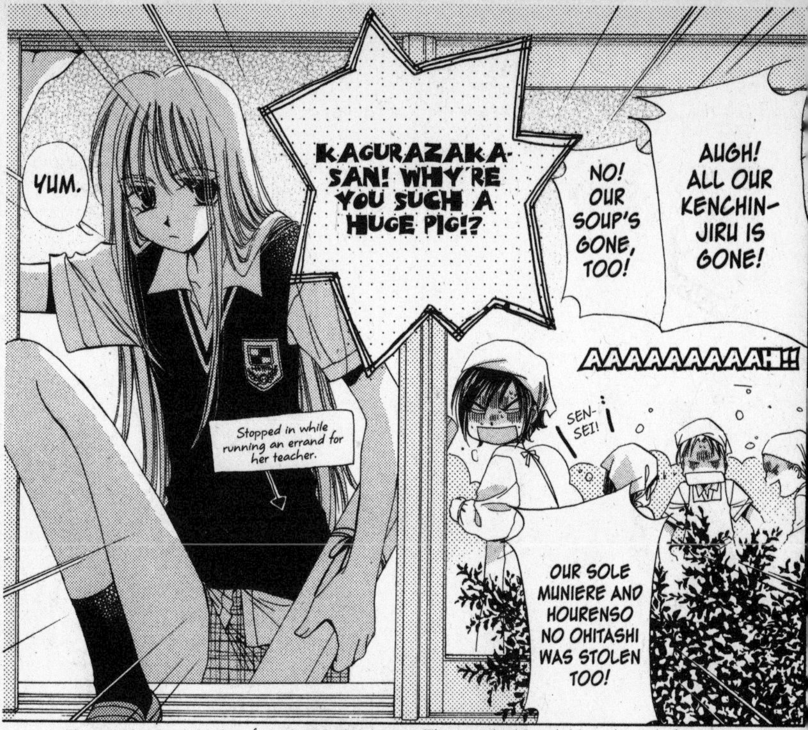
AUGH! ALL OUR KENCHIN-JIRU IS GONE!
NO! OUR SOUP'S GONE, TOO!
KAGURAZAKA-SAN! WHY'RE YOU SUCH A HUGE PIG!?
YUM.
AAAAAAAAAAH!!
SEN-SEI!
Stopped in while running an errand for her teacher.
OUR SOLE MUNIERE AND HOURENSO NO OHITASHI WAS STOLEN TOO!

*"Sole muniere" is a French dish. Sole is fried and coated with a citrusy sauce. *"Hourenso no ohitashi" = parboiled spinach covered with a citrusy sauce.

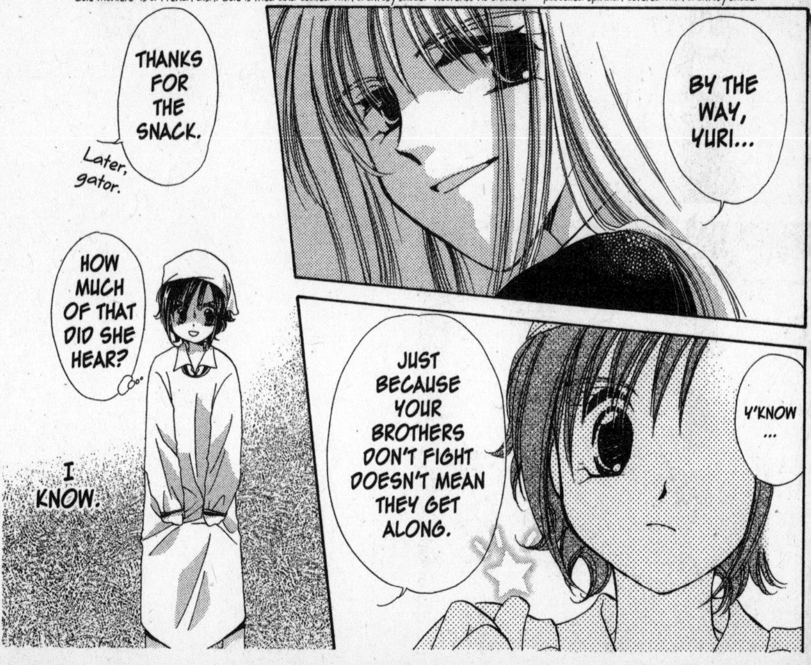
BY THE WAY, YURI...
THANKS FOR THE SNACK.
Later, gator.
Y'KNOW...
JUST BECAUSE YOUR BROTHERS DON'T FIGHT DOESN'T MEAN THEY GET ALONG.
HOW MUCH OF THAT DID SHE HEAR?
I KNOW.

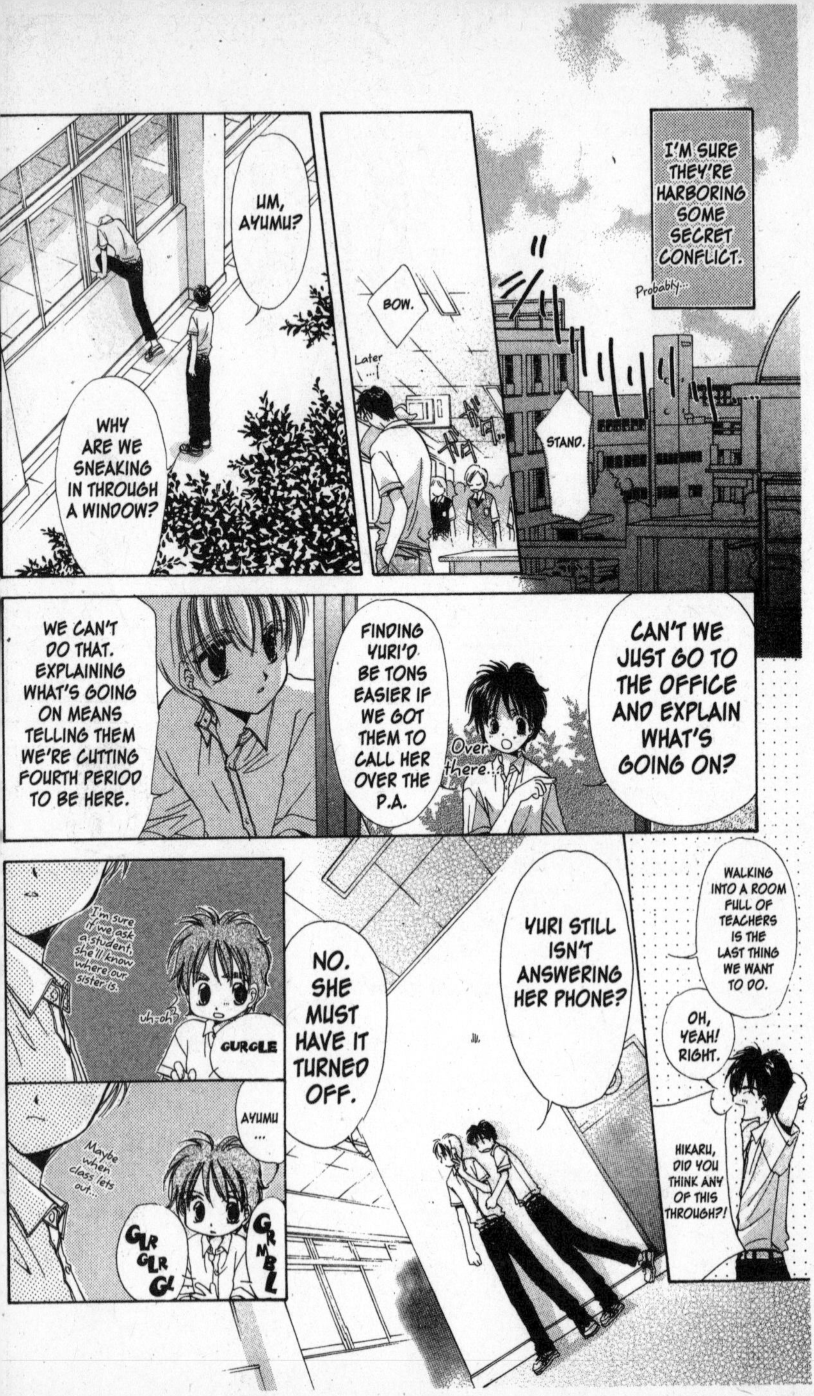
I'M SURE THEY'RE HARBORING SOME SECRET CONFLICT.
Probably...
STAND.
BOW.
Later ...!
UM, AYUMU?
WHY ARE WE SNEAKING IN THROUGH A WINDOW?
CAN'T WE JUST GO TO THE OFFICE AND EXPLAIN WHAT'S GOING ON?
FINDING YURI'D BE TONS EASIER IF WE GOT THEM TO CALL HER OVER THE P.A.
Over there...
WE CAN'T DO THAT. EXPLAINING WHAT'S GOING ON MEANS TELLING THEM WE'RE CUTTING FOURTH PERIOD TO BE HERE.
WALKING INTO A ROOM FULL OF TEACHERS IS THE LAST THING WE WANT TO DO.
OH, YEAH! RIGHT.
HIKARU, DID YOU THINK ANY OF THIS THROUGH?!
YURI STILL ISN'T ANSWERING HER PHONE?
NO. SHE MUST HAVE IT TURNED OFF.
I'm sure if we ask a student, she'll know where our sister is.
uh-oh?
GURGLE
AYUMU ...
Maybe when class lets out...
GLR GLR GL
GRMBL

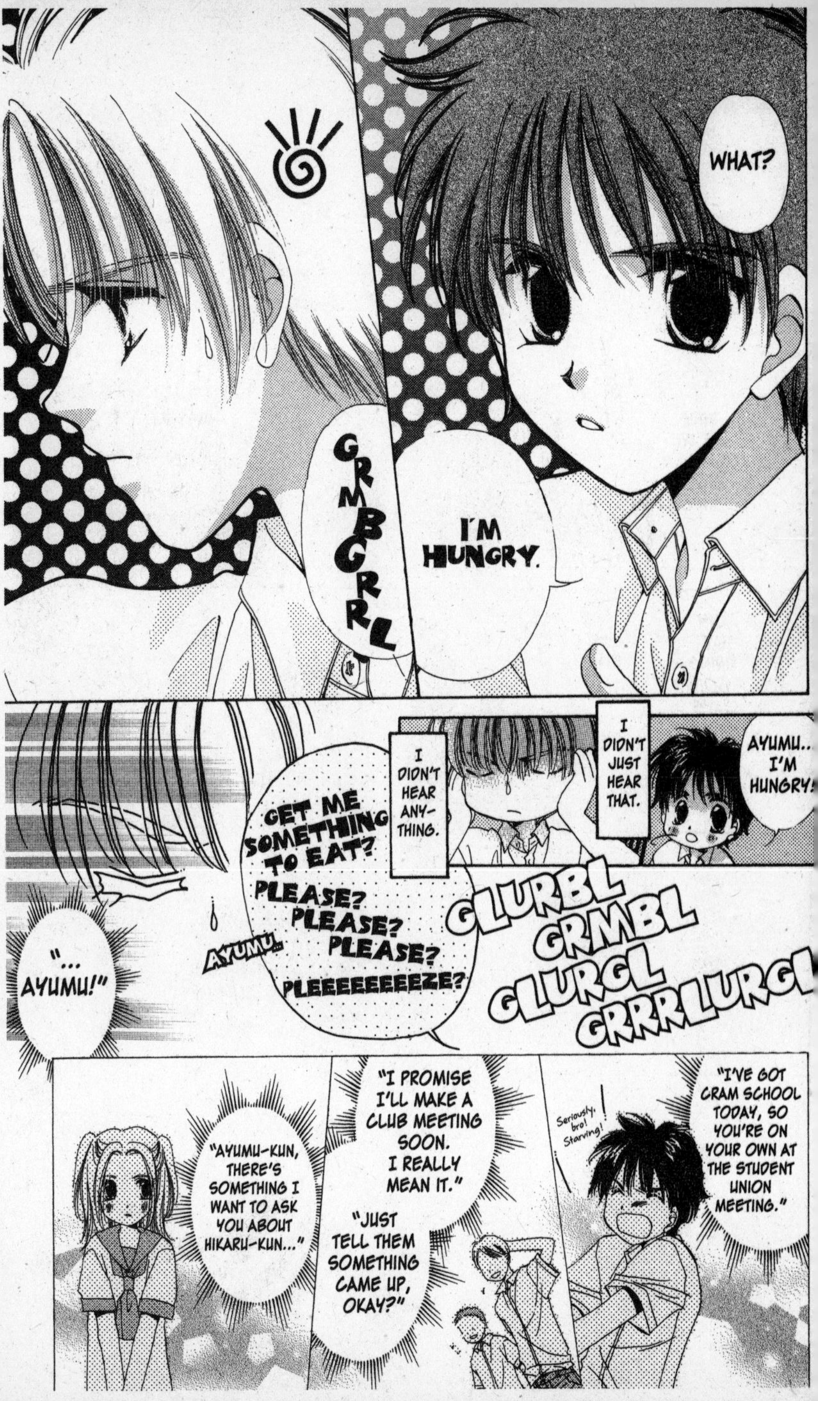
WHAT?
I'M HUNGRY.
GRMBGRRL
AYUMU... I'M HUNGRY!
I DIDN'T JUST HEAR THAT.
I DIDN'T HEAR ANY-THING.
GET ME SOMETHING TO EAT? PLEASE? PLEASE? PLEASE? PLEEEEEEEEZE?
GLURBL GRMBL GLURGL GRRRLURGL
AYUMU...
"... AYUMU!"
"I'VE GOT CRAM SCHOOL TODAY, SO YOU'RE ON YOUR OWN AT THE STUDENT UNION MEETING."
Seriously, bro! Starving!
"I PROMISE I'LL MAKE A CLUB MEETING SOON. I REALLY MEAN IT."
"JUST TELL THEM SOMETHING CAME UP, OKAY?"
"AYUMU-KUN, THERE'S SOMETHING I WANT TO ASK YOU ABOUT HIKARU-KUN..."

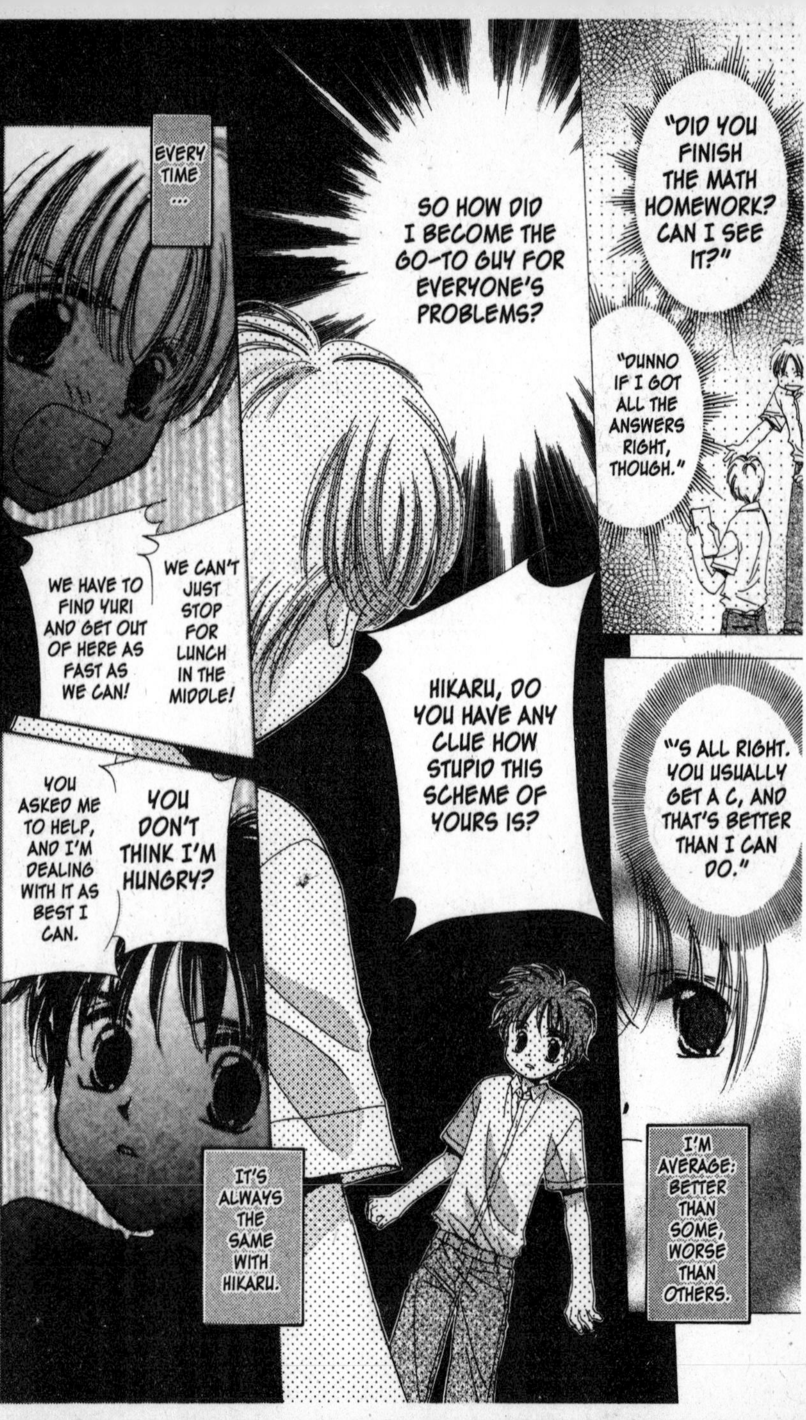
"DID YOU FINISH THE MATH HOMEWORK? CAN I SEE IT?"
"DUNNO IF I GOT ALL THE ANSWERS RIGHT, THOUGH."
SO HOW DID I BECOME THE GO-TO GUY FOR EVERYONE'S PROBLEMS?
EVERY TIME ...
WE CAN'T JUST STOP FOR LUNCH IN THE MIDDLE!
WE HAVE TO FIND YURI AND GET OUT OF HERE AS FAST AS WE CAN!
"'S ALL RIGHT. YOU USUALLY GET A C, AND THAT'S BETTER THAN I CAN DO."
I'M AVERAGE: BETTER THAN SOME, WORSE THAN OTHERS.
HIKARU, DO YOU HAVE ANY CLUE HOW STUPID THIS SCHEME OF YOURS IS?
YOU DON'T THINK I'M HUNGRY?
YOU ASKED ME TO HELP, AND I'M DEALING WITH IT AS BEST I CAN.
IT'S ALWAYS THE SAME WITH HIKARU.

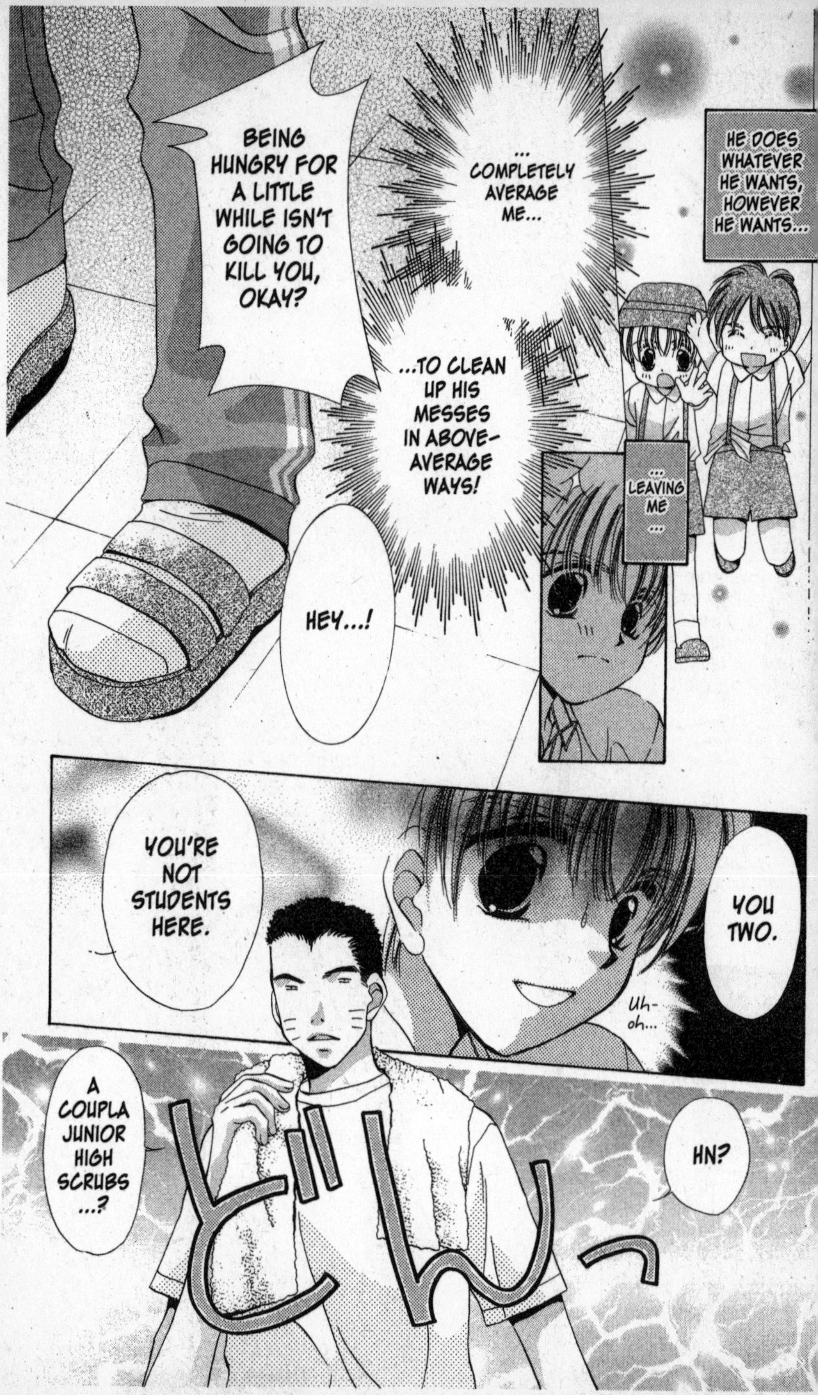
HE DOES WHATEVER HE WANTS, HOWEVER HE WANTS...
...LEAVING ME...
...COMPLETELY AVERAGE ME...
...TO CLEAN UP HIS MESSES IN ABOVE-AVERAGE WAYS!
BEING HUNGRY FOR A LITTLE WHILE ISN'T GOING TO KILL YOU, OKAY?
HEY...!
YOU TWO.
Uh-oh...
YOU'RE NOT STUDENTS HERE.
HN?
A COUPLA JUNIOR HIGH SCRUBS ...?

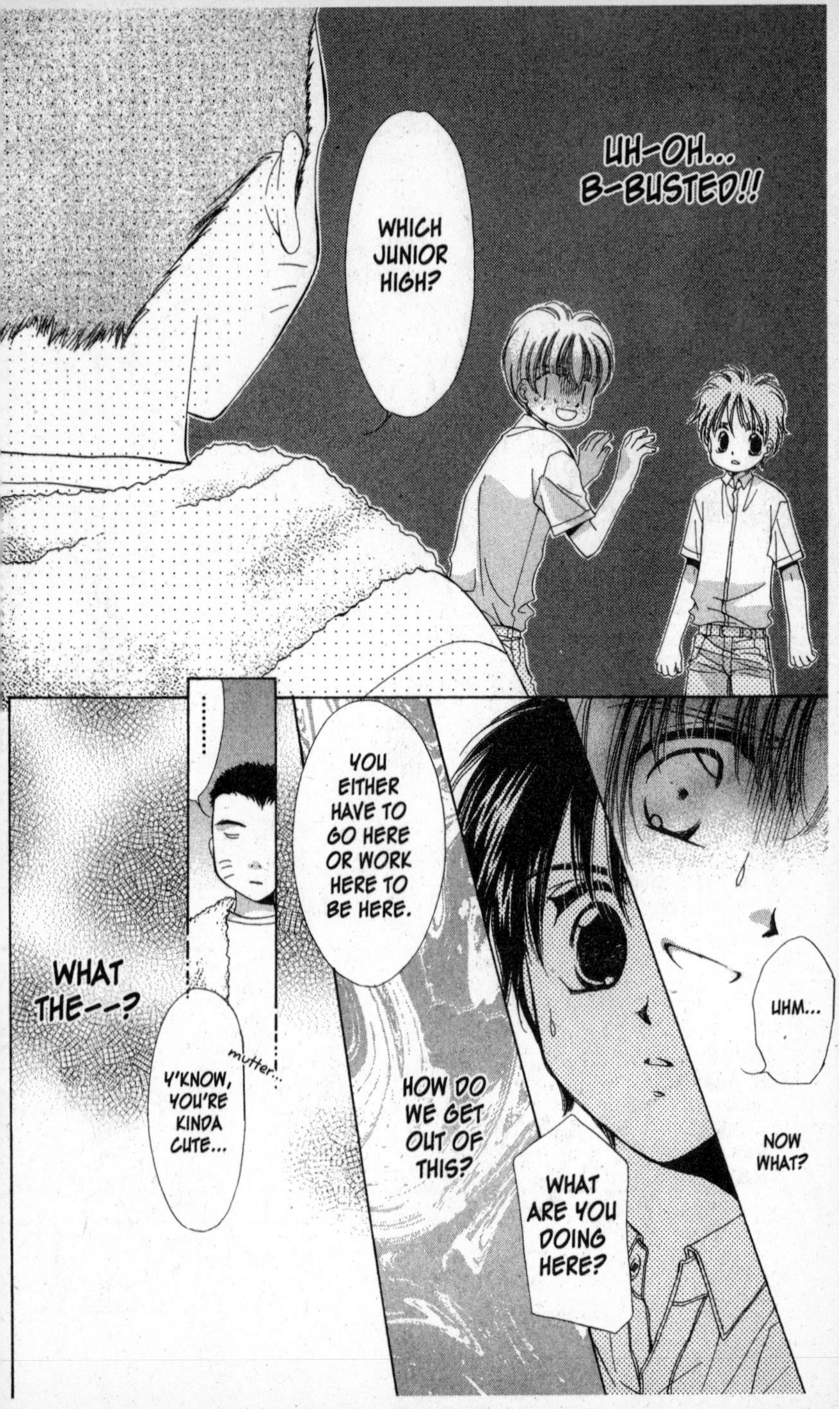

UH-OH... B-BUSTED!!
WHICH JUNIOR HIGH?
UHM...
NOW WHAT?
WHAT ARE YOU DOING HERE?
HOW DO WE GET OUT OF THIS?
YOU EITHER HAVE TO GO HERE OR WORK HERE TO BE HERE.
......
mutter...
Y'KNOW, YOU'RE KINDA CUTE...
WHAT THE--?

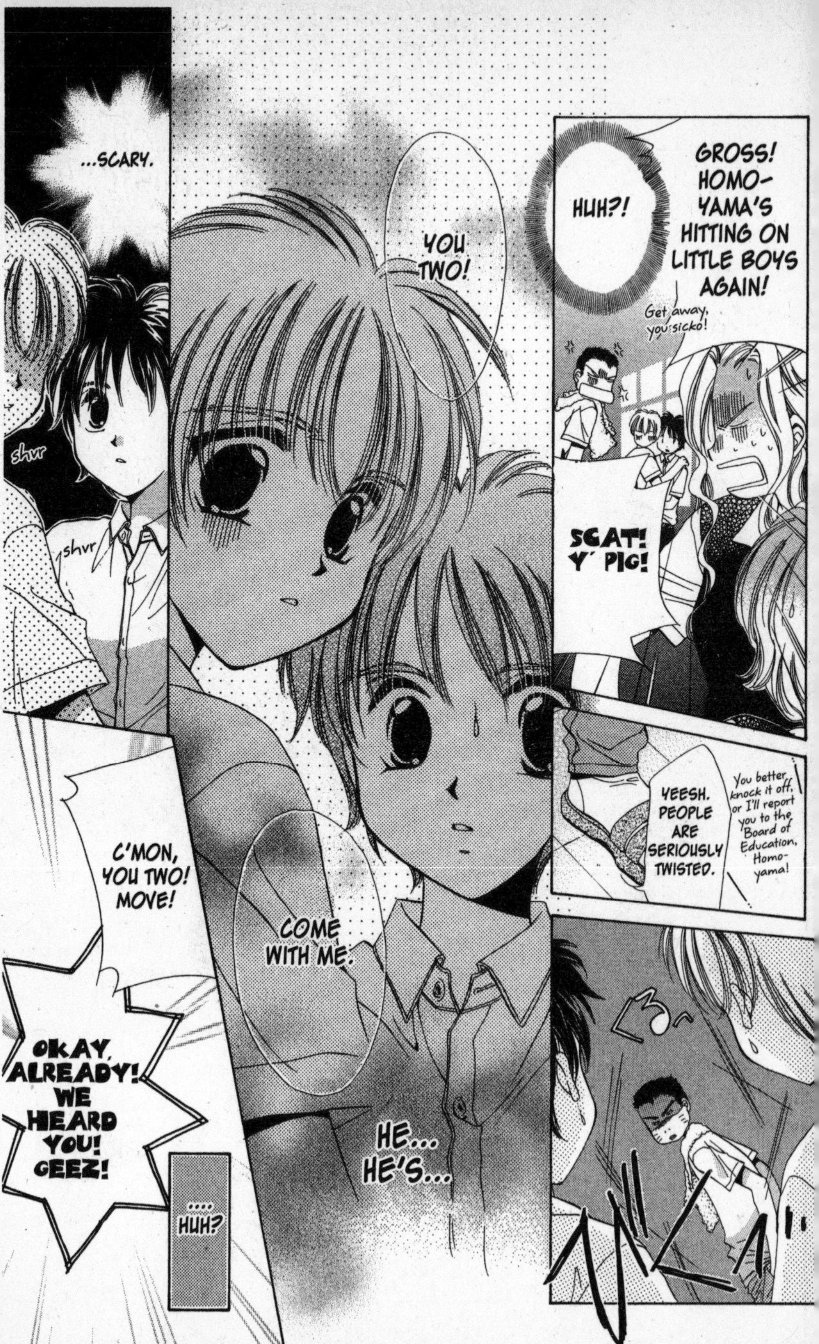
GROSS! HOMO-YAMA'S HITTING ON LITTLE BOYS AGAIN!
HUH?!
Get away, you sicko!
SCAT! Y' PIG!
You better knock it off, or I'll report you to the Board of Education, Homo-yama!
YEESH. PEOPLE ARE SERIOUSLY TWISTED.
YOU TWO!
COME WITH ME.
HE... HE'S...
...SCARY.
shvr
shvr
C'MON, YOU TWO! MOVE!
OKAY, ALREADY! WE HEARD YOU! GEEZ!
....HUH?

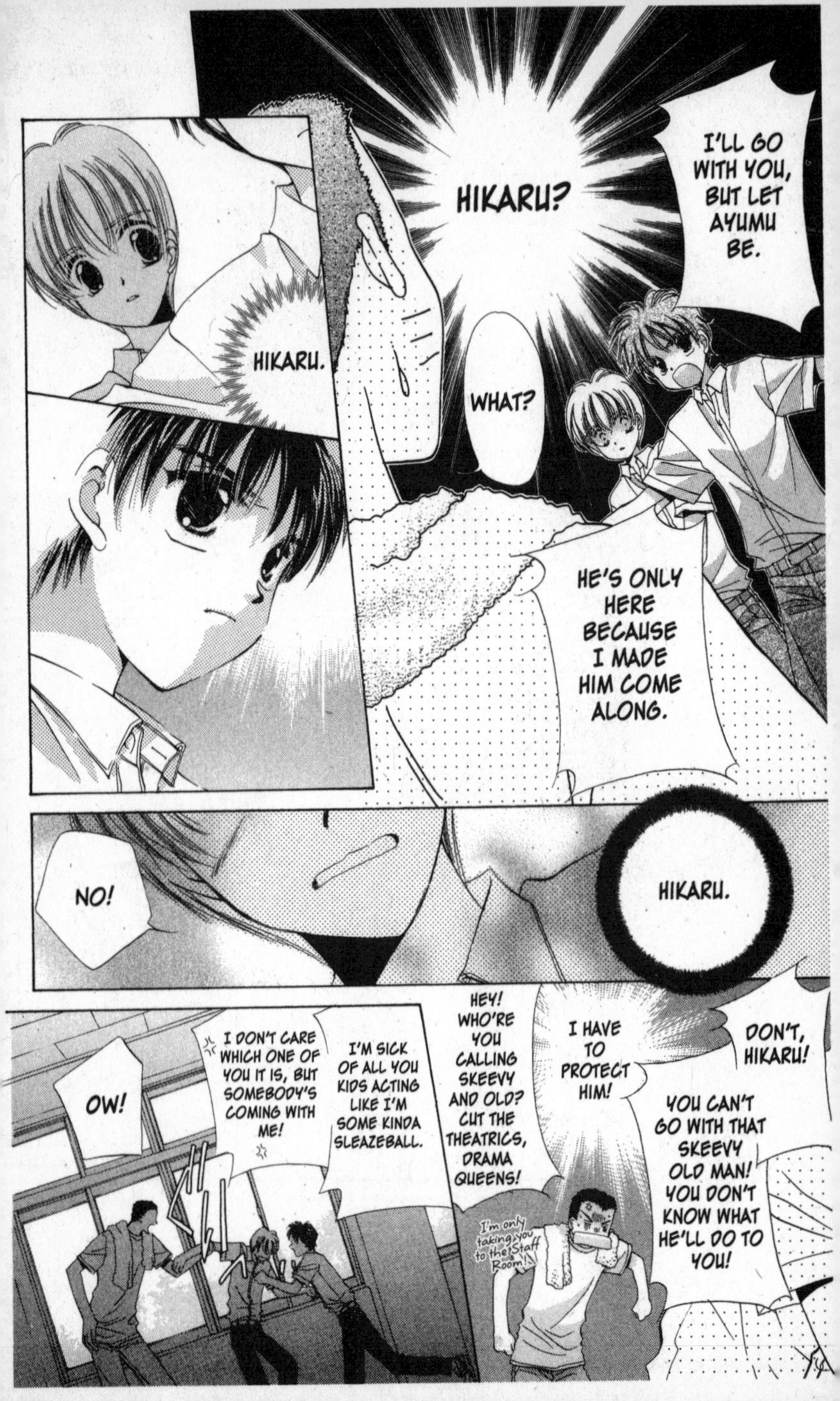
I'LL GO WITH YOU, BUT LET AYUMU BE.
HIKARU?
WHAT?
HE'S ONLY HERE BECAUSE I MADE HIM COME ALONG.
HIKARU.
HIKARU.
NO!
DON'T, HIKARU!
YOU CAN'T GO WITH THAT SKEEVY OLD MAN! YOU DON'T KNOW WHAT HE'LL DO TO YOU!
I HAVE TO PROTECT HIM!
HEY! WHO'RE YOU CALLING SKEEVY AND OLD? CUT THE THEATRICS, DRAMA QUEENS!
I'm only taking you to the Staff Room!
I'M SICK OF ALL YOU KIDS ACTING LIKE I'M SOME KINDA SLEAZEBALL.
I DON'T CARE WHICH ONE OF YOU IT IS, BUT SOMEBODY'S COMING WITH ME!
OW!

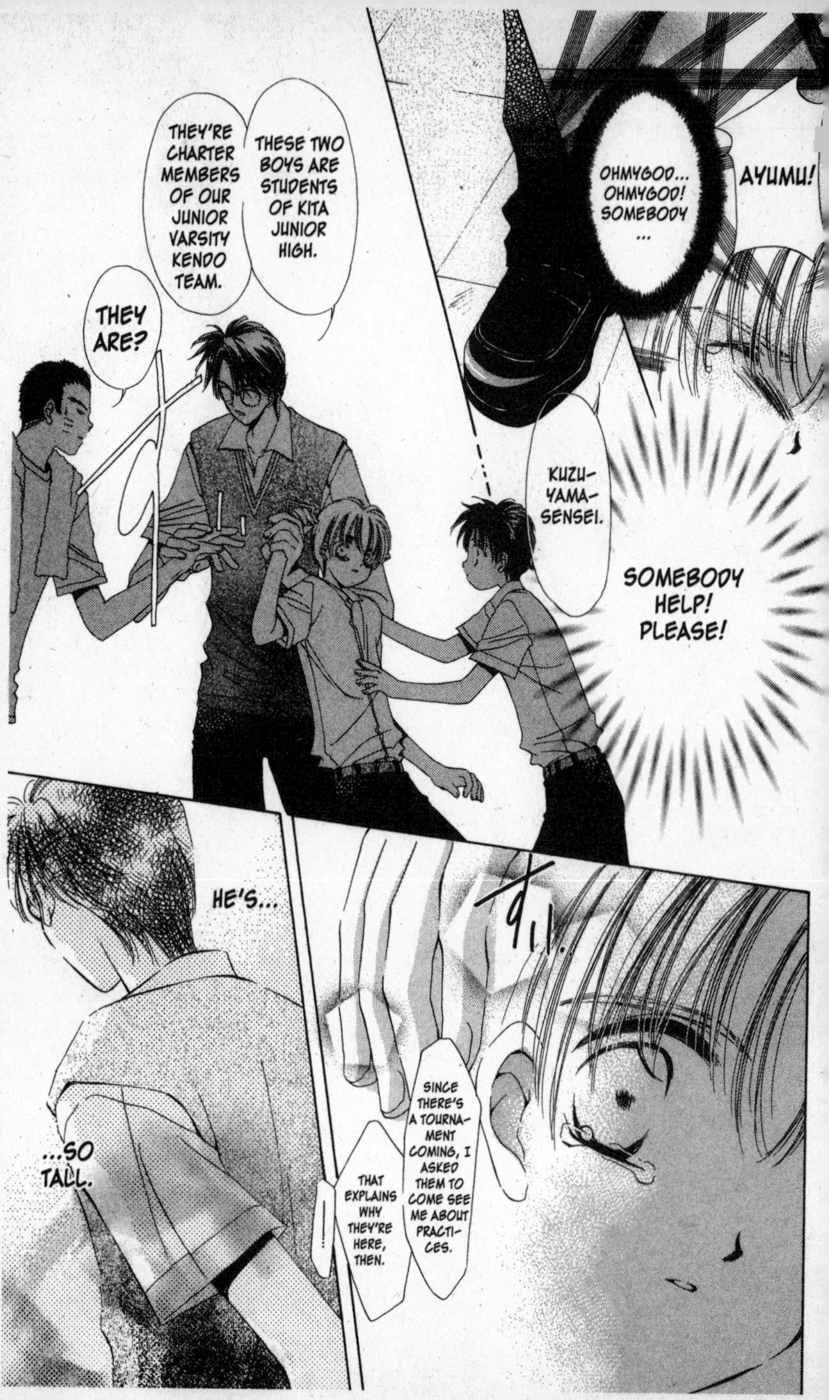
AYUMU!
OHMYGOD... OHMYGOD! SOMEBODY ...
SOMEBODY HELP! PLEASE!
KUZU-YAMA-SENSEI.
THESE TWO BOYS ARE STUDENTS OF KITA JUNIOR HIGH.
THEY'RE CHARTER MEMBERS OF OUR JUNIOR VARSITY KENDO TEAM.
THEY ARE?
SINCE THERE'S A TOURNA-MENT COMING, I ASKED THEM TO COME SEE ME ABOUT PRACTI-CES.
THAT EXPLAINS WHY THEY'RE HERE, THEN.
HE'S...
...SO TALL.

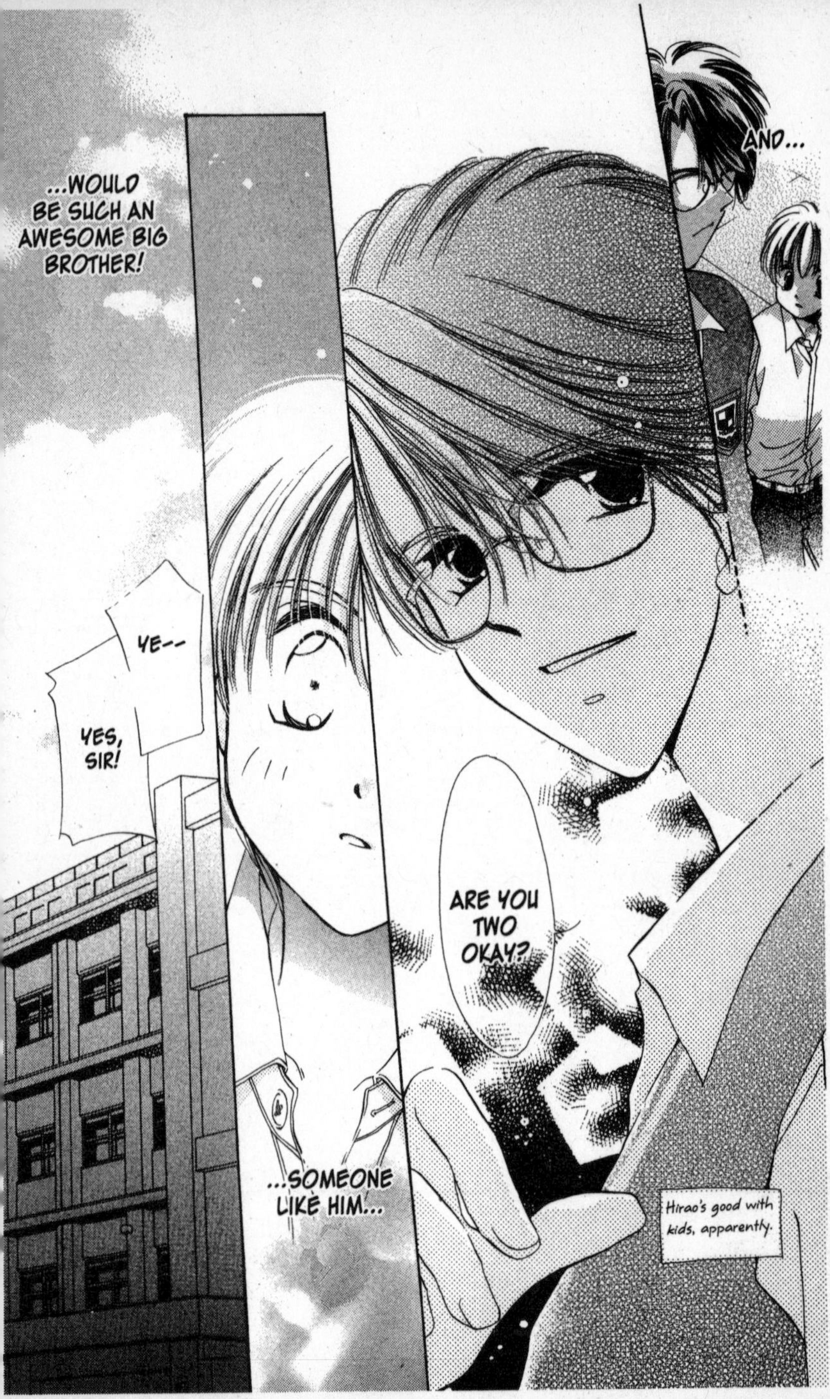
AND...
ARE YOU TWO OKAY?
YE--
YES, SIR!
...SOMEONE LIKE HIM...
...WOULD BE SUCH AN AWESOME BIG BROTHER!
Hirao's good with kids, apparently.

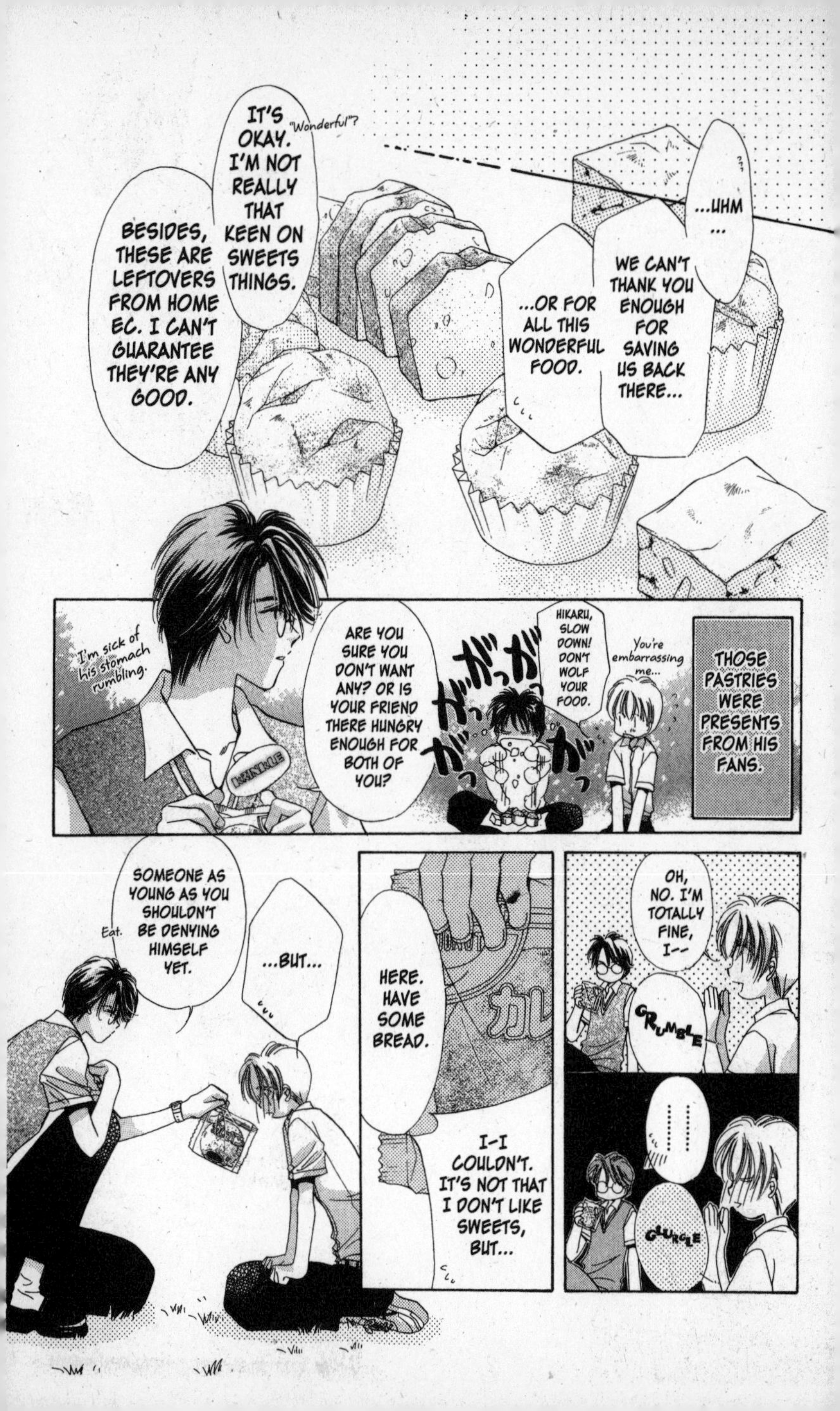
...UHM...
WE CAN'T THANK YOU ENOUGH FOR SAVING US BACK THERE...
...OR FOR ALL THIS WONDERFUL FOOD.
"Wonderful"?
IT'S OKAY. I'M NOT REALLY THAT KEEN ON SWEETS THINGS.
BESIDES, THESE ARE LEFTOVERS FROM HOME EC. I CAN'T GUARANTEE THEY'RE ANY GOOD.
THOSE PASTRIES WERE PRESENTS FROM HIS FANS.
You're embarrassing me...
HIKARU, SLOW DOWN! DON'T WOLF YOUR FOOD.
がっがっ
がっがっ
ARE YOU SURE YOU DON'T WANT ANY? OR IS YOUR FRIEND THERE HUNGRY ENOUGH FOR BOTH OF YOU?
I'm sick of his stomach rumbling.
WRINKLE
OH, NO. I'M TOTALLY FINE, I--
GRUMBLE
......
GLURGLE
HERE. HAVE SOME BREAD.
I-I COULDN'T. IT'S NOT THAT I DON'T LIKE SWEETS, BUT...
...BUT...
SOMEONE AS YOUNG AS YOU SHOULDN'T BE DENYING HIMSELF YET.
Eat.

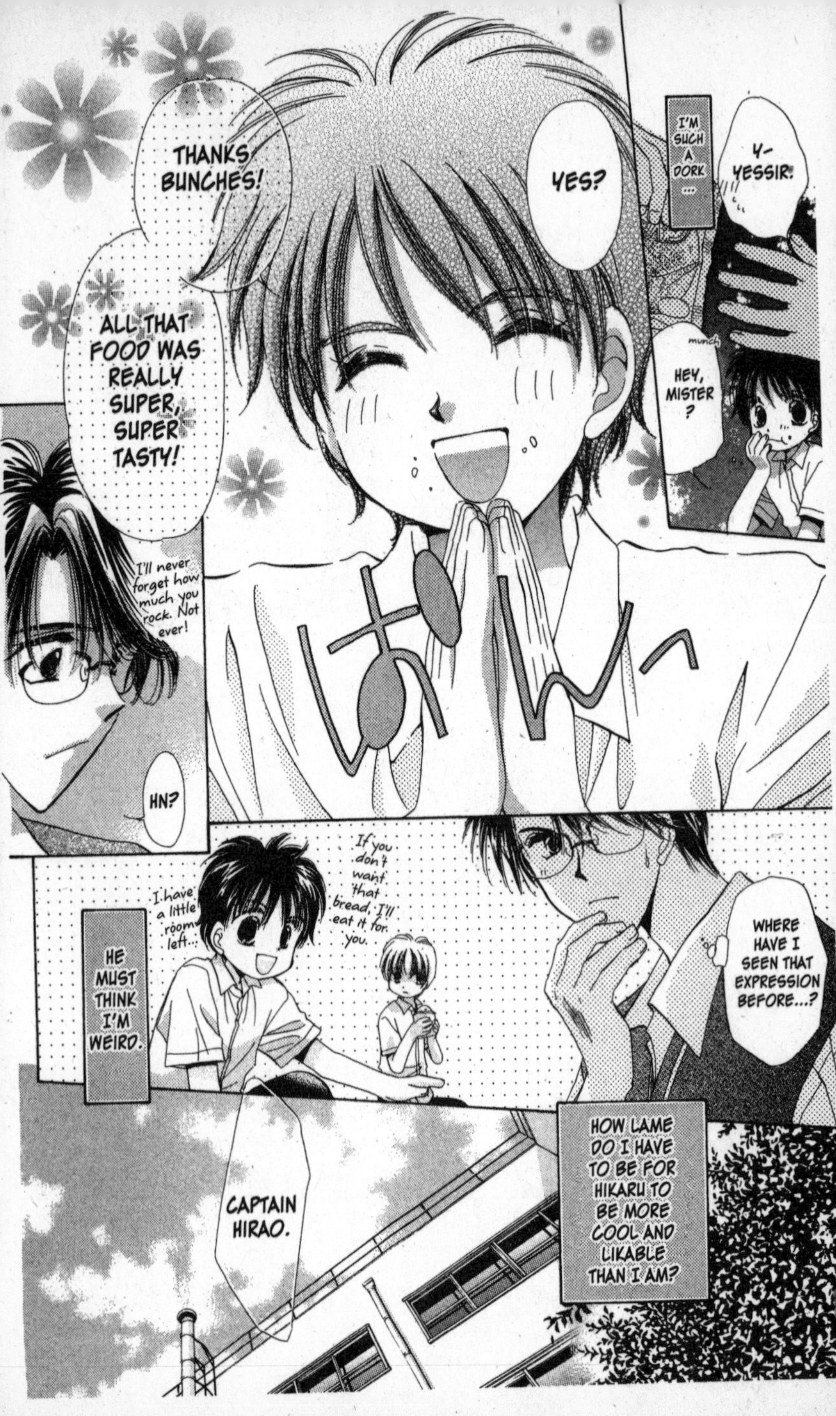
Y-YESSIR.
I'M SUCH A DORK...
munch
HEY, MISTER?
YES?
THANKS BUNCHES!
ALL THAT FOOD WAS REALLY SUPER, SUPER TASTY!
はい
I'll never forget how much you rock. Not ever!
HN?
WHERE HAVE I SEEN THAT EXPRESSION BEFORE...?
If you don't want that bread, I'll eat it for you.
I have a little room left...
HE MUST THINK I'M WEIRD.
HOW LAME DO I HAVE TO BE FOR HIKARU TO BE MORE COOL AND LIKABLE THAN I AM?
CAPTAIN HIRAO.

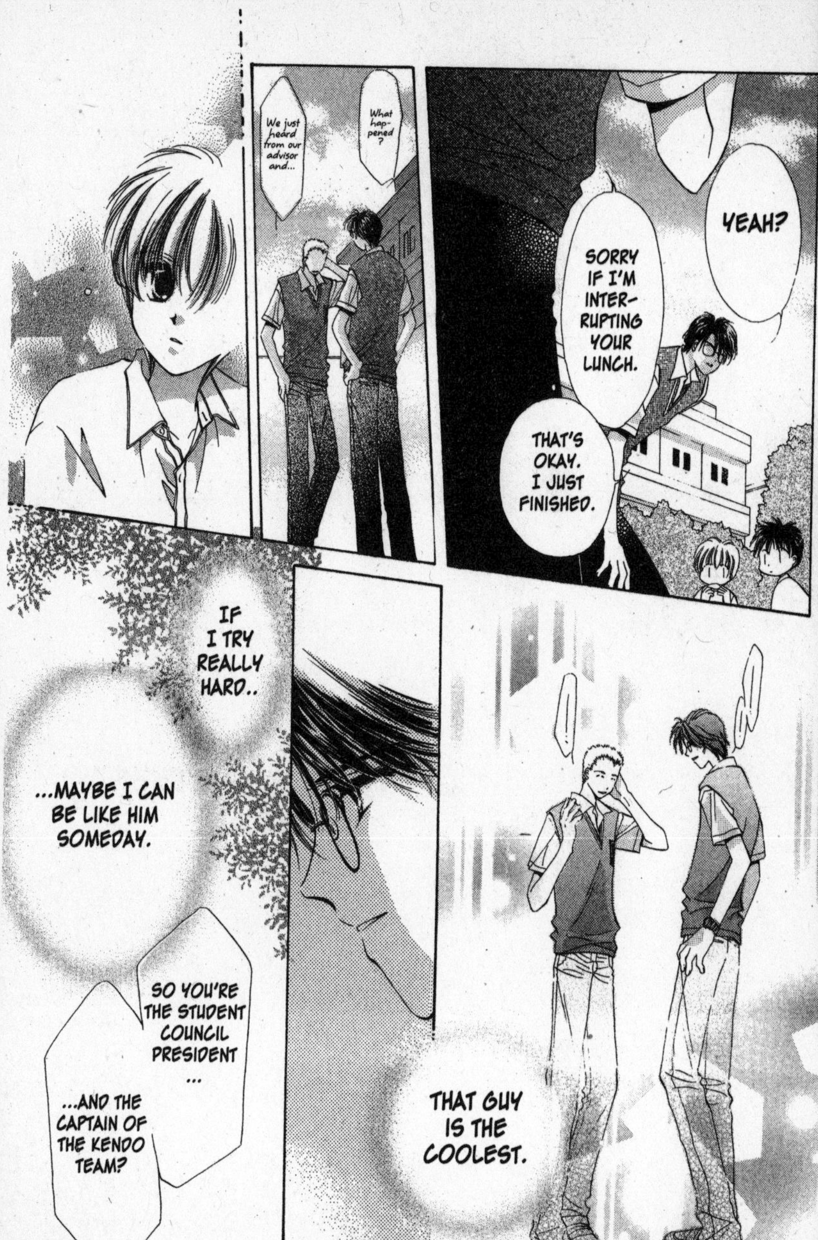
YEAH?
SORRY IF I'M INTER-RUPTING YOUR LUNCH.
THAT'S OKAY. I JUST FINISHED.
What hap-pened?
We just heard from our advisor and...
!
!
THAT GUY IS THE COOLEST.
IF I TRY REALLY HARD..
...MAYBE I CAN BE LIKE HIM SOMEDAY.
SO YOU'RE THE STUDENT COUNCIL PRESIDENT...
...AND THE CAPTAIN OF THE KENDO TEAM?

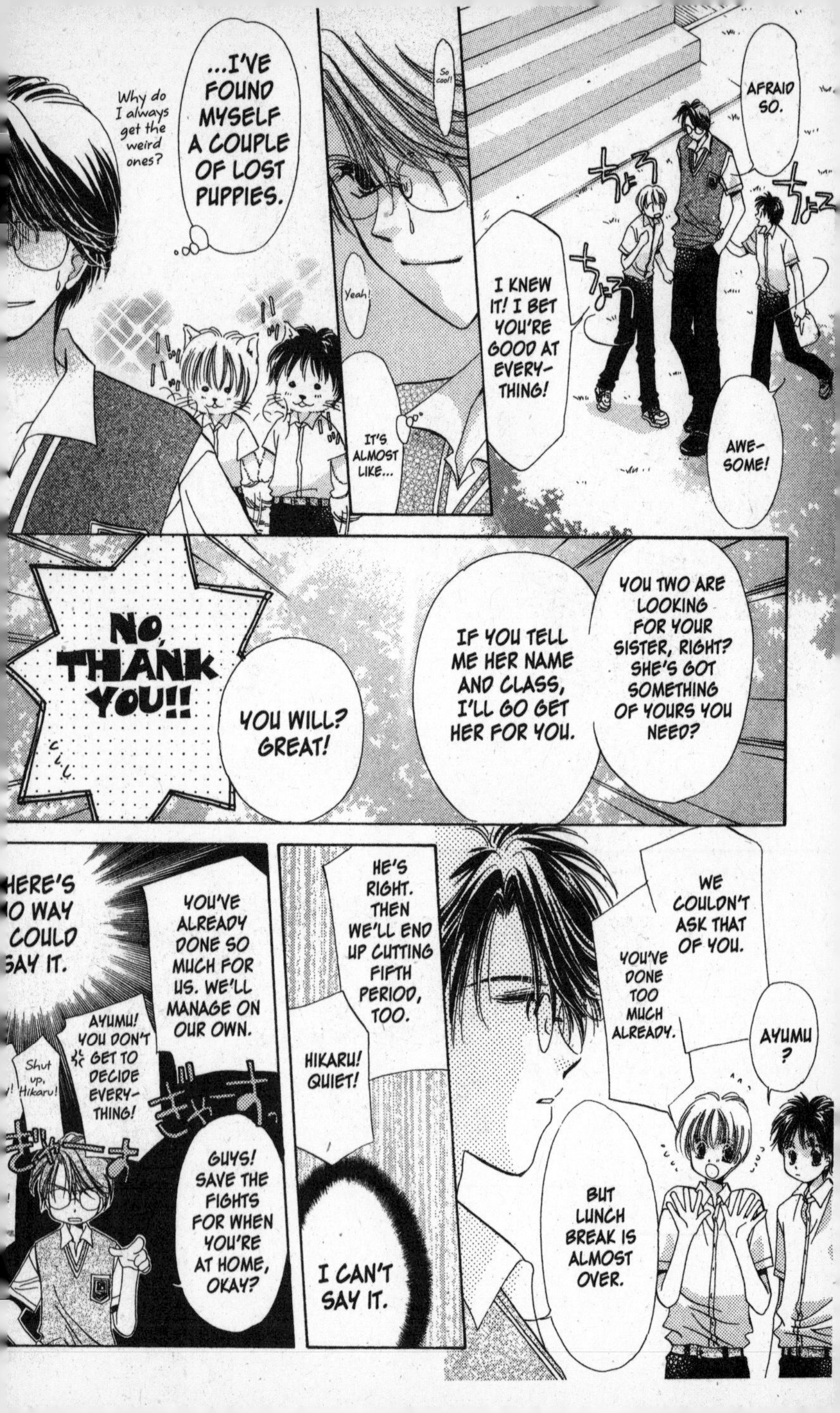
AFRAID SO.
ちょろ
ちょろ
ちょろ
I KNEW IT! I BET YOU'RE GOOD AT EVERY-THING!
AWE-SOME!
So cool!
Yeah!
IT'S ALMOST LIKE...
...I'VE FOUND MYSELF A COUPLE OF LOST PUPPIES.
Why do I always get the weird ones?
YOU TWO ARE LOOKING FOR YOUR SISTER, RIGHT? SHE'S GOT SOMETHING OF YOURS YOU NEED?
IF YOU TELL ME HER NAME AND CLASS, I'LL GO GET HER FOR YOU.
YOU WILL? GREAT!
NO, THANK YOU!!
WE COULDN'T ASK THAT OF YOU.
YOU'VE DONE TOO MUCH ALREADY.
AYUMU?
BUT LUNCH BREAK IS ALMOST OVER.
HE'S RIGHT. THEN WE'LL END UP CUTTING FIFTH PERIOD, TOO.
HIKARU! QUIET!
I CAN'T SAY IT.
HERE'S O WAY COULD SAY IT.
YOU'VE ALREADY DONE SO MUCH FOR US. WE'LL MANAGE ON OUR OWN.
AYUMU! YOU DON'T GET TO DECIDE EVERYTHING!
Shut up, Hikaru!
GUYS! SAVE THE FIGHTS FOR WHEN YOU'RE AT HOME, OKAY?

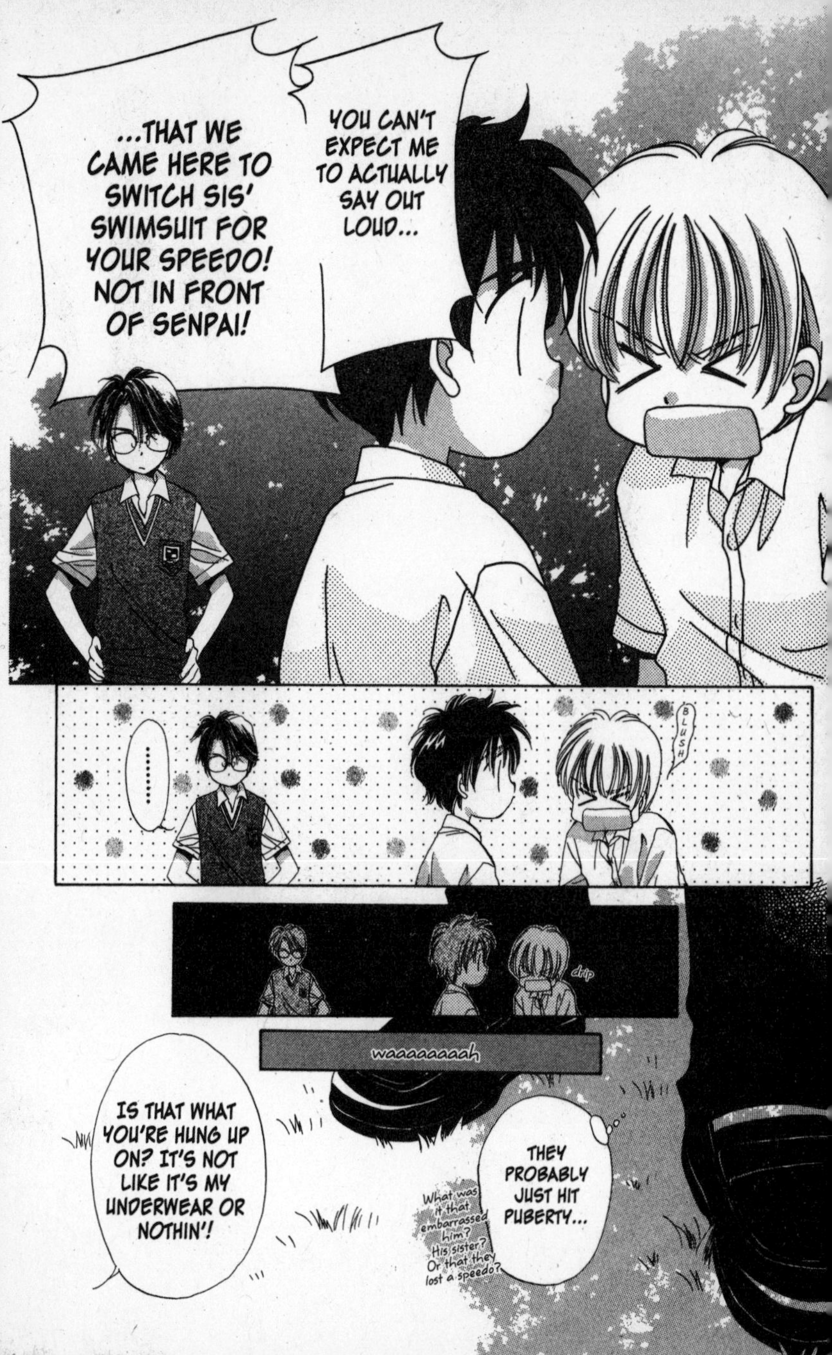
YOU CAN'T EXPECT ME TO ACTUALLY SAY OUT LOUD...
...THAT WE CAME HERE TO SWITCH SIS' SWIMSUIT FOR YOUR SPEEDO! NOT IN FRONT OF SENPAI!
BLUSH
....
drip
waaaaaaaah
IS THAT WHAT YOU'RE HUNG UP ON? IT'S NOT LIKE IT'S MY UNDERWEAR OR NOTHIN'!
THEY PROBABLY JUST HIT PUBERTY...
What was it that embarrassed him? His sister? Or that they lost a speedo?

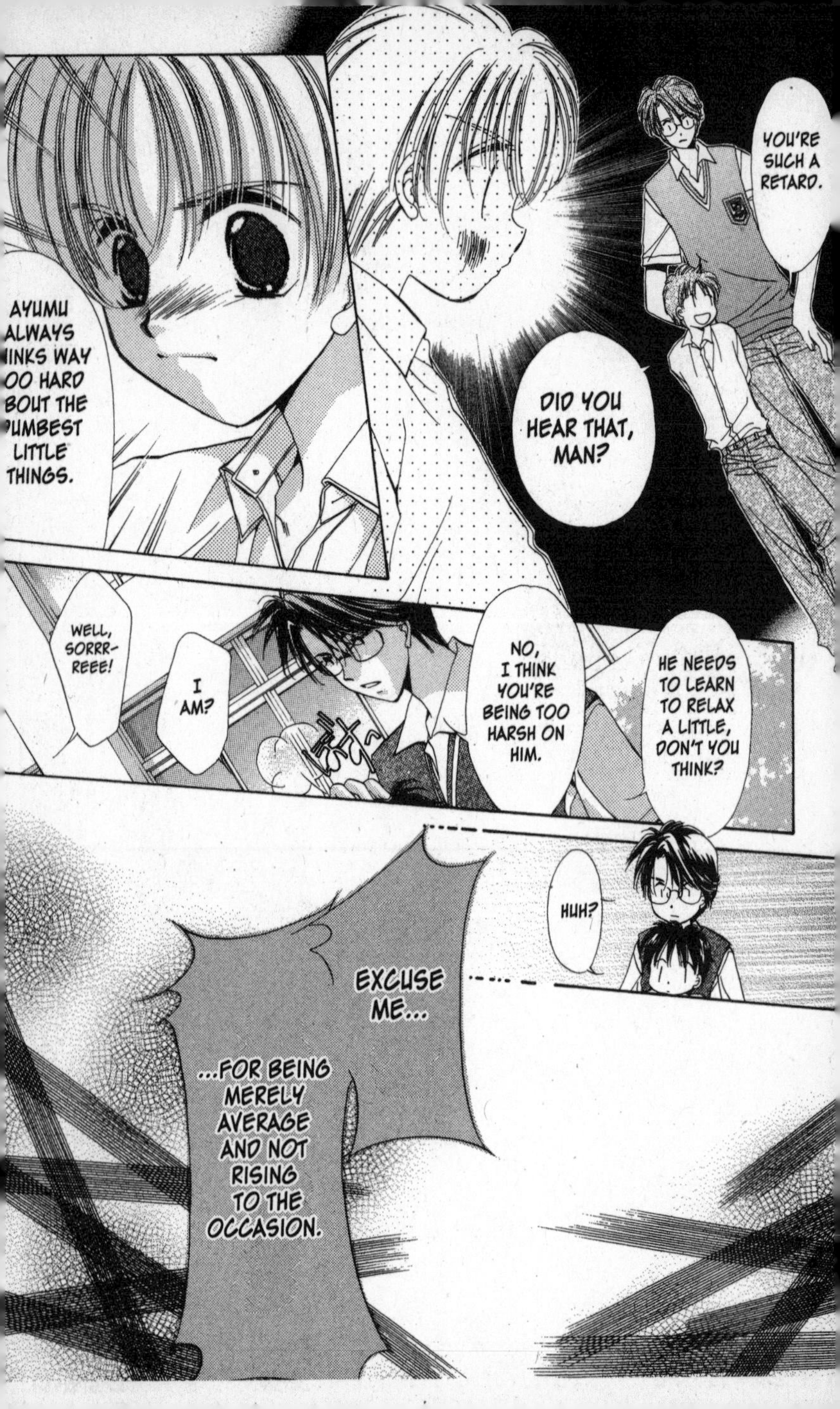
YOU'RE SUCH A RETARD.
DID YOU HEAR THAT, MAN?
AYUMU ALWAYS INKS WAY OO HARD BOUT THE UMBEST LITTLE THINGS.
HE NEEDS TO LEARN TO RELAX A LITTLE, DON'T YOU THINK?
NO, I THINK YOU'RE BEING TOO HARSH ON HIM.
I AM?
WELL, SORRR-REEE!
HUH?
EXCUSE ME...
...FOR BEING MERELY AVERAGE AND NOT RISING TO THE OCCASION.

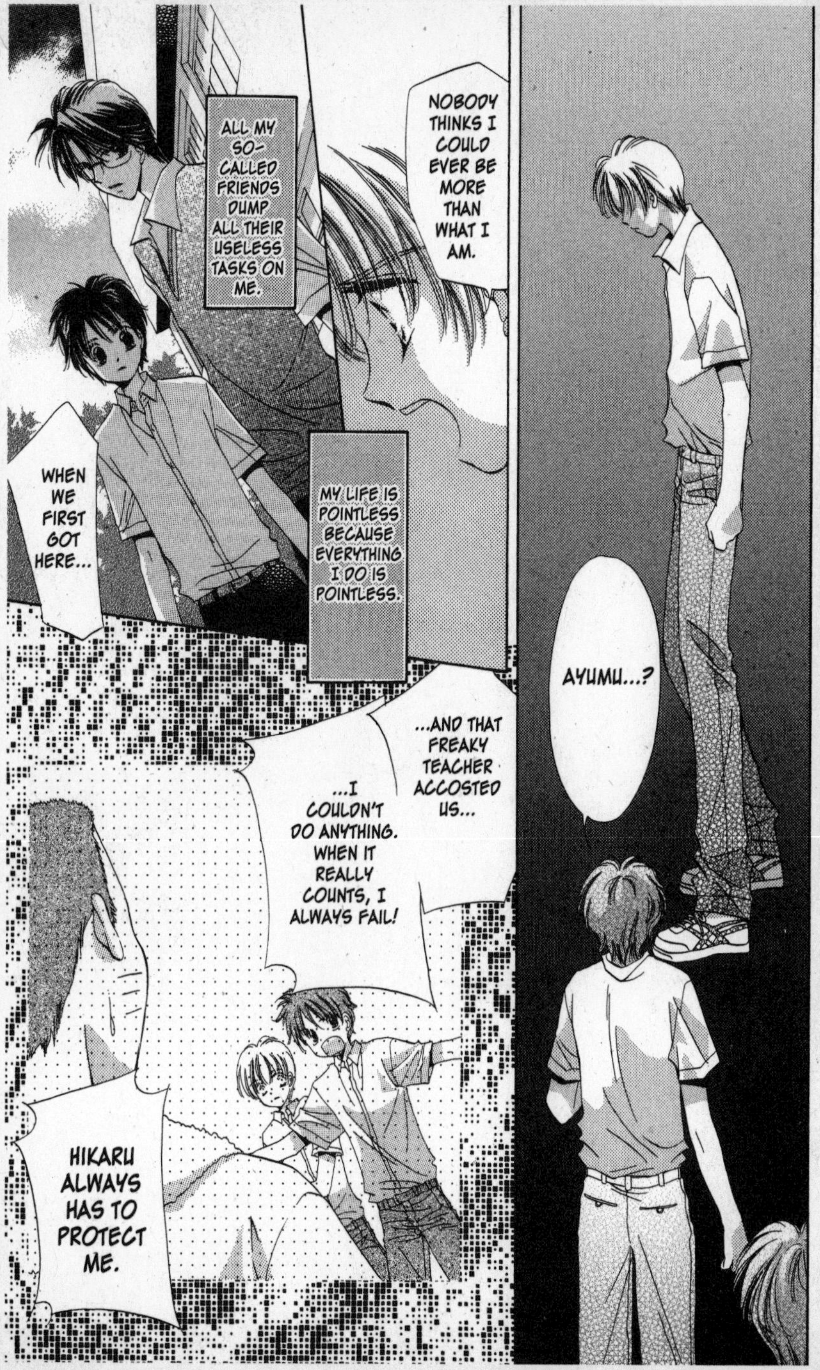
AYUMU...?
NOBODY THINKS I COULD EVER BE MORE THAN WHAT I AM.
MY LIFE IS POINTLESS BECAUSE EVERYTHING I DO IS POINTLESS.
ALL MY SO-CALLED FRIENDS DUMP ALL THEIR USELESS TASKS ON ME.
WHEN WE FIRST GOT HERE...
...AND THAT FREAKY TEACHER ACCOSTED US...
...I COULDN'T DO ANYTHING. WHEN IT REALLY COUNTS, I ALWAYS FAIL!
HIKARU ALWAYS HAS TO PROTECT ME.

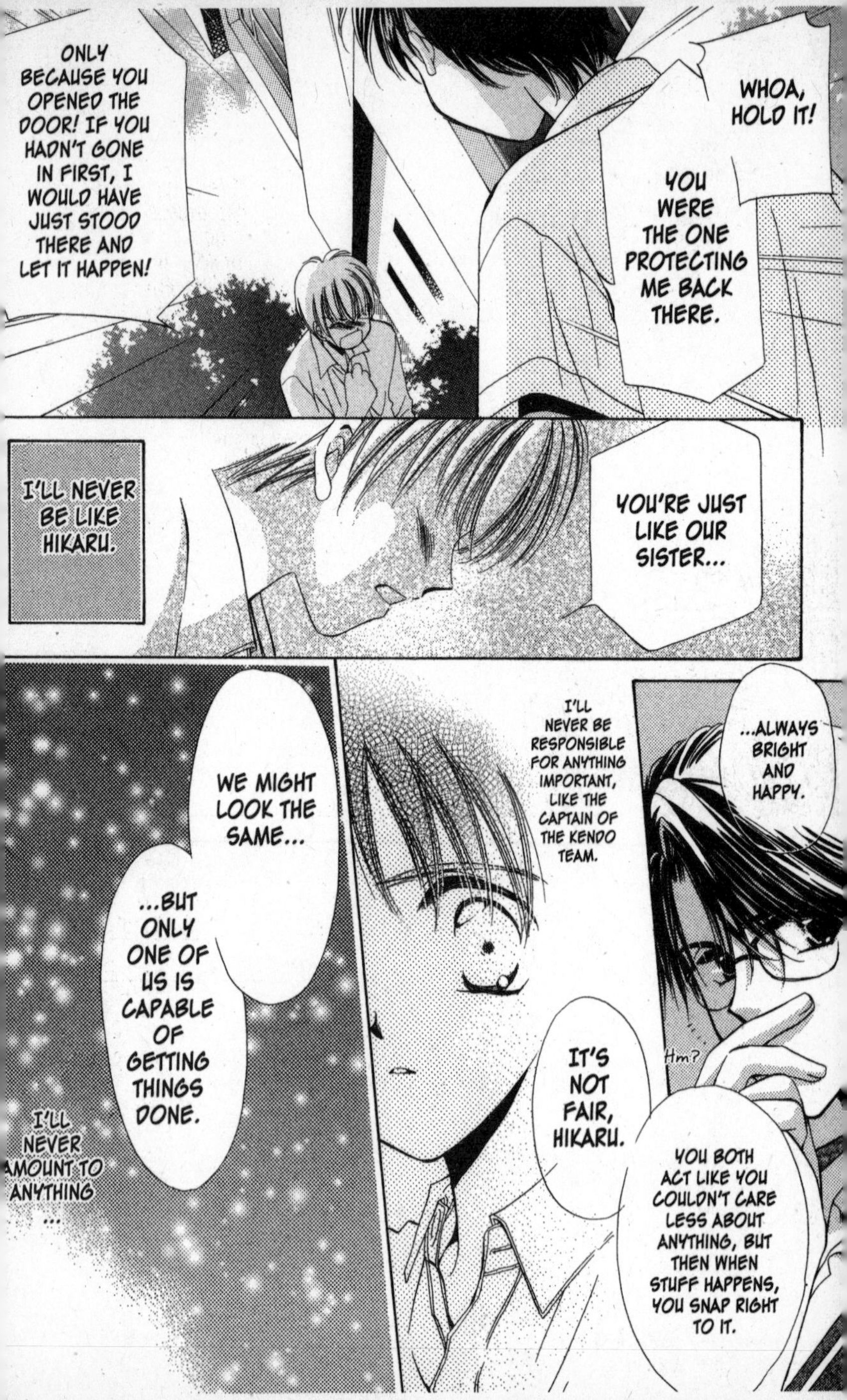
WHOA, HOLD IT!
YOU WERE THE ONE PROTECTING ME BACK THERE.
ONLY BECAUSE YOU OPENED THE DOOR! IF YOU HADN'T GONE IN FIRST, I WOULD HAVE JUST STOOD THERE AND LET IT HAPPEN!
YOU'RE JUST LIKE OUR SISTER...
I'LL NEVER BE LIKE HIKARU.
...ALWAYS BRIGHT AND HAPPY.
Hm?
YOU BOTH ACT LIKE YOU COULDN'T CARE LESS ABOUT ANYTHING, BUT THEN WHEN STUFF HAPPENS, YOU SNAP RIGHT TO IT.
I'LL NEVER BE RESPONSIBLE FOR ANYTHING IMPORTANT, LIKE THE CAPTAIN OF THE KENDO TEAM.
IT'S NOT FAIR, HIKARU.
WE MIGHT LOOK THE SAME...
...BUT ONLY ONE OF US IS CAPABLE OF GETTING THINGS DONE.
I'LL NEVER AMOUNT TO ANYTHING...

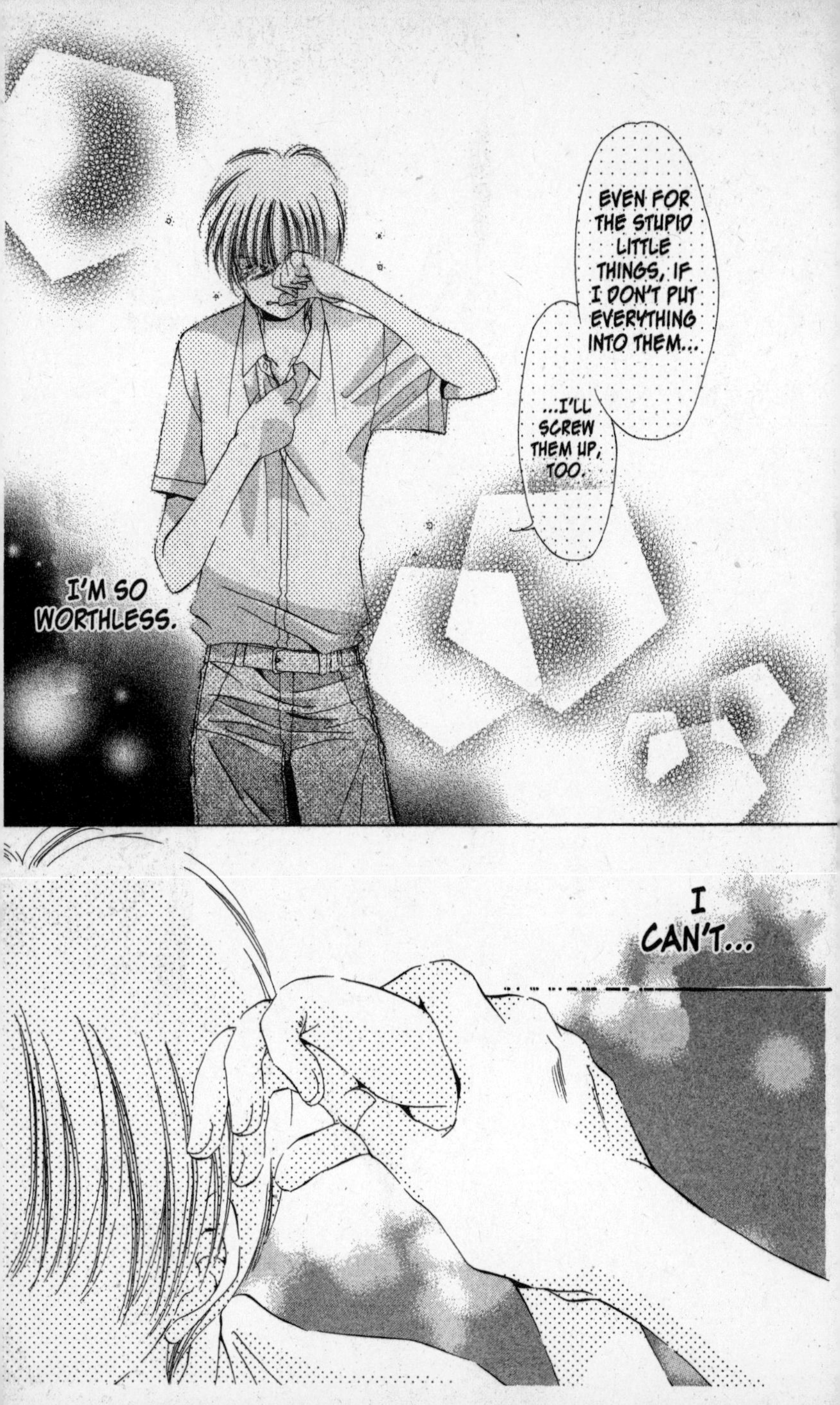
EVEN FOR THE STUPID LITTLE THINGS, IF I DON'T PUT EVERYTHING INTO THEM...
...I'LL SCREW THEM UP, TOO.
I'M SO WORTHLESS.
I CAN'T...

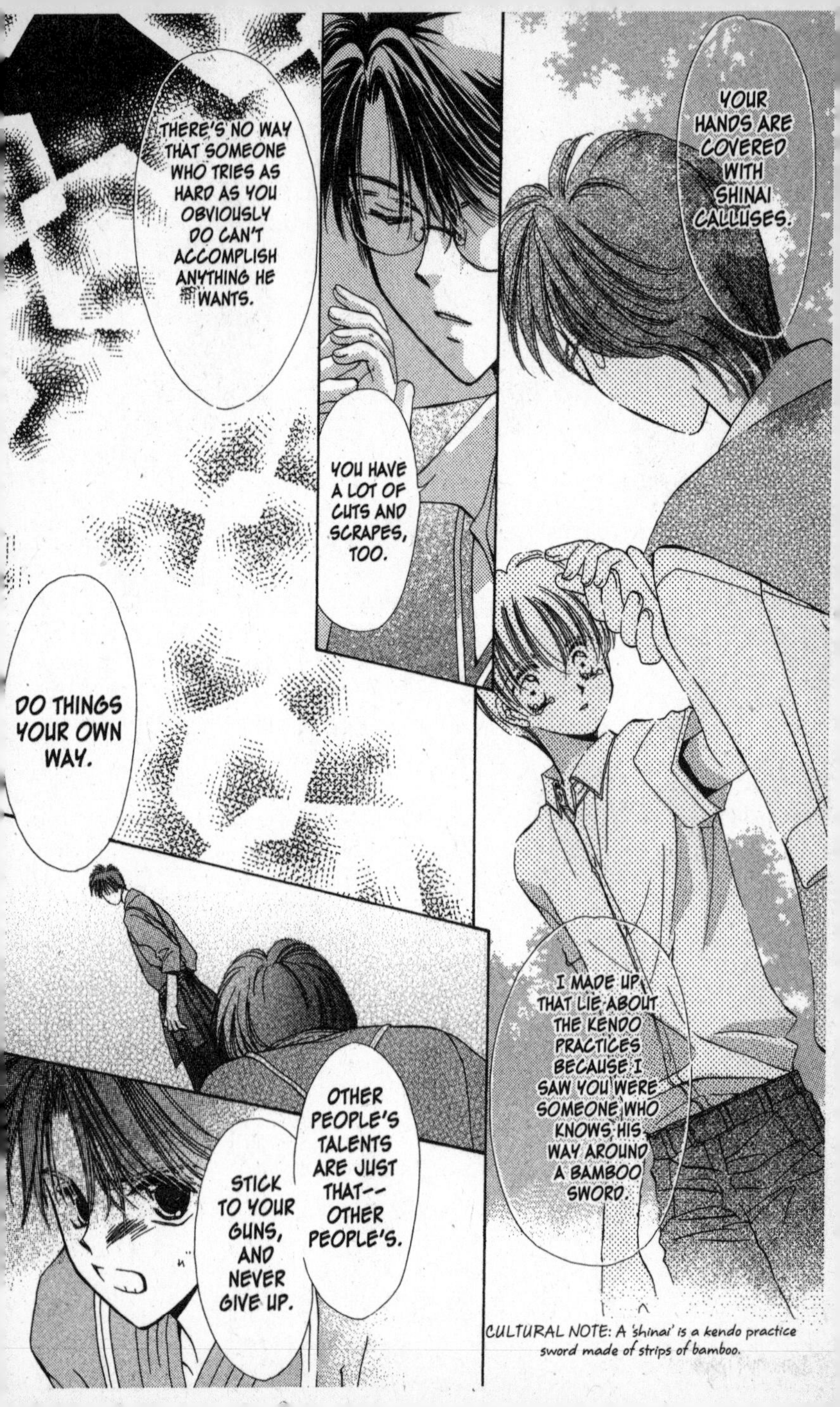
YOUR HANDS ARE COVERED WITH SHINAI CALLUSES.
I MADE UP THAT LIE ABOUT THE KENDO PRACTICES BECAUSE I SAW YOU WERE SOMEONE WHO KNOWS HIS WAY AROUND A BAMBOO SWORD.
YOU HAVE A LOT OF CUTS AND SCRAPES, TOO.
THERE'S NO WAY THAT SOMEONE WHO TRIES AS HARD AS YOU OBVIOUSLY DO CAN'T ACCOMPLISH ANYTHING HE WANTS.
DO THINGS YOUR OWN WAY.
OTHER PEOPLE'S TALENTS ARE JUST THAT--OTHER PEOPLE'S.
STICK TO YOUR GUNS, AND NEVER GIVE UP.

CULTURAL NOTE: A 'shinai' is a kendo practice sword made of strips of bamboo.

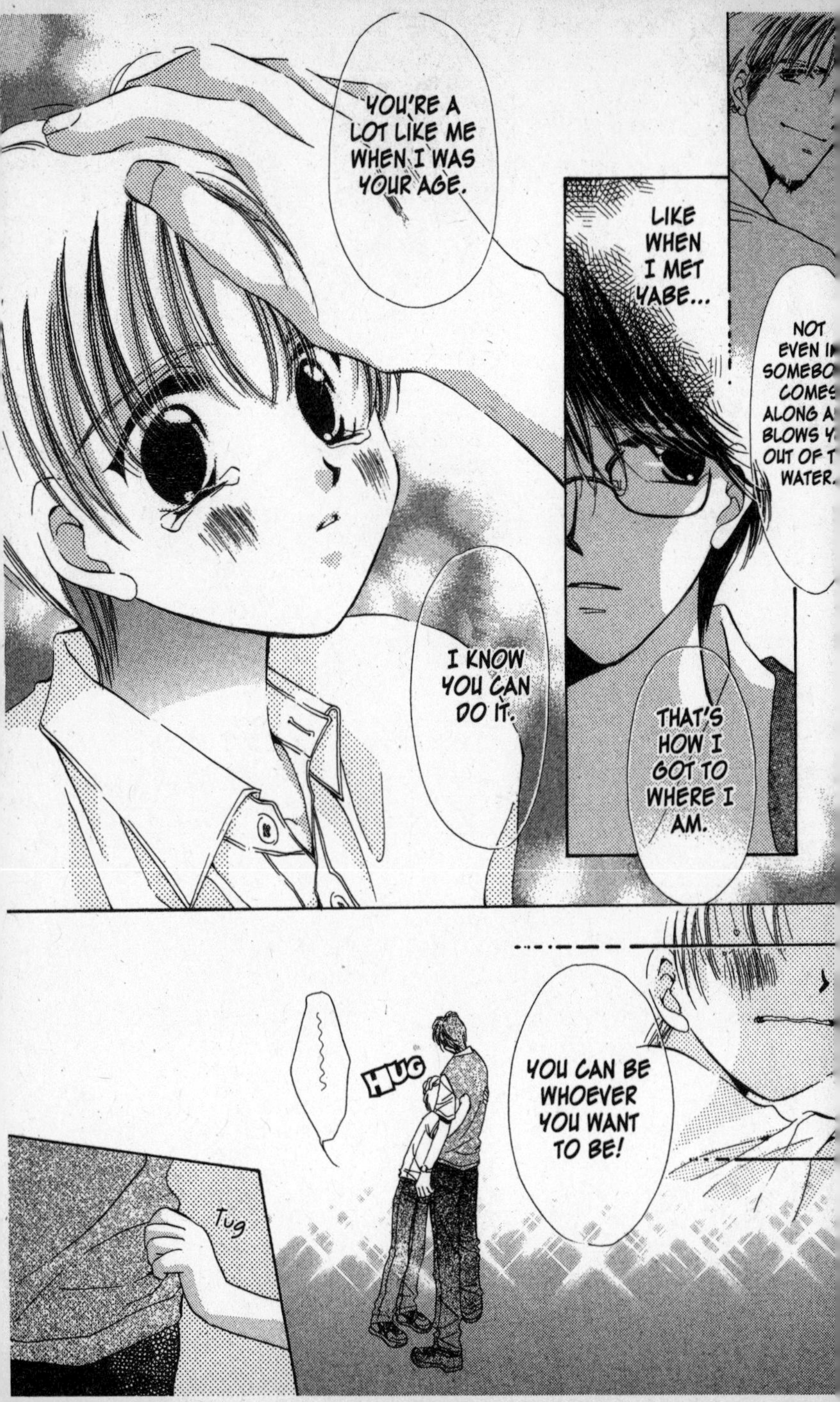
NOT EVEN I SOMEBO COMES ALONG A BLOWS Y OUT OF T WATER.
LIKE WHEN I MET YABE...
THAT'S HOW I GOT TO WHERE I AM.
YOU'RE A LOT LIKE ME WHEN I WAS YOUR AGE.
I KNOW YOU CAN DO IT.
YOU CAN BE WHOEVER YOU WANT TO BE!
HUG
Tug

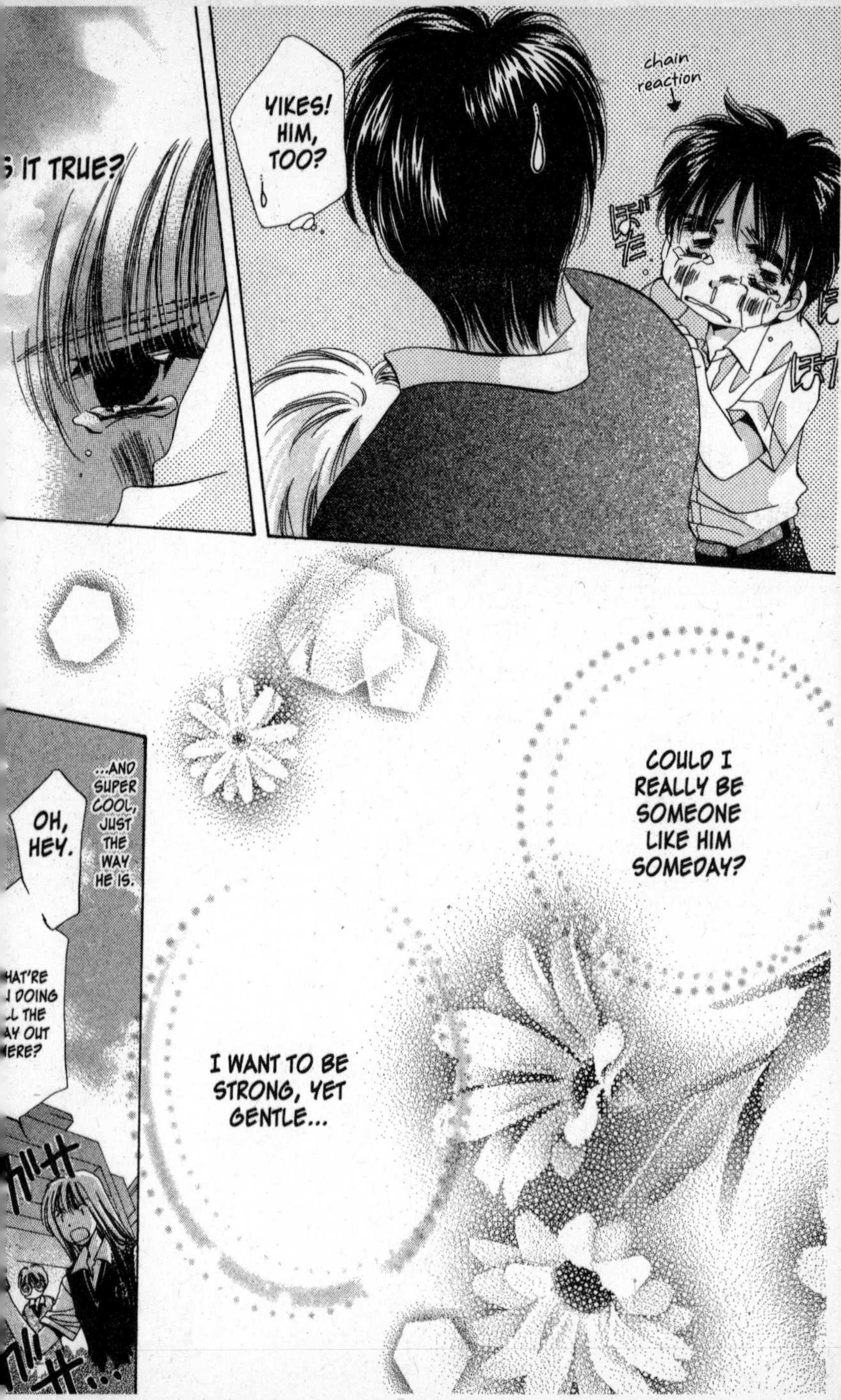
chain reaction
YIKES! HIM, TOO?
S IT TRUE?
COULD I REALLY BE SOMEONE LIKE HIM SOMEDAY?
I WANT TO BE STRONG, YET GENTLE...
...AND SUPER COOL, JUST THE WAY HE IS.
OH, HEY.
HAT'RE DOING LL THE AY OUT HERE?

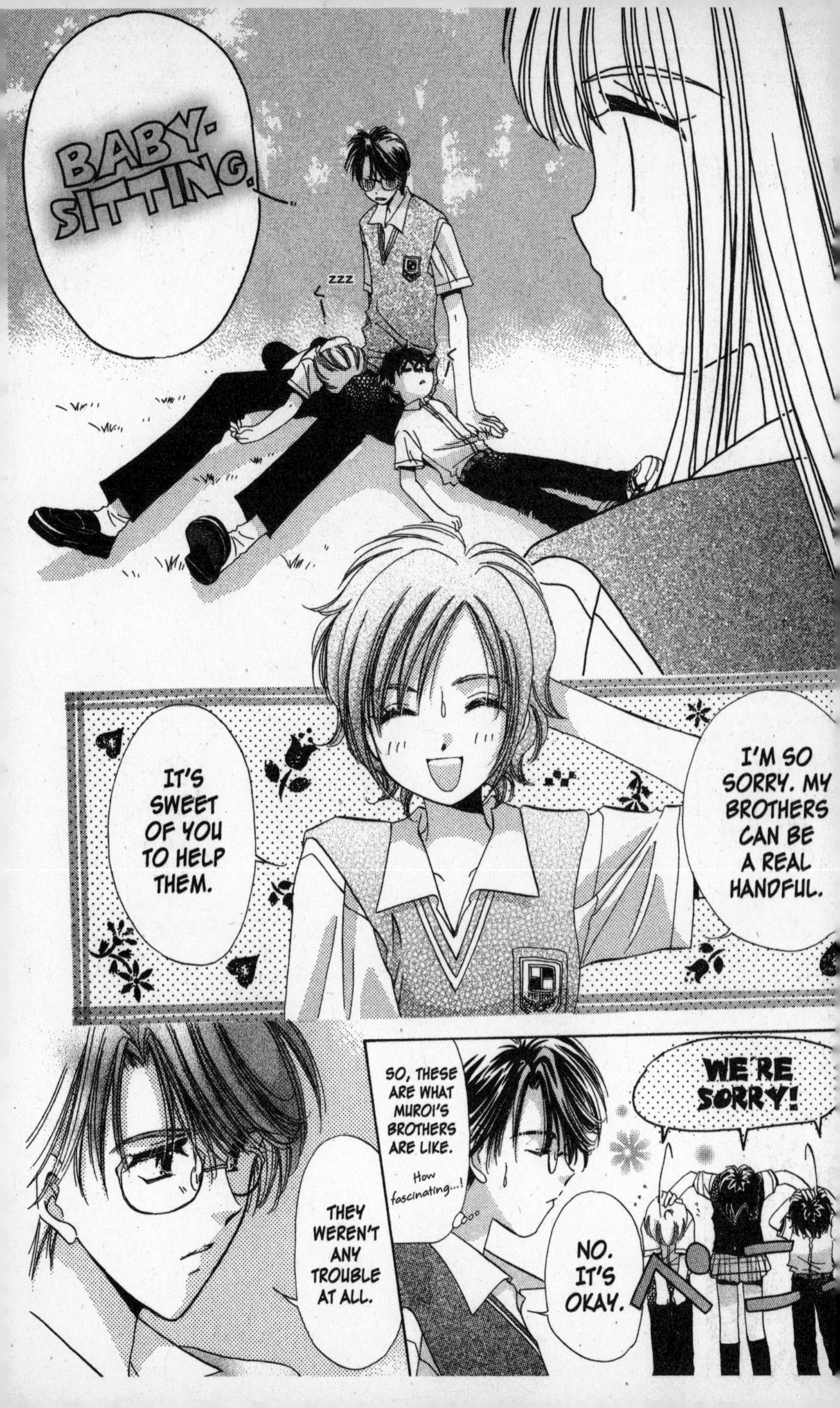
BABY-SITTING.
ZZZ
I'M SO SORRY. MY BROTHERS CAN BE A REAL HANDFUL.
IT'S SWEET OF YOU TO HELP THEM.
WE'RE SORRY!
NO. IT'S OKAY.
SO, THESE ARE WHAT MUROI'S BROTHERS ARE LIKE.
How fascinating...!
THEY WEREN'T ANY TROUBLE AT ALL.

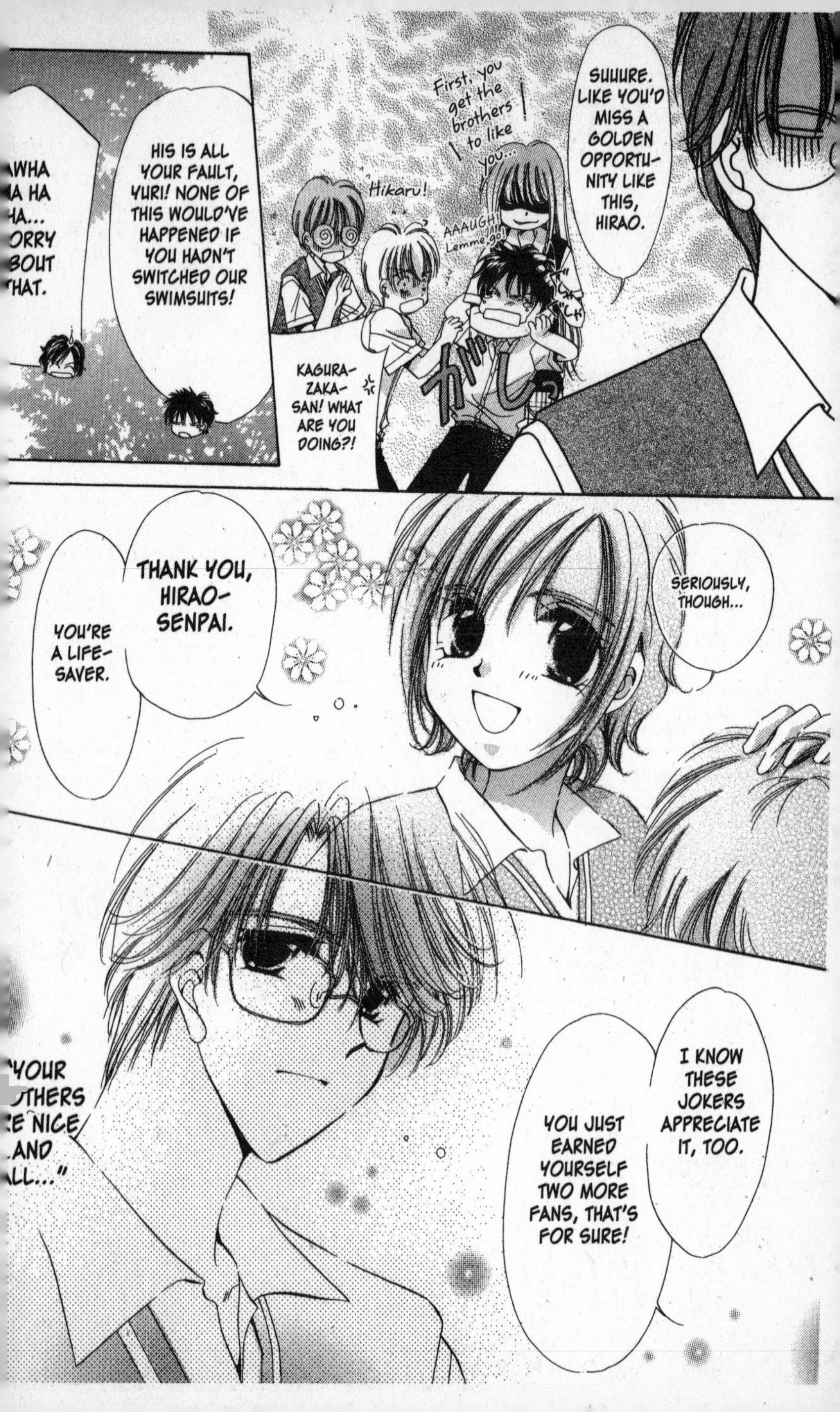

SUUURE. LIKE YOU'D MISS A GOLDEN OPPORTUNITY LIKE THIS, HIRAO.
First, you get the brothers to like you...
AAAUGH! Lemme go!
Hikaru!
KAGURAZAKA-SAN! WHAT ARE YOU DOING?!
HIS IS ALL YOUR FAULT, YURI! NONE OF THIS WOULD'VE HAPPENED IF YOU HADN'T SWITCHED OUR SWIMSUITS!
AWHA HA HA HA... ORRY BOUT THAT.
SERIOUSLY, THOUGH...
THANK YOU, HIRAO-SENPAI.
YOU'RE A LIFE-SAVER.
I KNOW THESE JOKERS APPRECIATE IT, TOO.
YOU JUST EARNED YOURSELF TWO MORE FANS, THAT'S FOR SURE!
"YOUR OTHERS E NICE AND LL..."

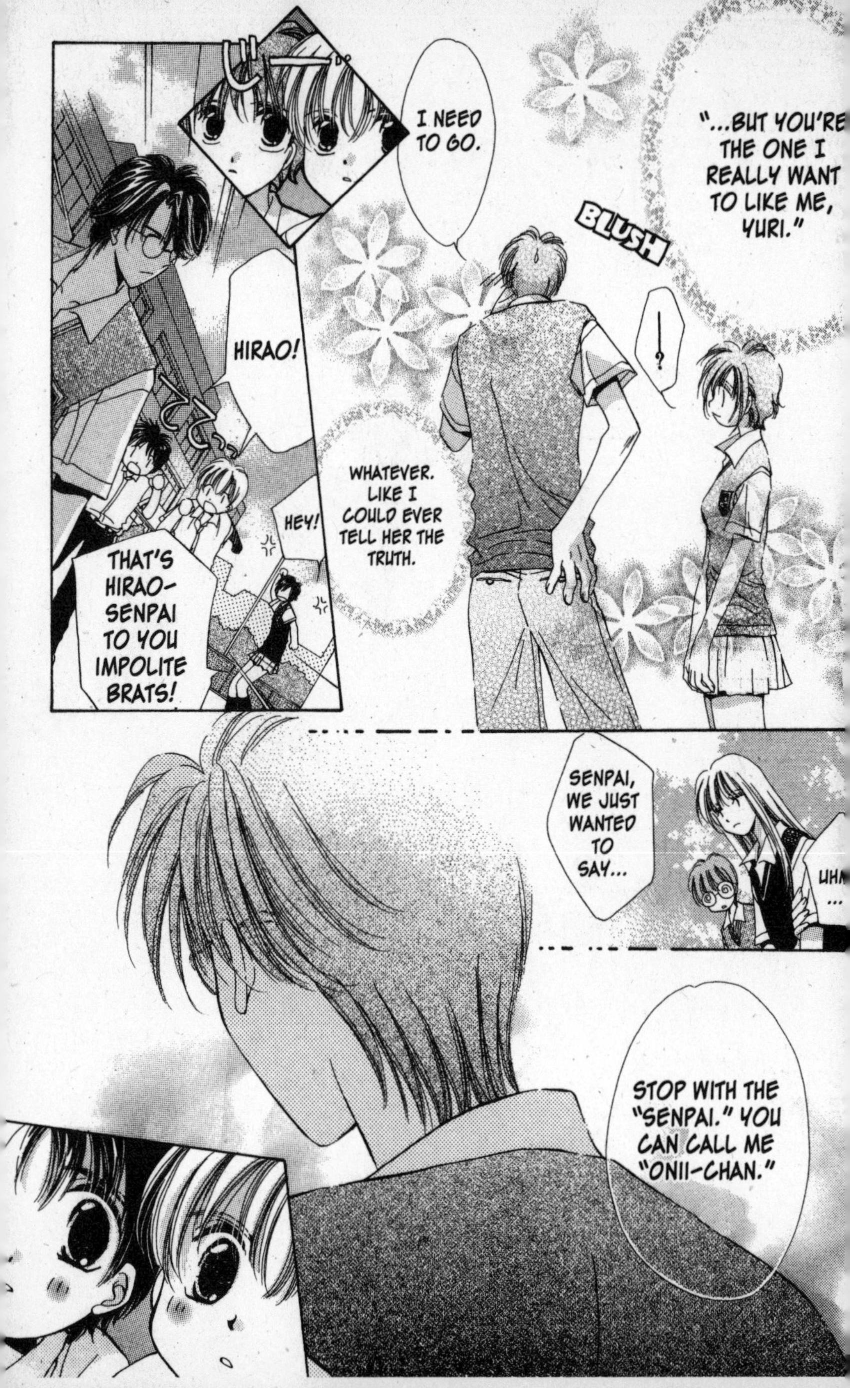
"...BUT YOU'RE THE ONE I REALLY WANT TO LIKE ME, YURI."
BLUSH
I NEED TO GO.
!?
WHATEVER. LIKE I COULD EVER TELL HER THE TRUTH.
HIRAO!
HEY!
THAT'S HIRAO-SENPAI TO YOU IMPOLITE BRATS!
UHM...
SENPAI, WE JUST WANTED TO SAY...
STOP WITH THE "SENPAI." YOU CAN CALL ME "ONII-CHAN."

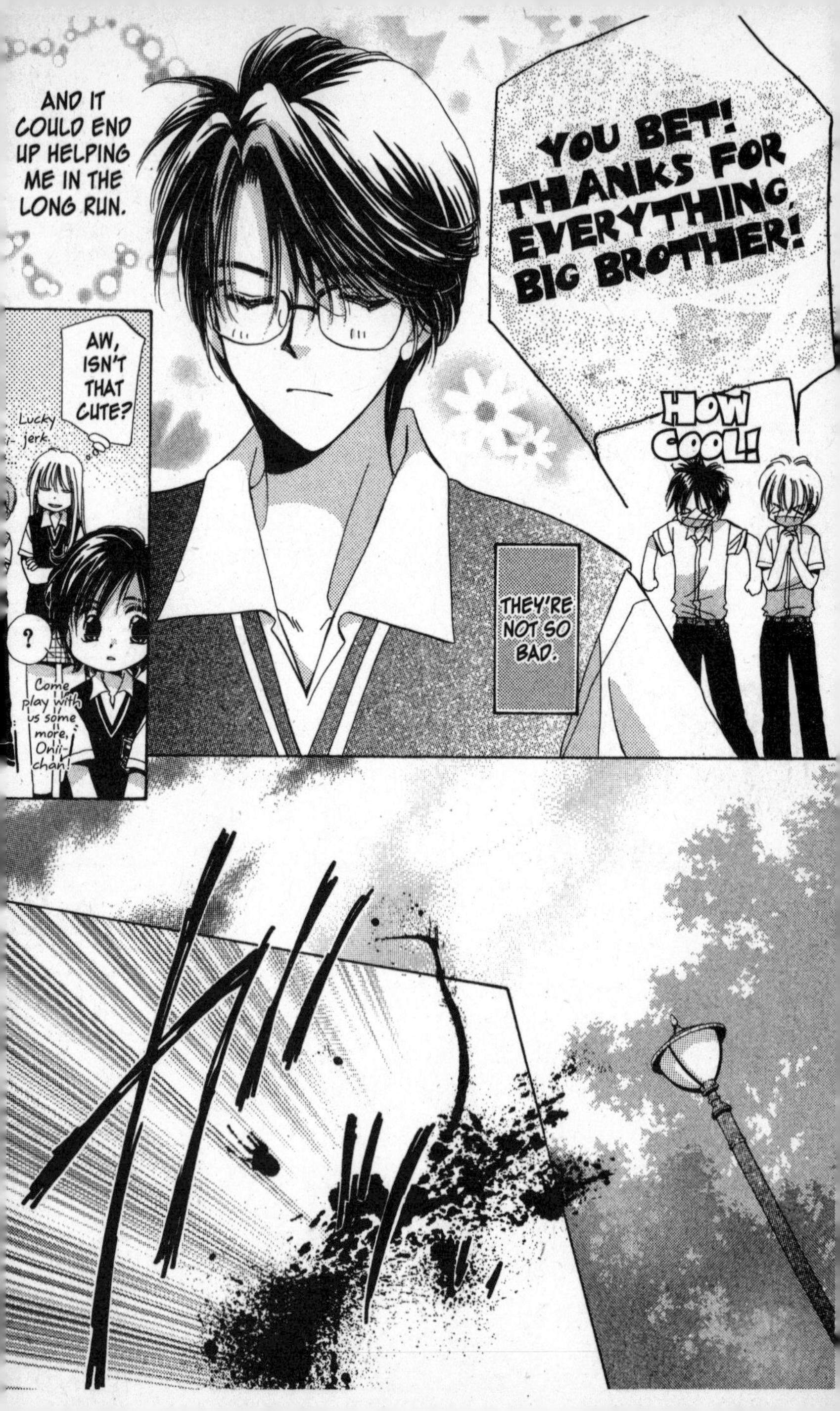
YOU BET! THANKS FOR EVERYTHING, BIG BROTHER!
HOW COOL!
AND IT COULD END UP HELPING ME IN THE LONG RUN.
THEY'RE NOT SO BAD.
AW, ISN'T THAT CUTE?
Lucky jerk.
?
Come play with us some more, Onii-chan!

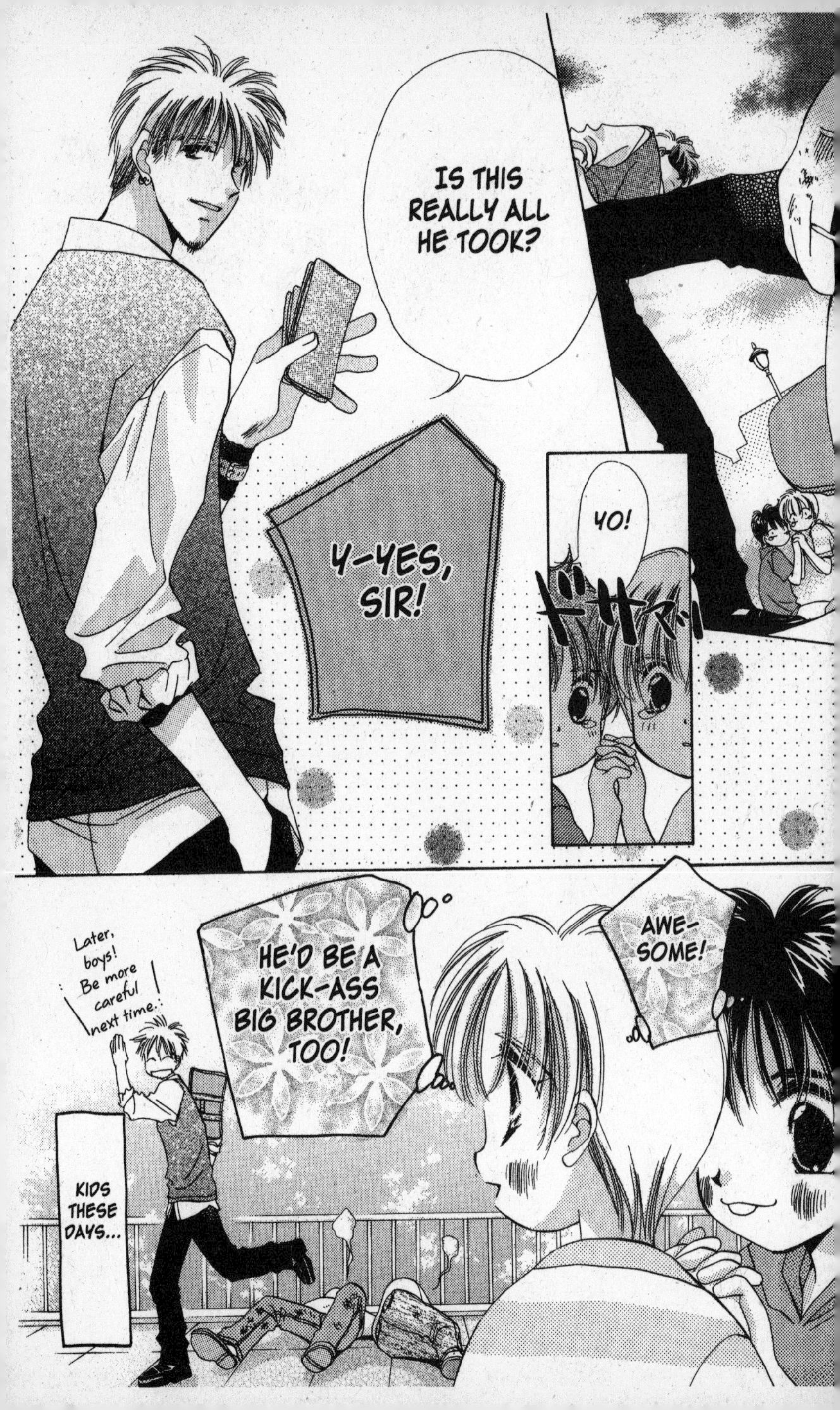

YO!
IS THIS REALLY ALL HE TOOK?
Y-YES, SIR!
AWE-SOME!
HE'D BE A KICK-ASS BIG BROTHER, TOO!
Later, boys! Be more careful next time.
KIDS THESE DAYS...

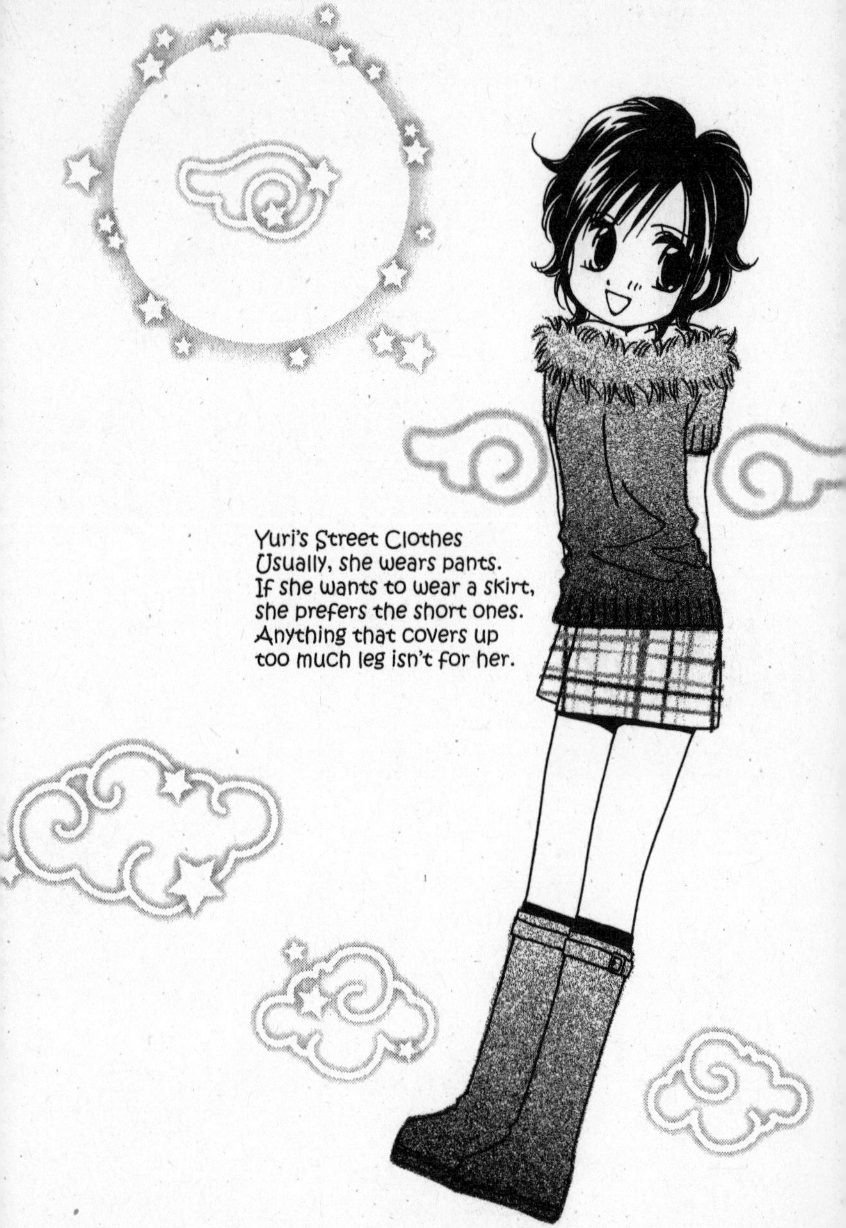
Yuri's Street Clothes
Usually, she wears pants.
If she wants to wear a skirt,
she prefers the short ones.
Anything that covers up
too much leg isn't for her.

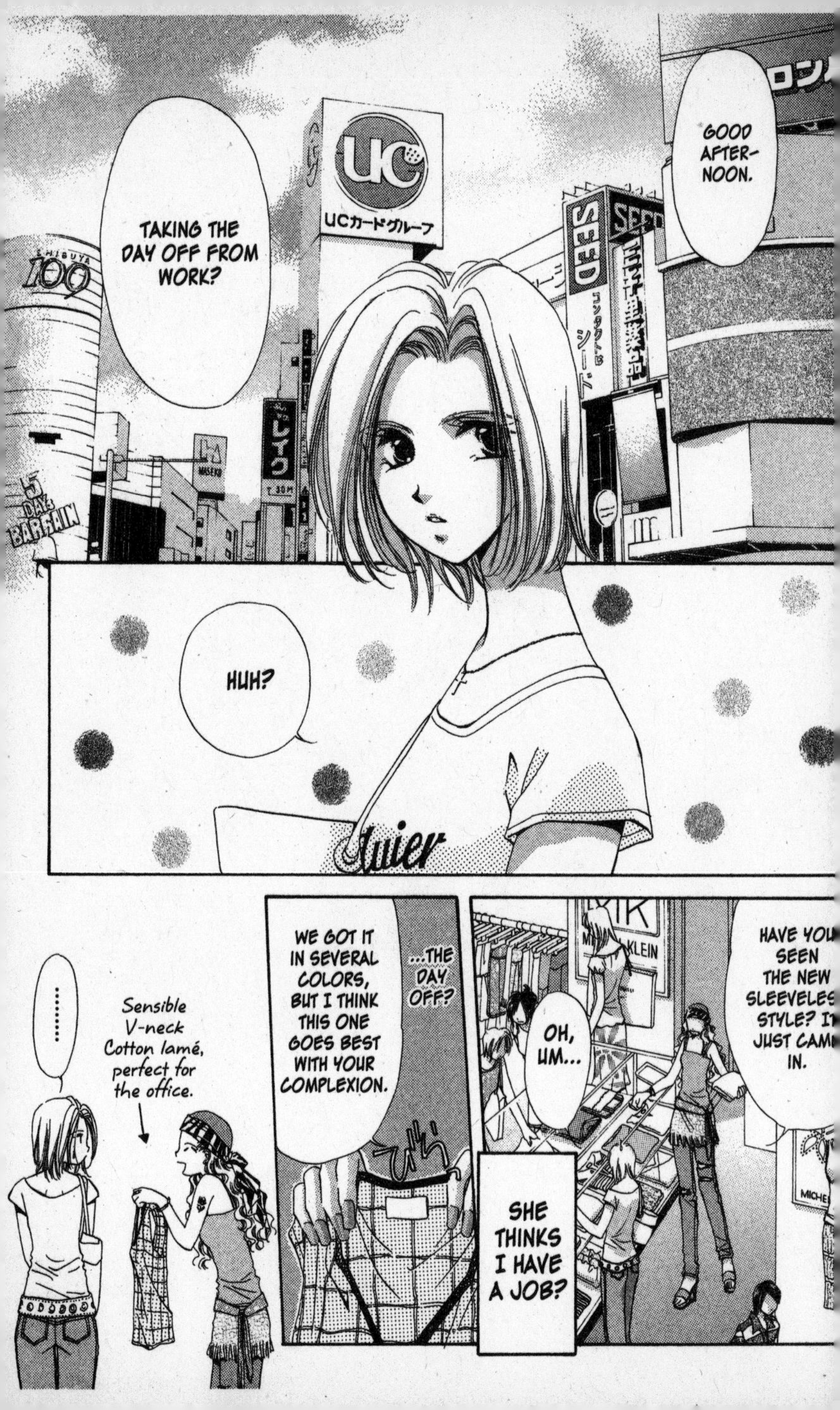
GOOD AFTERNOON.
TAKING THE DAY OFF FROM WORK?
SHIBUYA 109
UCカードグループ
SEED
5 DAYS BARGAIN
HUH?
HAVE YOU SEEN THE NEW SLEEVELES STYLE? IT JUST CAM IN.
OH, UM...
SHE THINKS I HAVE A JOB?
...THE DAY OFF?
WE GOT IT IN SEVERAL COLORS, BUT I THINK THIS ONE GOES BEST WITH YOUR COMPLEXION.
......
Sensible V-neck Cotton lamé, perfect for the office.

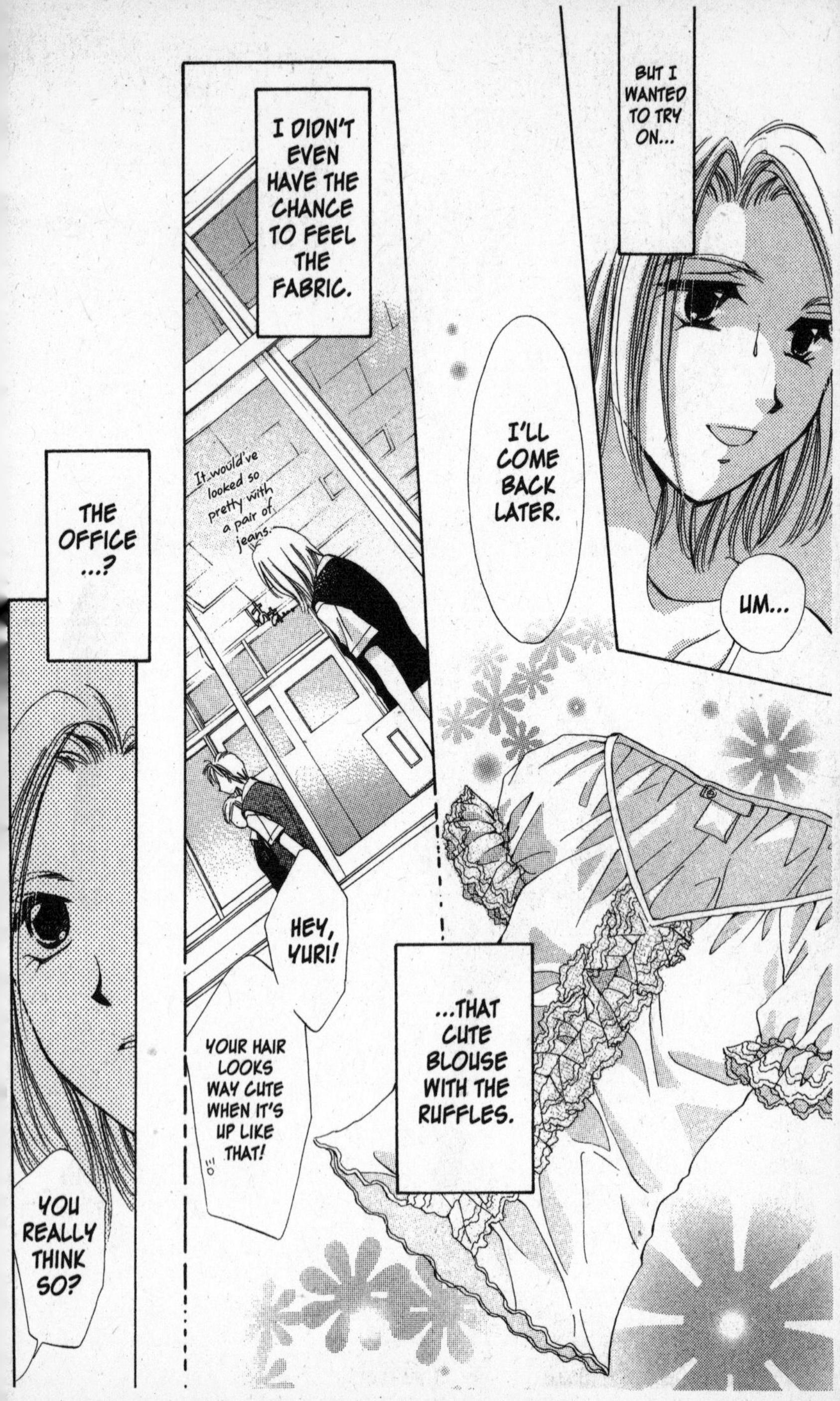

BUT I WANTED TO TRY ON...
UM...
I'LL COME BACK LATER.
...THAT CUTE BLOUSE WITH THE RUFFLES.
I DIDN'T EVEN HAVE THE CHANCE TO FEEL THE FABRIC.
It would've looked so pretty with a pair of jeans.
HEY, YURI!
YOUR HAIR LOOKS WAY CUTE WHEN IT'S UP LIKE THAT!
THE OFFICE ...?
YOU REALLY THINK SO?

Gatcha Gacha
MEIRIN
THANKS!
I WANTED THAT SHIRT... BECAUSE I KNOW SHE WOULD LOOK REALLY GOOD IN IT.

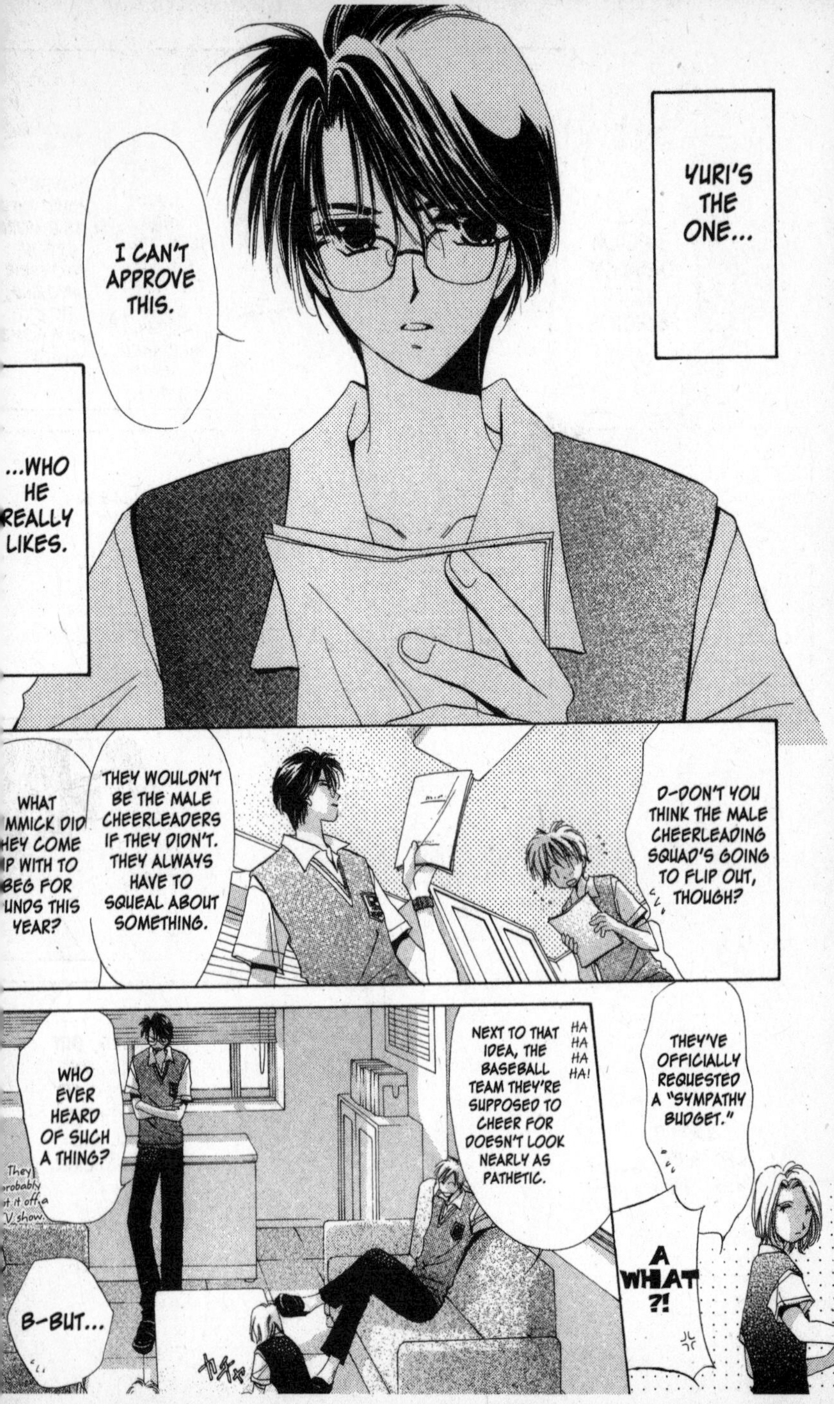
YURI'S THE ONE...
I CAN'T APPROVE THIS.
...WHO HE REALLY LIKES.
D-DON'T YOU THINK THE MALE CHEERLEADING SQUAD'S GOING TO FLIP OUT, THOUGH?
THEY WOULDN'T BE THE MALE CHEERLEADERS IF THEY DIDN'T. THEY ALWAYS HAVE TO SQUEAL ABOUT SOMETHING.
WHAT MMICK DID HEY COME P WITH TO BEG FOR UNDS THIS YEAR?
THEY'VE OFFICIALLY REQUESTED A "SYMPATHY BUDGET."
A WHAT ?!
NEXT TO THAT IDEA, THE BASEBALL TEAM THEY'RE SUPPOSED TO CHEER FOR DOESN'T LOOK NEARLY AS PATHETIC.
HA HA HA HA!
WHO EVER HEARD OF SUCH A THING?
They robably t it off a V show.
B-BUT...

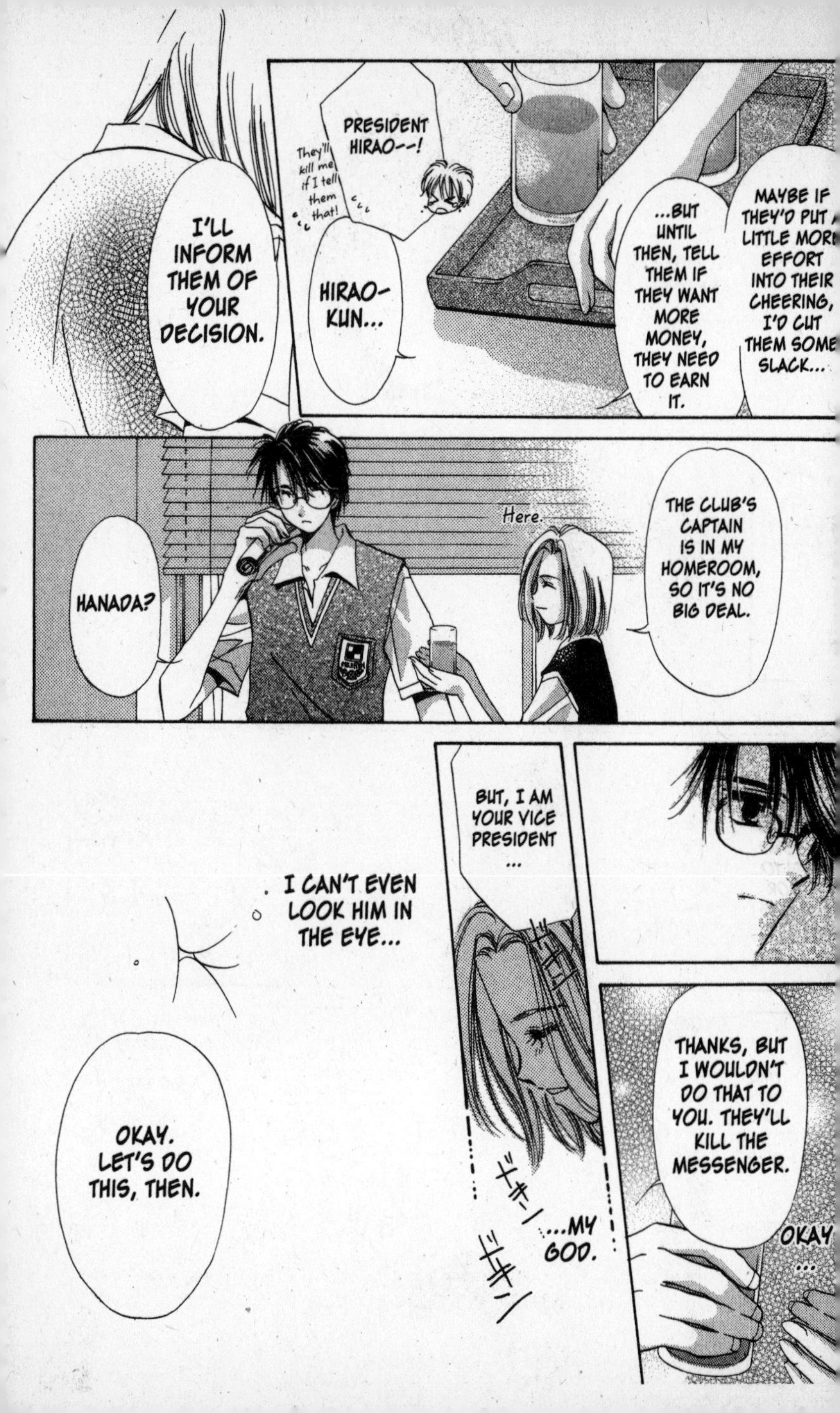
MAYBE IF THEY'D PUT A LITTLE MORE EFFORT INTO THEIR CHEERING, I'D CUT THEM SOME SLACK...
...BUT UNTIL THEN, TELL THEM IF THEY WANT MORE MONEY, THEY NEED TO EARN IT.
PRESIDENT HIRAO--!
They'll kill me if I tell them that!
HIRAO-KUN...
I'LL INFORM THEM OF YOUR DECISION.
THE CLUB'S CAPTAIN IS IN MY HOMEROOM, SO IT'S NO BIG DEAL.
Here.
HANADA?
THANKS, BUT I WOULDN'T DO THAT TO YOU. THEY'LL KILL THE MESSENGER.
OKAY...
BUT, I AM YOUR VICE PRESIDENT...
...MY GOD.
I CAN'T EVEN LOOK HIM IN THE EYE...
OKAY. LET'S DO THIS, THEN.

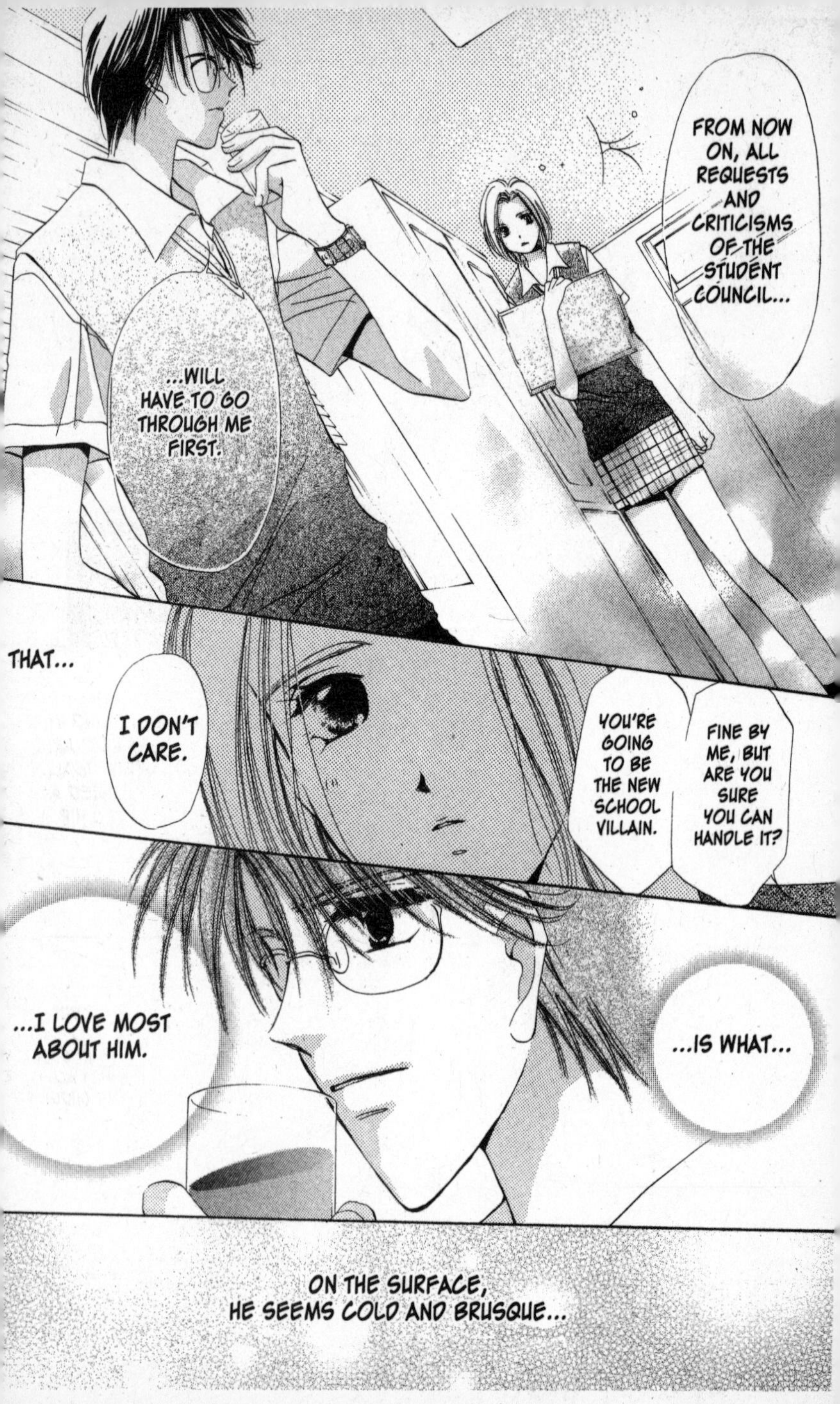
FROM NOW ON, ALL REQUESTS AND CRITICISMS OF THE STUDENT COUNCIL...
...WILL HAVE TO GO THROUGH ME FIRST.
FINE BY ME, BUT ARE YOU SURE YOU CAN HANDLE IT?
YOU'RE GOING TO BE THE NEW SCHOOL VILLAIN.
I DON'T CARE.
THAT...
...IS WHAT...
...I LOVE MOST ABOUT HIM.
ON THE SURFACE, HE SEEMS COLD AND BRUSQUE...

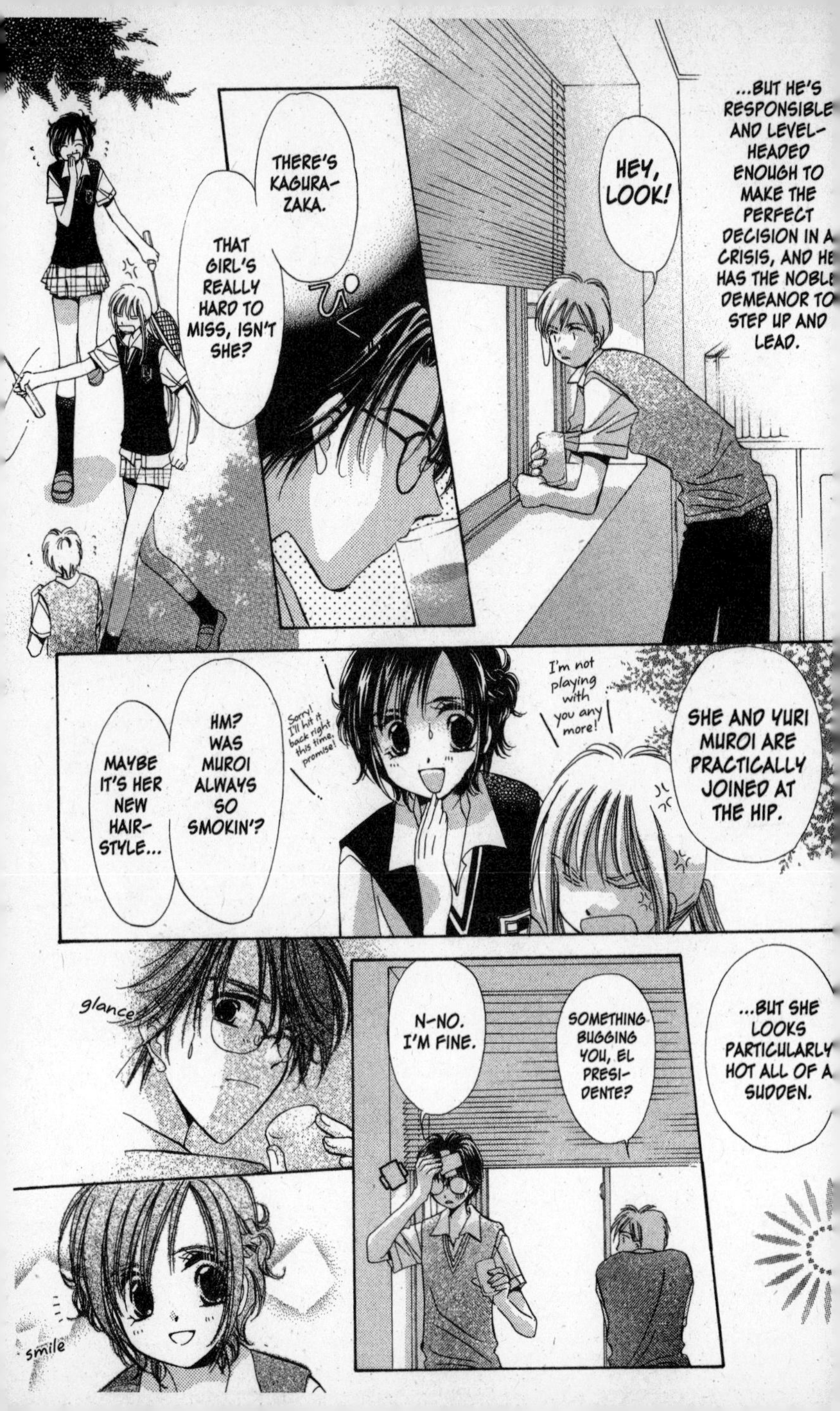
...BUT HE'S RESPONSIBLE AND LEVEL-HEADED ENOUGH TO MAKE THE PERFECT DECISION IN A CRISIS, AND HE HAS THE NOBLE DEMEANOR TO STEP UP AND LEAD.
HEY, LOOK!
THERE'S KAGURA-ZAKA.
THAT GIRL'S REALLY HARD TO MISS, ISN'T SHE?
SHE AND YURI MUROI ARE PRACTICALLY JOINED AT THE HIP.
I'm not playing with you any more!
Sorry! I'll hit it back right this time, promise!
HM? WAS MUROI ALWAYS SO SMOKIN'?
MAYBE IT'S HER NEW HAIR-STYLE...
...BUT SHE LOOKS PARTICULARLY HOT ALL OF A SUDDEN.
SOMETHING BUGGING YOU, EL PRESI-DENTE?
N-NO. I'M FINE.
glance
smile

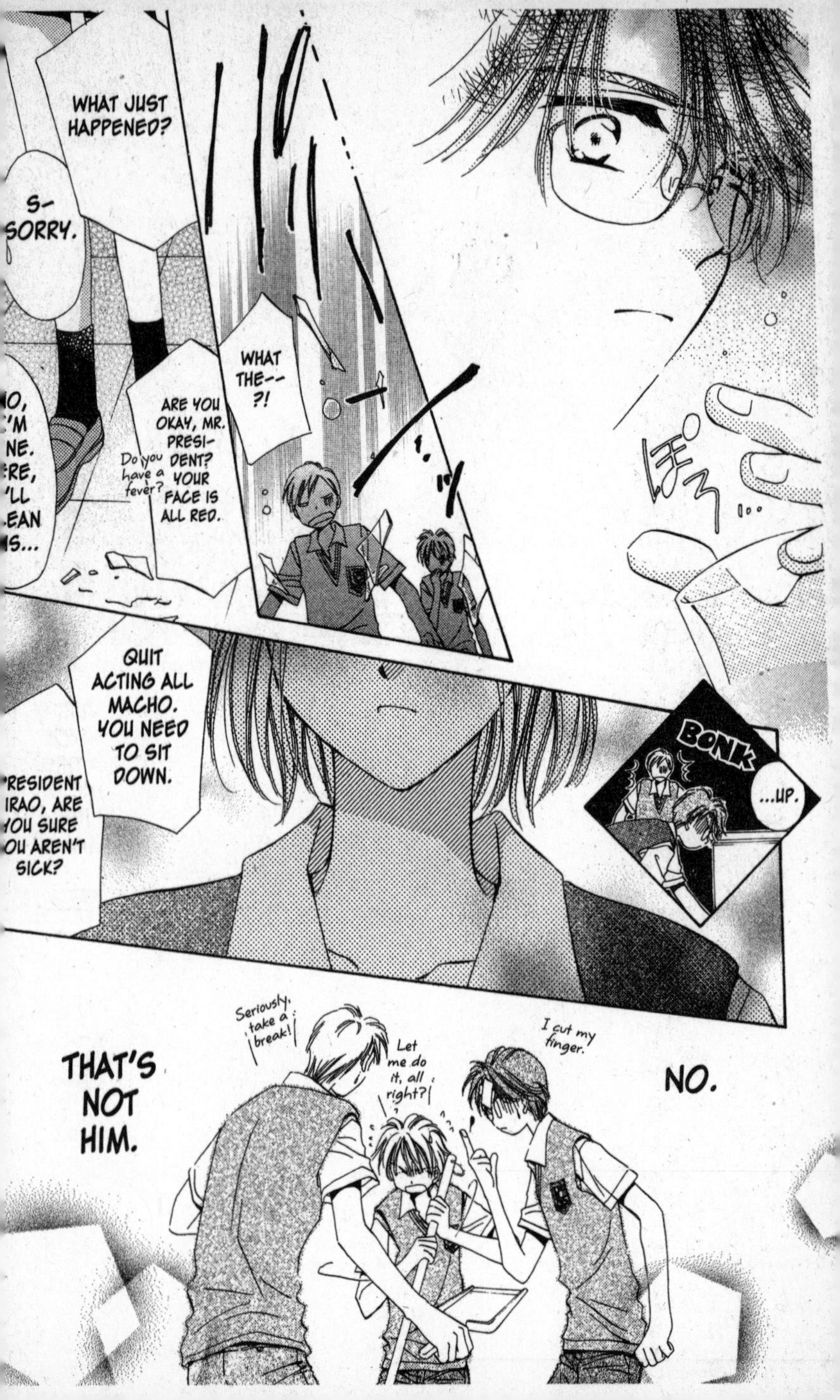

WHAT THE--?!
ARE YOU OKAY, MR. PRESIDENT? YOUR FACE IS ALL RED.
Do you have a fever?
WHAT JUST HAPPENED?
S-SORRY.
O, 'M NE. ERE, 'LL LEAN IS...
BONK
...UP.
QUIT ACTING ALL MACHO. YOU NEED TO SIT DOWN.
RESIDENT IRAO, ARE OU SURE OU AREN'T SICK?
NO.
I cut my finger.
Let me do it, all right?!
Seriously, take a break!
THAT'S NOT HIM.

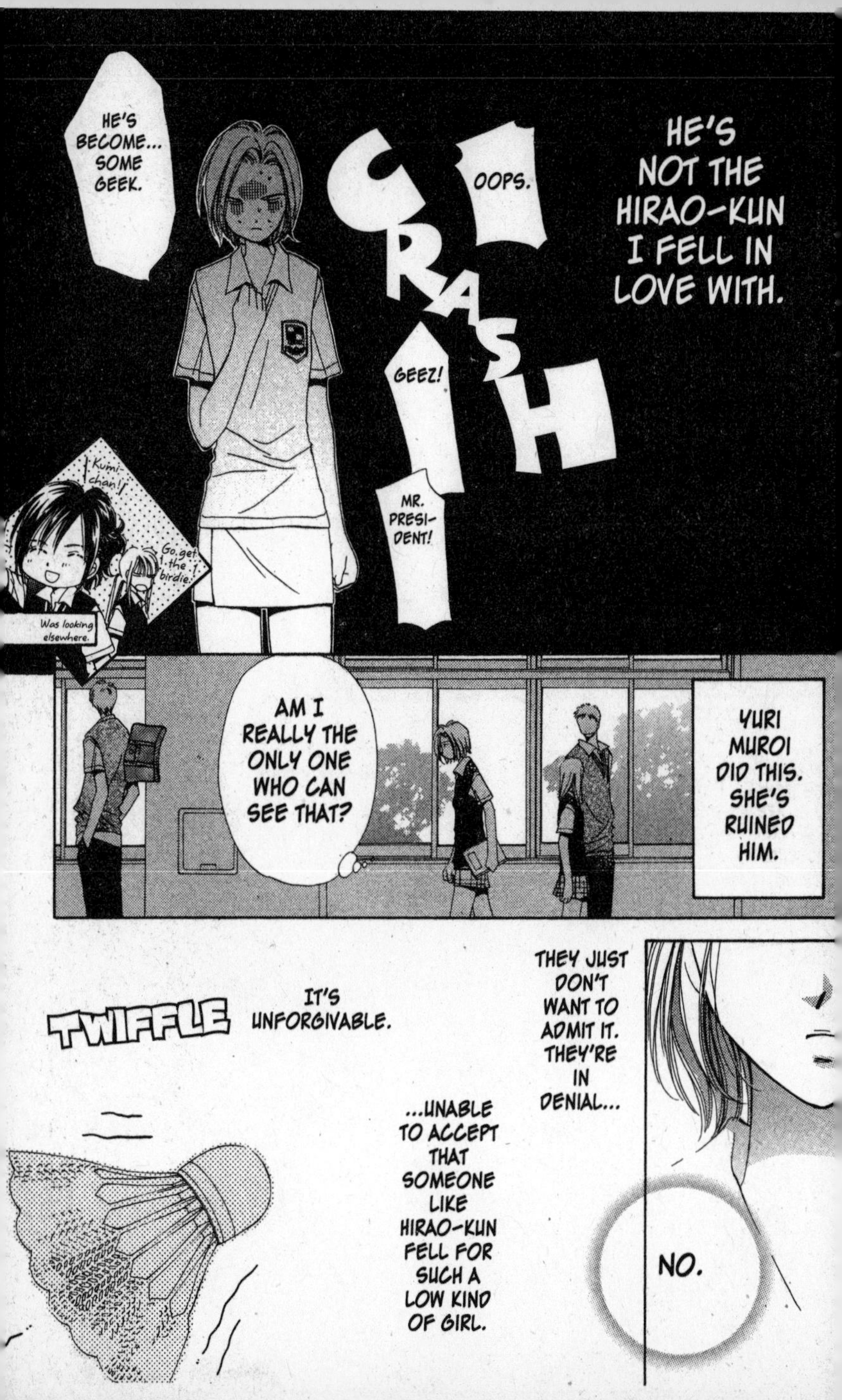
HE'S NOT THE HIRAO-KUN I FELL IN LOVE WITH.
CRASH
OOPS.
GEEZ!
MR. PRESIDENT!
HE'S BECOME... SOME GEEK.
Kumi-chan!!
Go get the birdie!
Was looking elsewhere.
YURI MUROI DID THIS. SHE'S RUINED HIM.
AM I REALLY THE ONLY ONE WHO CAN SEE THAT?
NO.
THEY JUST DON'T WANT TO ADMIT IT. THEY'RE IN DENIAL...
...UNABLE TO ACCEPT THAT SOMEONE LIKE HIRAO-KUN FELL FOR SUCH A LOW KIND OF GIRL.
IT'S UNFORGIVABLE.
TWIFFLE

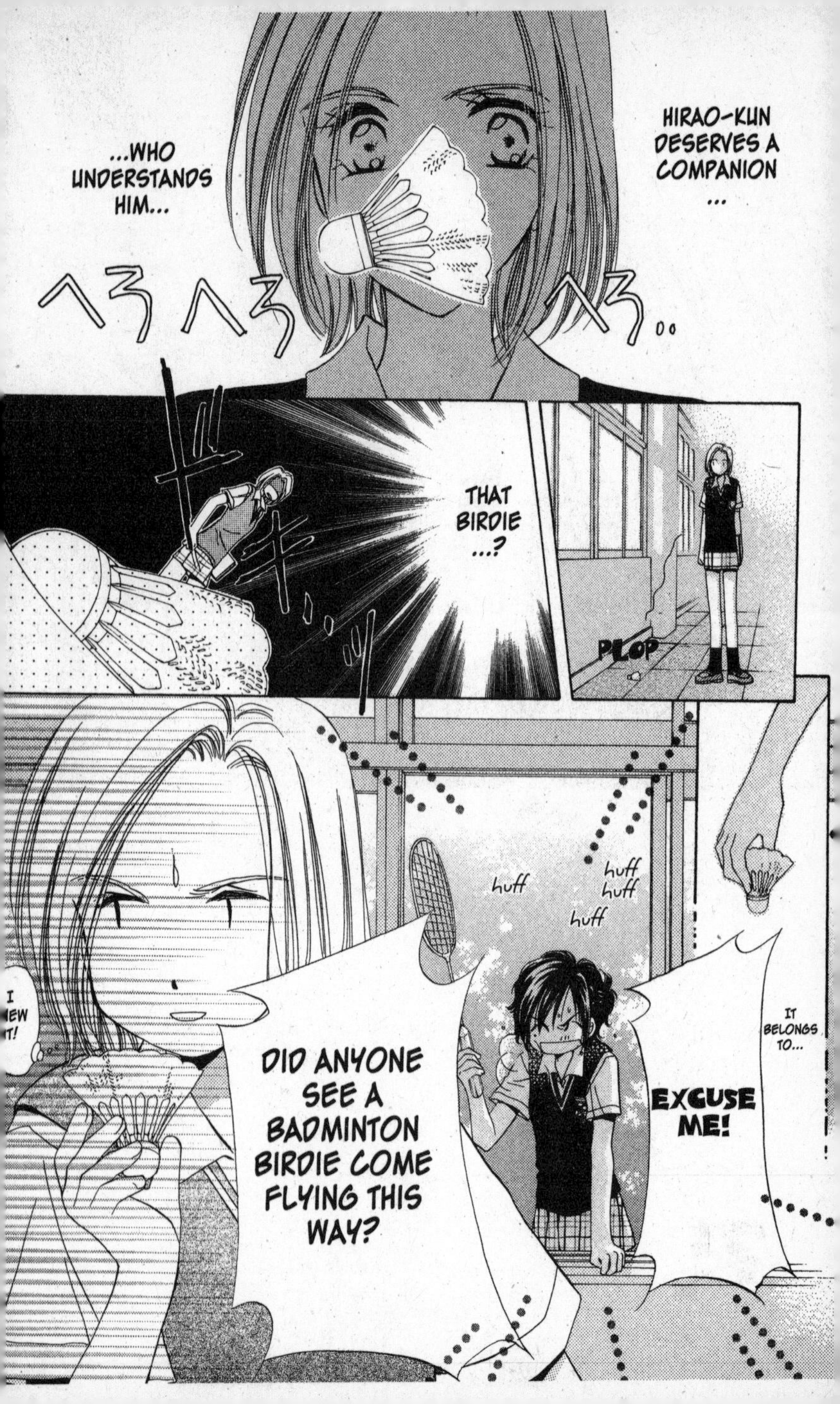
HIRAO-KUN DESERVES A COMPANION ...
...WHO UNDERSTANDS HIM...
へろへろへろ
PLOP
THAT BIRDIE ...?
IT BELONGS TO...
EXCUSE ME!
huff
huff huff
huff
DID ANYONE SEE A BADMINTON BIRDIE COME FLYING THIS WAY?

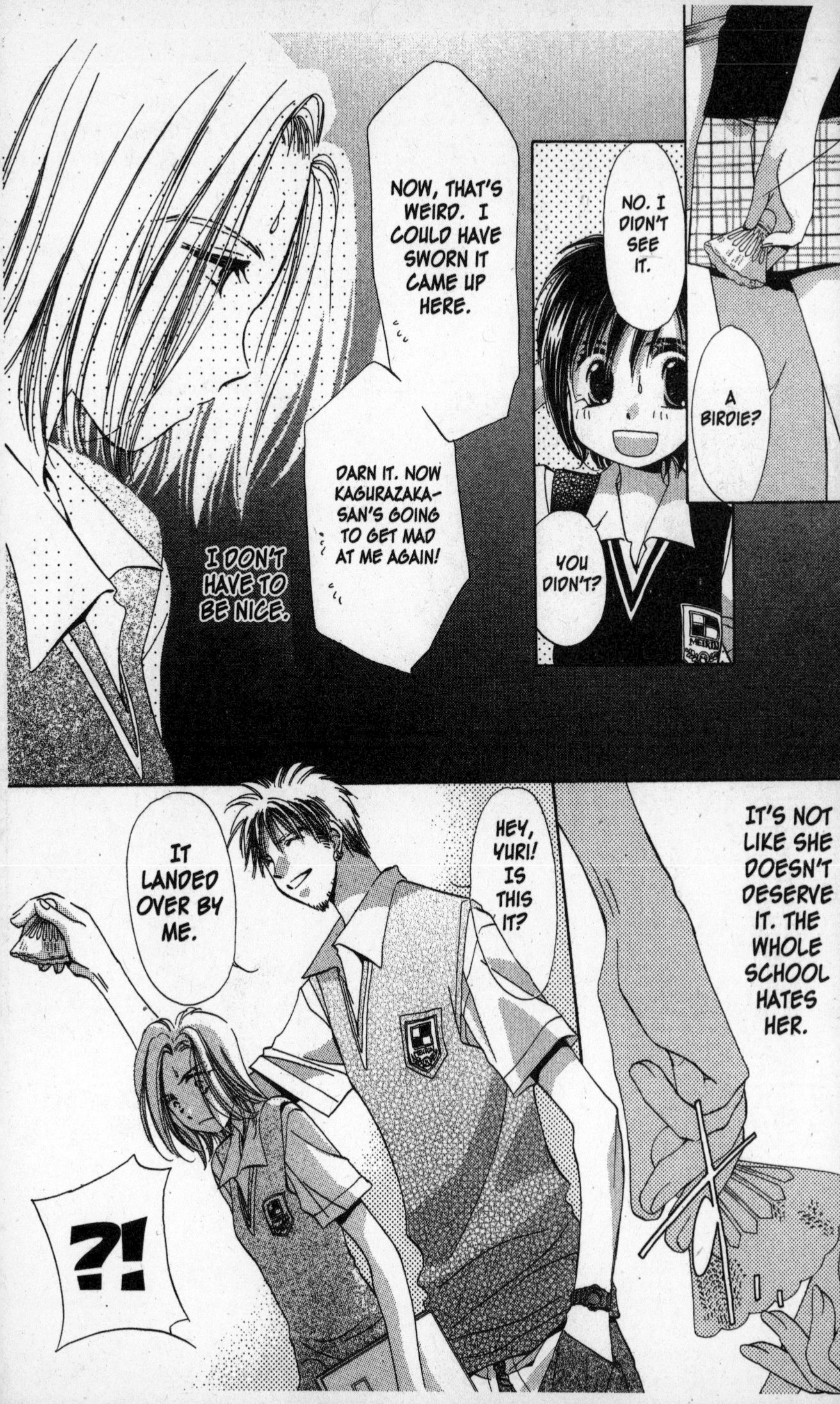

A BIRDIE?
NO. I DIDN'T SEE IT.
YOU DIDN'T?
NOW, THAT'S WEIRD. I COULD HAVE SWORN IT CAME UP HERE.
DARN IT. NOW KAGURAZAKA-SAN'S GOING TO GET MAD AT ME AGAIN!
I DON'T HAVE TO BE NICE.
IT'S NOT LIKE SHE DOESN'T DESERVE IT. THE WHOLE SCHOOL HATES HER.
HEY, YURI! IS THIS IT?
IT LANDED OVER BY ME.
?!

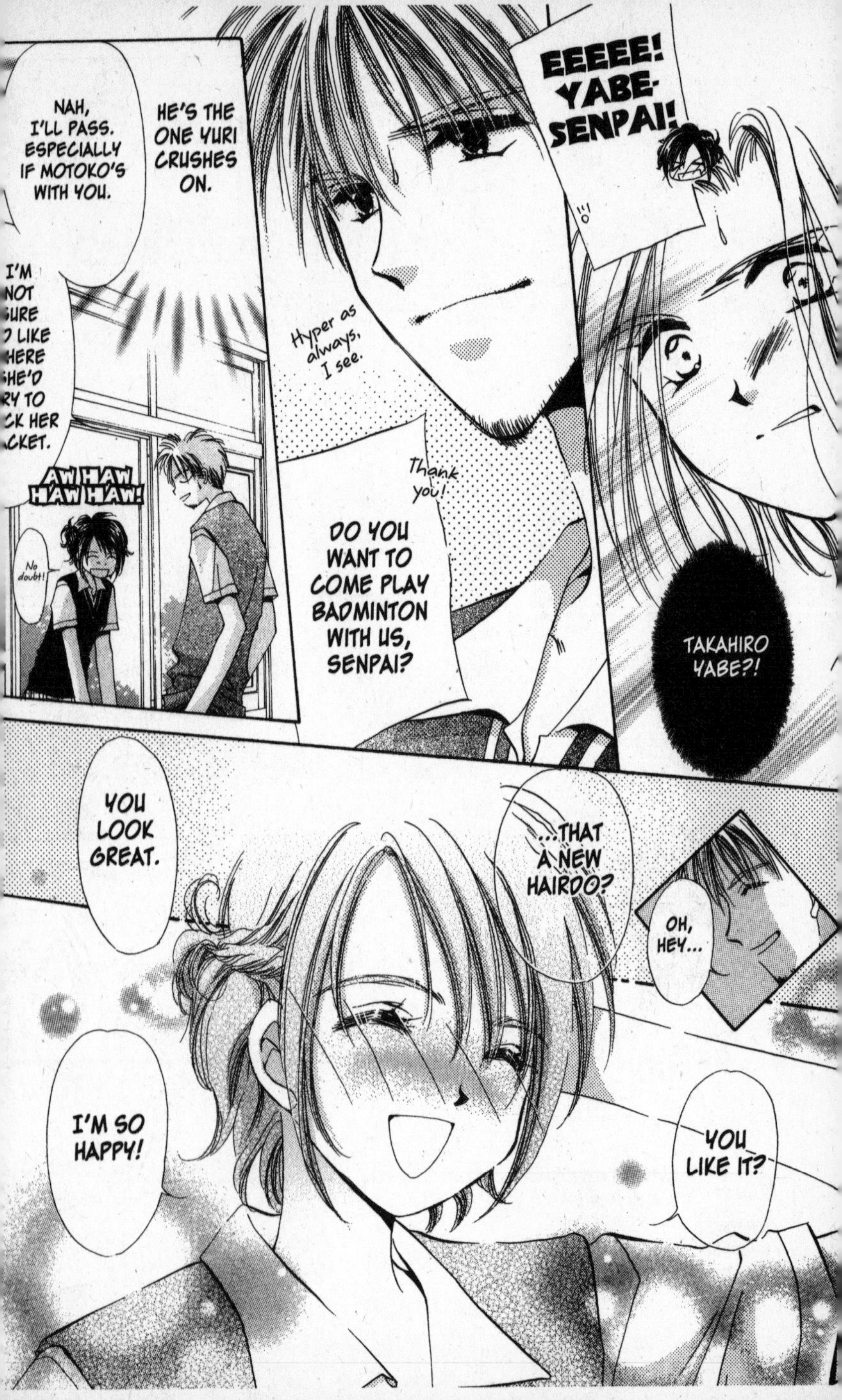
EEEEE! YABE-SENPAI!
TAKAHIRO YABE?!
Hyper as always, I see.
Thank you!
DO YOU WANT TO COME PLAY BADMINTON WITH US, SENPAI?
HE'S THE ONE YURI CRUSHES ON.
NAH, I'LL PASS. ESPECIALLY IF MOTOKO'S WITH YOU.
I'M NOT SURE
AW HAW HAW HAW!
No doubt!
OH, HEY...
...THAT A NEW HAIRDO?
YOU LIKE IT?
YOU LOOK GREAT.
I'M SO HAPPY!

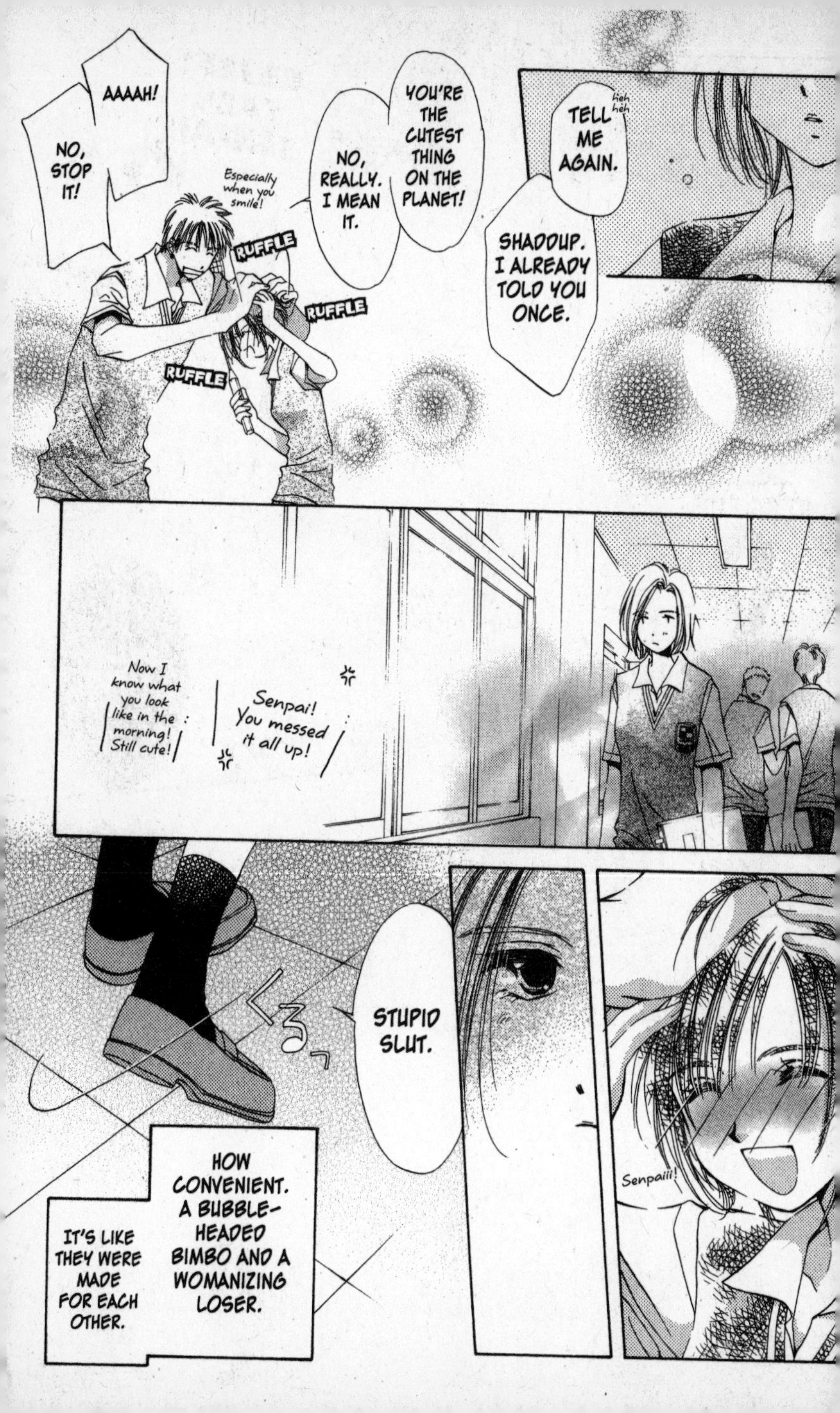
heh heh
TELL ME AGAIN.
SHADDUP. I ALREADY TOLD YOU ONCE.
YOU'RE THE CUTEST THING ON THE PLANET!
NO, REALLY. I MEAN IT.
Especially when you smile!
AAAAH!
NO, STOP IT!
RUFFLE
RUFFLE
RUFFLE
Senpai! You messed it all up!
Now I know what you look like in the morning! Still cute!
Senpaiii!
STUPID SLUT.
くる
HOW CONVENIENT. A BUBBLE-HEADED BIMBO AND A WOMANIZING LOSER.
IT'S LIKE THEY WERE MADE FOR EACH OTHER.

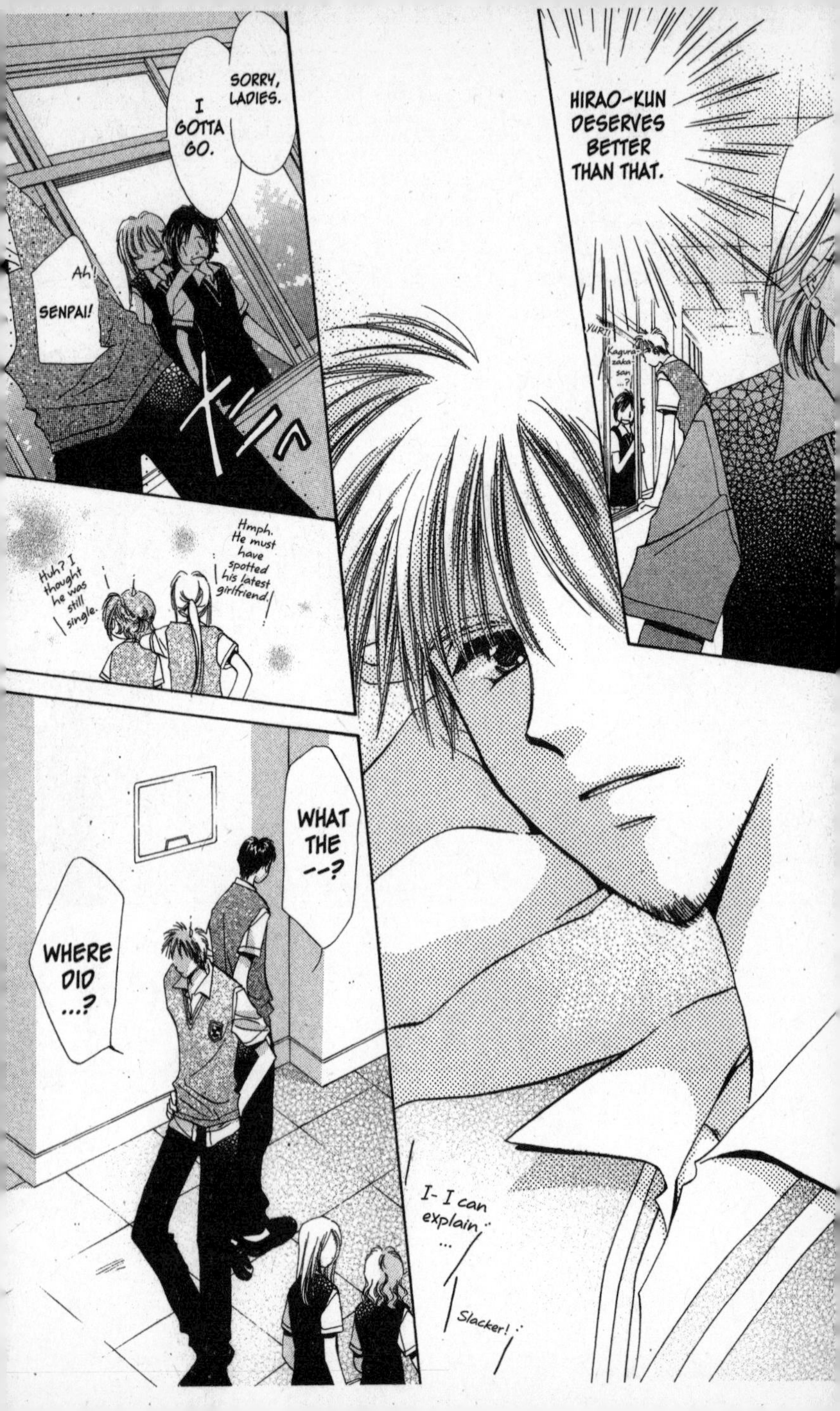
HIRAO-KUN DESERVES BETTER THAN THAT.
YURI!
Kagura-zaka-san ...?
I- I can explain ...
Slacker!
SORRY, LADIES. I GOTTA GO.
Ah! SENPAI!
Hmph. He must have spotted his latest girlfriend.
Huh? I thought he was still single.
WHAT THE --?
WHERE DID ...?

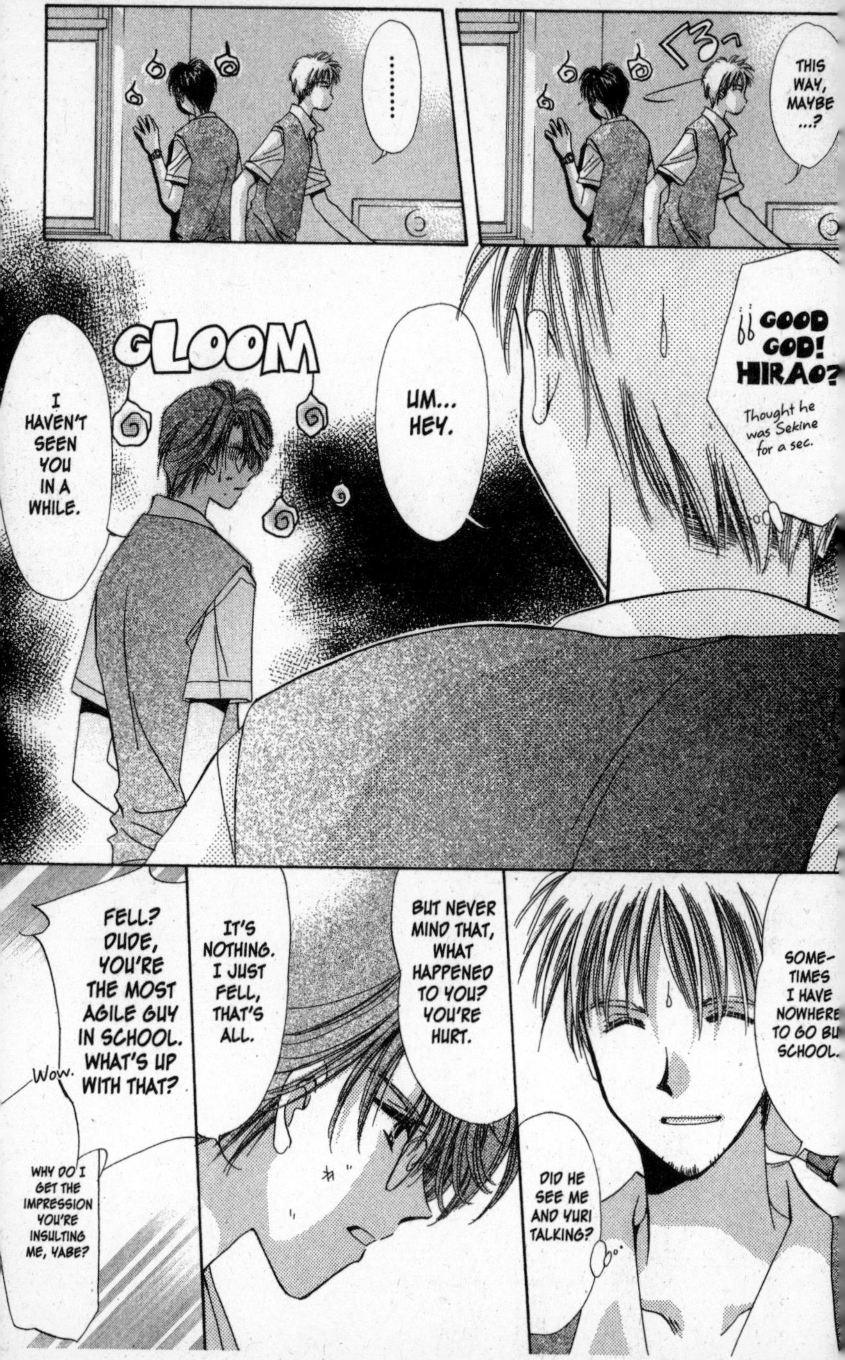
THIS WAY, MAYBE ...?
....
GOOD GOD! HIRAO?
Thought he was Sekine for a sec.
UM... HEY.
GLOOM
I HAVEN'T SEEN YOU IN A WHILE.
SOME-TIMES I HAVE NOWHERE TO GO BU SCHOOL.
DID HE SEE ME AND YURI TALKING?
BUT NEVER MIND THAT, WHAT HAPPENED TO YOU? YOU'RE HURT.
IT'S NOTHING. I JUST FELL, THAT'S ALL.
FELL? DUDE, YOU'RE THE MOST AGILE GUY IN SCHOOL. WHAT'S UP WITH THAT?
Wow.
WHY DO I GET THE IMPRESSION YOU'RE INSULTING ME, YABE?

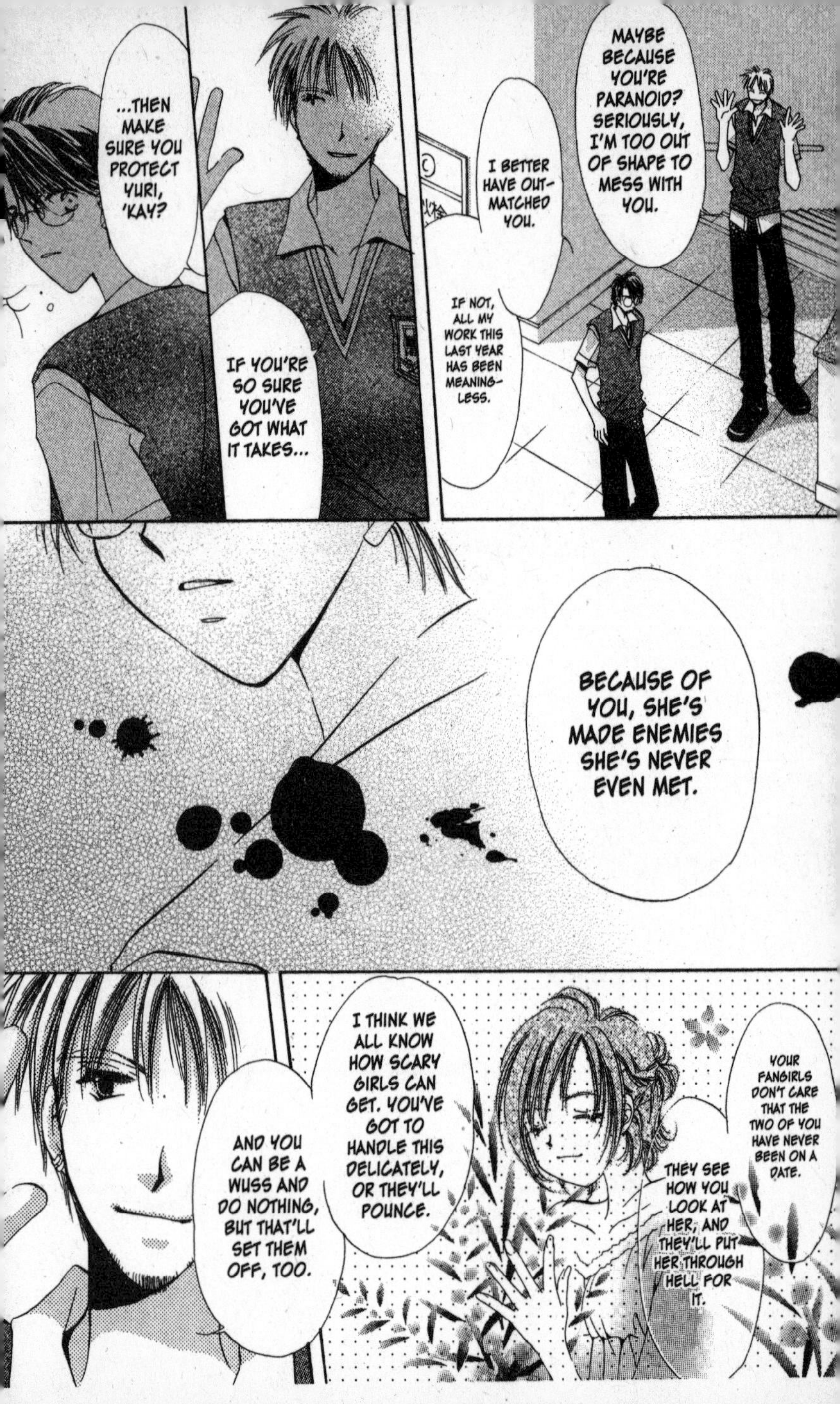
MAYBE BECAUSE YOU'RE PARANOID? SERIOUSLY, I'M TOO OUT OF SHAPE TO MESS WITH YOU.
I BETTER HAVE OUT-MATCHED YOU.
IF NOT, ALL MY WORK THIS LAST YEAR HAS BEEN MEANING-LESS.
IF YOU'RE SO SURE YOU'VE GOT WHAT IT TAKES...
...THEN MAKE SURE YOU PROTECT YURI, 'KAY?
BECAUSE OF YOU, SHE'S MADE ENEMIES SHE'S NEVER EVEN MET.
YOUR FANGIRLS DON'T CARE THAT THE TWO OF YOU HAVE NEVER BEEN ON A DATE.
THEY SEE HOW YOU LOOK AT HER, AND THEY'LL PUT HER THROUGH HELL FOR IT.
I THINK WE ALL KNOW HOW SCARY GIRLS CAN GET. YOU'VE GOT TO HANDLE THIS DELICATELY, OR THEY'LL POUNCE.
AND YOU CAN BE A WUSS AND DO NOTHING, BUT THAT'LL SET THEM OFF, TOO.

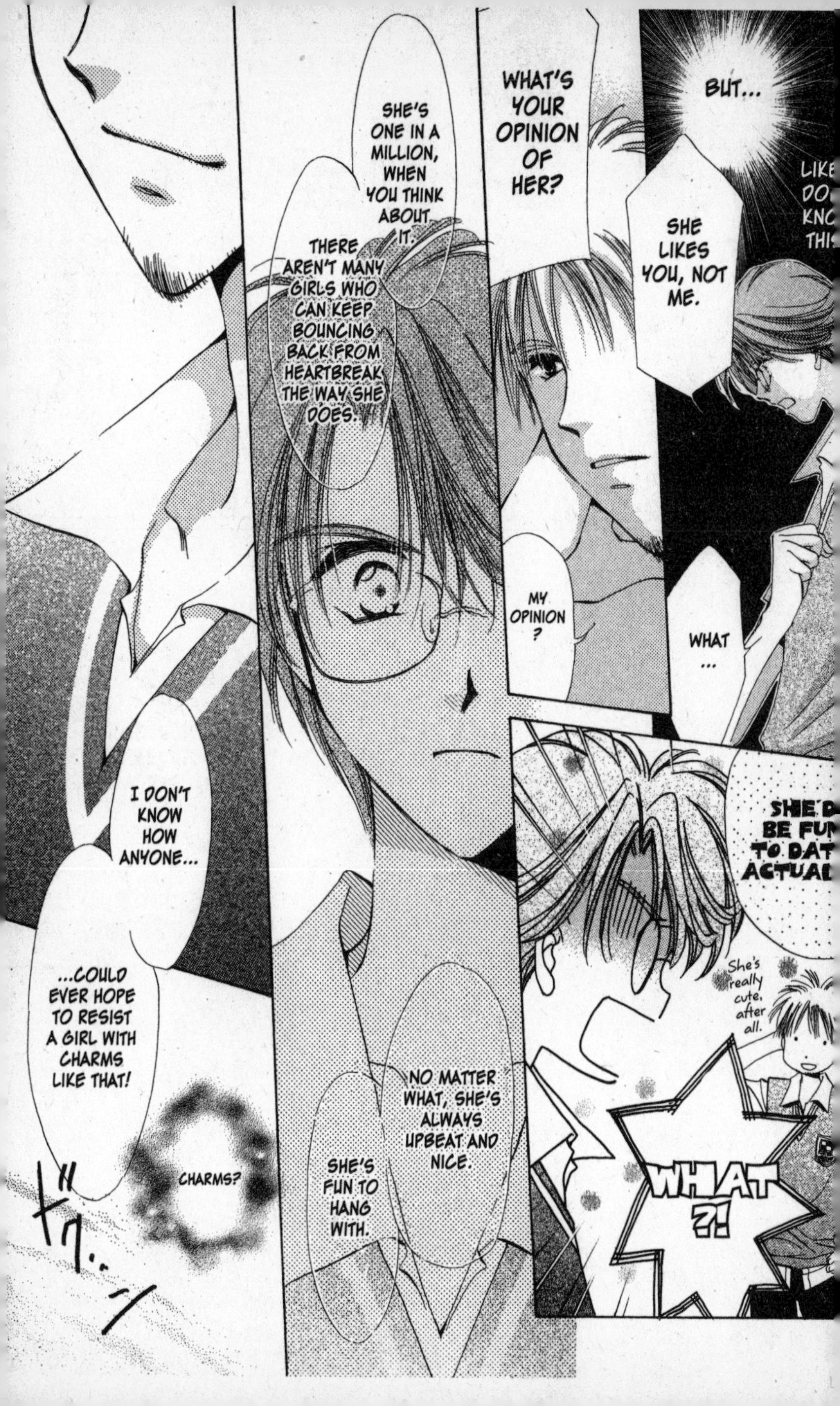

BUT...
SHE LIKES YOU, NOT ME.
WHAT ...
WHAT'S YOUR OPINION OF HER?
MY OPINION?
She's really cute, after all.
WHAT ?!
SHE'S ONE IN A MILLION, WHEN YOU THINK ABOUT IT.
THERE AREN'T MANY GIRLS WHO CAN KEEP BOUNCING BACK FROM HEARTBREAK THE WAY SHE DOES.
NO MATTER WHAT, SHE'S ALWAYS UPBEAT AND NICE.
SHE'S FUN TO HANG WITH.
I DON'T KNOW HOW ANYONE...
...COULD EVER HOPE TO RESIST A GIRL WITH CHARMS LIKE THAT!
CHARMS?

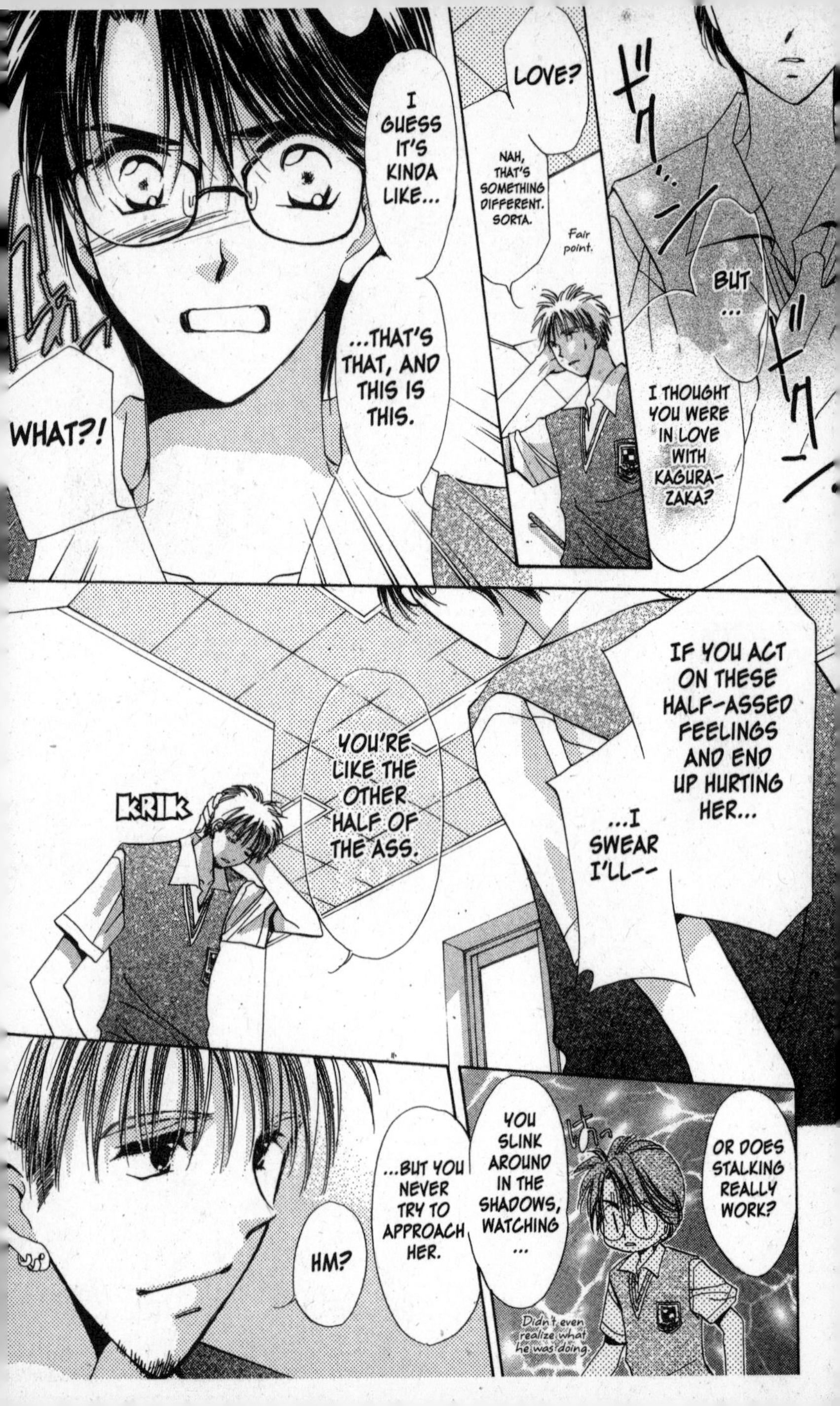
BUT ...
I THOUGHT YOU WERE IN LOVE WITH KAGURA-ZAKA?
LOVE?
NAH, THAT'S SOMETHING DIFFERENT. SORTA.
Fair point.
I GUESS IT'S KINDA LIKE...
...THAT'S THAT, AND THIS IS THIS.
WHAT?!
IF YOU ACT ON THESE HALF-ASSED FEELINGS AND END UP HURTING HER...
...I SWEAR I'LL--
YOU'RE LIKE THE OTHER HALF OF THE ASS.
KRIK
OR DOES STALKING REALLY WORK?
YOU SLINK AROUND IN THE SHADOWS, WATCHING ...
Didn't even realize what he was doing.
...BUT YOU NEVER TRY TO APPROACH HER.
HM?

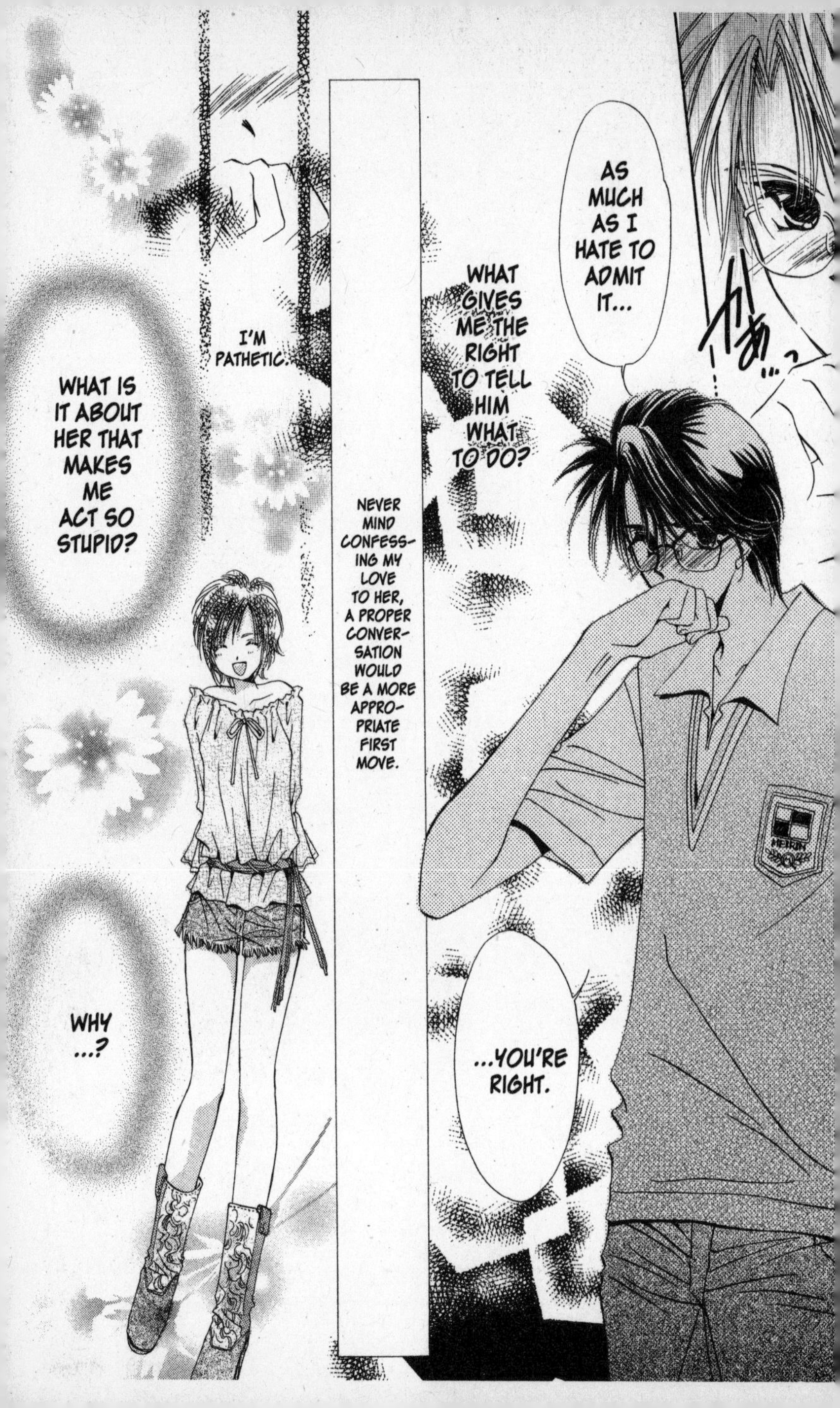
AS MUCH AS I HATE TO ADMIT IT...
WHAT GIVES ME THE RIGHT TO TELL HIM WHAT TO DO?
...YOU'RE RIGHT.
NEVER MIND CONFESSING MY LOVE TO HER, A PROPER CONVERSATION WOULD BE A MORE APPROPRIATE FIRST MOVE.
I'M PATHETIC.
WHAT IS IT ABOUT HER THAT MAKES ME ACT SO STUPID?
WHY ...?

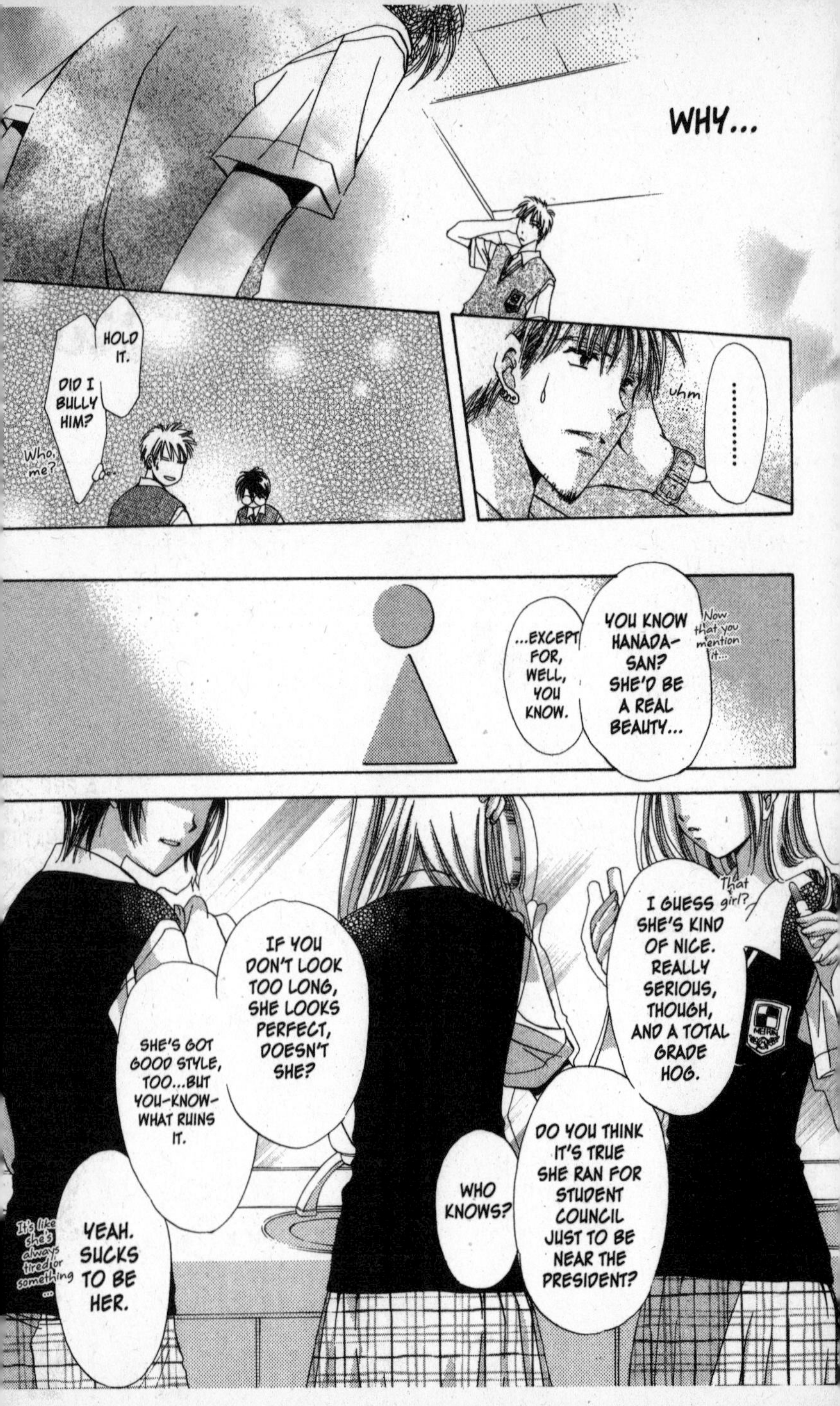
WHY...
uhm...
......
HOLD IT.
DID I BULLY HIM?
Who, me?
Now that you mention it...
YOU KNOW HANADA-SAN? SHE'D BE A REAL BEAUTY...
...EXCEPT FOR, WELL, YOU KNOW.
That girl?
I GUESS SHE'S KIND OF NICE. REALLY SERIOUS, THOUGH, AND A TOTAL GRADE HOG.
IF YOU DON'T LOOK TOO LONG, SHE LOOKS PERFECT, DOESN'T SHE?
DO YOU THINK IT'S TRUE SHE RAN FOR STUDENT COUNCIL JUST TO BE NEAR THE PRESIDENT?
WHO KNOWS?
SHE'S GOT GOOD STYLE, TOO...BUT YOU-KNOW-WHAT RUINS IT.
YEAH. SUCKS TO BE HER.
It's like she's always tired or something...

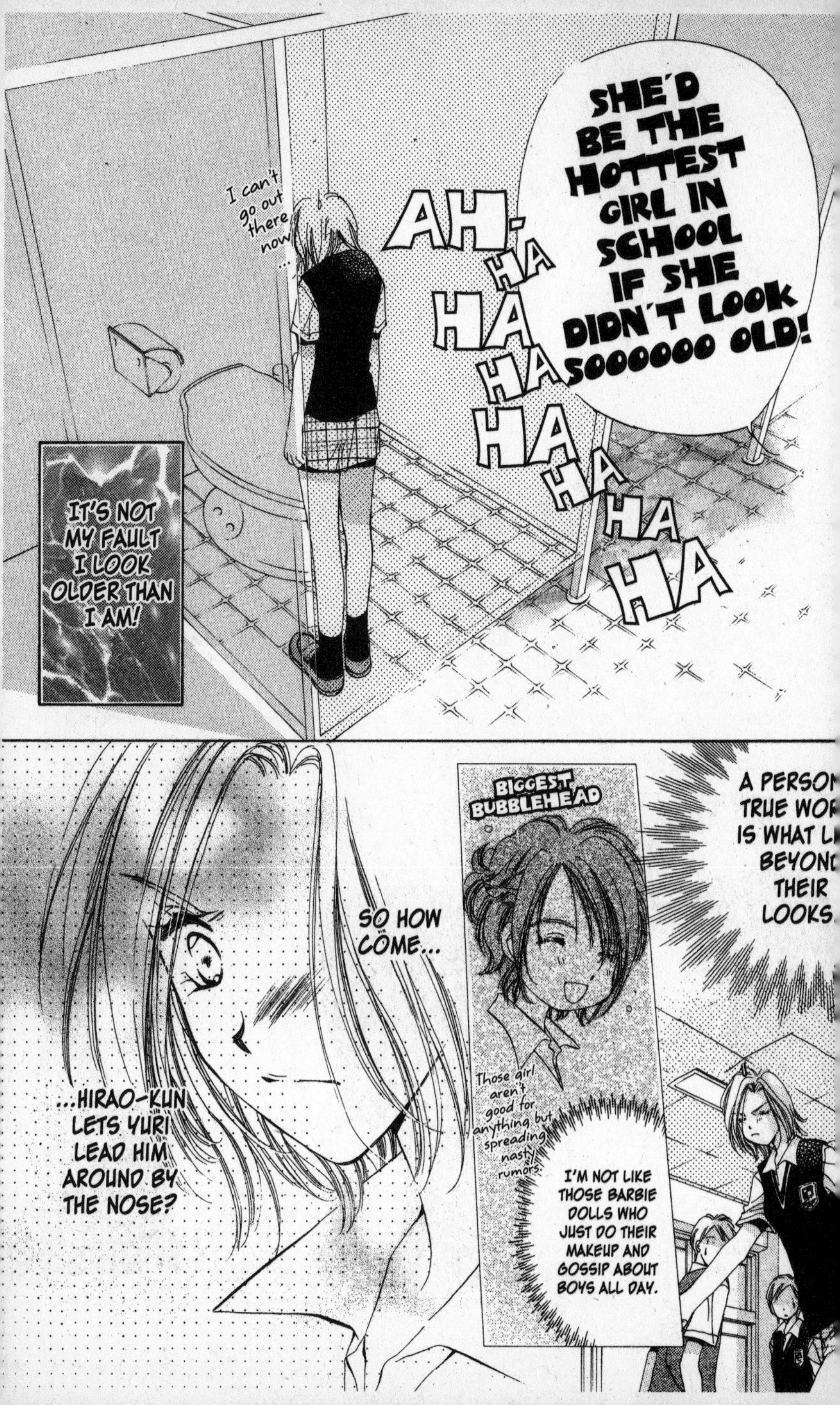
SHE'D BE THE HOTTEST GIRL IN SCHOOL IF SHE DIDN'T LOOK SOOOOOO OLD!
AH-HA HA HA HA HA HA HA HA
I can't go out there now...
IT'S NOT MY FAULT I LOOK OLDER THAN I AM!
A PERSO TRUE WO IS WHAT L BEYON THEIR LOOKS.
BIGGEST BUBBLEHEAD
I'M NOT LIKE THOSE BARBIE DOLLS WHO JUST DO THEIR MAKEUP AND GOSSIP ABOUT BOYS ALL DAY.
Those girl aren't good for anything but spreading nasty rumors.
SO HOW COME...
...HIRAO-KUN LETS YURI LEAD HIM AROUND BY THE NOSE?

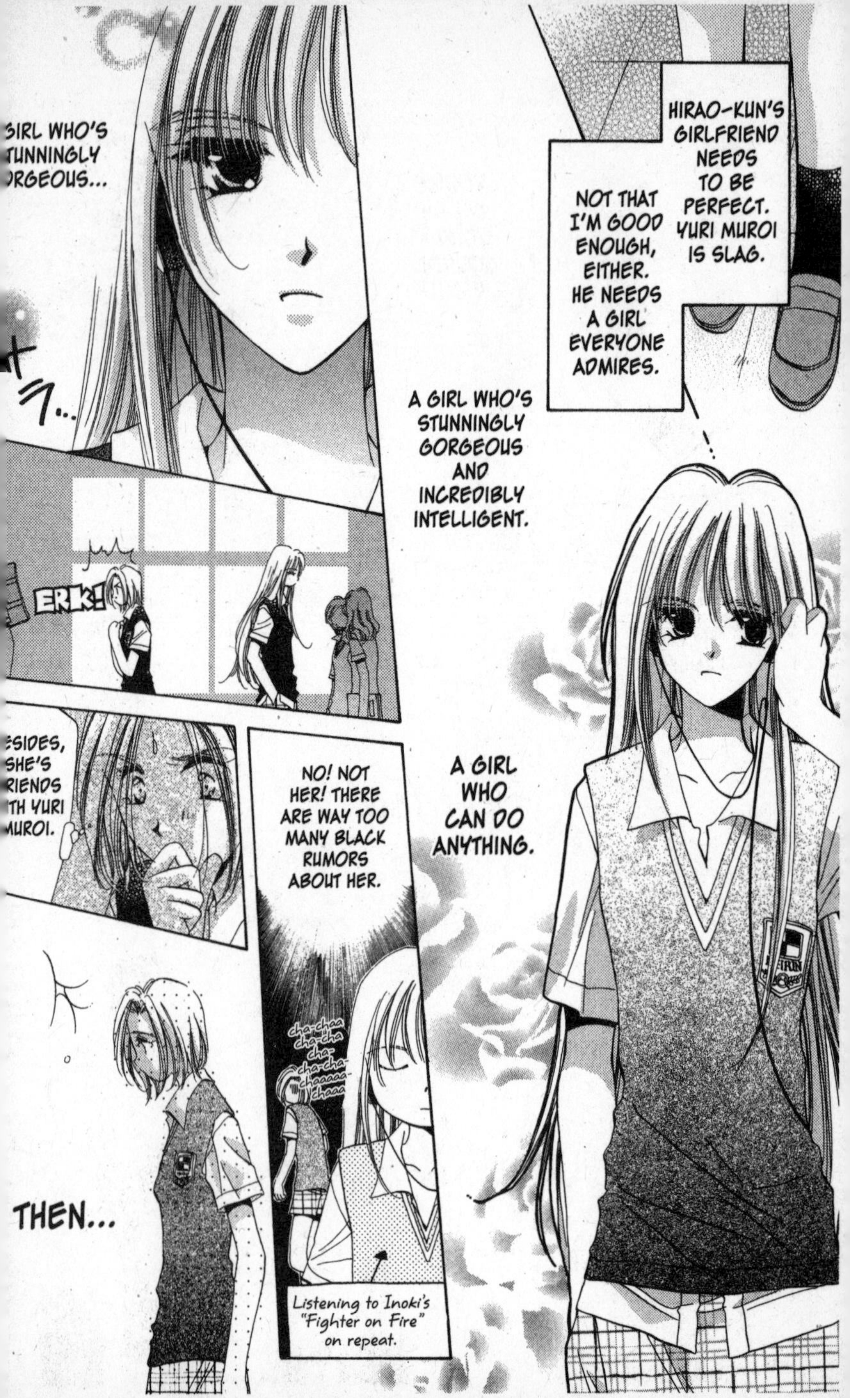

HIRAO-KUN'S GIRLFRIEND NEEDS TO BE PERFECT. YURI MUROI IS SLAG.
NOT THAT I'M GOOD ENOUGH, EITHER. HE NEEDS A GIRL EVERYONE ADMIRES.
A GIRL WHO'S STUNNINGLY GORGEOUS AND INCREDIBLY INTELLIGENT.
A GIRL WHO CAN DO ANYTHING.
GIRL WHO'S STUNNINGLY ORGEOUS...
ERK!
NO! NOT HER! THERE ARE WAY TOO MANY BLACK RUMORS ABOUT HER.
cha-chaa cha-cha cha- cha-cha-chaaaaa-chaaa
Listening to Inoki's "Fighter on Fire" on repeat.
ESIDES, SHE'S RIENDS TH YURI MUROI.
THEN...

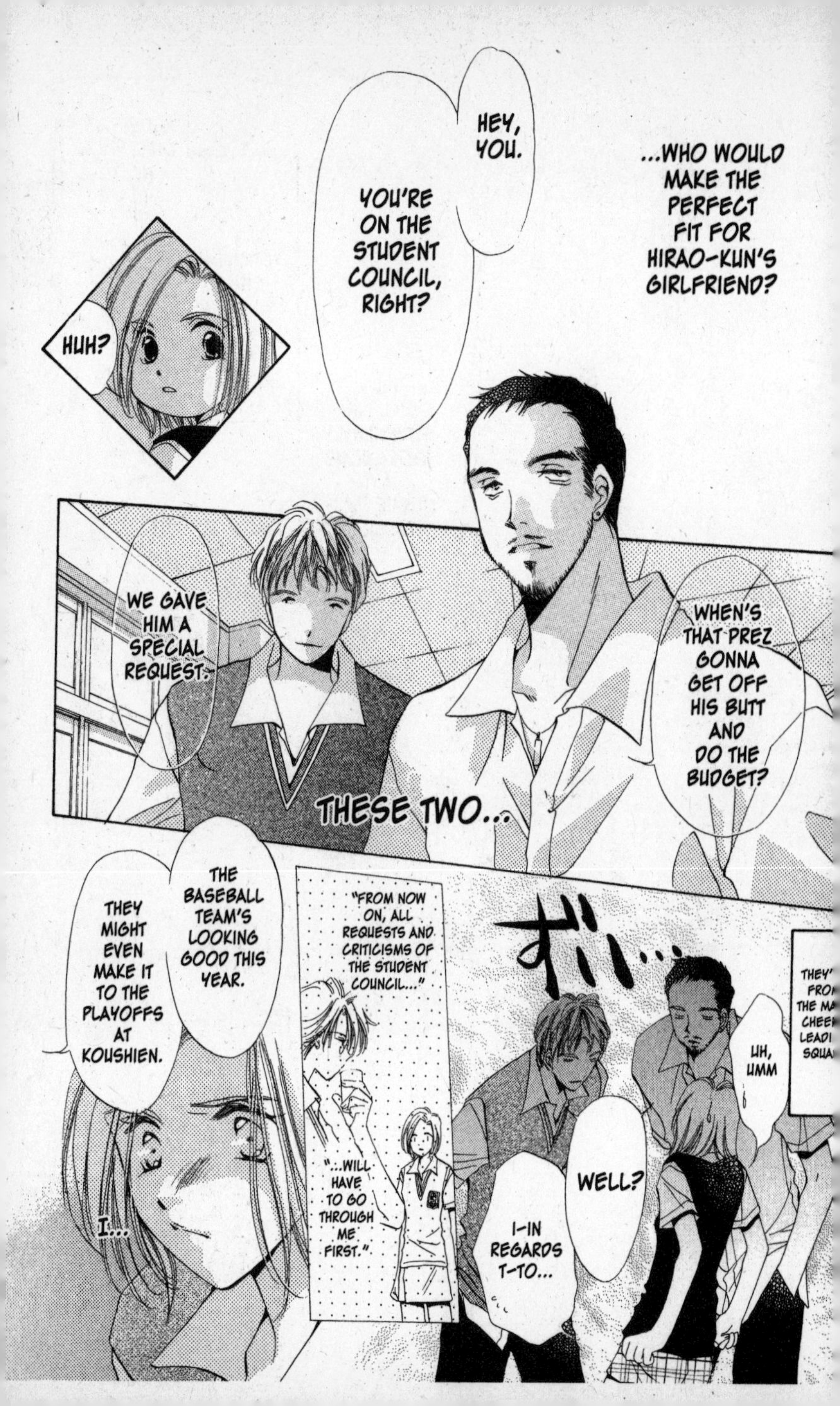
...WHO WOULD MAKE THE PERFECT FIT FOR HIRAO-KUN'S GIRLFRIEND?
HEY, YOU.
YOU'RE ON THE STUDENT COUNCIL, RIGHT?
HUH?
WHEN'S THAT PREZ GONNA GET OFF HIS BUTT AND DO THE BUDGET?
WE GAVE HIM A SPECIAL REQUEST.
THESE TWO...
UH, UMM
ずい...
WELL?
I-IN REGARDS T-TO...
"FROM NOW ON, ALL REQUESTS AND CRITICISMS OF THE STUDENT COUNCIL..."
"...WILL HAVE TO GO THROUGH ME FIRST."
THE BASEBALL TEAM'S LOOKING GOOD THIS YEAR.
THEY MIGHT EVEN MAKE IT TO THE PLAYOFFS AT KOUSHIEN.
I...

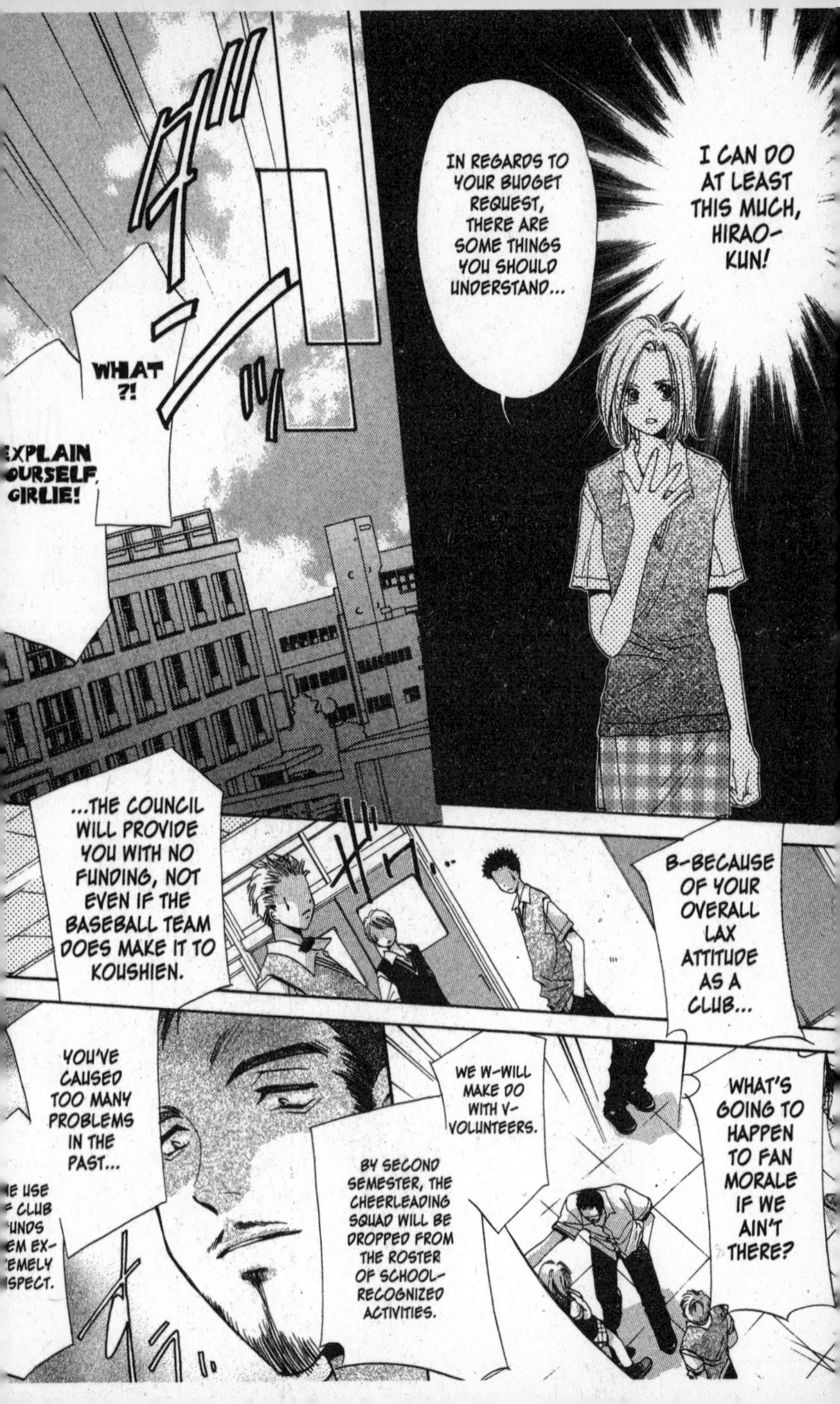
I CAN DO AT LEAST THIS MUCH, HIRAO-KUN!
IN REGARDS TO YOUR BUDGET REQUEST, THERE ARE SOME THINGS YOU SHOULD UNDERSTAND...
WHAT ?!
XPLAIN OURSELF, GIRLIE!
B-BECAUSE OF YOUR OVERALL LAX ATTITUDE AS A CLUB...
...THE COUNCIL WILL PROVIDE YOU WITH NO FUNDING, NOT EVEN IF THE BASEBALL TEAM DOES MAKE IT TO KOUSHIEN.
WHAT'S GOING TO HAPPEN TO FAN MORALE IF WE AIN'T THERE?
WE W-WILL MAKE DO WITH V-VOLUNTEERS.
BY SECOND SEMESTER, THE CHEERLEADING SQUAD WILL BE DROPPED FROM THE ROSTER OF SCHOOL-RECOGNIZED ACTIVITIES.
YOU'VE CAUSED TOO MANY PROBLEMS IN THE PAST...
E USE F CLUB UNDS EM EX- EMELY SPECT.

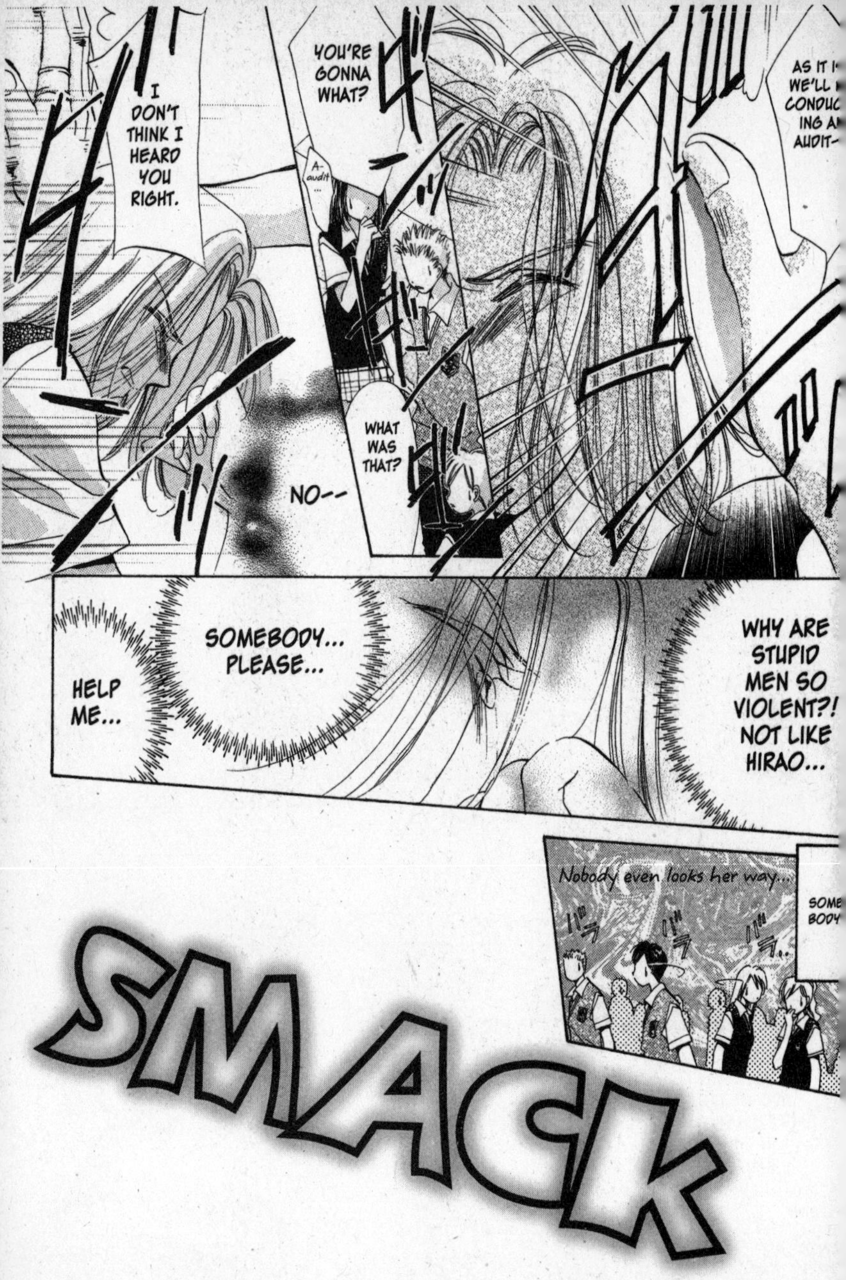
AS IT I
WE'LL
CONDUC
ING A
AUDIT-
YOU'RE GONNA WHAT?
A-audit...
WHAT WAS THAT?
I DON'T THINK I HEARD YOU RIGHT.
NO--
WHY ARE STUPID MEN SO VIOLENT?! NOT LIKE HIRAO...
SOMEBODY... PLEASE...
HELP ME...
SOME BODY
Nobody even looks her way...
SMACK

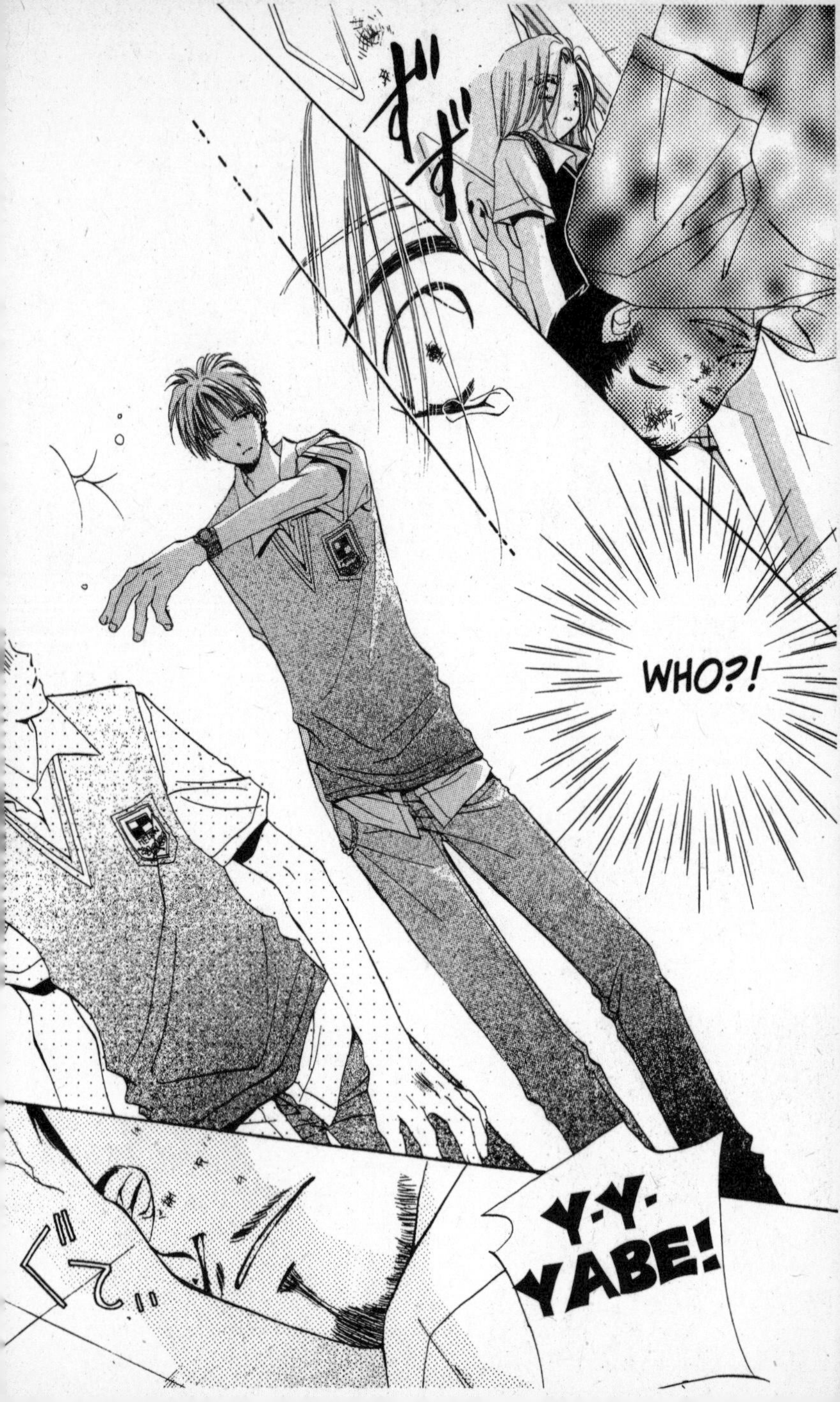
ずず
WHO?!
Y-Y-YABE!

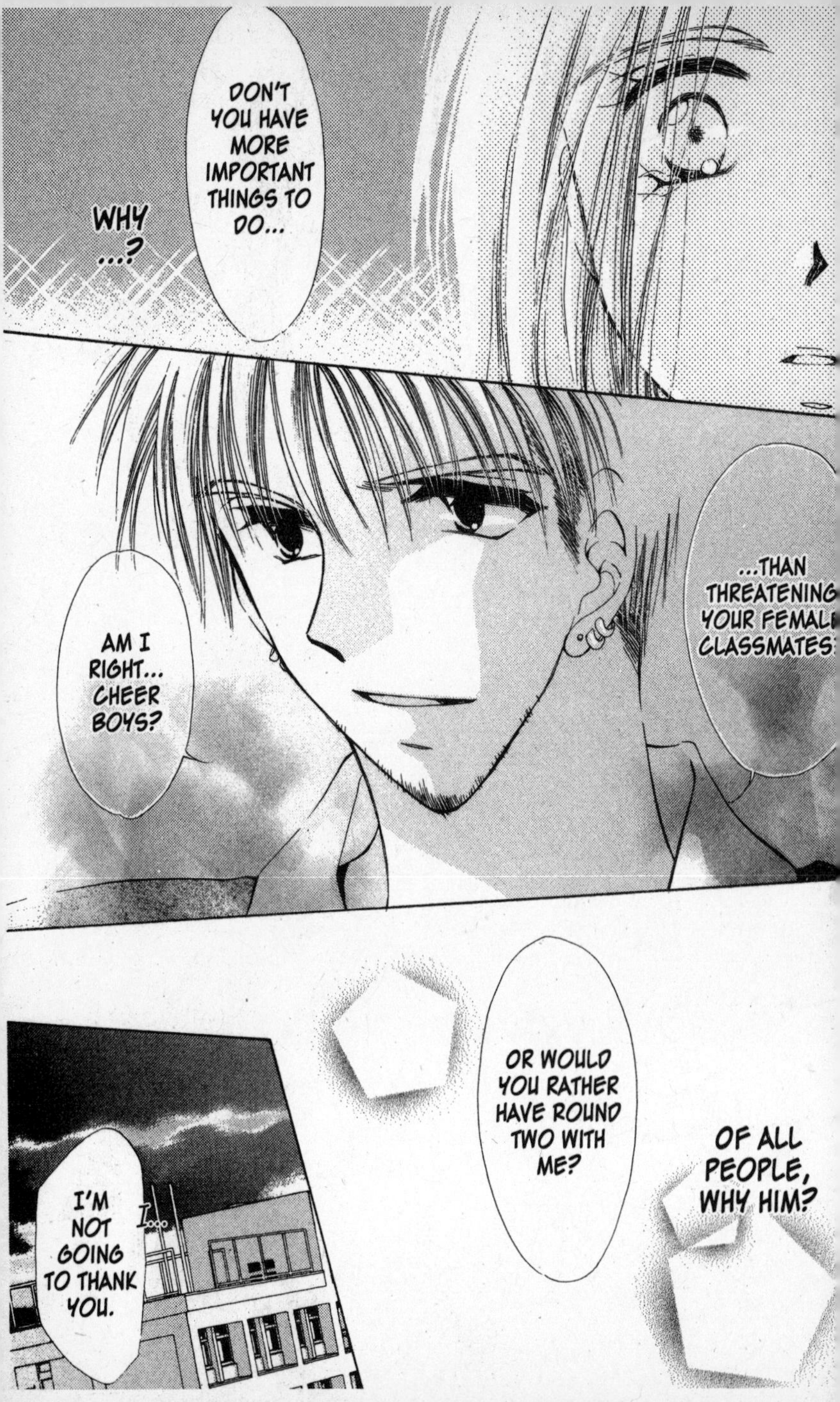
DON'T YOU HAVE MORE IMPORTANT THINGS TO DO...
WHY ...?
...THAN THREATENING YOUR FEMALE CLASSMATES?
AM I RIGHT... CHEER BOYS?
OR WOULD YOU RATHER HAVE ROUND TWO WITH ME?
OF ALL PEOPLE, WHY HIM?
I...
I'M NOT GOING TO THANK YOU.

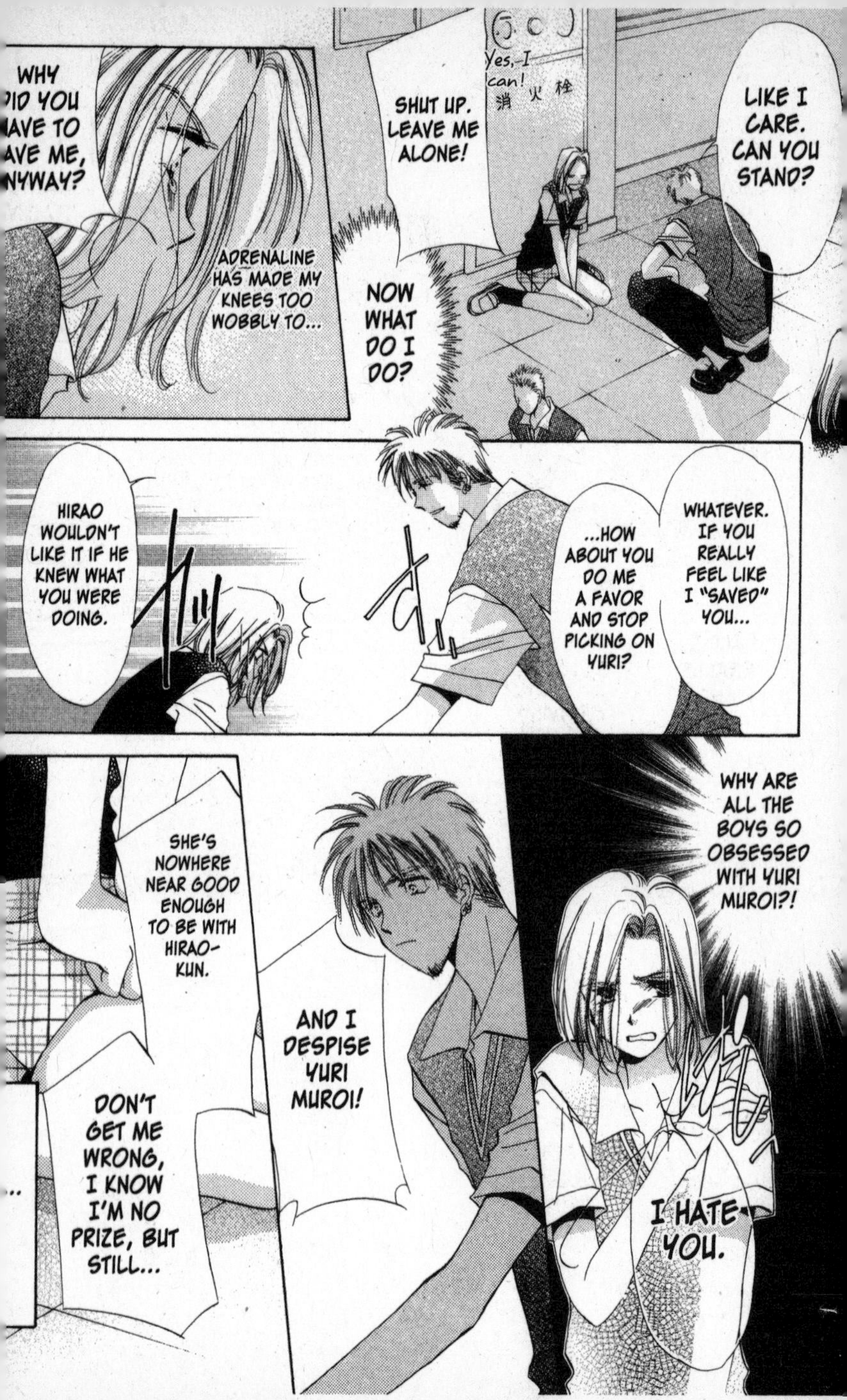
LIKE I CARE. CAN YOU STAND?
Yes, I can!
消火栓
SHUT UP. LEAVE ME ALONE!
NOW WHAT DO I DO?
ADRENALINE HAS MADE MY KNEES TOO WOBBLY TO...
WHY ID YOU AVE TO AVE ME, NYWAY?
WHATEVER. IF YOU REALLY FEEL LIKE I "SAVED" YOU...
...HOW ABOUT YOU DO ME A FAVOR AND STOP PICKING ON YURI?
HIRAO WOULDN'T LIKE IT IF HE KNEW WHAT YOU WERE DOING.
WHY ARE ALL THE BOYS SO OBSESSED WITH YURI MUROI?!
I HATE YOU.
SHE'S NOWHERE NEAR GOOD ENOUGH TO BE WITH HIRAO-KUN.
AND I DESPISE YURI MUROI!
DON'T GET ME WRONG, I KNOW I'M NO PRIZE, BUT STILL...
...

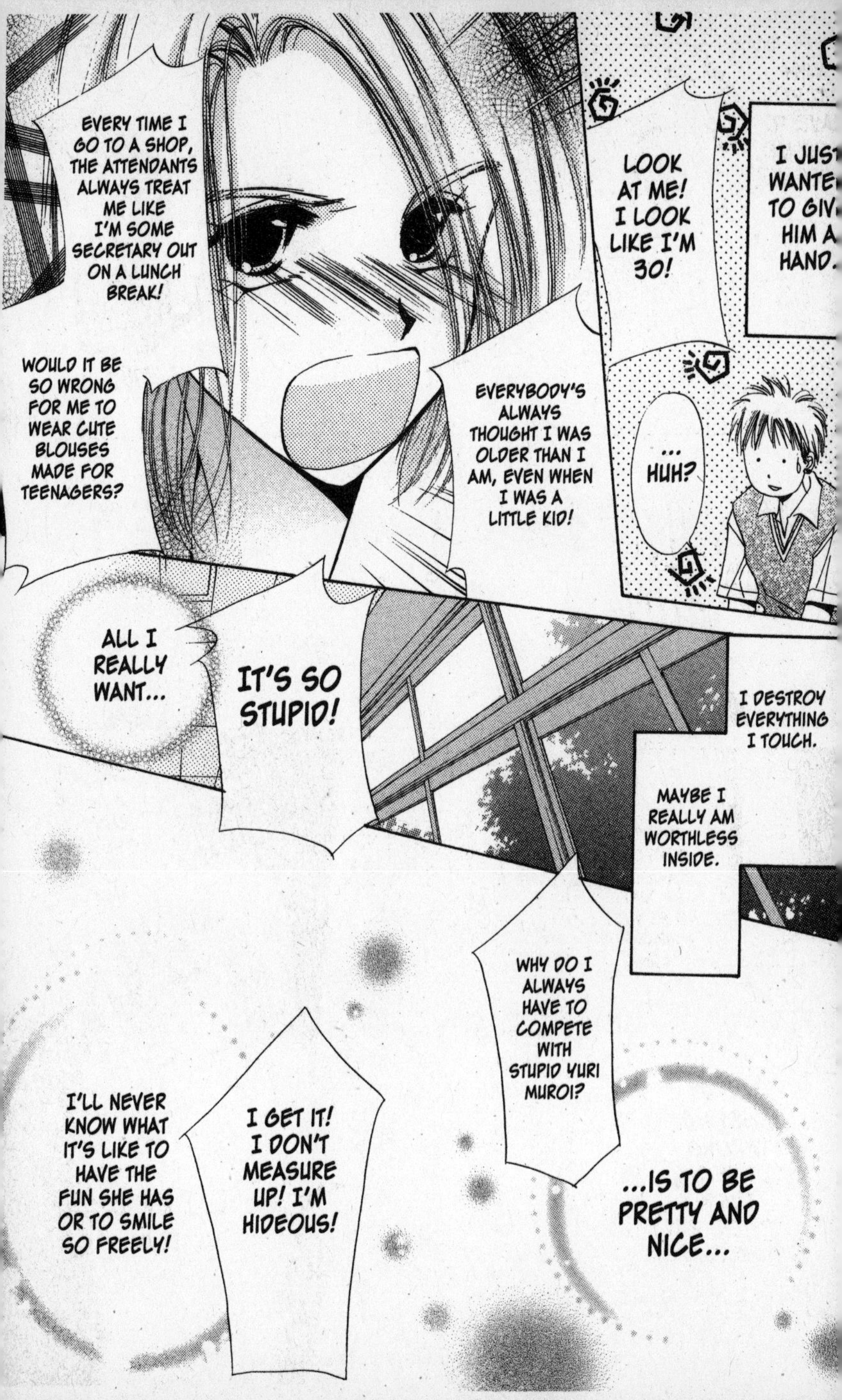
I JUS WANTE TO GIV HIM A HAND.
LOOK AT ME! I LOOK LIKE I'M 30!
... HUH?
EVERYBODY'S ALWAYS THOUGHT I WAS OLDER THAN I AM, EVEN WHEN I WAS A LITTLE KID!
EVERY TIME I GO TO A SHOP, THE ATTENDANTS ALWAYS TREAT ME LIKE I'M SOME SECRETARY OUT ON A LUNCH BREAK!
WOULD IT BE SO WRONG FOR ME TO WEAR CUTE BLOUSES MADE FOR TEENAGERS?
I DESTROY EVERYTHING I TOUCH.
MAYBE I REALLY AM WORTHLESS INSIDE.
IT'S SO STUPID!
ALL I REALLY WANT...
WHY DO I ALWAYS HAVE TO COMPETE WITH STUPID YURI MUROI?
...IS TO BE PRETTY AND NICE...
I GET IT! I DON'T MEASURE UP! I'M HIDEOUS!
I'LL NEVER KNOW WHAT IT'S LIKE TO HAVE THE FUN SHE HAS OR TO SMILE SO FREELY!

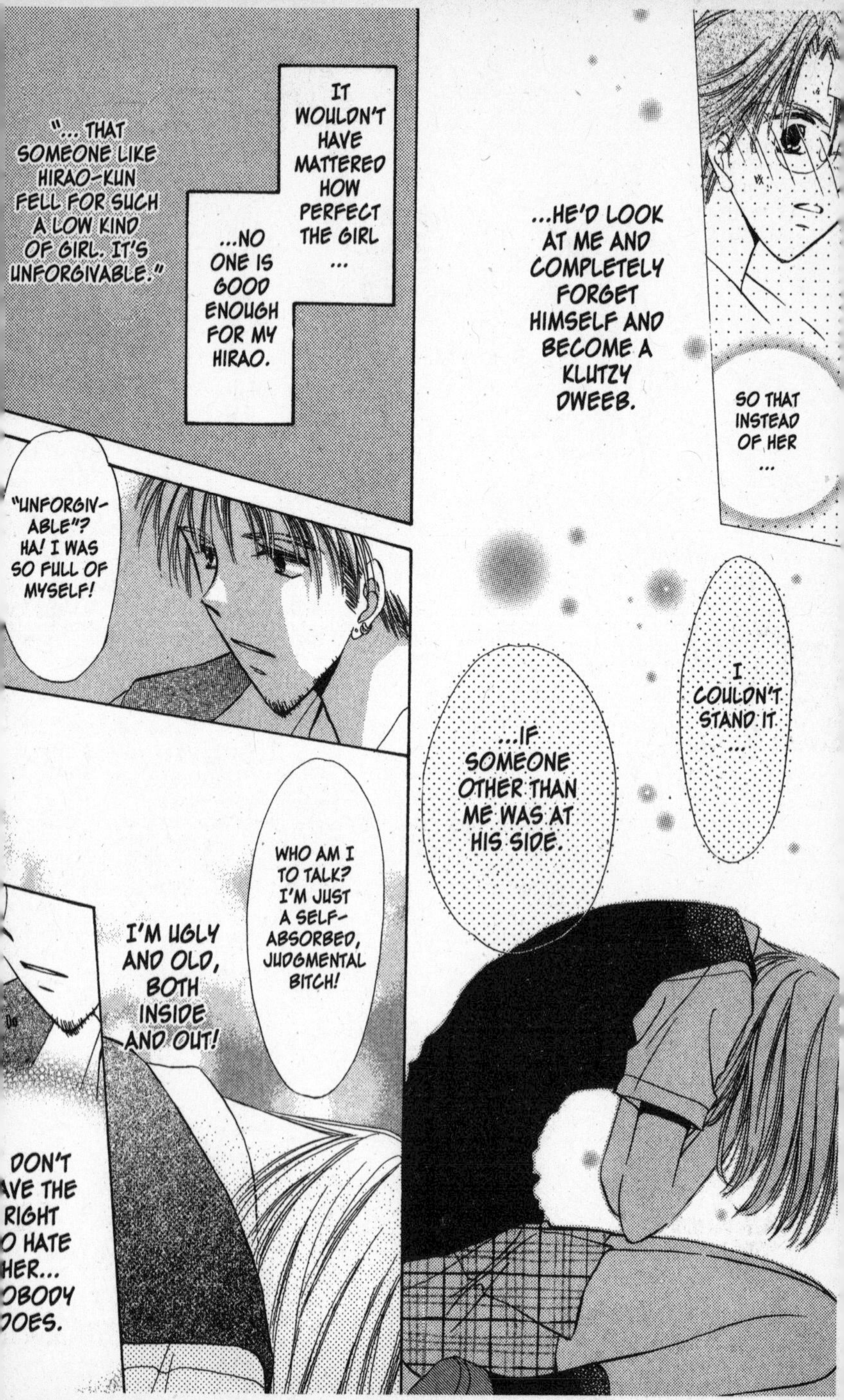
SO THAT INSTEAD OF HER ...
...HE'D LOOK AT ME AND COMPLETELY FORGET HIMSELF AND BECOME A KLUTZY DWEEB.
I COULDN'T STAND IT ...
...IF SOMEONE OTHER THAN ME WAS AT HIS SIDE.
IT WOULDN'T HAVE MATTERED HOW PERFECT THE GIRL ...
...NO ONE IS GOOD ENOUGH FOR MY HIRAO.
"... THAT SOMEONE LIKE HIRAO-KUN FELL FOR SUCH A LOW KIND OF GIRL. IT'S UNFORGIVABLE."
"UNFORGIV-ABLE"? HA! I WAS SO FULL OF MYSELF!
WHO AM I TO TALK? I'M JUST A SELF-ABSORBED, JUDGMENTAL BITCH!
I'M UGLY AND OLD, BOTH INSIDE AND OUT!
DON'T AVE THE RIGHT O HATE HER... OBODY OES.

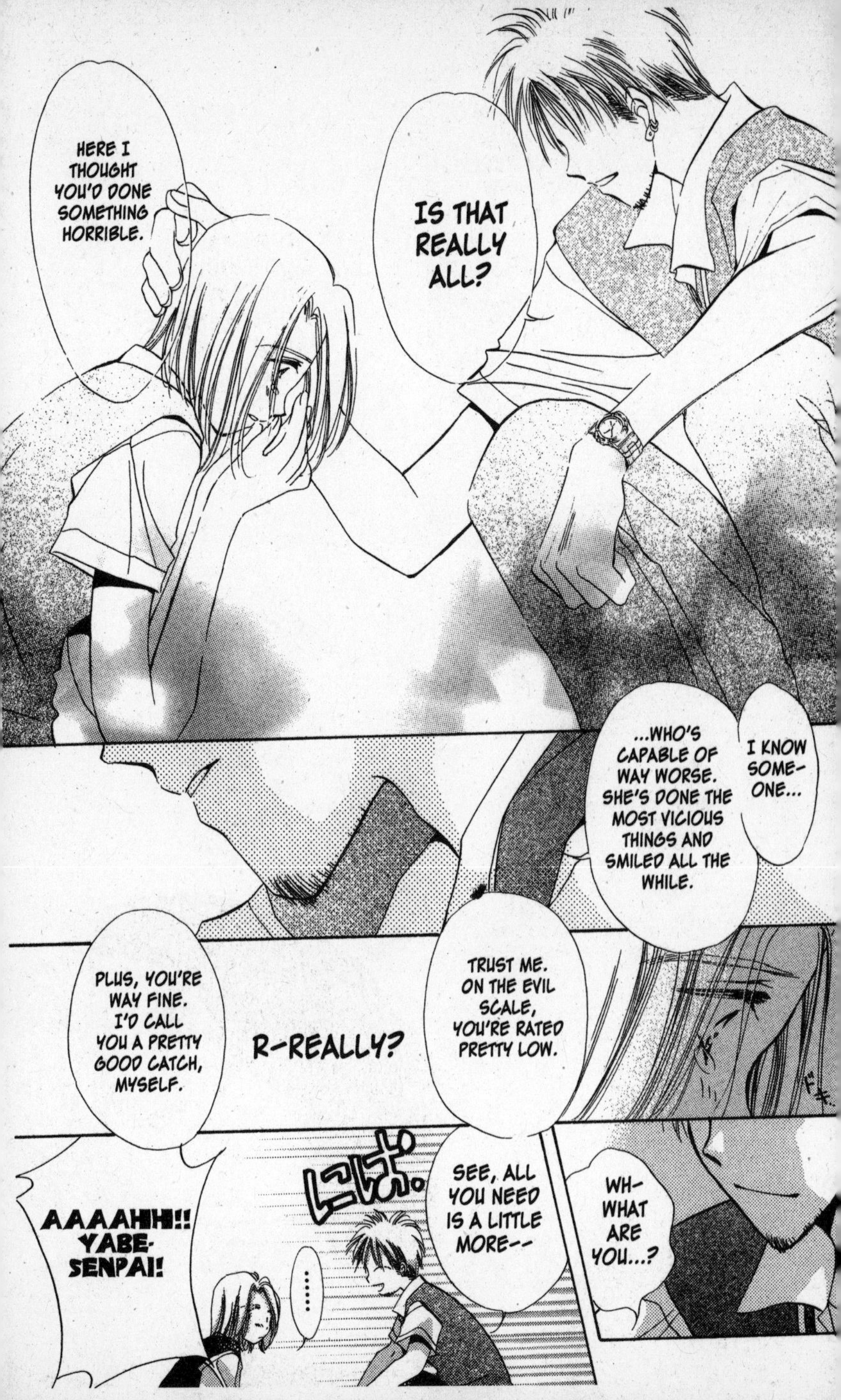
IS THAT REALLY ALL?
HERE I THOUGHT YOU'D DONE SOMETHING HORRIBLE.
I KNOW SOME-ONE...
...WHO'S CAPABLE OF WAY WORSE. SHE'S DONE THE MOST VICIOUS THINGS AND SMILED ALL THE WHILE.
TRUST ME. ON THE EVIL SCALE, YOU'RE RATED PRETTY LOW.
R-REALLY?
PLUS, YOU'RE WAY FINE. I'D CALL YOU A PRETTY GOOD CATCH, MYSELF.
WH- WHAT ARE YOU...?
SEE, ALL YOU NEED IS A LITTLE MORE--
にぱ。
AAAAHH!! YABE-SENPAI!
......

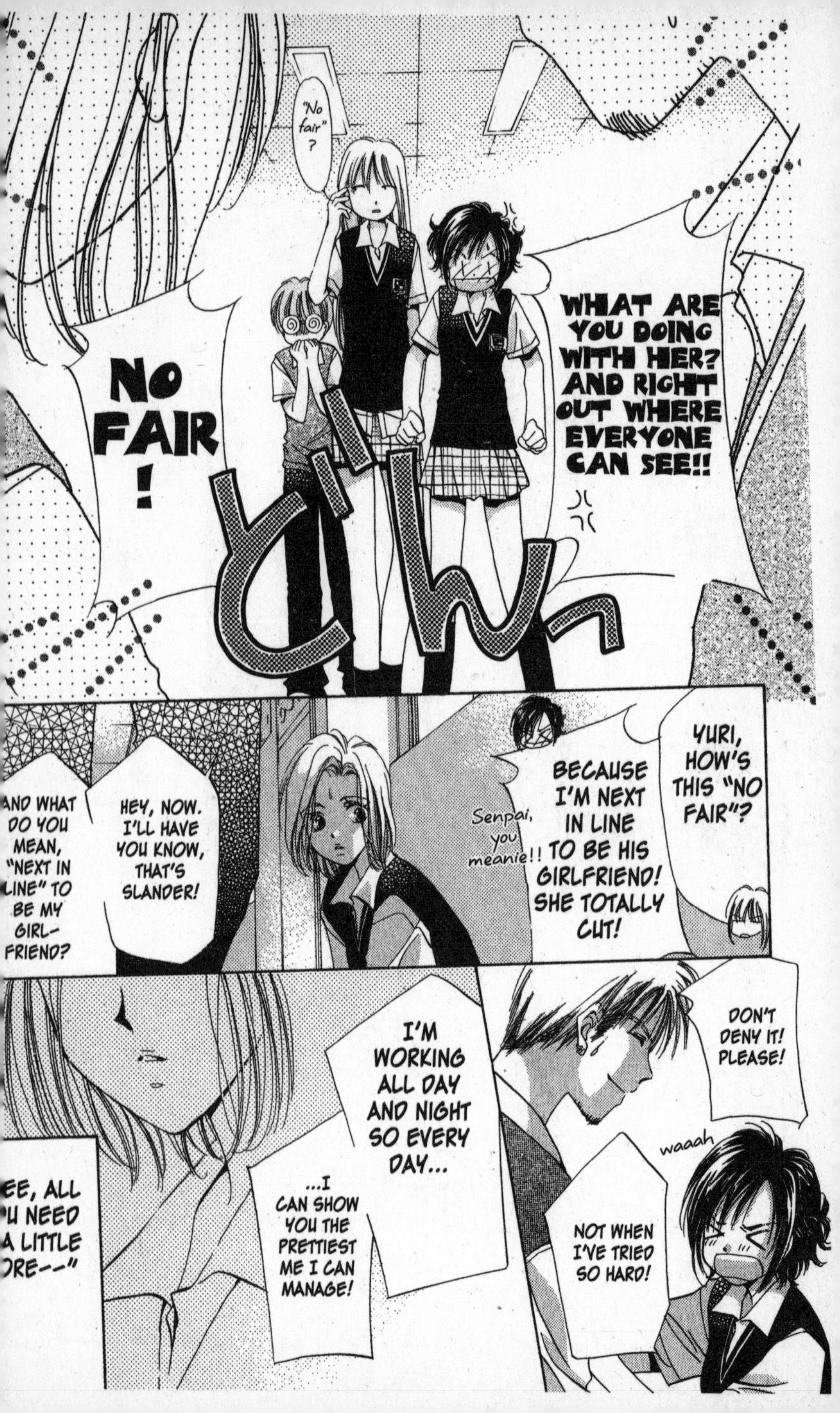
"No fair"?
WHAT ARE YOU DOING WITH HER? AND RIGHT OUT WHERE EVERYONE CAN SEE!!
NO FAIR!
どん
YURI, HOW'S THIS "NO FAIR"?
BECAUSE I'M NEXT IN LINE TO BE HIS GIRLFRIEND! SHE TOTALLY CUT!
Senpai, you meanie!!
HEY, NOW. I'LL HAVE YOU KNOW, THAT'S SLANDER!
AND WHAT DO YOU MEAN, "NEXT IN LINE" TO BE MY GIRLFRIEND?
DON'T DENY IT! PLEASE!
waaah
NOT WHEN I'VE TRIED SO HARD!
I'M WORKING ALL DAY AND NIGHT SO EVERY DAY...
...I CAN SHOW YOU THE PRETTIEST ME I CAN MANAGE!
EE, ALL U NEED A LITTLE ORE--"

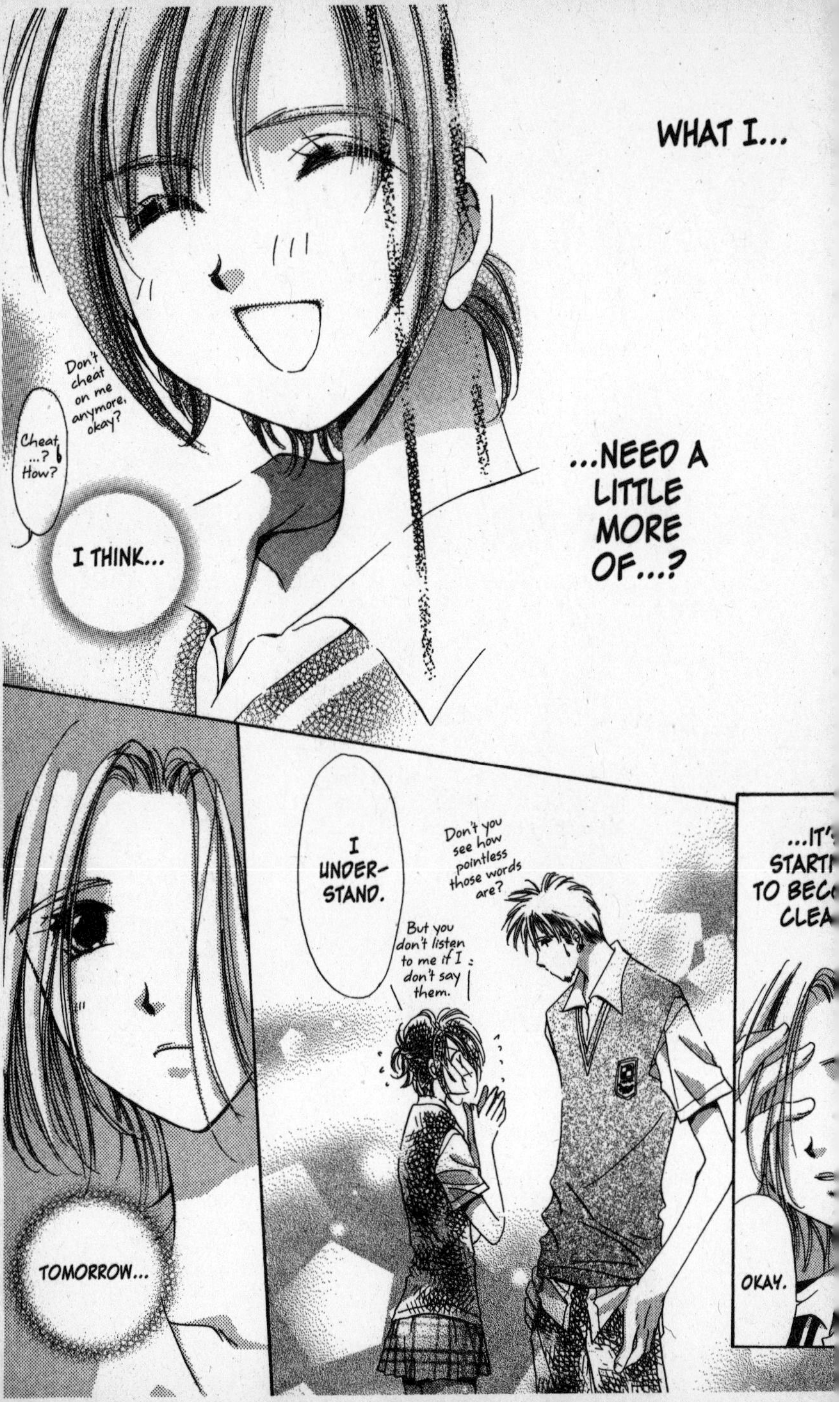

WHAT I...
...NEED A LITTLE MORE OF...?
Don't cheat on me anymore, okay?
Cheat ...? How?
I THINK...
...IT'S STARTI TO BECO CLEA
OKAY.
Don't you see how pointless those words are?
But you don't listen to me if I don't say them.
I UNDERSTAND.
TOMORROW...

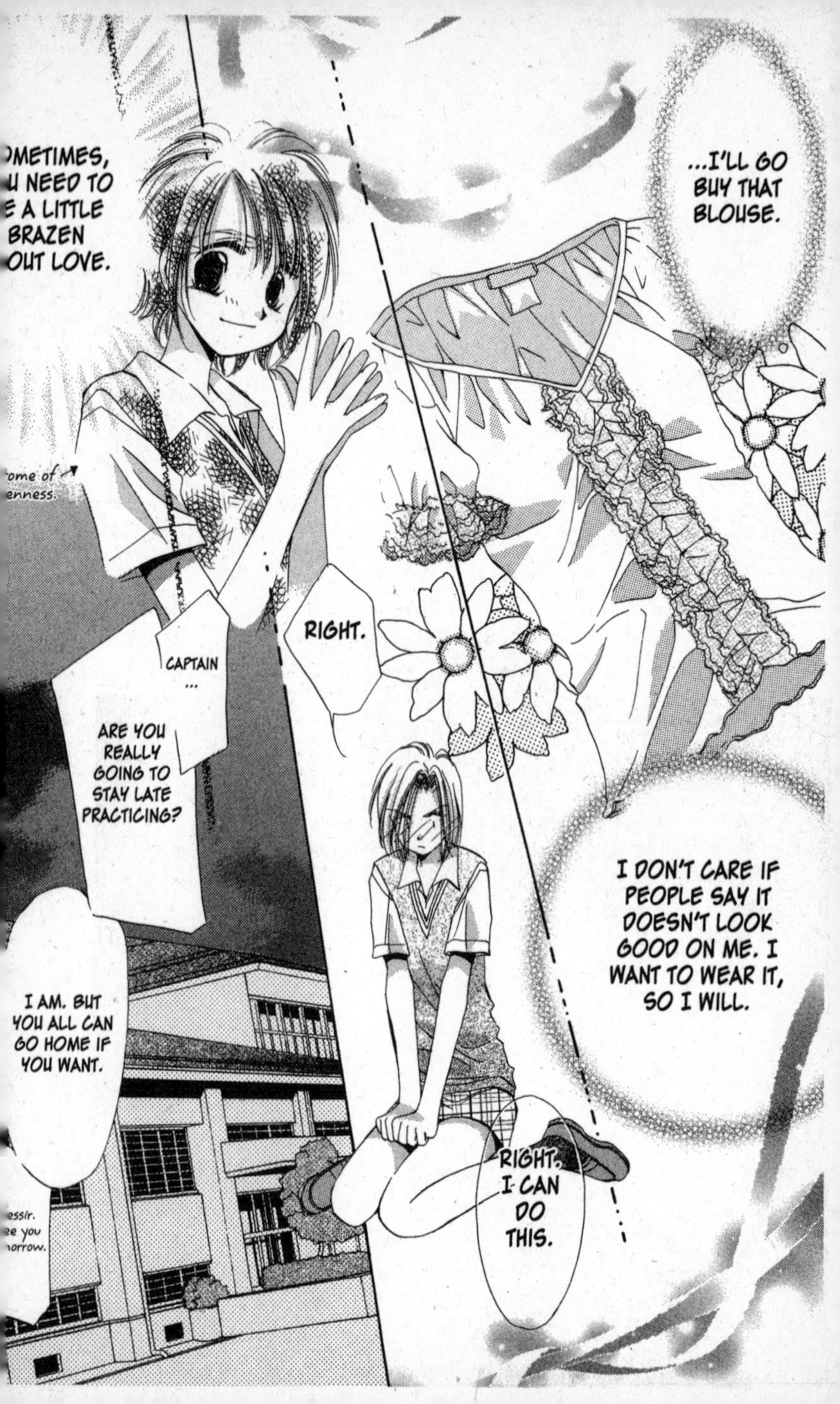
...I'LL GO BUY THAT BLOUSE.
I DON'T CARE IF PEOPLE SAY IT DOESN'T LOOK GOOD ON ME. I WANT TO WEAR IT, SO I WILL.
RIGHT. I CAN DO THIS.
METIMES, U NEED TO E A LITTLE BRAZEN OUT LOVE.
ome of enness.
CAPTAIN ...
ARE YOU REALLY GOING TO STAY LATE PRACTICING?
RIGHT.
I AM. BUT YOU ALL CAN GO HOME IF YOU WANT.
essir. ee you norrow.

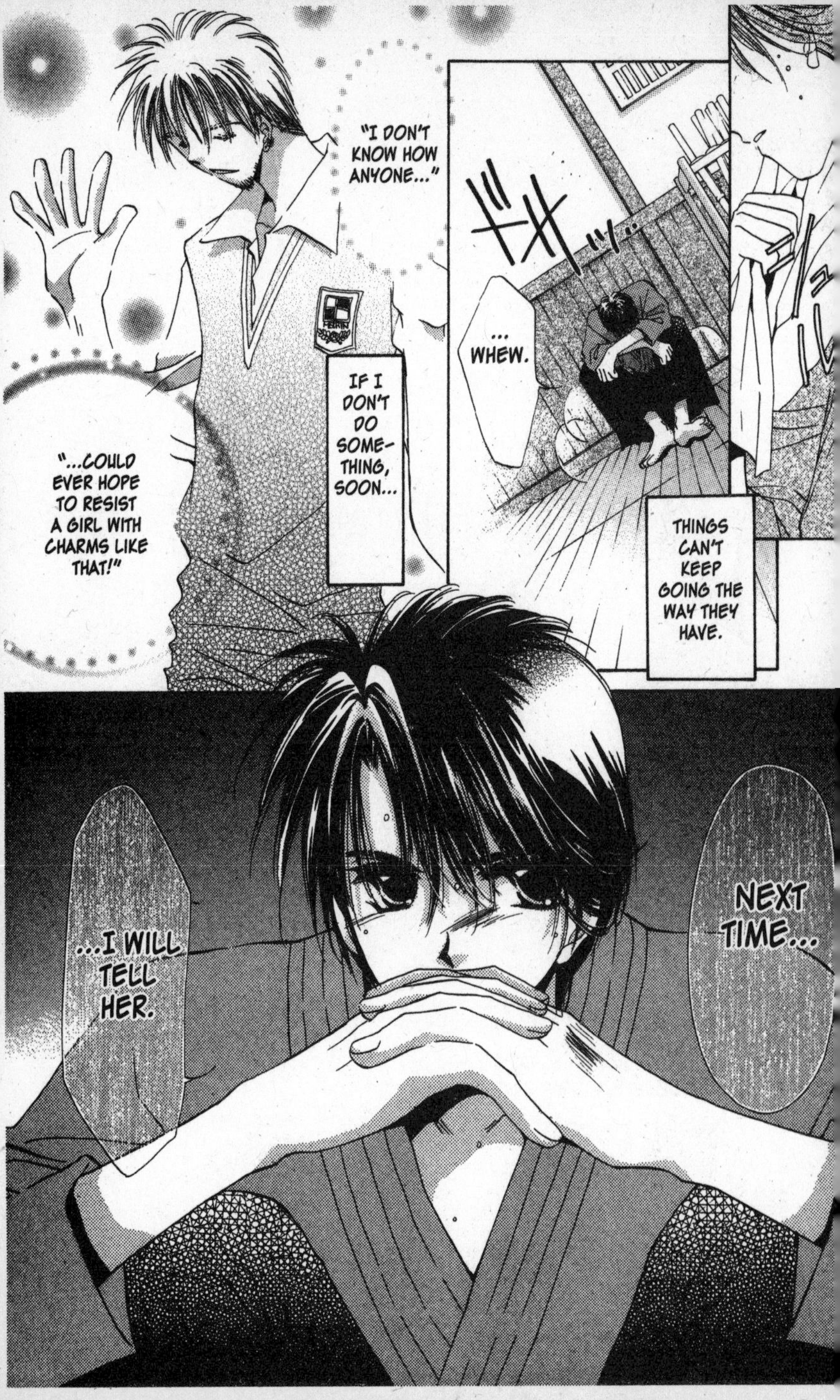
... WHEW.
THINGS CAN'T KEEP GOING THE WAY THEY HAVE.
"I DON'T KNOW HOW ANYONE..."
IF I DON'T DO SOME-THING, SOON...
"...COULD EVER HOPE TO RESIST A GIRL WITH CHARMS LIKE THAT!"
NEXT TIME...
...I WILL TELL HER.

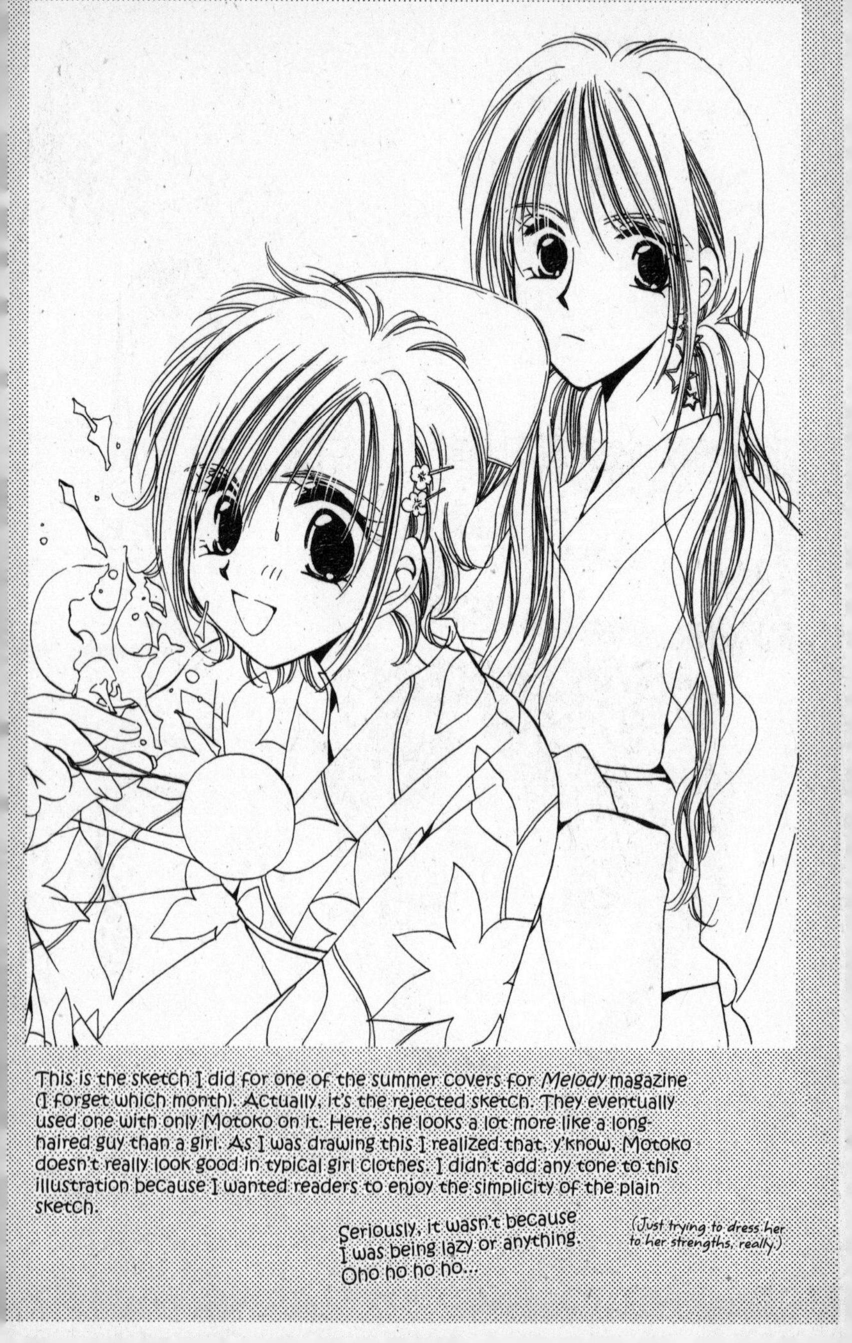

This is the sketch I did for one of the summer covers for *Melody* magazine (I forget which month). Actually, it's the rejected sketch. They eventually used one with only Motoko on it. Here, she looks a lot more like a long-haired guy than a girl. As I was drawing this I realized that, y'know, Motoko doesn't really look good in typical girl clothes. I didn't add any tone to this illustration because I wanted readers to enjoy the simplicity of the plain sketch.

Seriously, it wasn't because I was being lazy or anything. Oho ho ho ho...

(Just trying to dress her to her strengths, really.)

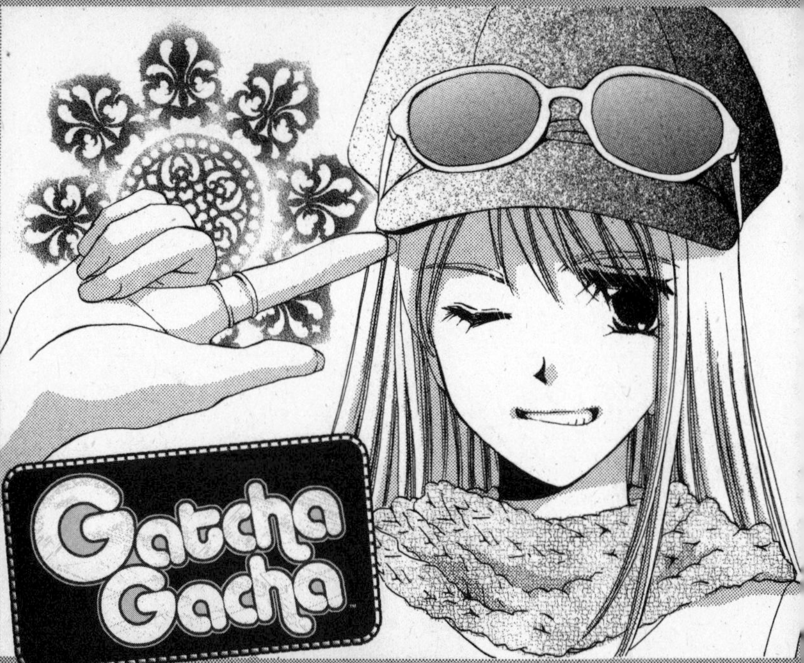
Gatcha Gacha™
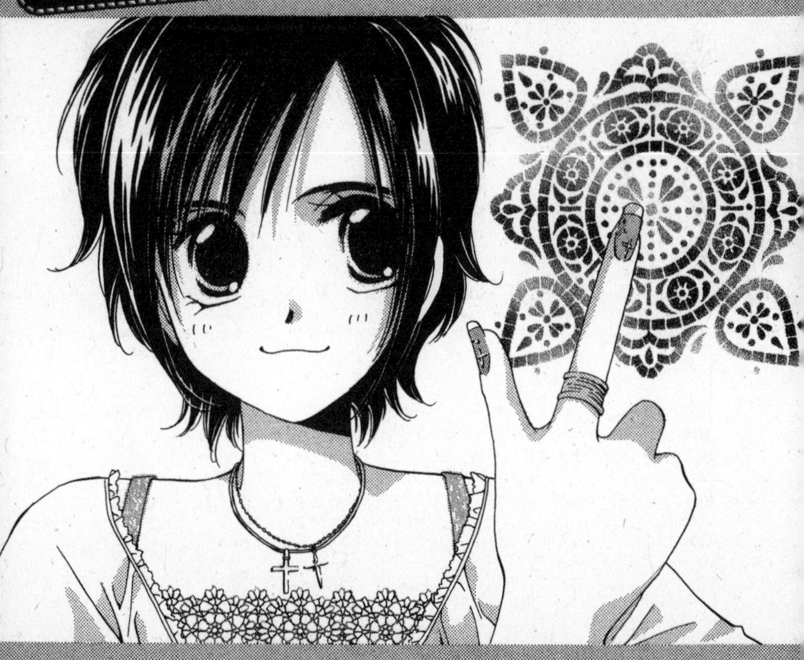

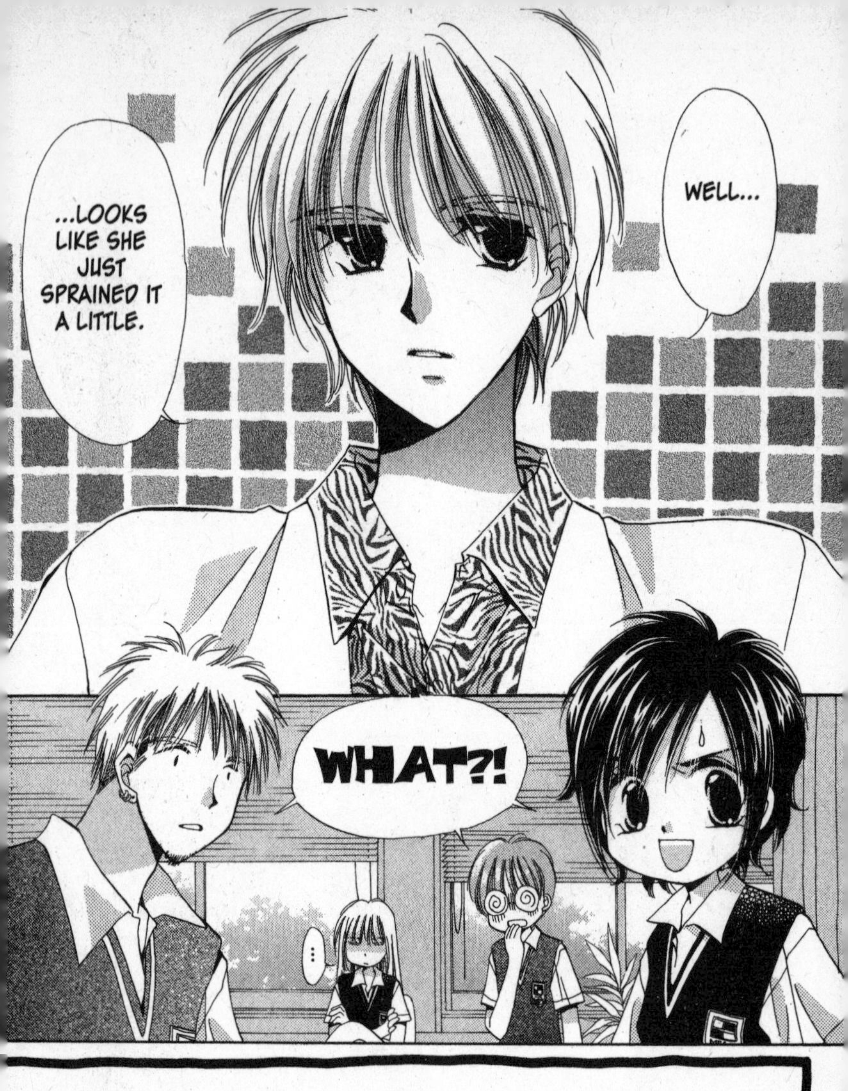
WELL...
...LOOKS LIKE SHE JUST SPRAINED IT A LITTLE.
WHAT?!
...

Band of Brothers.

I don't know why, but I've always really liked war movies.

(*L.A. Confidential* was another good one. It's not a war movie, but it was still really good. I started liking Russell Crowe after I watched it.)

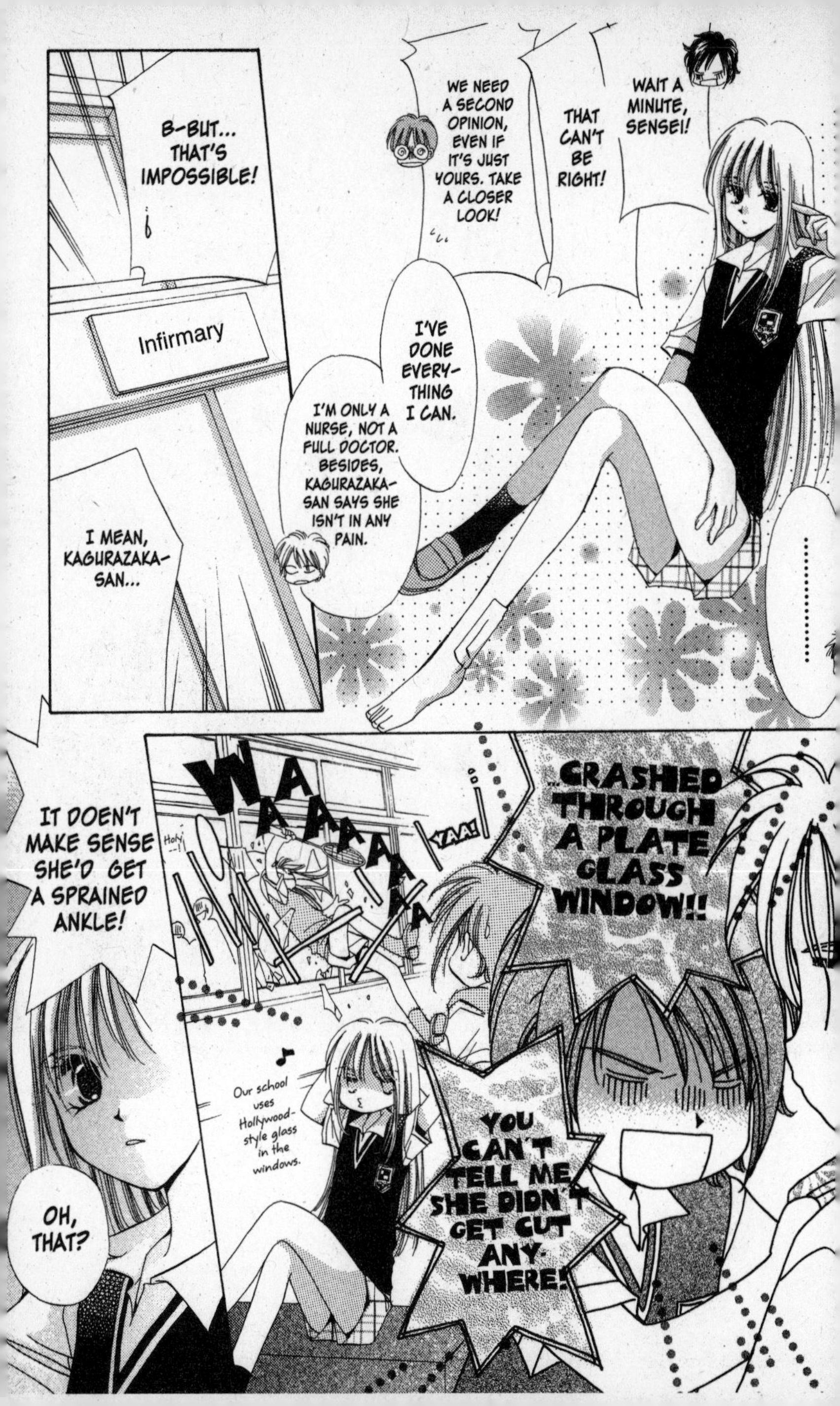
WAIT A MINUTE, SENSEI!
THAT CAN'T BE RIGHT!
WE NEED A SECOND OPINION, EVEN IF IT'S JUST YOURS. TAKE A CLOSER LOOK!
I'VE DONE EVERYTHING I CAN.
I'M ONLY A NURSE, NOT A FULL DOCTOR. BESIDES, KAGURAZAKA-SAN SAYS SHE ISN'T IN ANY PAIN.
B-BUT... THAT'S IMPOSSIBLE!
Infirmary
I MEAN, KAGURAZAKA-SAN...
IT DOESN'T MAKE SENSE SHE'D GET A SPRAINED ANKLE!
...CRASHED THROUGH A PLATE GLASS WINDOW!!
WAAAAAAAA
YAA!
Holy--!
YOU CAN'T TELL ME SHE DIDN'T GET CUT ANYWHERE!
Our school uses Hollywood-style glass in the windows.
OH, THAT?

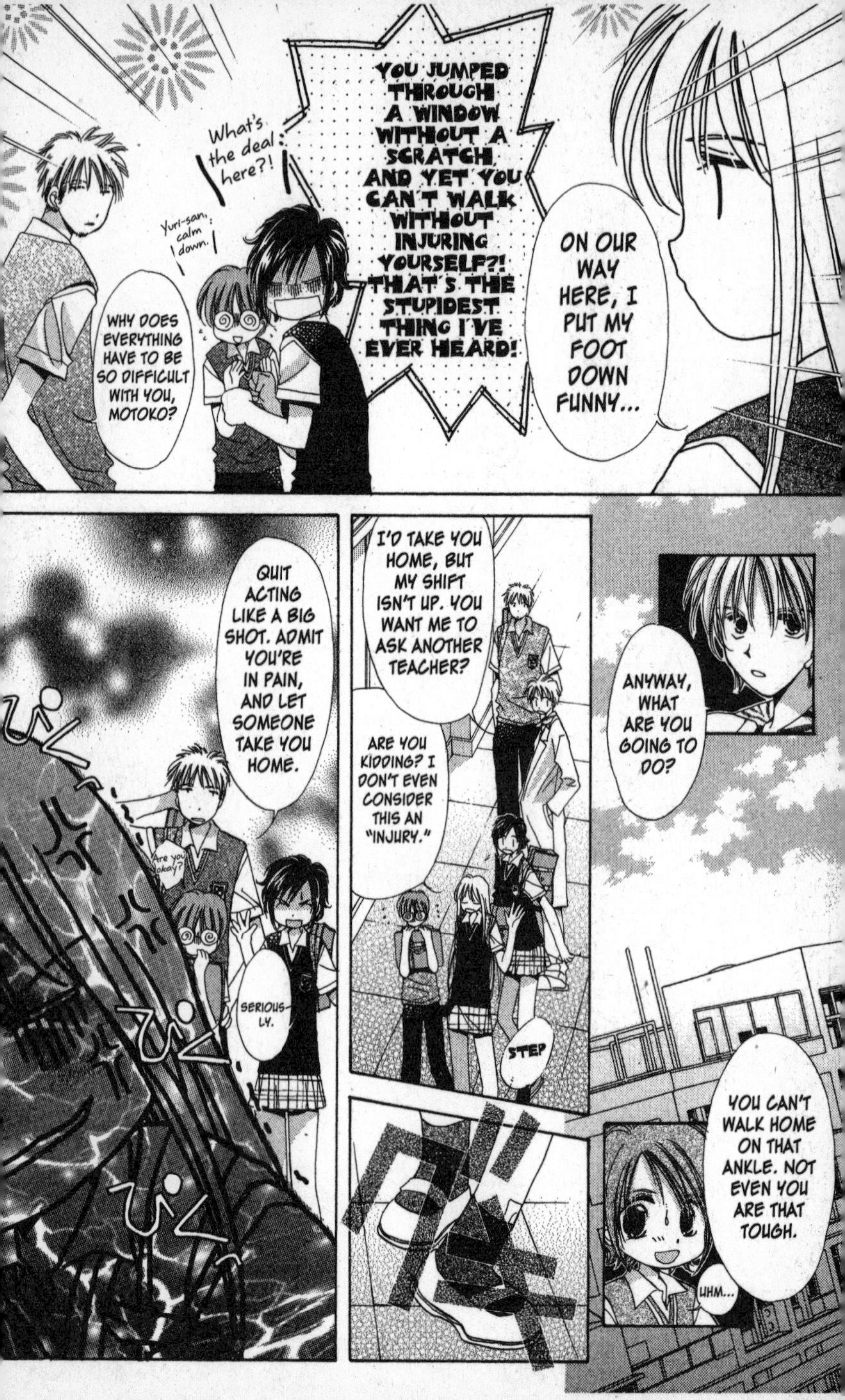
ON OUR WAY HERE, I PUT MY FOOT DOWN FUNNY...
YOU JUMPED THROUGH A WINDOW WITHOUT A SCRATCH, AND YET YOU CAN'T WALK WITHOUT INJURING YOURSELF?! THAT'S THE STUPIDEST THING I'VE EVER HEARD!
What's the deal here?!
Yuri-san, calm down.
WHY DOES EVERYTHING HAVE TO BE SO DIFFICULT WITH YOU, MOTOKO?
ANYWAY, WHAT ARE YOU GOING TO DO?
YOU CAN'T WALK HOME ON THAT ANKLE. NOT EVEN YOU ARE THAT TOUGH.
UHM...
I'D TAKE YOU HOME, BUT MY SHIFT ISN'T UP. YOU WANT ME TO ASK ANOTHER TEACHER?
ARE YOU KIDDING? I DON'T EVEN CONSIDER THIS AN "INJURY."
STEP
QUIT ACTING LIKE A BIG SHOT. ADMIT YOU'RE IN PAIN, AND LET SOMEONE TAKE YOU HOME.
Are you okay?
SERIOUS-LY.

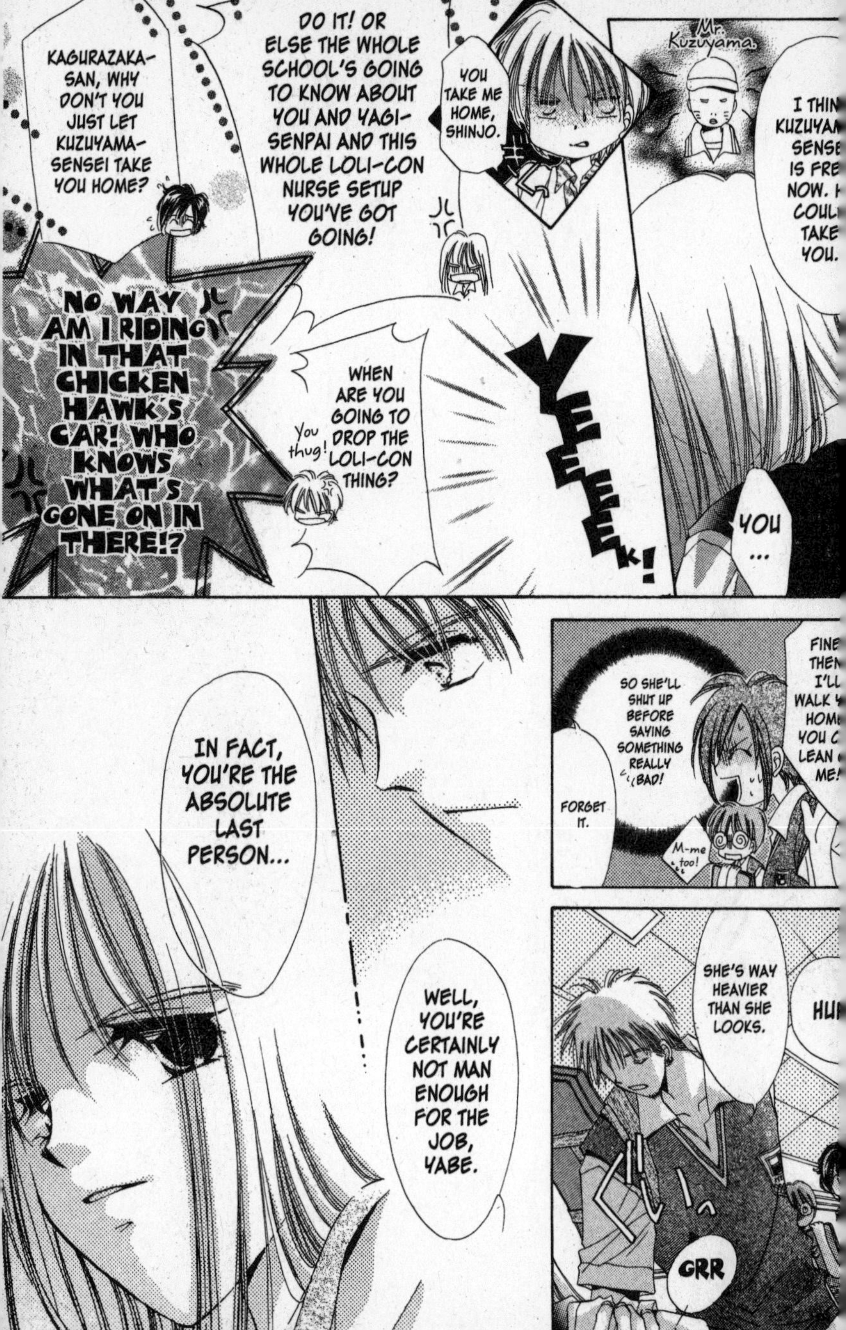

Mr. Kuzuyama.
I THIN KUZUYAM SENSE IS FRE NOW. COULI TAKE YOU.
YOU ...
YOU TAKE ME HOME, SHINJO.
YEEEEEK!
WHEN ARE YOU GOING TO DROP THE LOLI-CON THING?
You thug!
DO IT! OR ELSE THE WHOLE SCHOOL'S GOING TO KNOW ABOUT YOU AND YAGI-SENPAI AND THIS WHOLE LOLI-CON NURSE SETUP YOU'VE GOT GOING!
KAGURAZAKA-SAN, WHY DON'T YOU JUST LET KUZUYAMA-SENSEI TAKE YOU HOME?
NO WAY AM I RIDING IN THAT CHICKEN HAWK'S CAR! WHO KNOWS WHAT'S GONE ON IN THERE!?
FINE THEN I'LL WALK HOME YOU C LEAN ME!
SO SHE'LL SHUT UP BEFORE SAYING SOMETHING REALLY BAD!
FORGET IT.
M-me too!
HU
SHE'S WAY HEAVIER THAN SHE LOOKS.
GRR
WELL, YOU'RE CERTAINLY NOT MAN ENOUGH FOR THE JOB, YABE.
IN FACT, YOU'RE THE ABSOLUTE LAST PERSON...

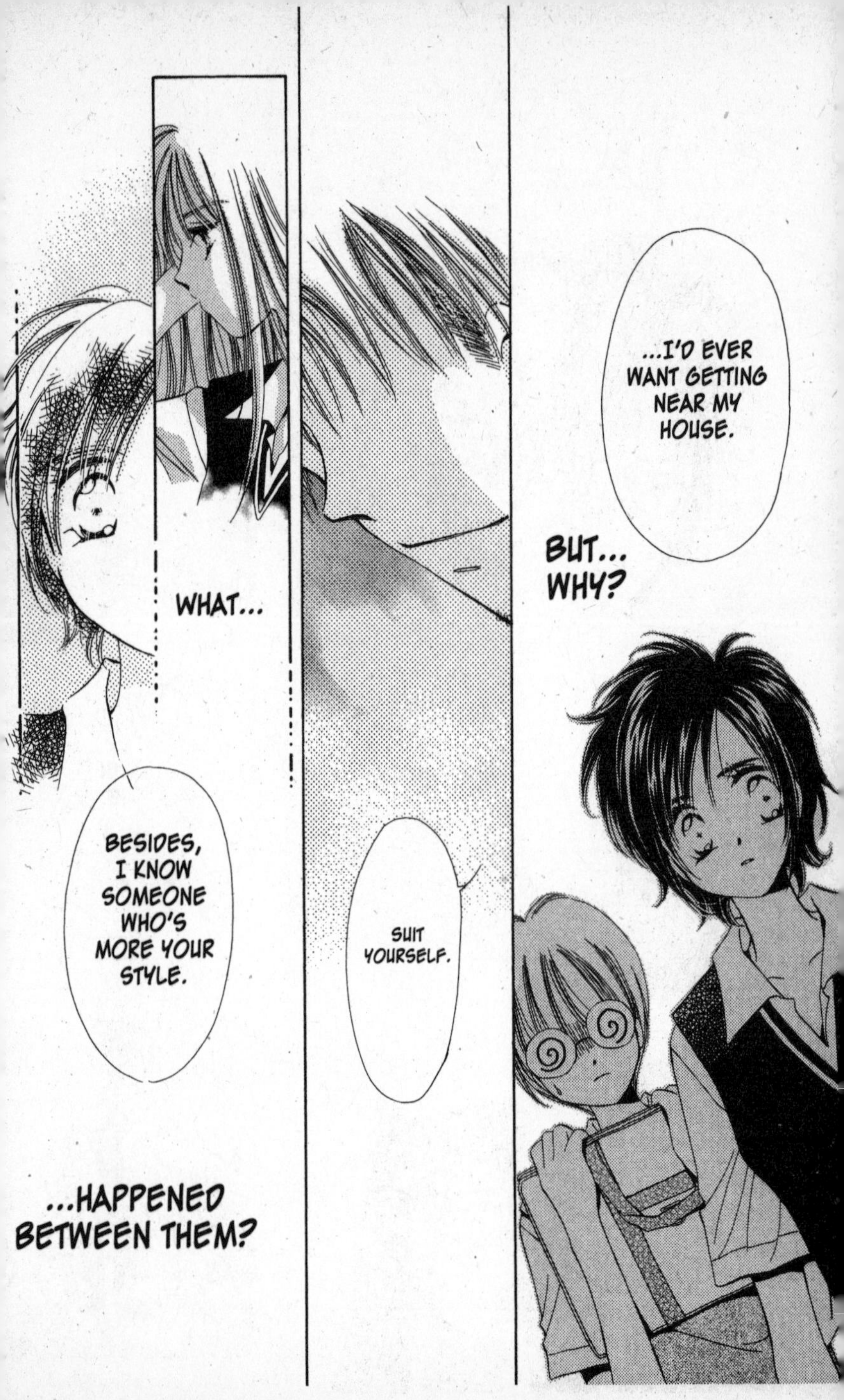
...I'D EVER WANT GETTING NEAR MY HOUSE.
BUT... WHY?
SUIT YOURSELF.
WHAT...
BESIDES, I KNOW SOMEONE WHO'S MORE YOUR STYLE.
...HAPPENED BETWEEN THEM?

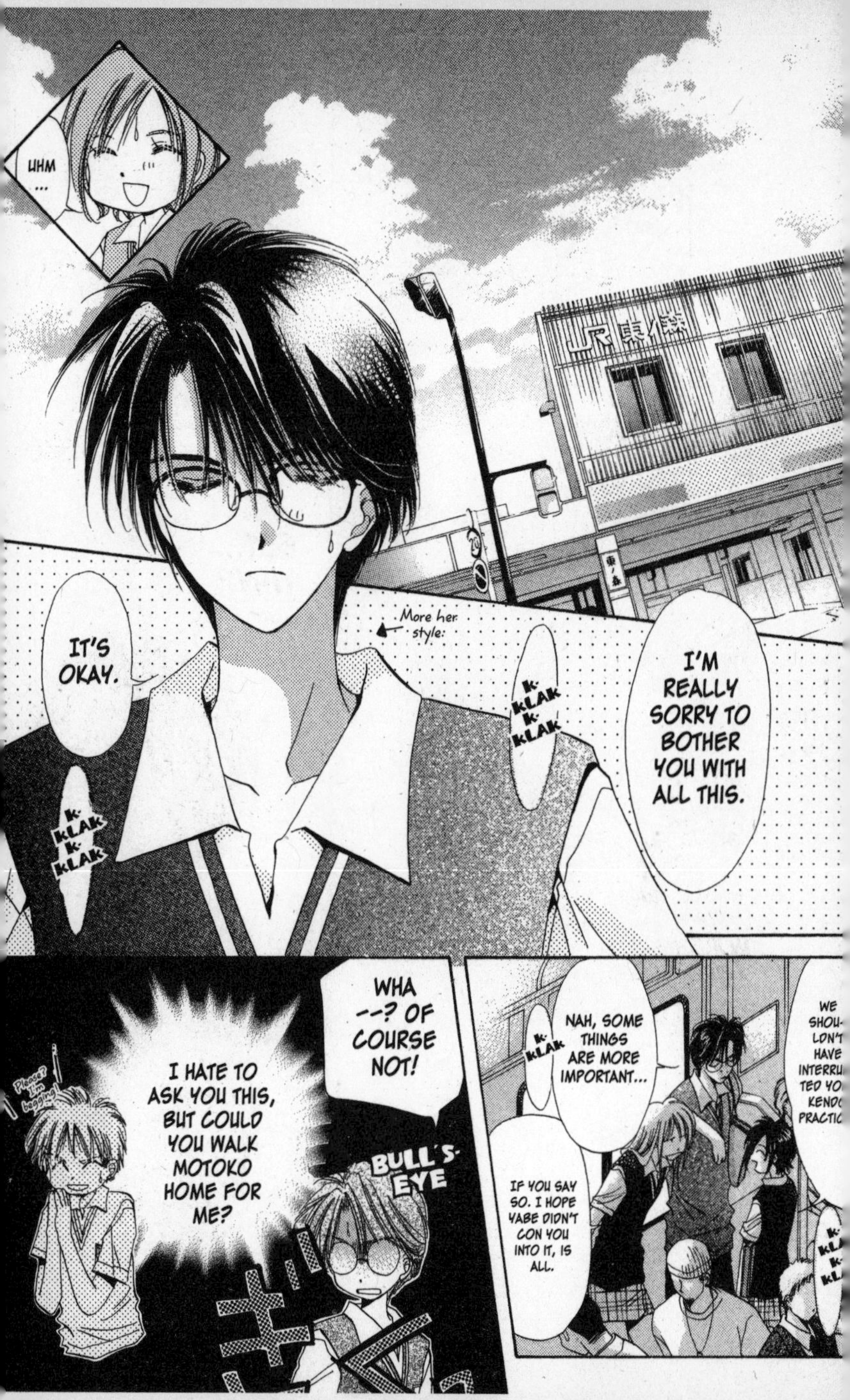
UHM ...
I'M REALLY SORRY TO BOTHER YOU WITH ALL THIS.
K-KLAK K-KLAK
More her style.
IT'S OKAY.
K-KLAK K-KLAK
WE SHOU- LDN'T HAVE INTERRU TED YO KENDO PRACTIC
K-KLAK K-KLAK
NAH, SOME THINGS ARE MORE IMPORTANT...
K-KLAK
IF YOU SAY SO. I HOPE YABE DIDN'T CON YOU INTO IT, IS ALL.
WHA --? OF COURSE NOT!
BULL'S-EYE
I HATE TO ASK YOU THIS, BUT COULD YOU WALK MOTOKO HOME FOR ME?
Please? I'm begging!

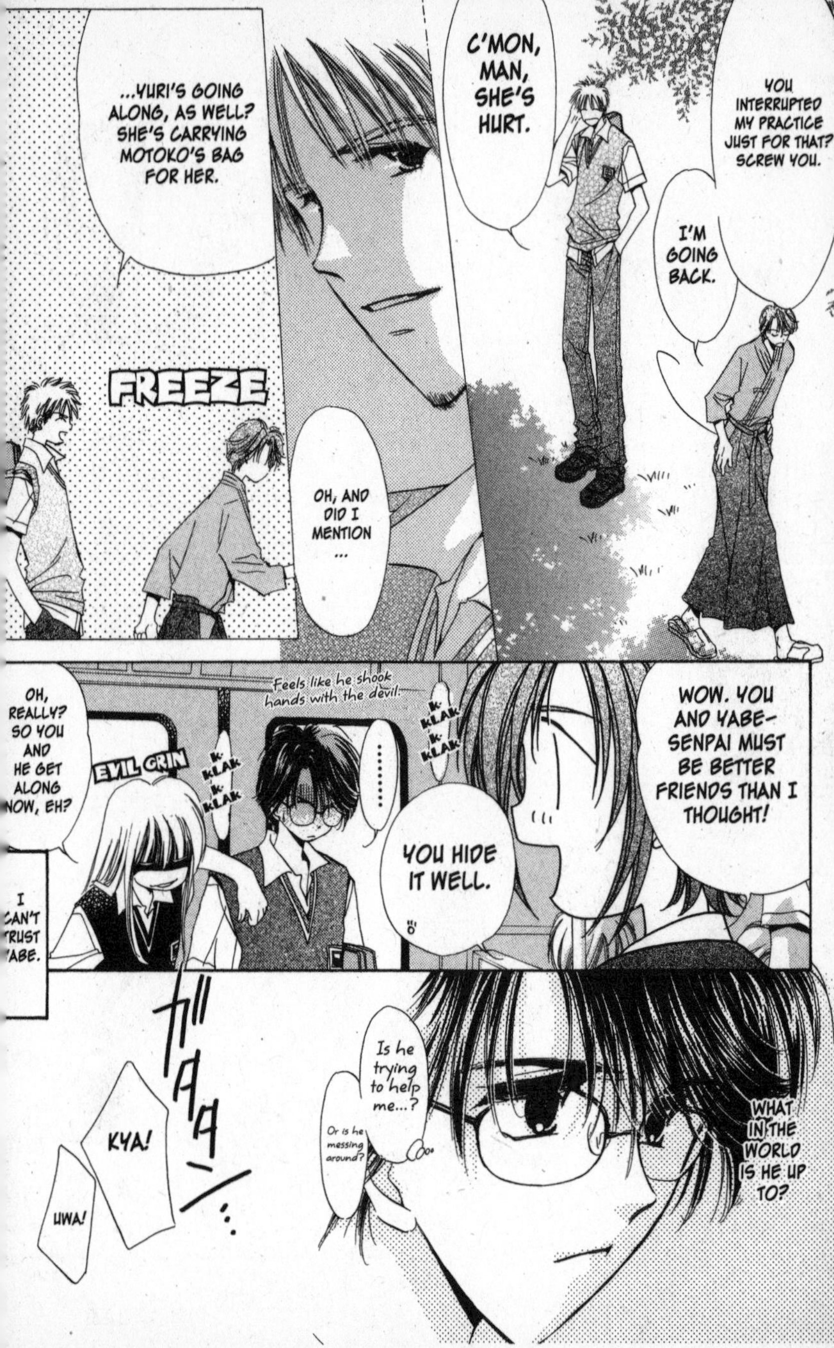

YOU INTERRUPTED MY PRACTICE JUST FOR THAT? SCREW YOU.
C'MON, MAN, SHE'S HURT.
I'M GOING BACK.
OH, AND DID I MENTION ...
...YURI'S GOING ALONG, AS WELL? SHE'S CARRYING MOTOKO'S BAG FOR HER.
FREEZE
WOW. YOU AND YABE-SENPAI MUST BE BETTER FRIENDS THAN I THOUGHT!
YOU HIDE IT WELL.
K-KLAK K-KLAK
Feels like he shook hands with the devil.
....
K-KLAK K-KLAK
EVIL GRIN
OH, REALLY? SO YOU AND HE GET ALONG NOW, EH?
I CAN'T TRUST YABE.
WHAT IN THE WORLD IS HE UP TO?
Is he trying to help me...?
Or is he messing around?
ガタタ
KYA!
UWA!

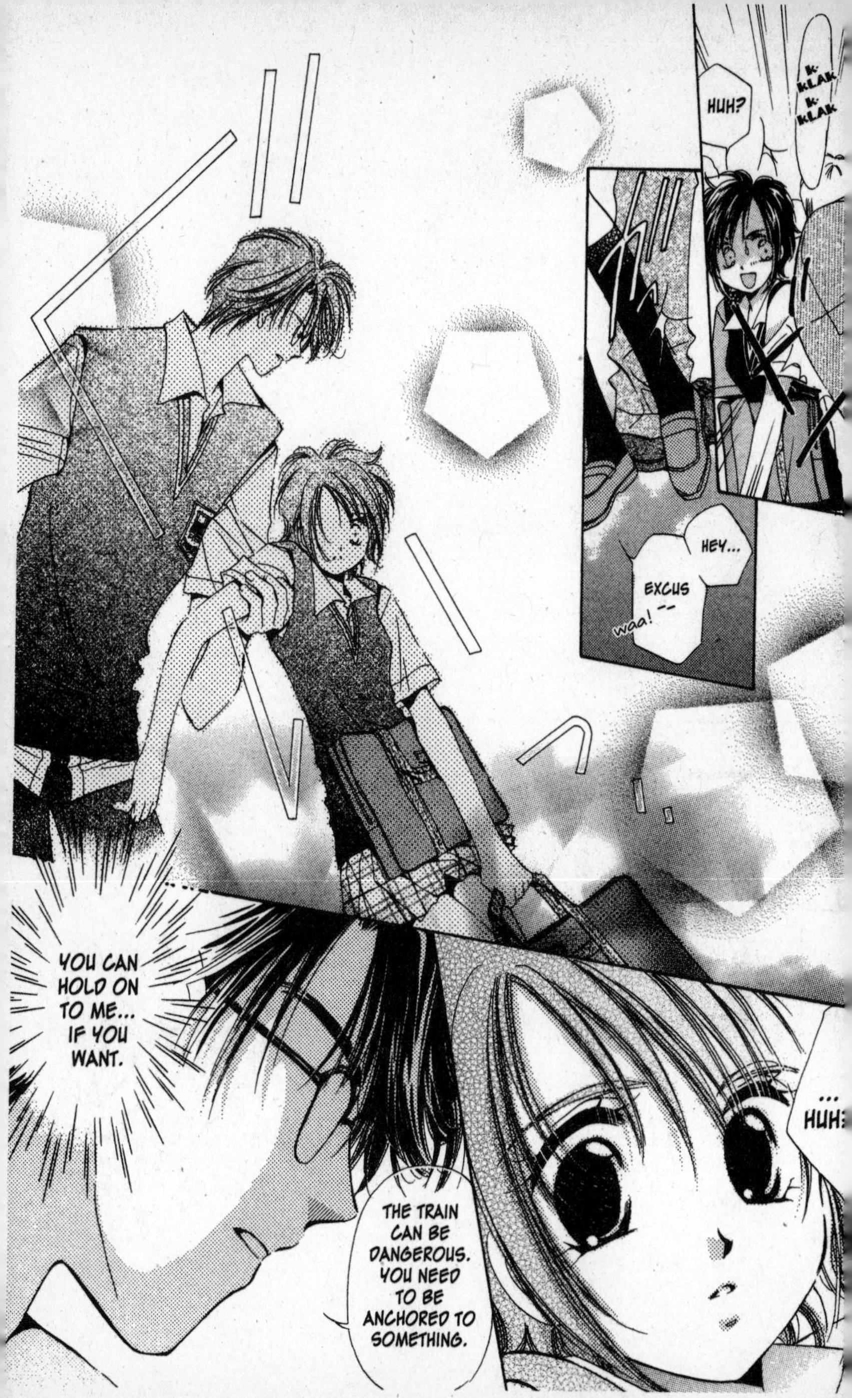

K-KLAK K-KLAK
HUH?
HEY...
EXCUS--
waa!
... HUH
YOU CAN HOLD ON TO ME... IF YOU WANT.
THE TRAIN CAN BE DANGEROUS. YOU NEED TO BE ANCHORED TO SOMETHING.

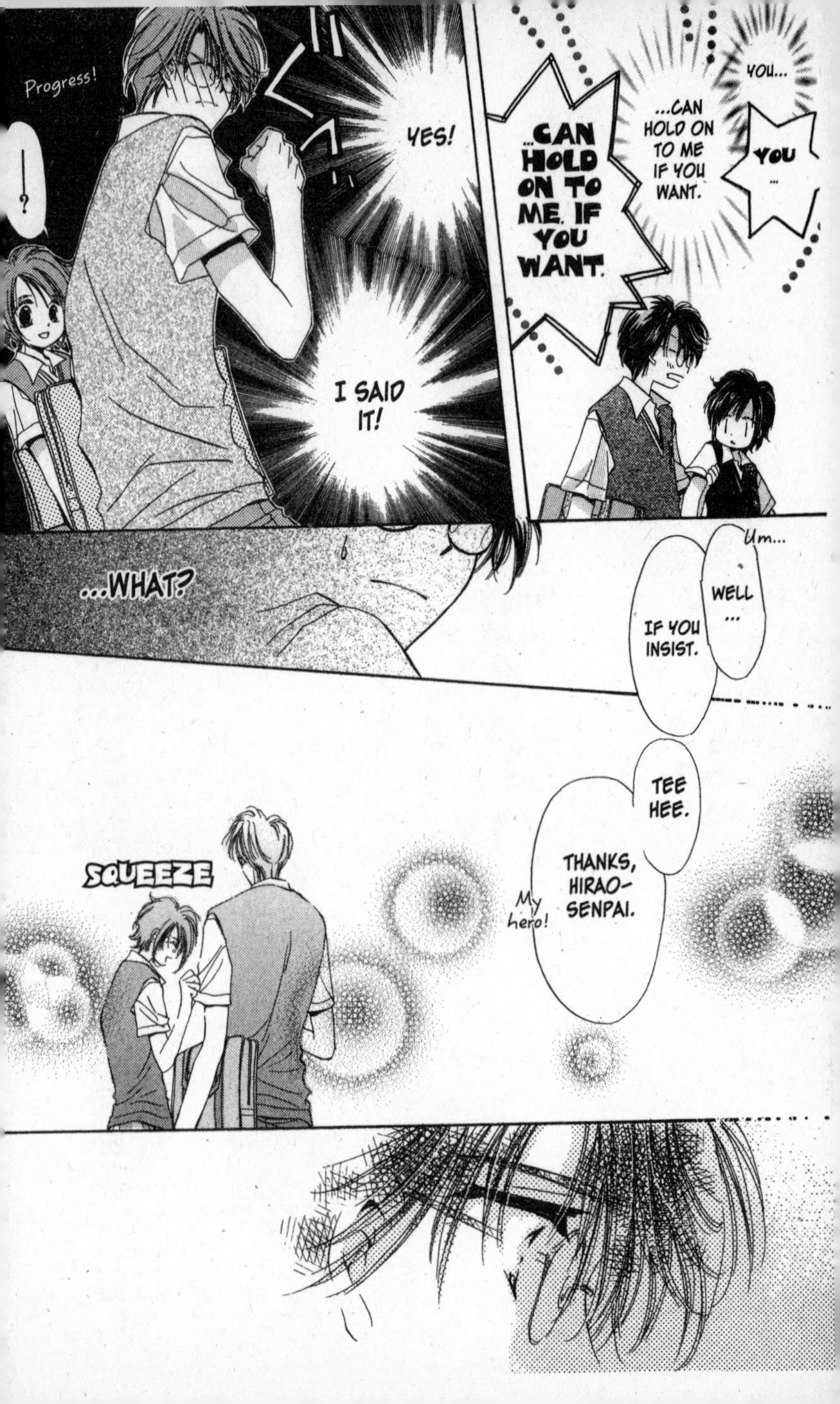
YOU...
YOU ...
...CAN HOLD ON TO ME IF YOU WANT.
...CAN HOLD ON TO ME. IF YOU WANT.
YES!
I SAID IT!
Progress!
—?
Um...
WELL ...
IF YOU INSIST.
...WHAT?
TEE HEE.
THANKS, HIRAO-SENPAI.
My hero!
SQUEEZE

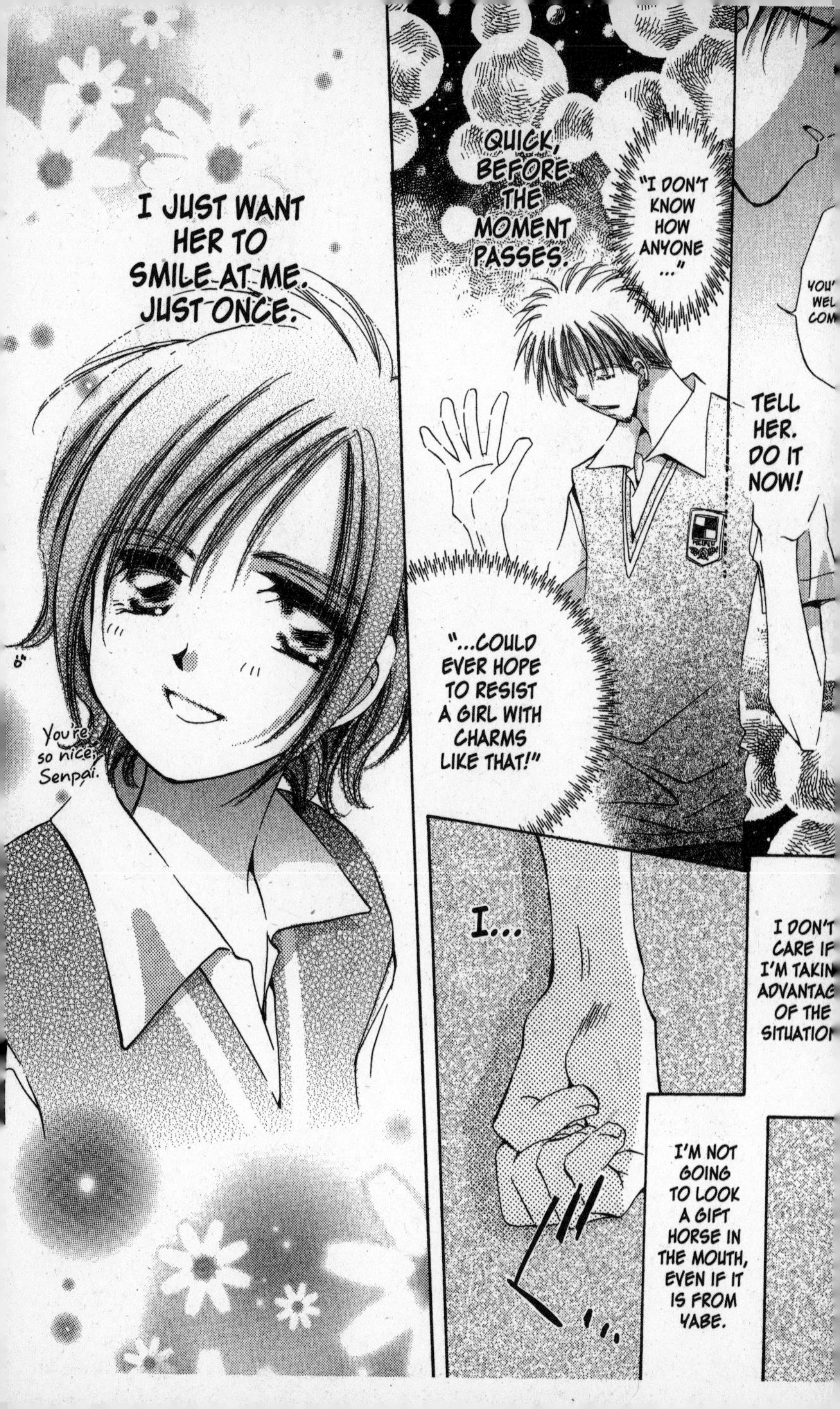
YOU'
WEL
COM
TELL HER. DO IT NOW!
QUICK, BEFORE THE MOMENT PASSES.
"I DON'T KNOW HOW ANYONE..."
"...COULD EVER HOPE TO RESIST A GIRL WITH CHARMS LIKE THAT!"
I DON'T CARE IF I'M TAKIN ADVANTAG OF THE SITUATIO
I'M NOT GOING TO LOOK A GIFT HORSE IN THE MOUTH, EVEN IF IT IS FROM YABE.
I...
I JUST WANT HER TO SMILE AT ME. JUST ONCE.
You're so nice, Senpai.

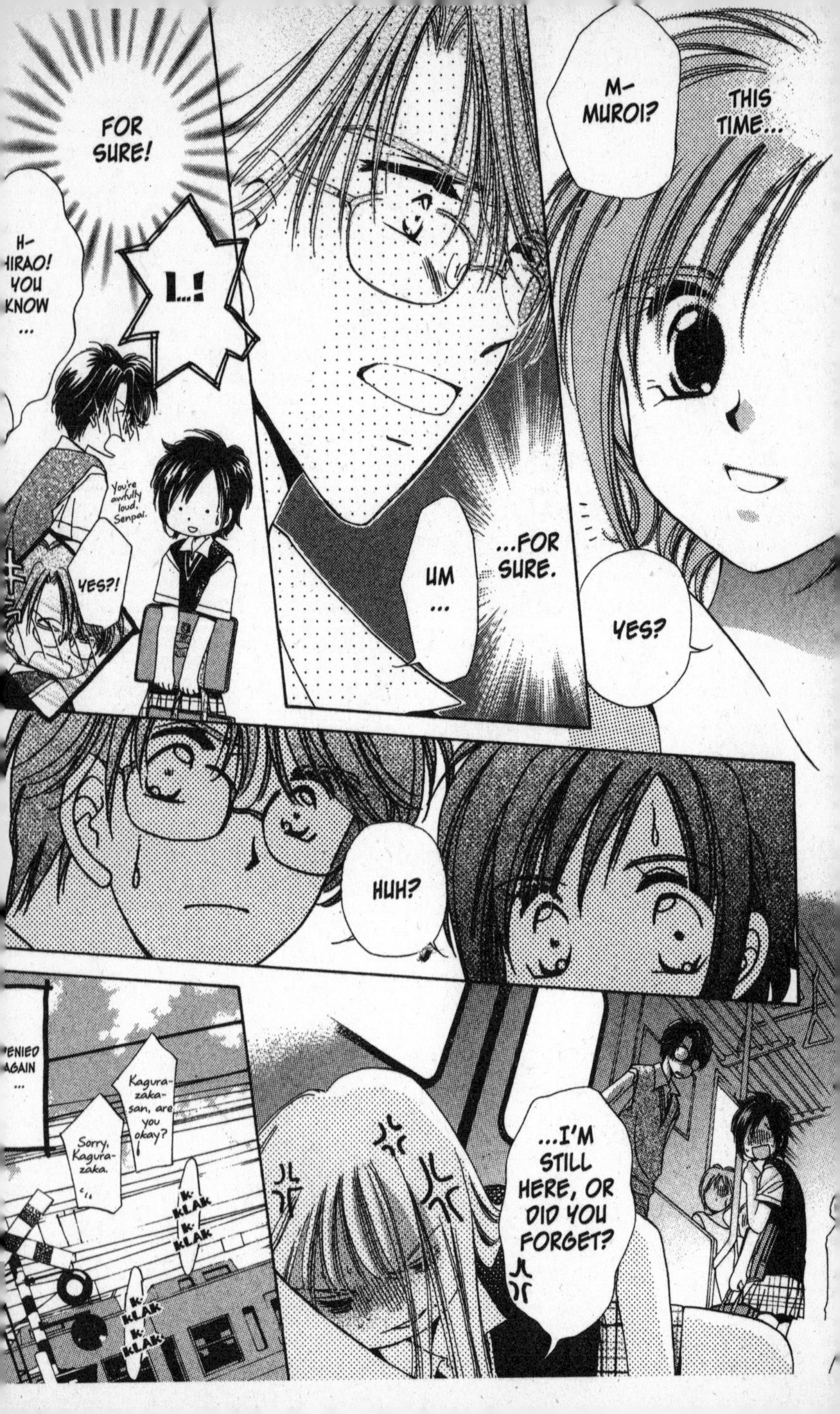
THIS TIME...
M-MUROI?
YES?
...FOR SURE.
UM...
FOR SURE!
I...!
H-HIRAO! YOU KNOW...
You're awfully loud, Senpai.
YES?!
HUH?
...I'M STILL HERE, OR DID YOU FORGET?
ENIED AGAIN ...
Kagura-zaka-san, are you okay?
Sorry, Kagura-zaka.
K-KLAK K-KLAK
K-KLAK K-KLAK

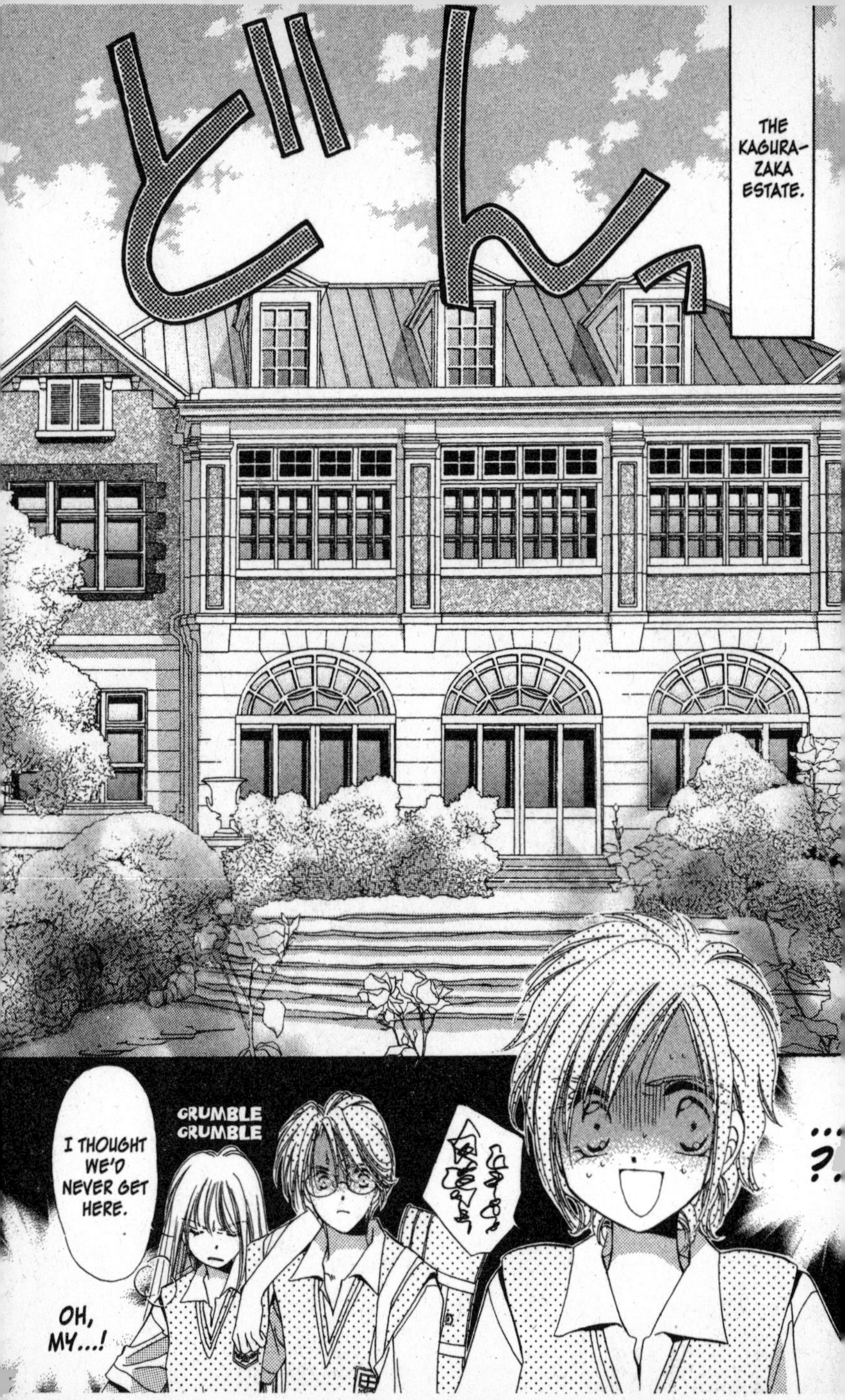

どん
THE KAGURA-ZAKA ESTATE.
...?!
GRUMBLE GRUMBLE
I THOUGHT WE'D NEVER GET HERE.
OH, MY...!

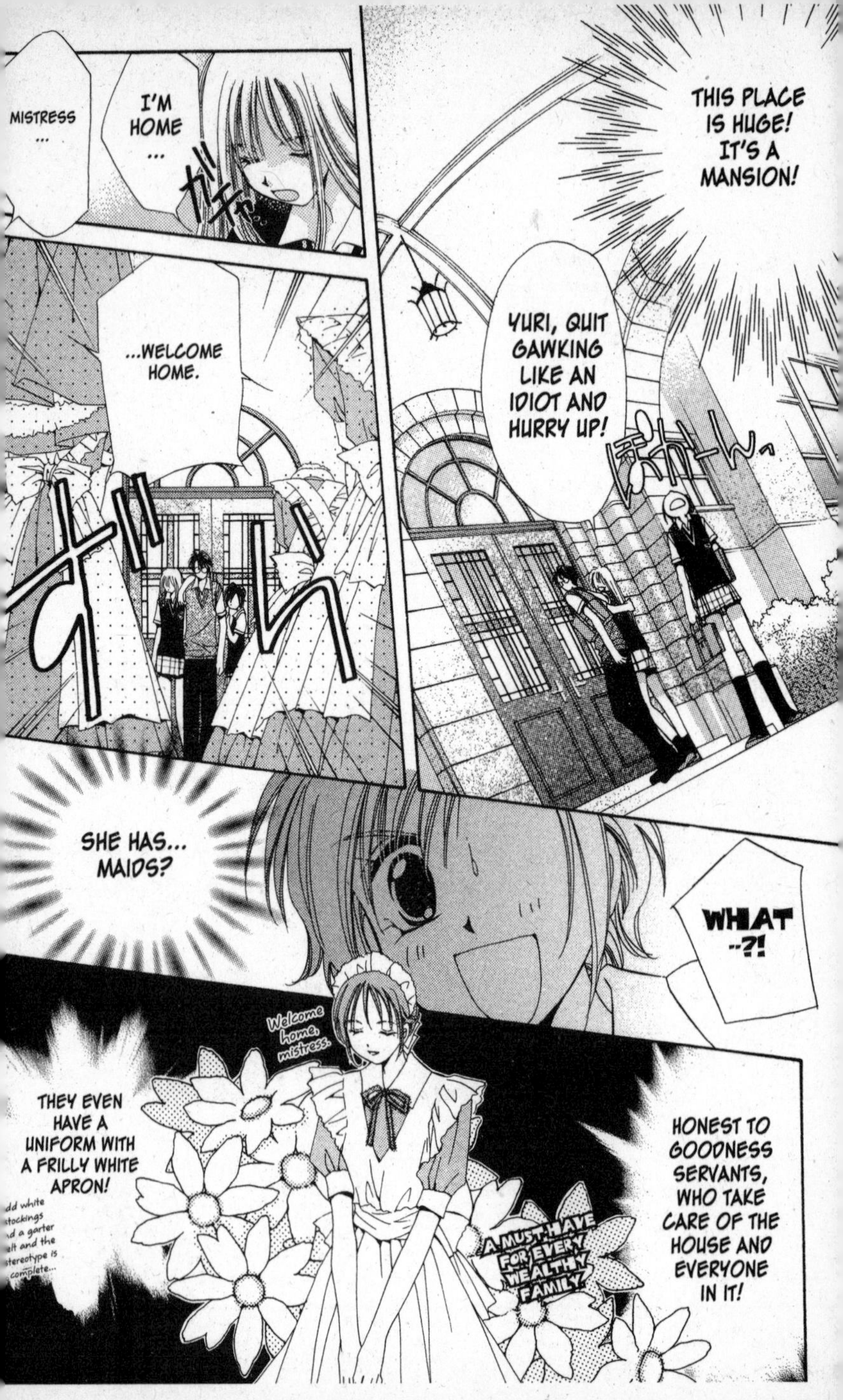
THIS PLACE IS HUGE! IT'S A MANSION!
YURI, QUIT GAWKING LIKE AN IDIOT AND HURRY UP!
ぽかーん。
I'M HOME ...
ガチャ
MISTRESS ...
...WELCOME HOME.
WHAT --?!
SHE HAS... MAIDS?
HONEST TO GOODNESS SERVANTS, WHO TAKE CARE OF THE HOUSE AND EVERYONE IN IT!
A MUST-HAVE FOR EVERY WEALTHY FAMILY
Welcome home, mistress.
THEY EVEN HAVE A UNIFORM WITH A FRILLY WHITE APRON!
dd white stockings
d a garter
lt and the
stereotype is
complete...

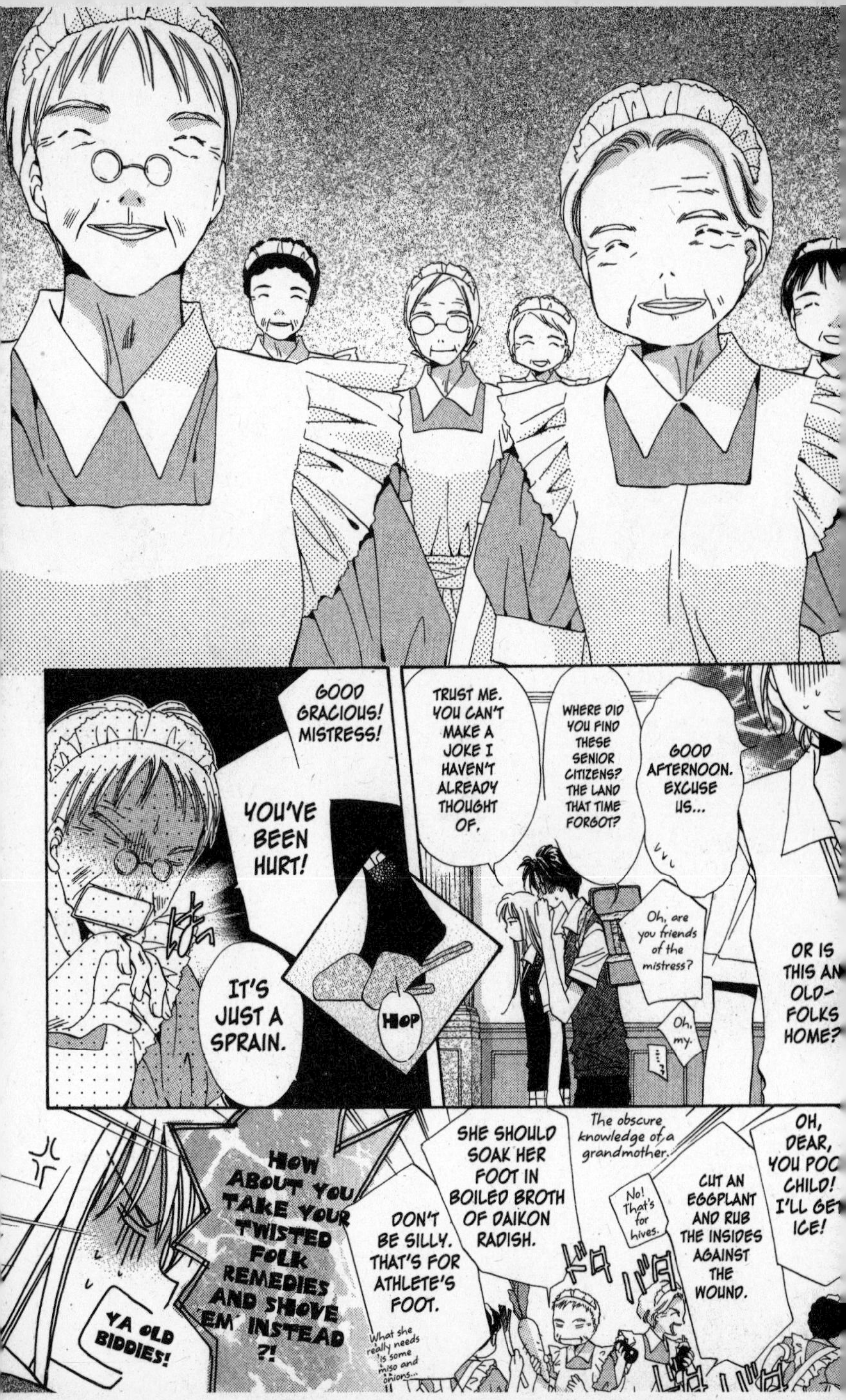
GOOD AFTERNOON. EXCUSE US...
WHERE DID YOU FIND THESE SENIOR CITIZENS? THE LAND THAT TIME FORGOT?
OR IS THIS AN OLD-FOLKS HOME?
TRUST ME. YOU CAN'T MAKE A JOKE I HAVEN'T ALREADY THOUGHT OF.
Oh, are you friends of the mistress?
Oh, my.
...
GOOD GRACIOUS! MISTRESS!
YOU'VE BEEN HURT!
HOP
IT'S JUST A SPRAIN.
OH, DEAR, YOU POO CHILD! I'LL GE ICE!
CUT AN EGGPLANT AND RUB THE INSIDES AGAINST THE WOUND.
ドタ
バタ
No! That's for hives.
The obscure knowledge of a grandmother.
SHE SHOULD SOAK HER FOOT IN BOILED BROTH OF DAIKON RADISH.
DON'T BE SILLY. THAT'S FOR ATHLETE'S FOOT.
What she really needs is some miso and onions...
HOW ABOUT YOU TAKE YOUR TWISTED FOLK REMEDIES AND SHOVE 'EM INSTEAD ?!
YA OLD BIDDIES!

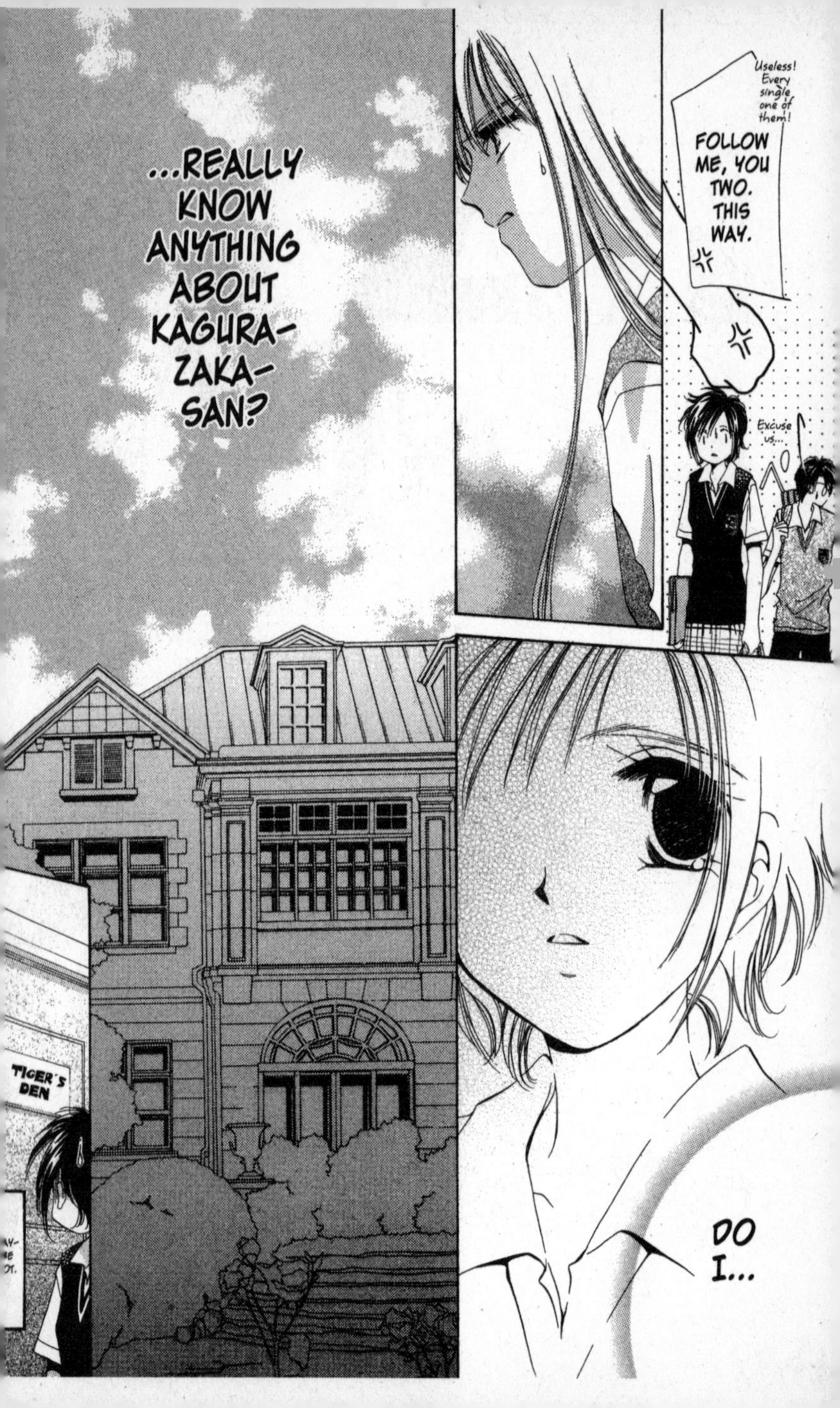
Useless! Every single one of them!
FOLLOW ME, YOU TWO. THIS WAY.
Excuse us...
DO I...
...REALLY KNOW ANYTHING ABOUT KAGURA-ZAKA-SAN?
TIGER'S DEN

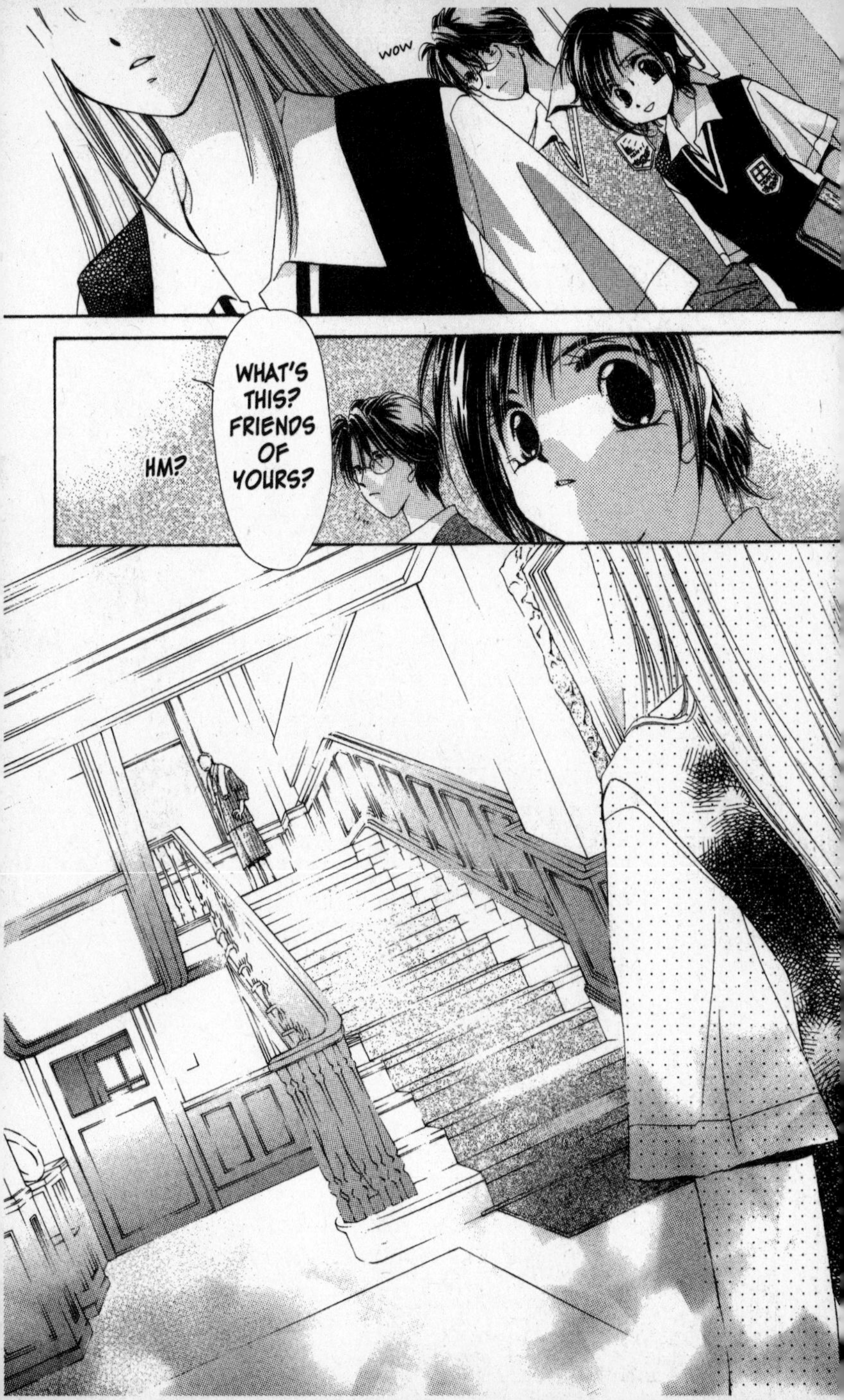
WOW
WHAT'S THIS? FRIENDS OF YOURS?
HM?

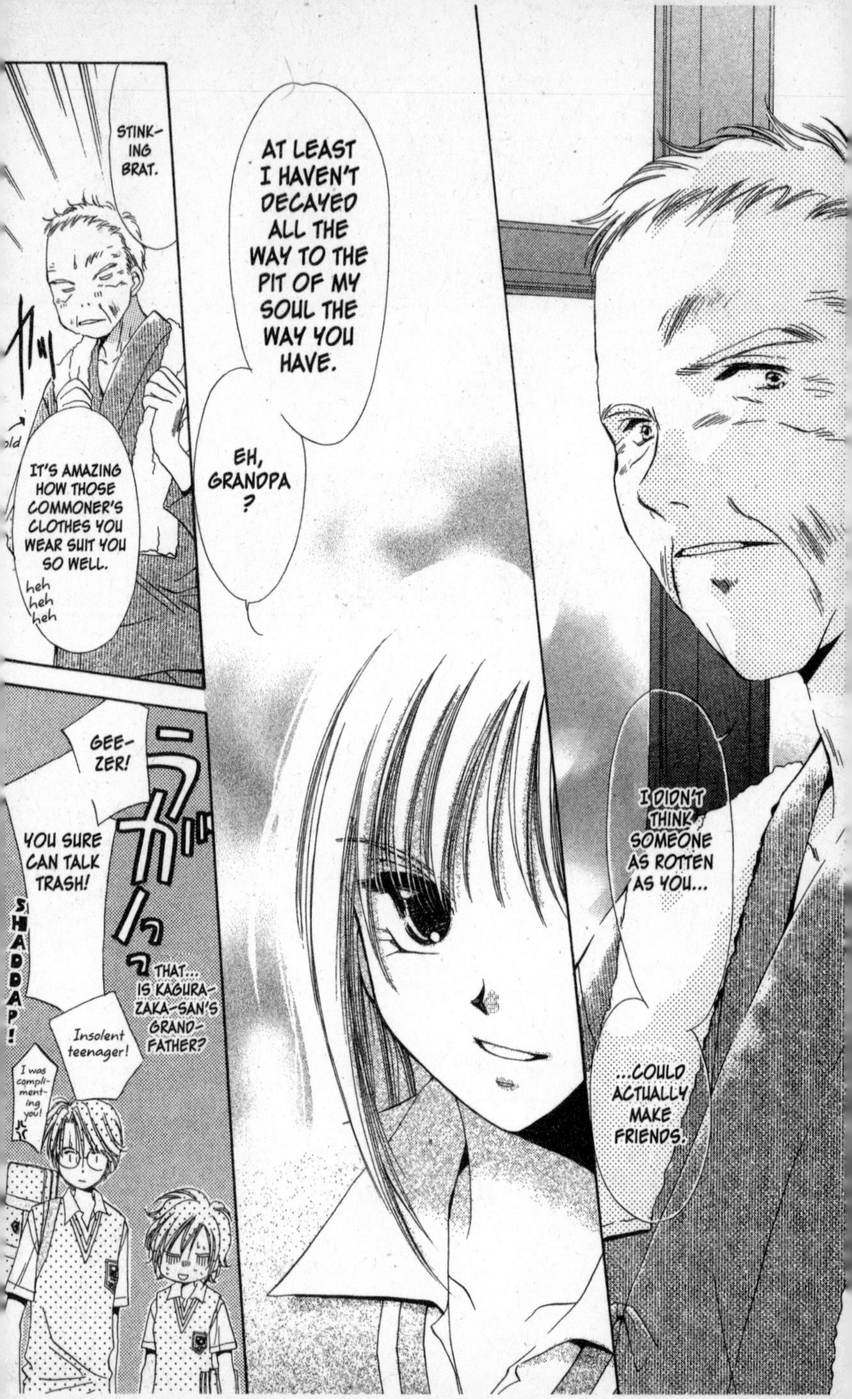
I DIDN'T THINK SOMEONE AS ROTTEN AS YOU...
...COULD ACTUALLY MAKE FRIENDS.
AT LEAST I HAVEN'T DECAYED ALL THE WAY TO THE PIT OF MY SOUL THE WAY YOU HAVE.
EH, GRANDPA?
STINK-ING BRAT.
IT'S AMAZING HOW THOSE COMMONER'S CLOTHES YOU WEAR SUIT YOU SO WELL.
heh heh heh
THAT... IS KAGURA-ZAKA-SAN'S GRAND-FATHER?
GEE-ZER!
YOU SURE CAN TALK TRASH!
SHADDAP!
Insolent teenager!
I was compli-ment-ing you!

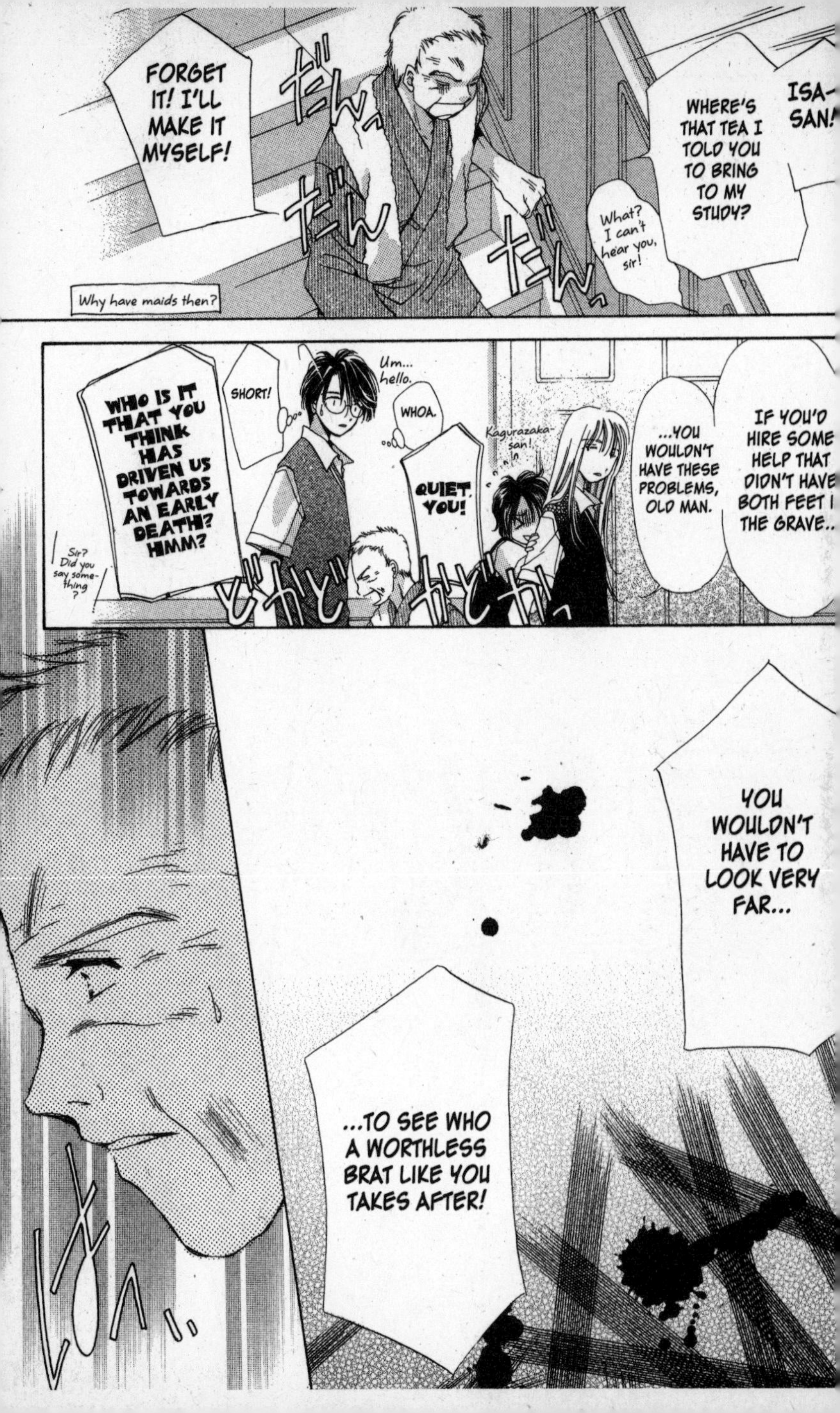
ISA-SAN!
WHERE'S THAT TEA I TOLD YOU TO BRING TO MY STUDY?
What? I can't hear you, sir!
FORGET IT! I'LL MAKE IT MYSELF!
Why have maids then?
IF YOU'D HIRE SOME HELP THAT DIDN'T HAVE BOTH FEET I THE GRAVE...
...YOU WOULDN'T HAVE THESE PROBLEMS, OLD MAN.
Kagurazaka-san!
QUIET, YOU!
WHOA.
Um... hello.
SHORT!
WHO IS IT THAT YOU THINK HAS DRIVEN US TOWARDS AN EARLY DEATH? HMM?
Sir? Did you say some-thing?
YOU WOULDN'T HAVE TO LOOK VERY FAR...
...TO SEE WHO A WORTHLESS BRAT LIKE YOU TAKES AFTER!

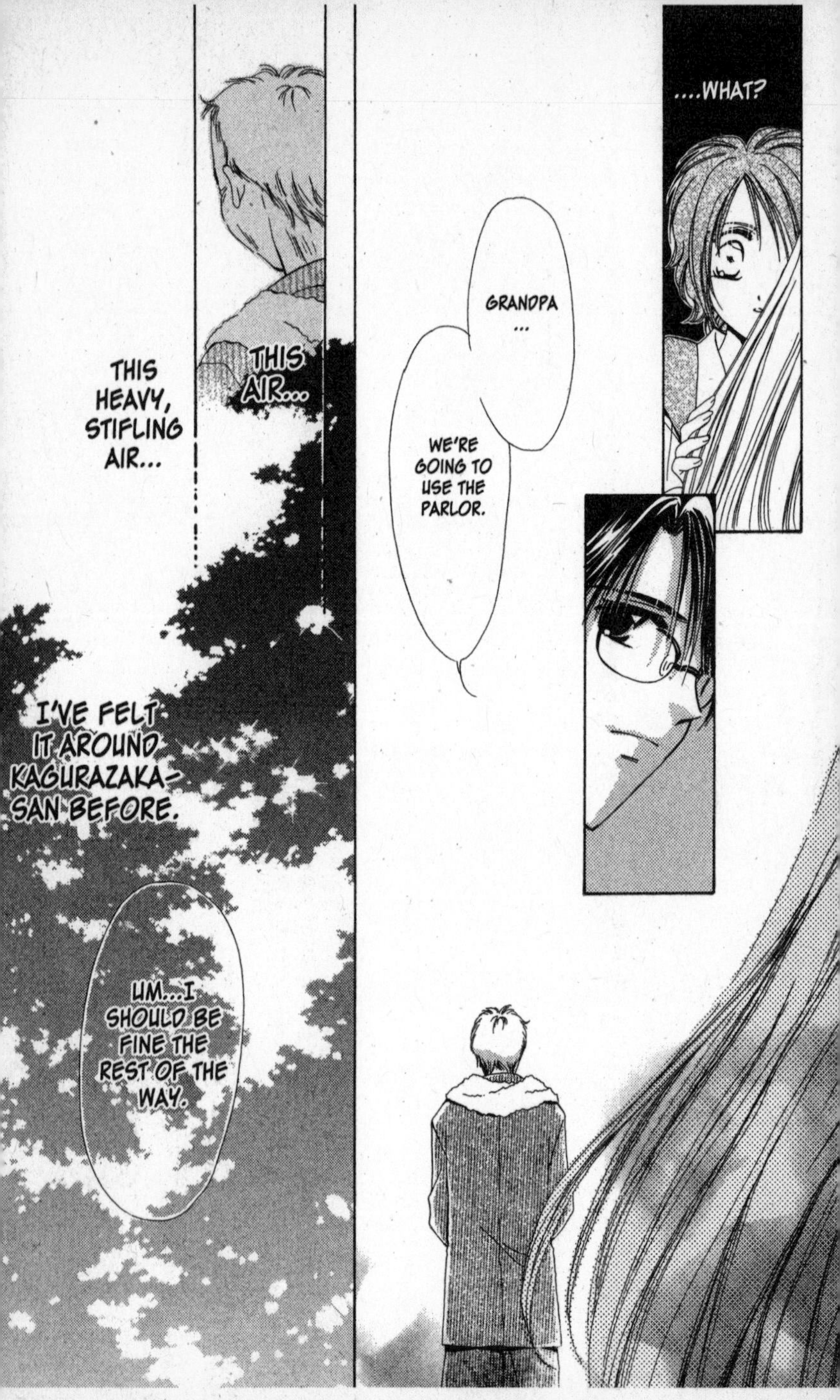
....WHAT?
GRANDPA ...
WE'RE GOING TO USE THE PARLOR.
THIS AIR...
THIS HEAVY, STIFLING AIR...
I'VE FELT IT AROUND KAGURAZAKA-SAN BEFORE.
UM...I SHOULD BE FINE THE REST OF THE WAY.

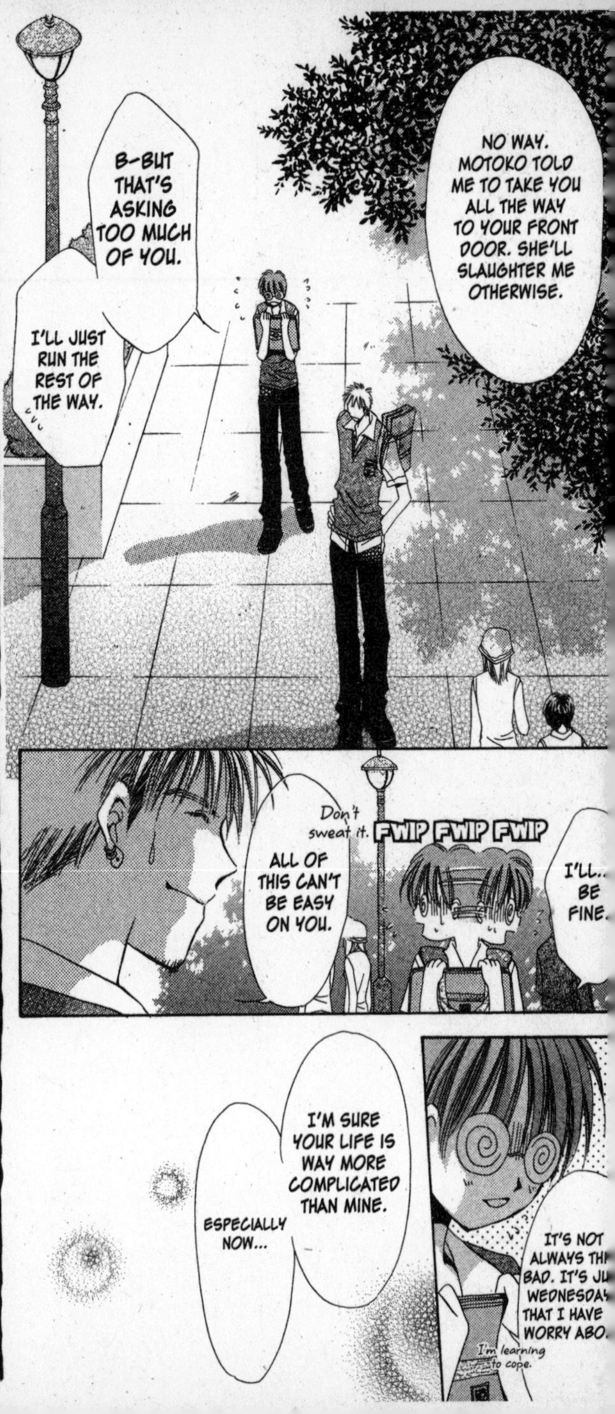
NO WAY. MOTOKO TOLD ME TO TAKE YOU ALL THE WAY TO YOUR FRONT DOOR. SHE'LL SLAUGHTER ME OTHERWISE.
B-BUT THAT'S ASKING TOO MUCH OF YOU.
I'LL JUST RUN THE REST OF THE WAY.
I'LL... BE FINE.
FWIP FWIP FWIP
Don't sweat it.
ALL OF THIS CAN'T BE EASY ON YOU.
IT'S NOT ALWAYS THI BAD. IT'S JU WEDNESDA THAT I HAVE WORRY ABO.
I'm learning to cope.
I'M SURE YOUR LIFE IS WAY MORE COMPLICATED THAN MINE.
ESPECIALLY NOW...

Today, we'll visit a character we saw for the first time way back in Chapter 2, Mr. Homoya--er, Mr. Kuzuyama. The vast majority of the shojo manga fans out there, both boys and girls, aren't particularly fond of him.

Truth be told, I kinda like the guy. I want to draw him again sometime if there's an opportunity in the story. Would you mind?

Masao Kuzuyama

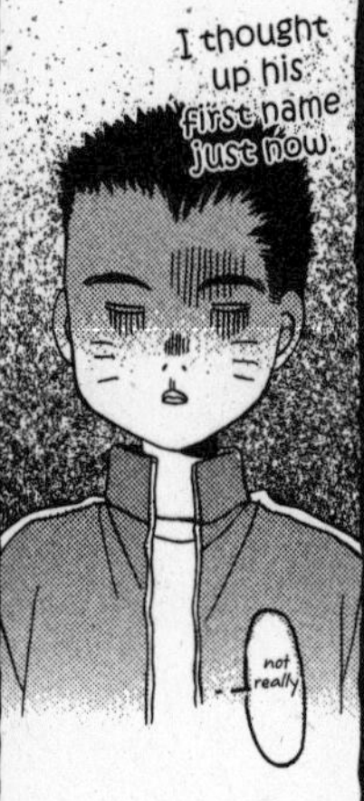
I thought up his first name just now.
not really

He's not a bad guy. He's just misunderstood.

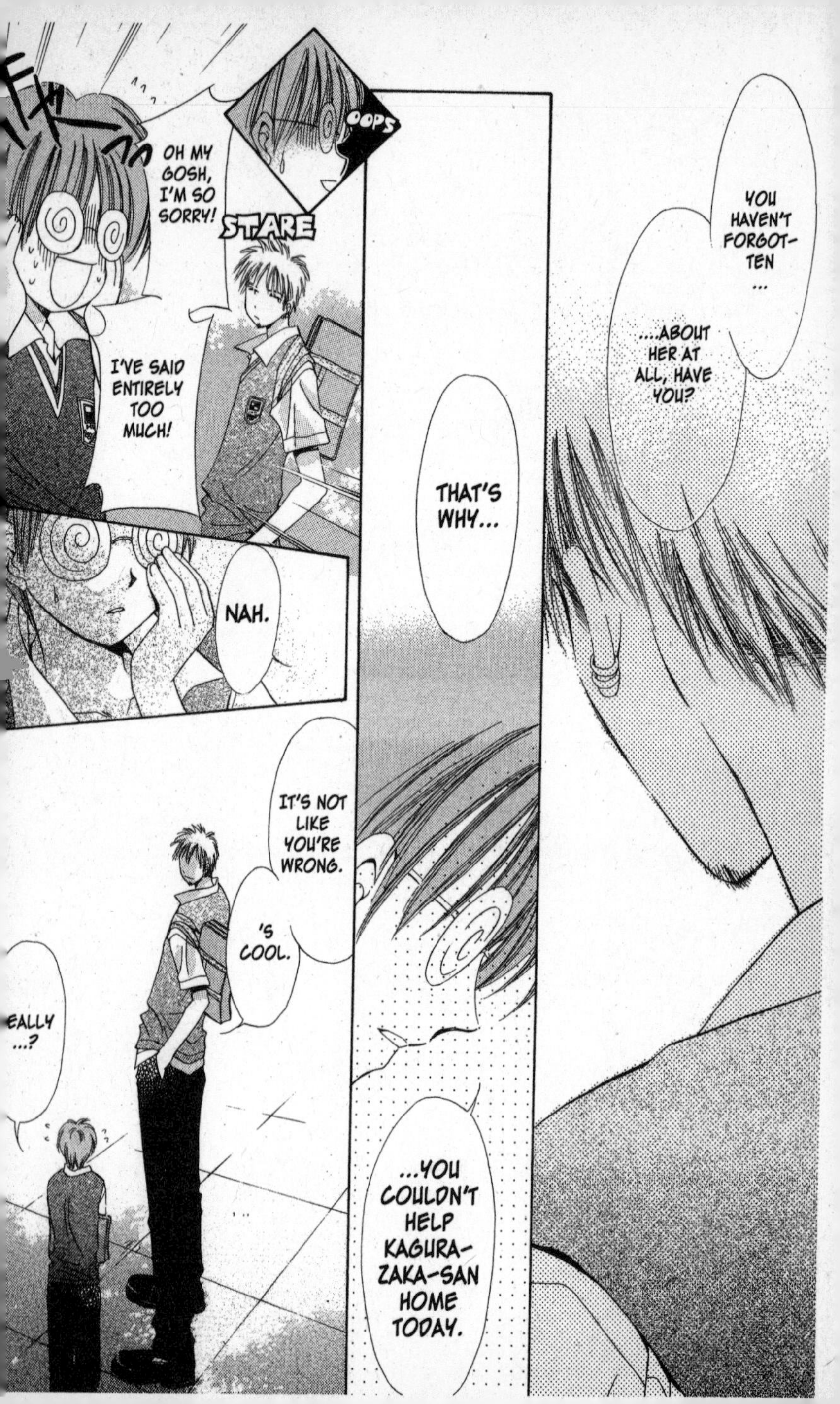
YOU HAVEN'T FORGOT-TEN ...
....ABOUT HER AT ALL, HAVE YOU?
THAT'S WHY...
...YOU COULDN'T HELP KAGURA-ZAKA-SAN HOME TODAY.
OOPS
OH MY GOSH, I'M SO SORRY!
STARE
I'VE SAID ENTIRELY TOO MUCH!
NAH.
IT'S NOT LIKE YOU'RE WRONG.
'S COOL.
EALLY ...?
...

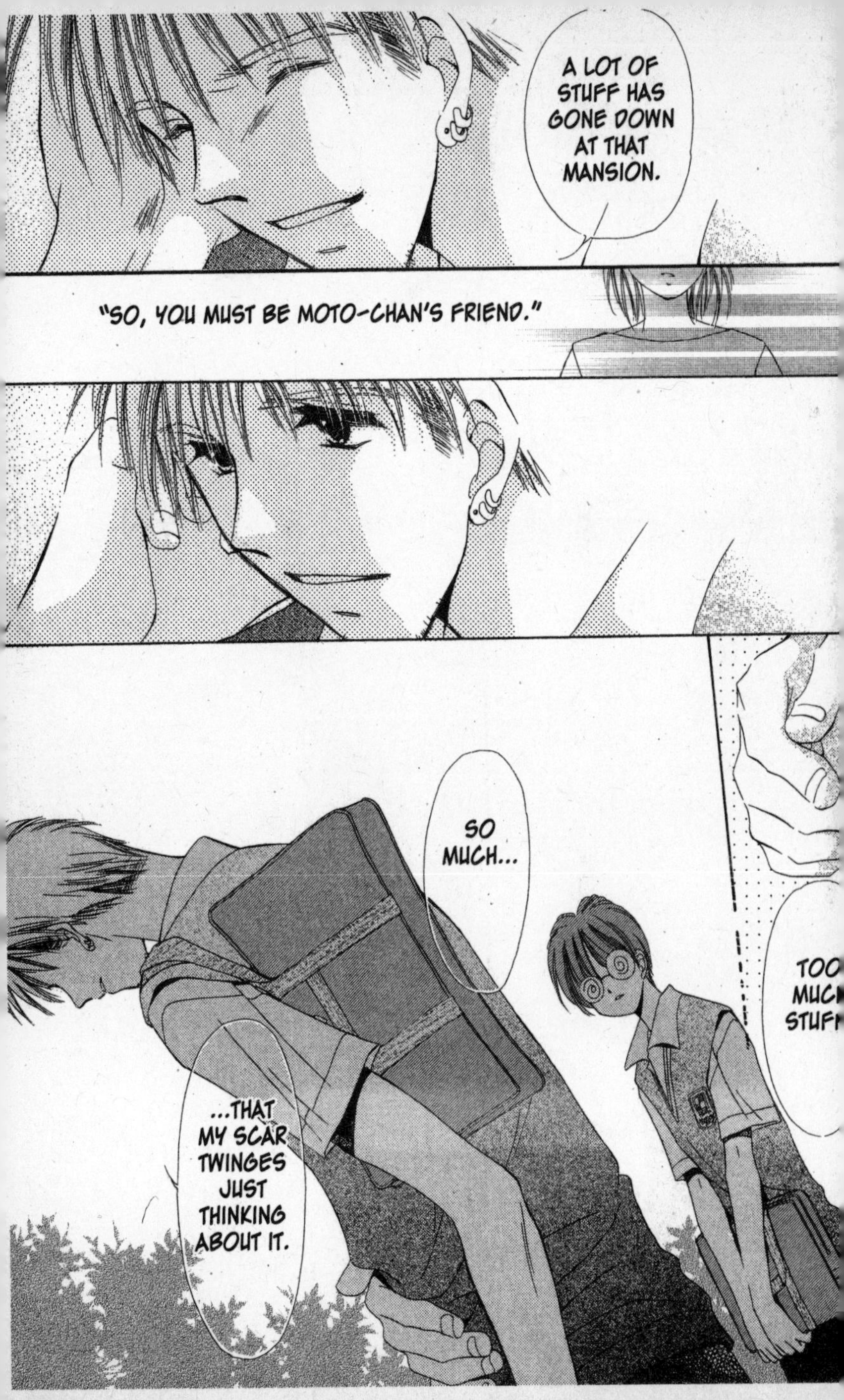
A LOT OF STUFF HAS GONE DOWN AT THAT MANSION.
"SO, YOU MUST BE MOTO-CHAN'S FRIEND."
TOO MUCH STUFF
SO MUCH...
...THAT MY SCAR TWINGES JUST THINKING ABOUT IT.

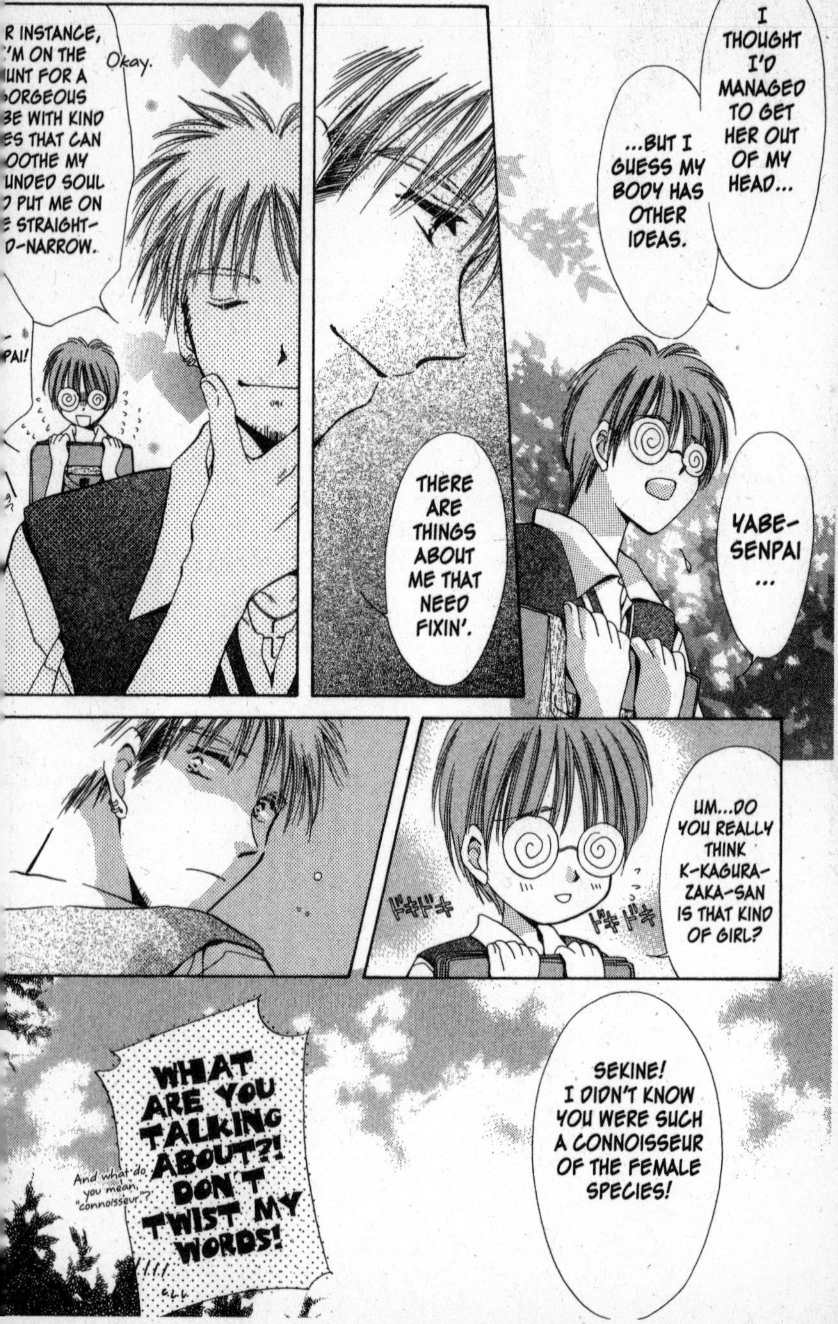
I THOUGHT I'D MANAGED TO GET HER OUT OF MY HEAD...
...BUT I GUESS MY BODY HAS OTHER IDEAS.
YABE-SENPAI...
THERE ARE THINGS ABOUT ME THAT NEED FIXIN'.
R INSTANCE, 'M ON THE IUNT FOR A ORGEOUS BE WITH KIND ES THAT CAN OOTHE MY UNDED SOUL D PUT ME ON E STRAIGHT-D-NARROW.
Okay.
PAI!
UM...DO YOU REALLY THINK K-KAGURA-ZAKA-SAN IS THAT KIND OF GIRL?
ドキドキ
ドキドキ
SEKINE! I DIDN'T KNOW YOU WERE SUCH A CONNOISSEUR OF THE FEMALE SPECIES!
WHAT ARE YOU TALKING ABOUT?! DON'T TWIST MY WORDS!
And what do you mean, "connoisseur"?

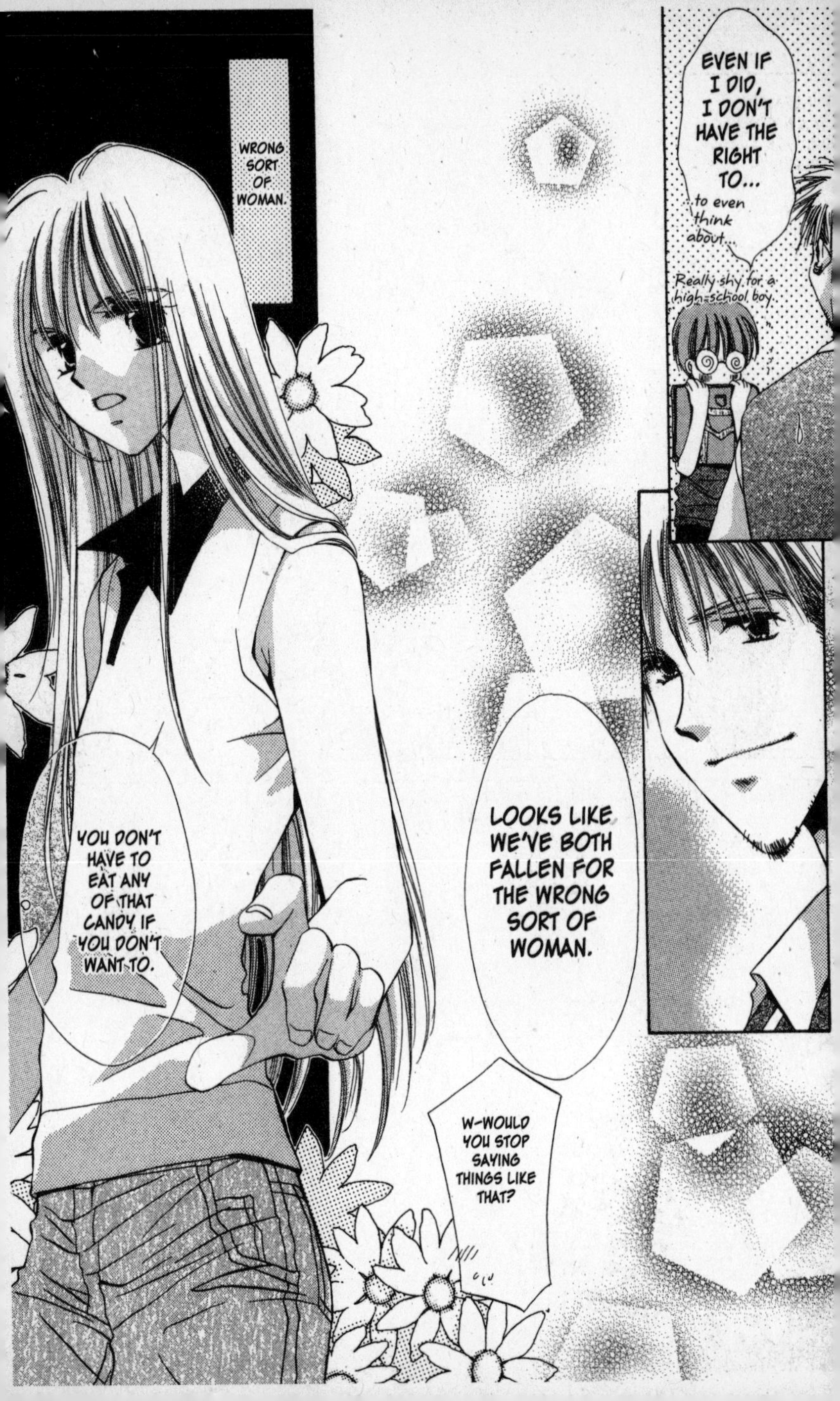
EVEN IF I DID, I DON'T HAVE THE RIGHT TO...
to even think about...
Really shy for a high-school boy.
LOOKS LIKE WE'VE BOTH FALLEN FOR THE WRONG SORT OF WOMAN.
W-WOULD YOU STOP SAYING THINGS LIKE THAT?
WRONG SORT OF WOMAN.
YOU DON'T HAVE TO EAT ANY OF THAT CANDY IF YOU DON'T WANT TO.

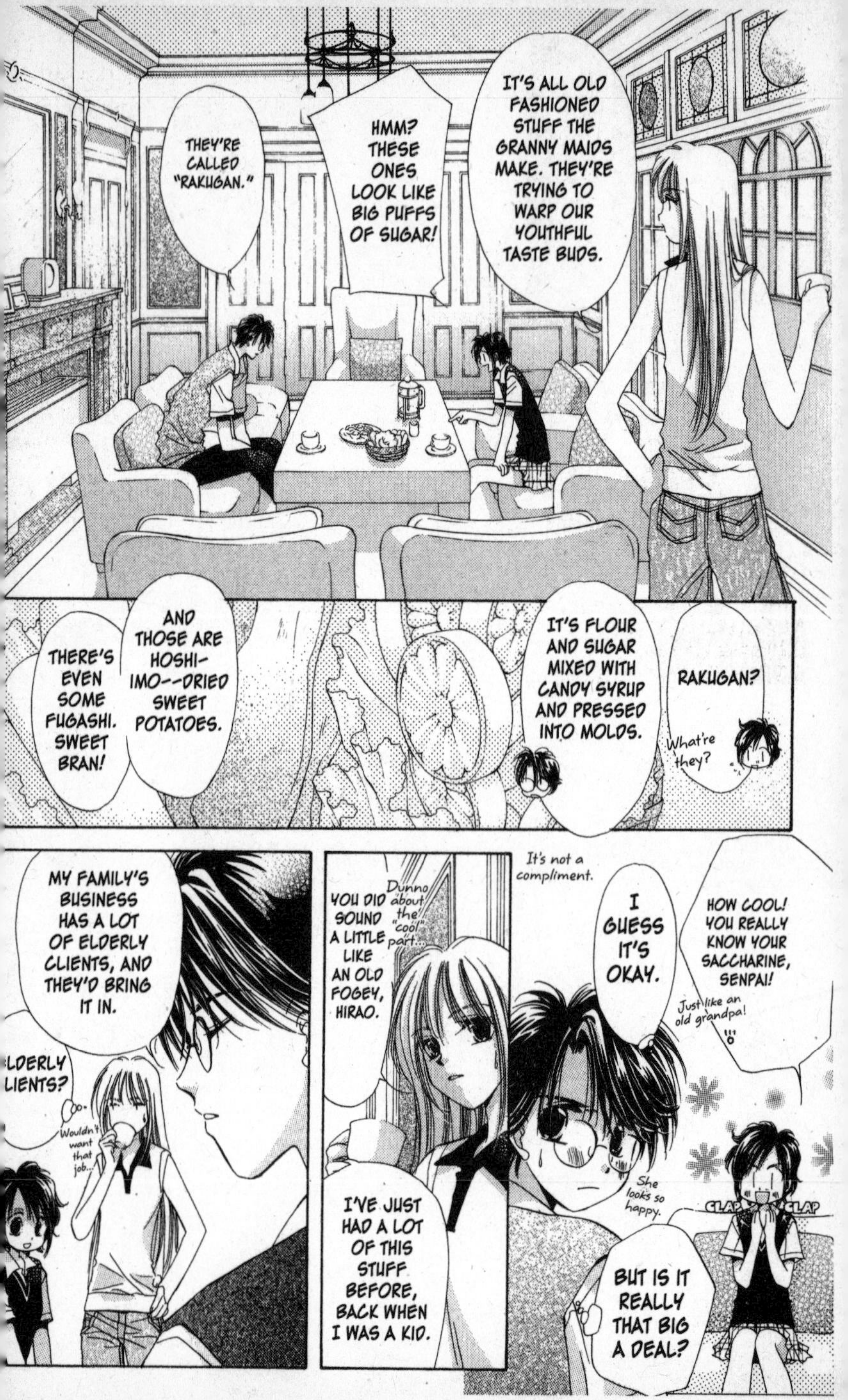
IT'S ALL OLD FASHIONED STUFF THE GRANNY MAIDS MAKE. THEY'RE TRYING TO WARP OUR YOUTHFUL TASTE BUDS.
HMM? THESE ONES LOOK LIKE BIG PUFFS OF SUGAR!
THEY'RE CALLED "RAKUGAN."
RAKUGAN?
What're they?
IT'S FLOUR AND SUGAR MIXED WITH CANDY SYRUP AND PRESSED INTO MOLDS.
AND THOSE ARE HOSHI-IMO--DRIED SWEET POTATOES.
THERE'S EVEN SOME FUGASHI. SWEET BRAN!
HOW COOL! YOU REALLY KNOW YOUR SACCHARINE, SENPAI!
Just like an old grandpa!
It's not a compliment.
I GUESS IT'S OKAY.
She looks so happy.
CLAP CLAP
BUT IS IT REALLY THAT BIG A DEAL?
Dunno about the "cool" part...
YOU DID SOUND A LITTLE LIKE AN OLD FOGEY, HIRAO.
I'VE JUST HAD A LOT OF THIS STUFF BEFORE, BACK WHEN I WAS A KID.
MY FAMILY'S BUSINESS HAS A LOT OF ELDERLY CLIENTS, AND THEY'D BRING IT IN.
LDERLY LIENTS?
Wouldn't want that job...

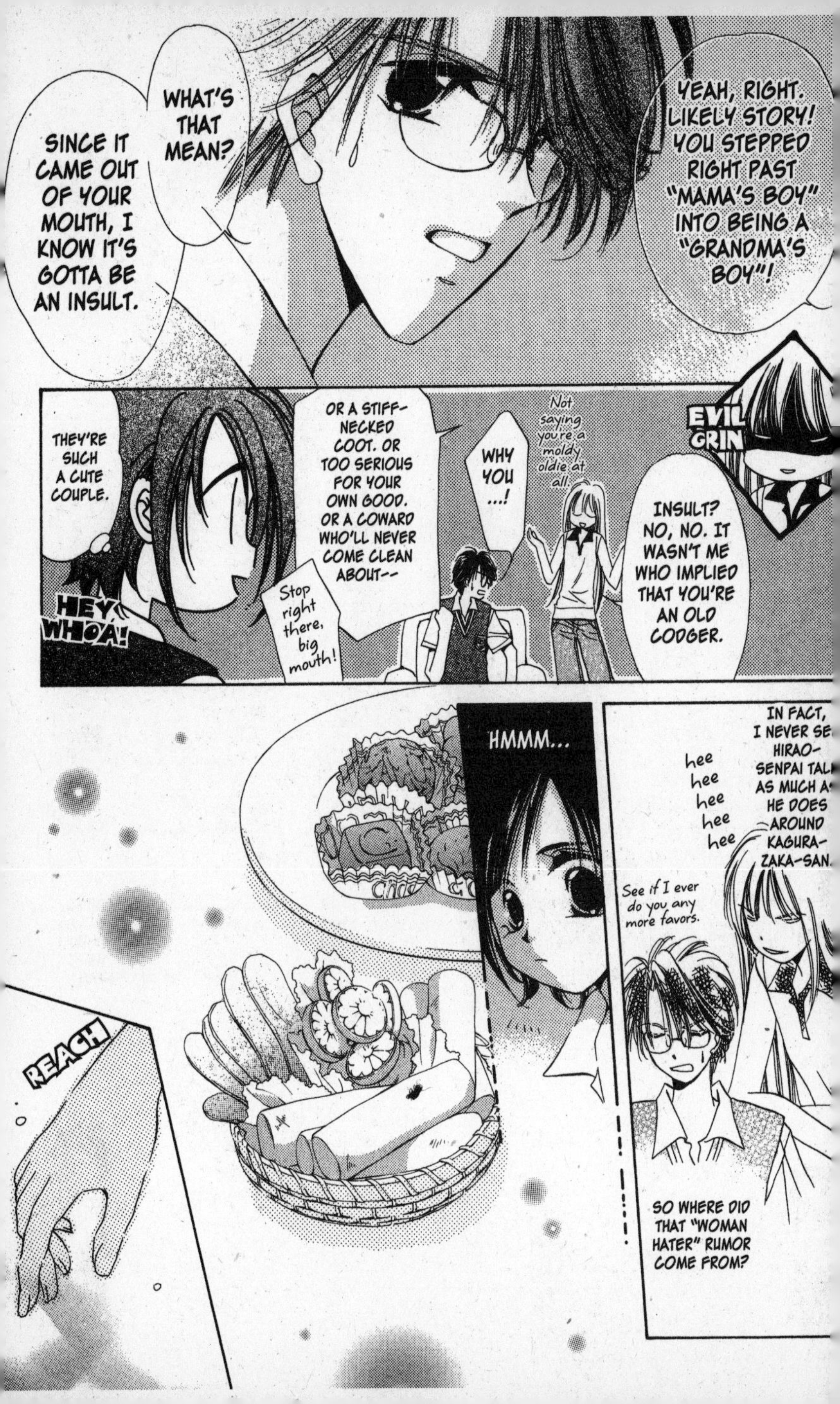
YEAH, RIGHT. LIKELY STORY! YOU STEPPED RIGHT PAST "MAMA'S BOY" INTO BEING A "GRANDMA'S BOY"!
WHAT'S THAT MEAN?
SINCE IT CAME OUT OF YOUR MOUTH, I KNOW IT'S GOTTA BE AN INSULT.
EVIL GRIN
INSULT? NO, NO. IT WASN'T ME WHO IMPLIED THAT YOU'RE AN OLD CODGER.
Not saying you're a moldy oldie at all.
WHY YOU ...!
OR A STIFF-NECKED COOT. OR TOO SERIOUS FOR YOUR OWN GOOD. OR A COWARD WHO'LL NEVER COME CLEAN ABOUT--
Stop right there, big mouth!
THEY'RE SUCH A CUTE COUPLE.
HEY, WHOA!
IN FACT, I NEVER SE HIRAO-SENPAI TAL AS MUCH A HE DOES AROUND KAGURA-ZAKA-SAN.
hee hee hee hee hee
See if I ever do you any more favors.
SO WHERE DID THAT "WOMAN HATER" RUMOR COME FROM?
HMMM...
REACH

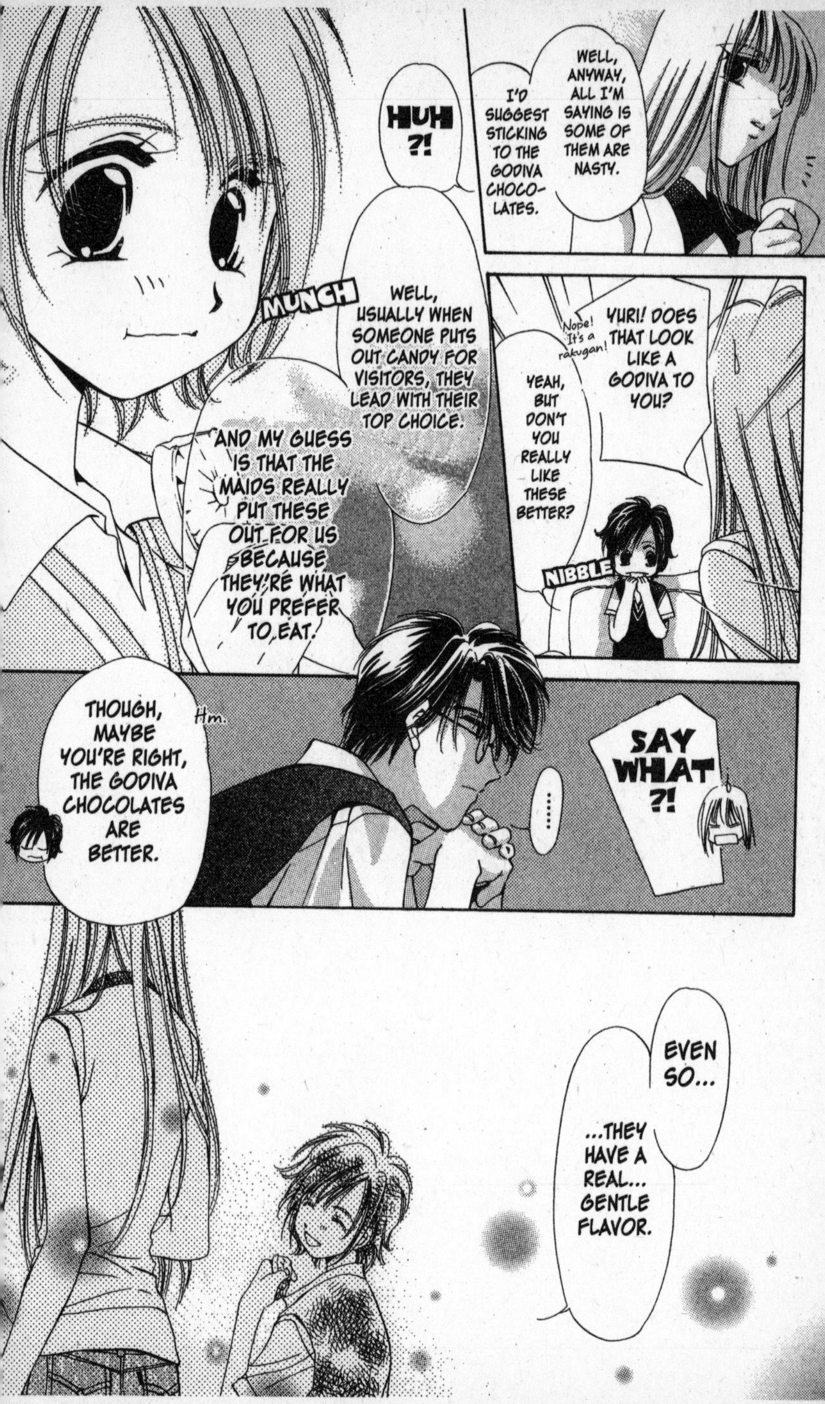
WELL, ANYWAY, ALL I'M SAYING IS SOME OF THEM ARE NASTY.
I'D SUGGEST STICKING TO THE GODIVA CHOCO-LATES.
YURI! DOES THAT LOOK LIKE A GODIVA TO YOU?
Nope! It's a rakugan!
YEAH, BUT DON'T YOU REALLY LIKE THESE BETTER?
NIBBLE
HUH?!
MUNCH
WELL, USUALLY WHEN SOMEONE PUTS OUT CANDY FOR VISITORS, THEY LEAD WITH THEIR TOP CHOICE.
AND MY GUESS IS THAT THE MAIDS REALLY PUT THESE OUT FOR US BECAUSE THEY'RE WHAT YOU PREFER TO EAT.
SAY WHAT?!
......
Hm.
THOUGH, MAYBE YOU'RE RIGHT, THE GODIVA CHOCOLATES ARE BETTER.
EVEN SO...
...THEY HAVE A REAL... GENTLE FLAVOR.

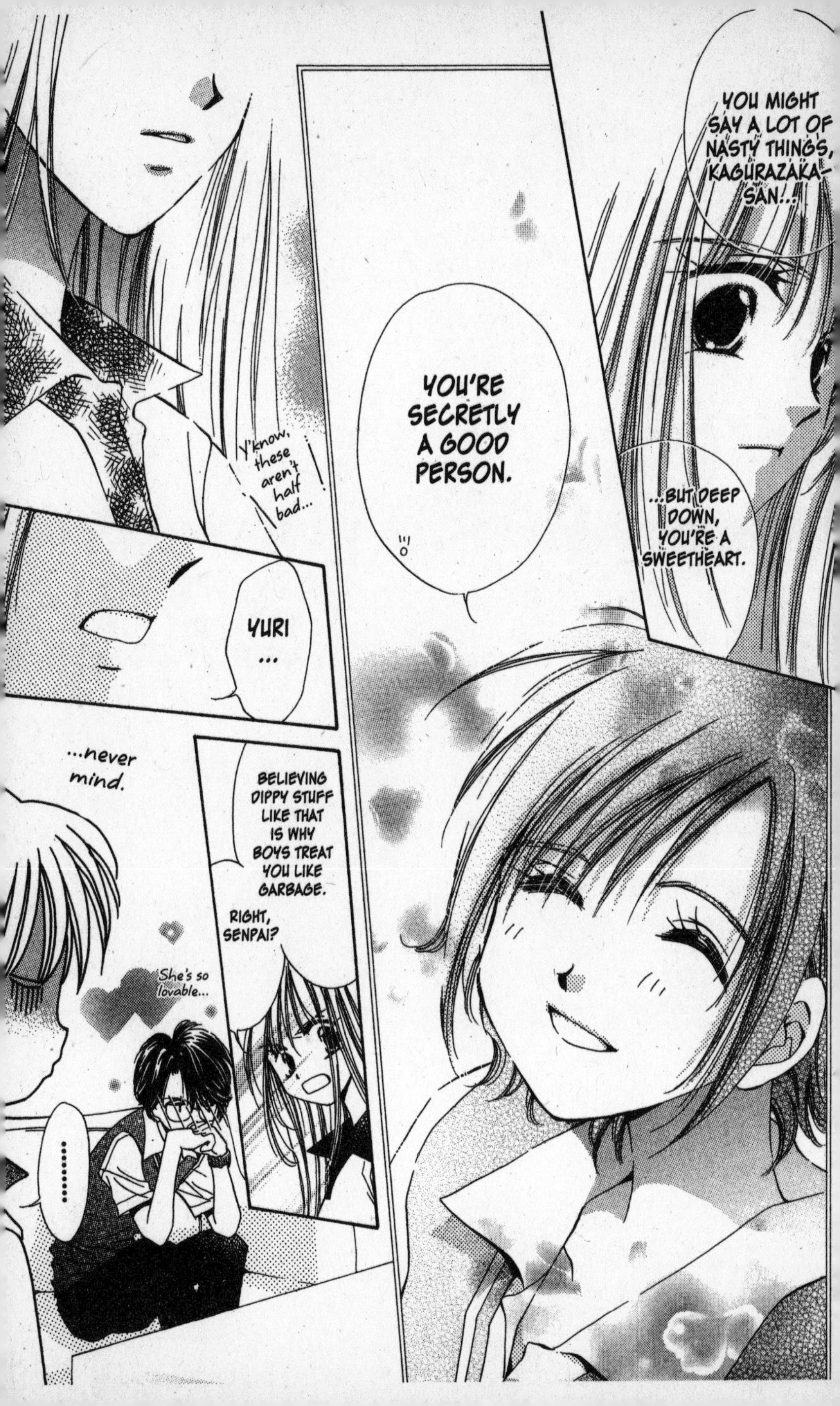
YOU MIGHT SAY A LOT OF NASTY THINGS, KAGURAZAKA-SAN...
...BUT DEEP DOWN, YOU'RE A SWEETHEART.
YOU'RE SECRETLY A GOOD PERSON.
!!
Y'know, these aren't half bad...
YURI ...
BELIEVING DIPPY STUFF LIKE THAT IS WHY BOYS TREAT YOU LIKE GARBAGE.
RIGHT, SENPAI?
...never mind.
She's so lovable...
....

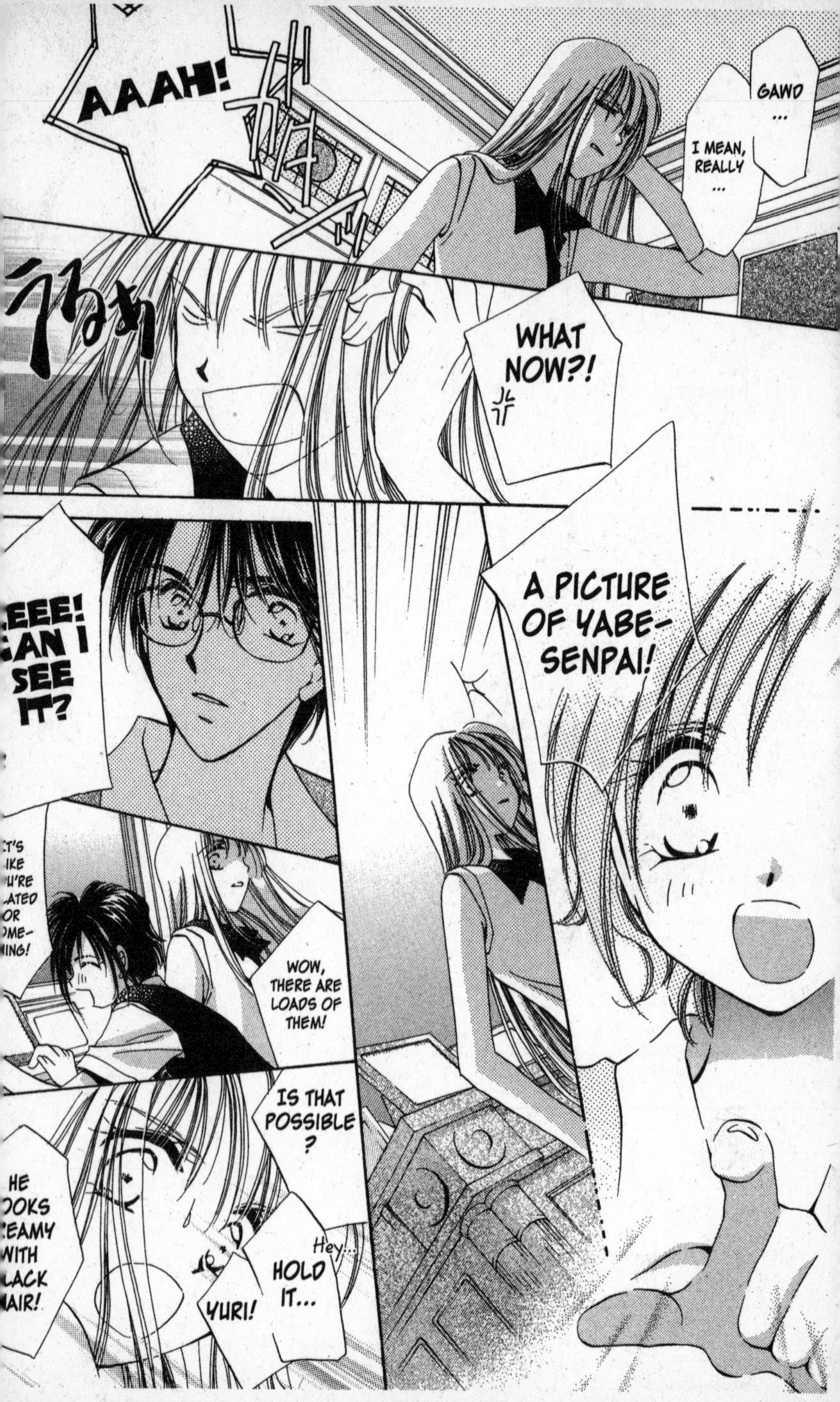
GAWD ...
I MEAN, REALLY ...
AAAH!
WHAT NOW?!
A PICTURE OF YABE-SENPAI!
EEEE! CAN I SEE IT?
WOW, THERE ARE LOADS OF THEM!
IT'S LIKE YOU'RE RELATED OR SOMETHING!
IS THAT POSSIBLE ?
Hey...
HOLD IT...
YURI!
HE LOOKS CREAMY WITH BLACK HAIR!

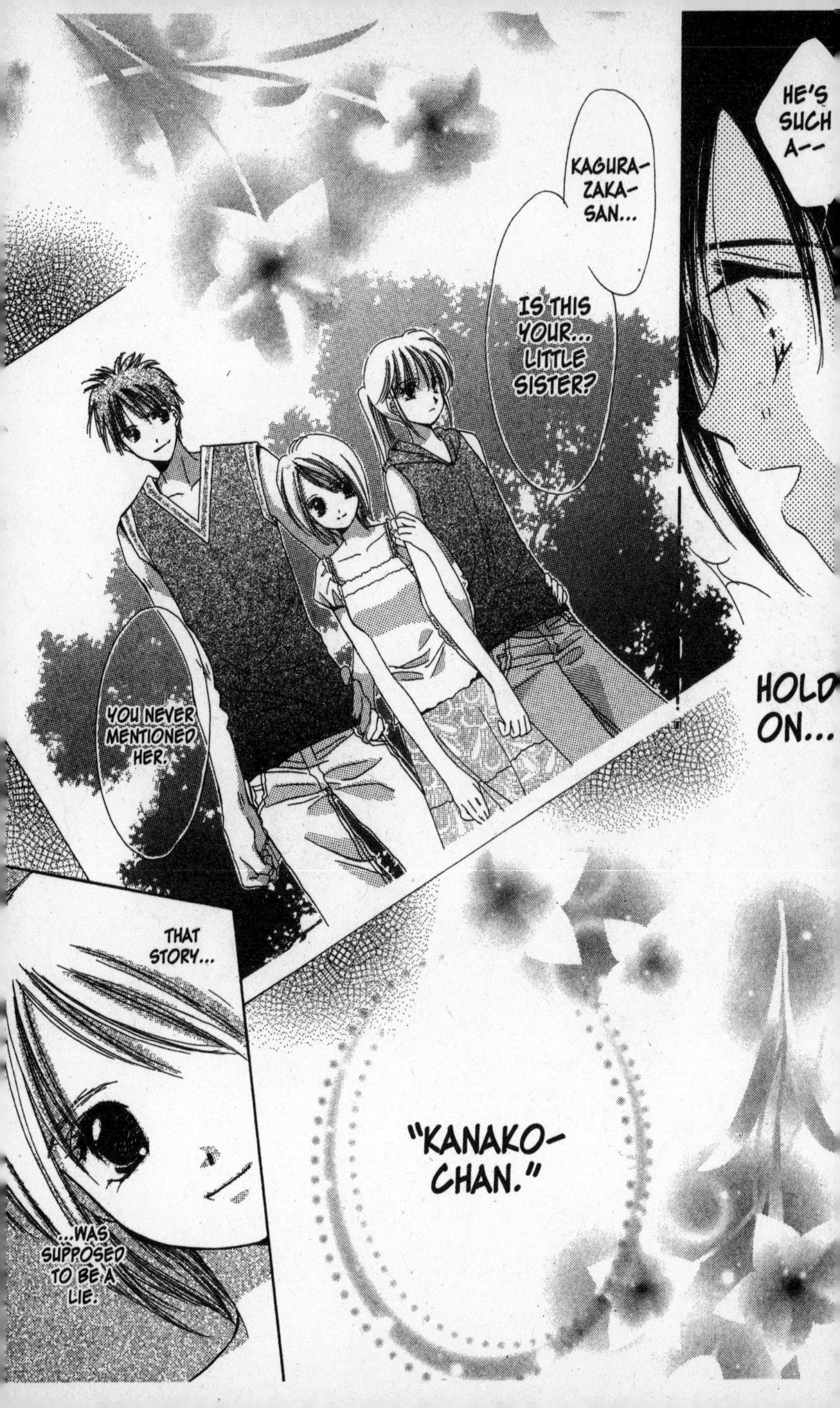

HE'S SUCH A--
KAGURA-ZAKA-SAN...
IS THIS YOUR... LITTLE SISTER?
YOU NEVER MENTIONED HER.
HOLD ON...
"KANAKO-CHAN."
THAT STORY...
...WAS SUPPOSED TO BE A LIE.

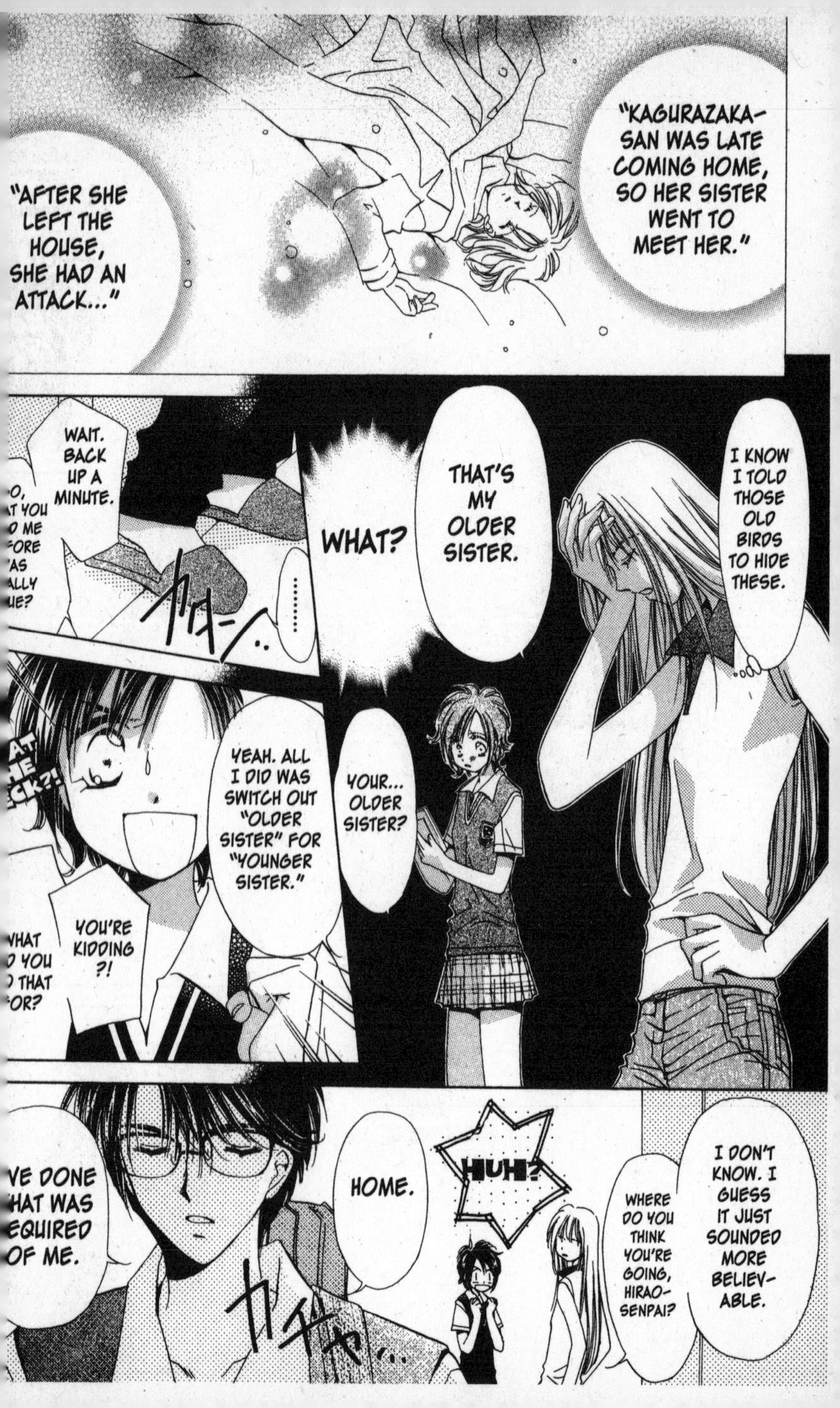

"KAGURAZAKA-SAN WAS LATE COMING HOME, SO HER SISTER WENT TO MEET HER."
"AFTER SHE LEFT THE HOUSE, SHE HAD AN ATTACK..."
I KNOW I TOLD THOSE OLD BIRDS TO HIDE THESE.
THAT'S MY OLDER SISTER.
WHAT?
YOUR... OLDER SISTER?
WAIT. BACK UP A MINUTE.
......
YEAH. ALL I DID WAS SWITCH OUT "OLDER SISTER" FOR "YOUNGER SISTER."
YOU'RE KIDDING?!
I DON'T KNOW. I GUESS IT JUST SOUNDED MORE BELIEV-ABLE.
WHERE DO YOU THINK YOU'RE GOING, HIRAO-SENPAI?
HUH?
HOME.

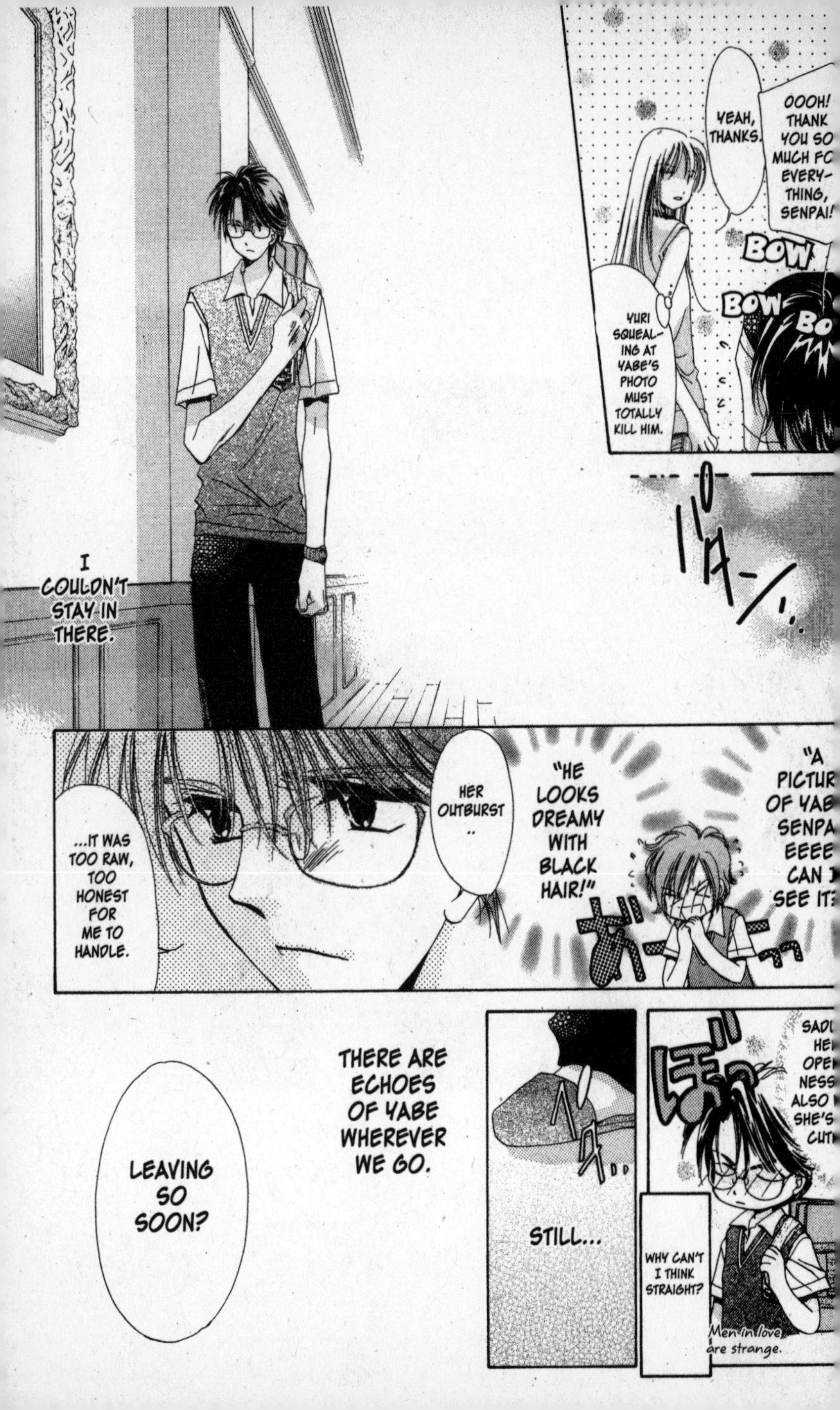

OOOH! THANK YOU SO MUCH FO EVERY- THING, SENPAI!
YEAH, THANKS.
BOW
BOW
BO
YURI SQUEAL- ING AT YABE'S PHOTO MUST TOTALLY KILL HIM.
バターン
I COULDN'T STAY IN THERE.
"A PICTUR OF YAB SENPA EEEE CAN I SEE IT
"HE LOOKS DREAMY WITH BLACK HAIR!"
HER OUTBURST ..
...IT WAS TOO RAW, TOO HONEST FOR ME TO HANDLE.
SADL HE OPE NESS ALSO SHE'S CUT
STILL...
WHY CAN'T I THINK STRAIGHT?
Men in love are strange.
THERE ARE ECHOES OF YABE WHEREVER WE GO.
LEAVING SO SOON?

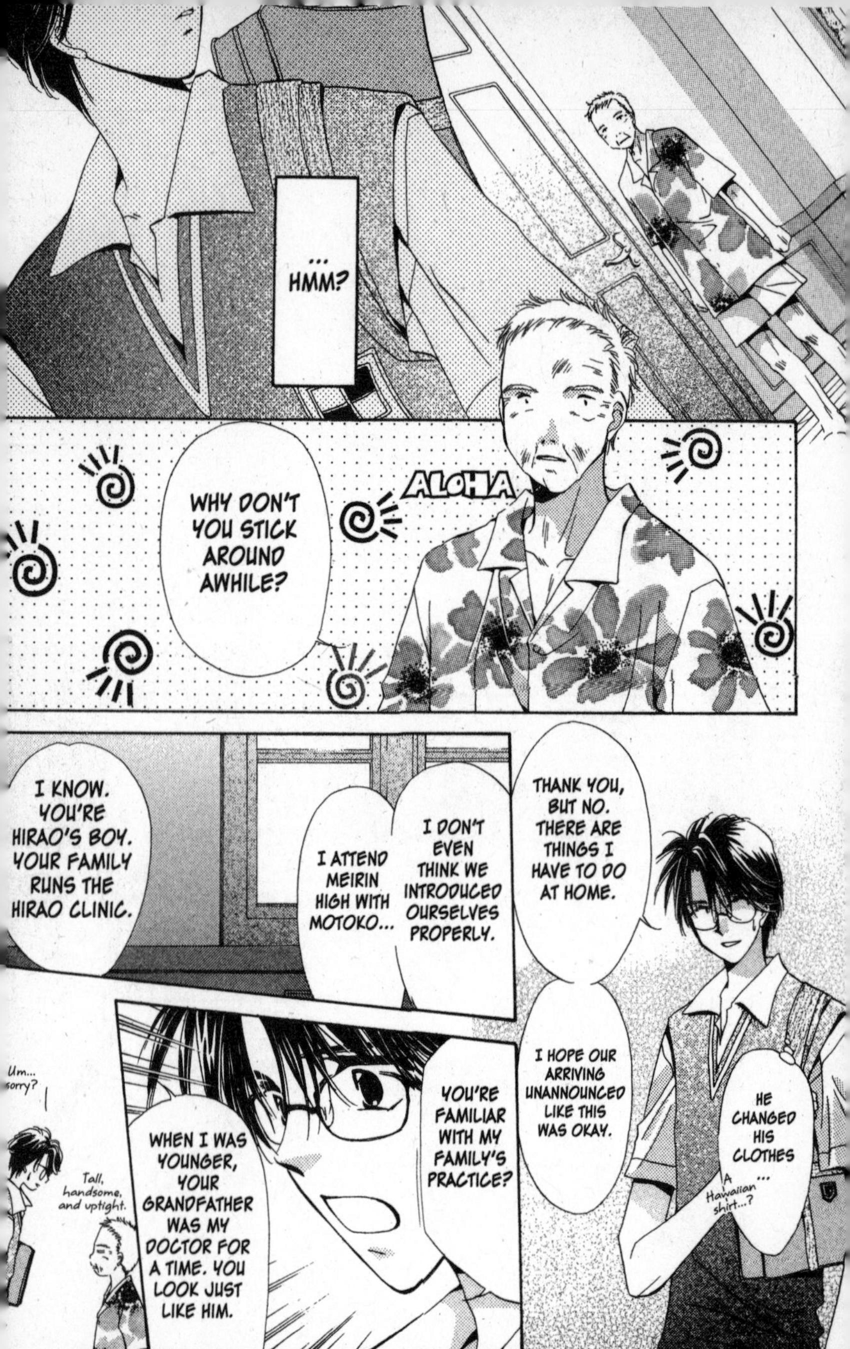
... HMM?
ALOHA
WHY DON'T YOU STICK AROUND AWHILE?
THANK YOU, BUT NO. THERE ARE THINGS I HAVE TO DO AT HOME.
I HOPE OUR ARRIVING UNANNOUNCED LIKE THIS WAS OKAY.
HE CHANGED HIS CLOTHES ...
A Hawaiian shirt...?
I DON'T EVEN THINK WE INTRODUCED OURSELVES PROPERLY.
I ATTEND MEIRIN HIGH WITH MOTOKO...
I KNOW. YOU'RE HIRAO'S BOY. YOUR FAMILY RUNS THE HIRAO CLINIC.
YOU'RE FAMILIAR WITH MY FAMILY'S PRACTICE?
WHEN I WAS YOUNGER, YOUR GRANDFATHER WAS MY DOCTOR FOR A TIME. YOU LOOK JUST LIKE HIM.
Tall, handsome, and uptight.
Um... sorry?

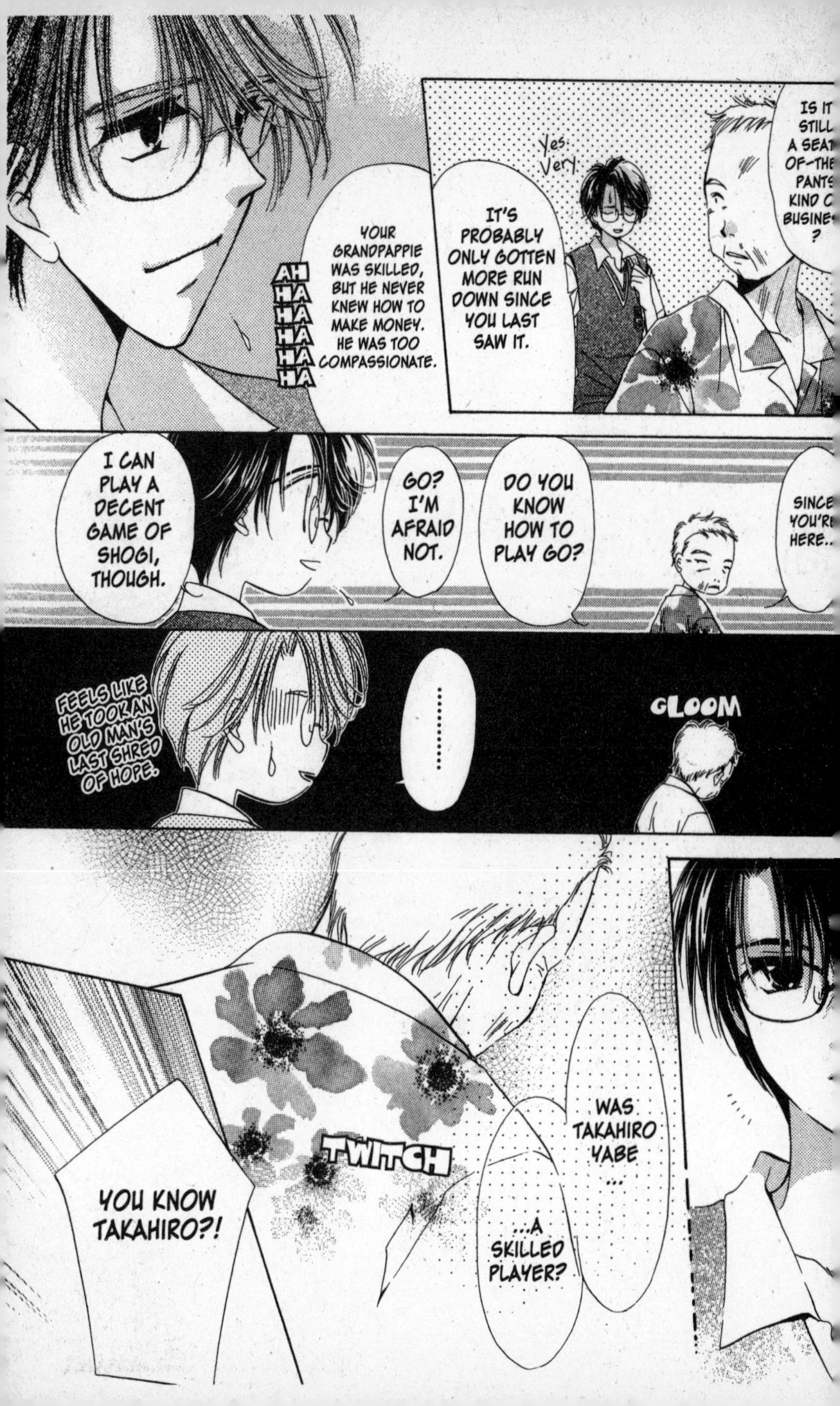
IS IT STILL A SEAT OF-THE PANTS KIND C BUSINE ?
Yes. Very.
IT'S PROBABLY ONLY GOTTEN MORE RUN DOWN SINCE YOU LAST SAW IT.
YOUR GRANDPAPPIE WAS SKILLED, BUT HE NEVER KNEW HOW TO MAKE MONEY. HE WAS TOO COMPASSIONATE.
AH HA HA HA HA HA HA
SINCE YOU'R HERE..
DO YOU KNOW HOW TO PLAY GO?
GO? I'M AFRAID NOT.
I CAN PLAY A DECENT GAME OF SHOGI, THOUGH.
GLOOM
......
FEELS LIKE HE TOOK AN OLD MAN'S LAST SHRED OF HOPE.
WAS TAKAHIRO YABE ...
...A SKILLED PLAYER?
TWITCH
YOU KNOW TAKAHIRO?!

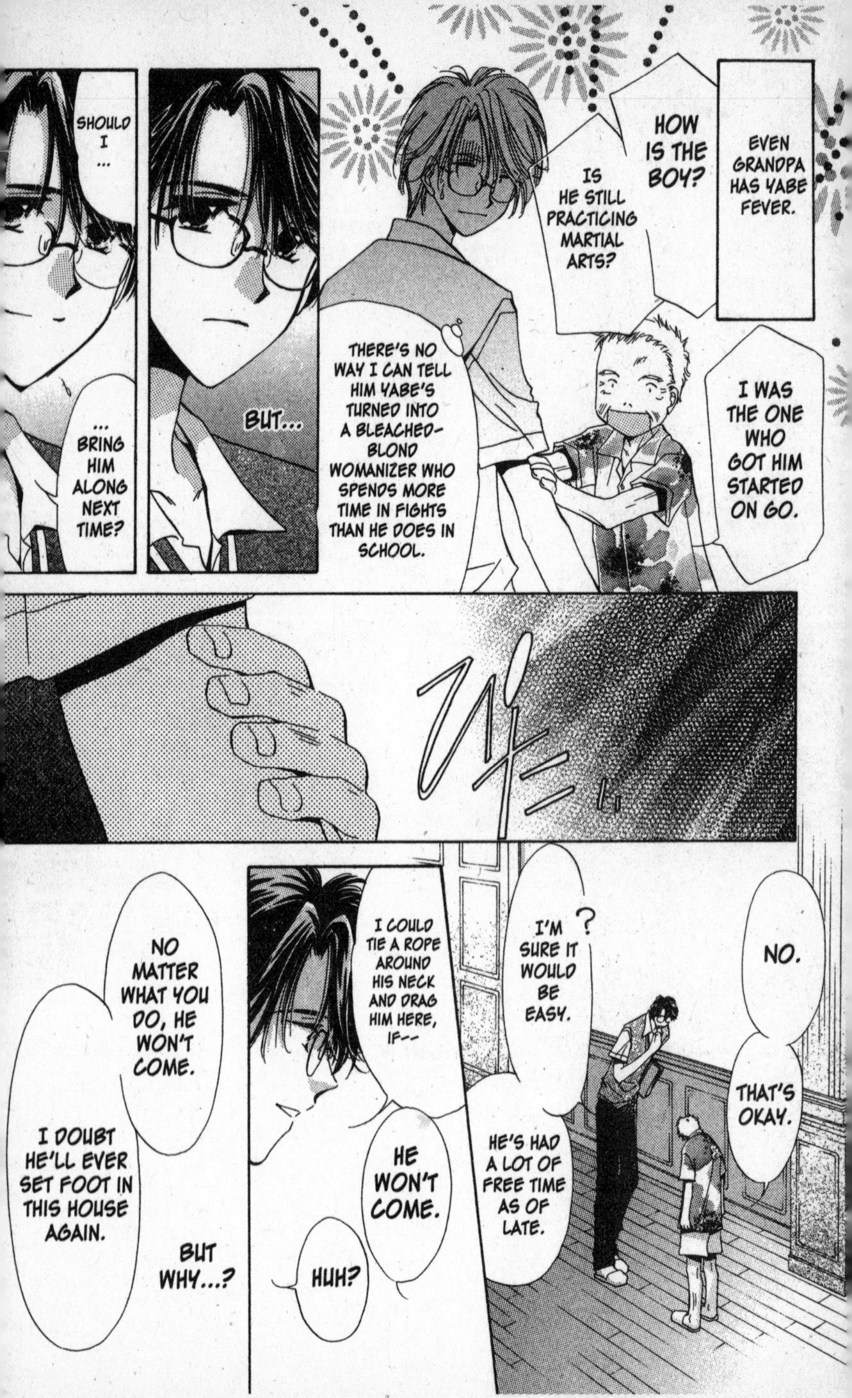
EVEN GRANDPA HAS YABE FEVER.
HOW IS THE BOY?
IS HE STILL PRACTICING MARTIAL ARTS?
I WAS THE ONE WHO GOT HIM STARTED ON GO.
THERE'S NO WAY I CAN TELL HIM YABE'S TURNED INTO A BLEACHED-BLOND WOMANIZER WHO SPENDS MORE TIME IN FIGHTS THAN HE DOES IN SCHOOL.
BUT...
SHOULD I ...
... BRING HIM ALONG NEXT TIME?
NO.
THAT'S OKAY.
I'M SURE IT WOULD BE EASY.
?
HE'S HAD A LOT OF FREE TIME AS OF LATE.
I COULD TIE A ROPE AROUND HIS NECK AND DRAG HIM HERE, IF--
HE WON'T COME.
HUH?
NO MATTER WHAT YOU DO, HE WON'T COME.
BUT WHY...?
I DOUBT HE'LL EVER SET FOOT IN THIS HOUSE AGAIN.

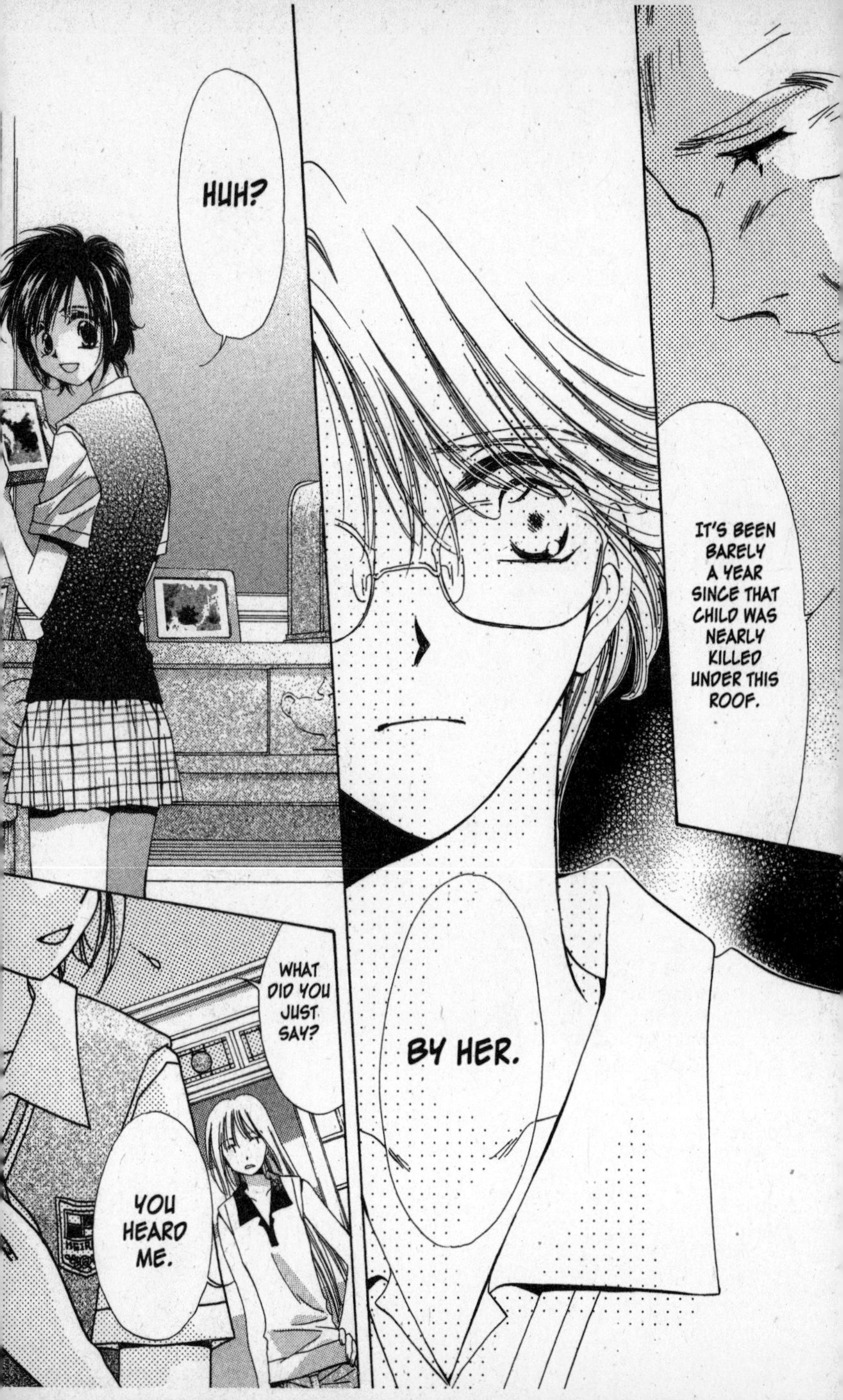
IT'S BEEN BARELY A YEAR SINCE THAT CHILD WAS NEARLY KILLED UNDER THIS ROOF.
BY HER.
HUH?
WHAT DID YOU JUST SAY?
YOU HEARD ME.

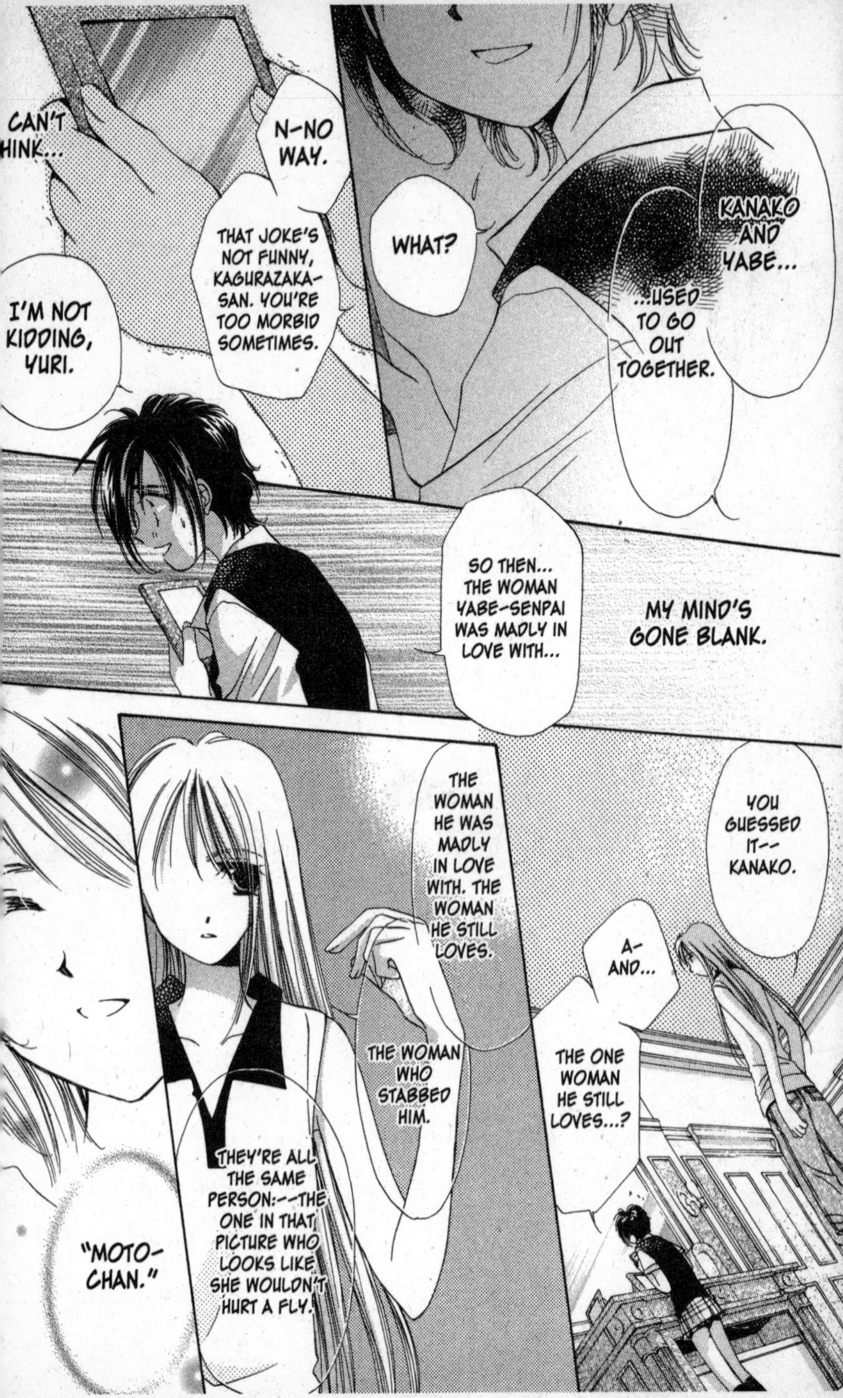
KANAKO AND YABE...
...USED TO GO OUT TOGETHER.
WHAT?
N-NO WAY.
THAT JOKE'S NOT FUNNY, KAGURAZAKA-SAN. YOU'RE TOO MORBID SOMETIMES.
CAN'T HINK...
I'M NOT KIDDING, YURI.
MY MIND'S GONE BLANK.
SO THEN... THE WOMAN YABE-SENPAI WAS MADLY IN LOVE WITH...
YOU GUESSED IT-- KANAKO.
A- AND...
THE ONE WOMAN HE STILL LOVES...?
THE WOMAN HE WAS MADLY IN LOVE WITH. THE WOMAN HE STILL LOVES.
THE WOMAN WHO STABBED HIM.
THEY'RE ALL THE SAME PERSON:--THE ONE IN THAT PICTURE WHO LOOKS LIKE SHE WOULDN'T HURT A FLY.
"MOTO-CHAN."

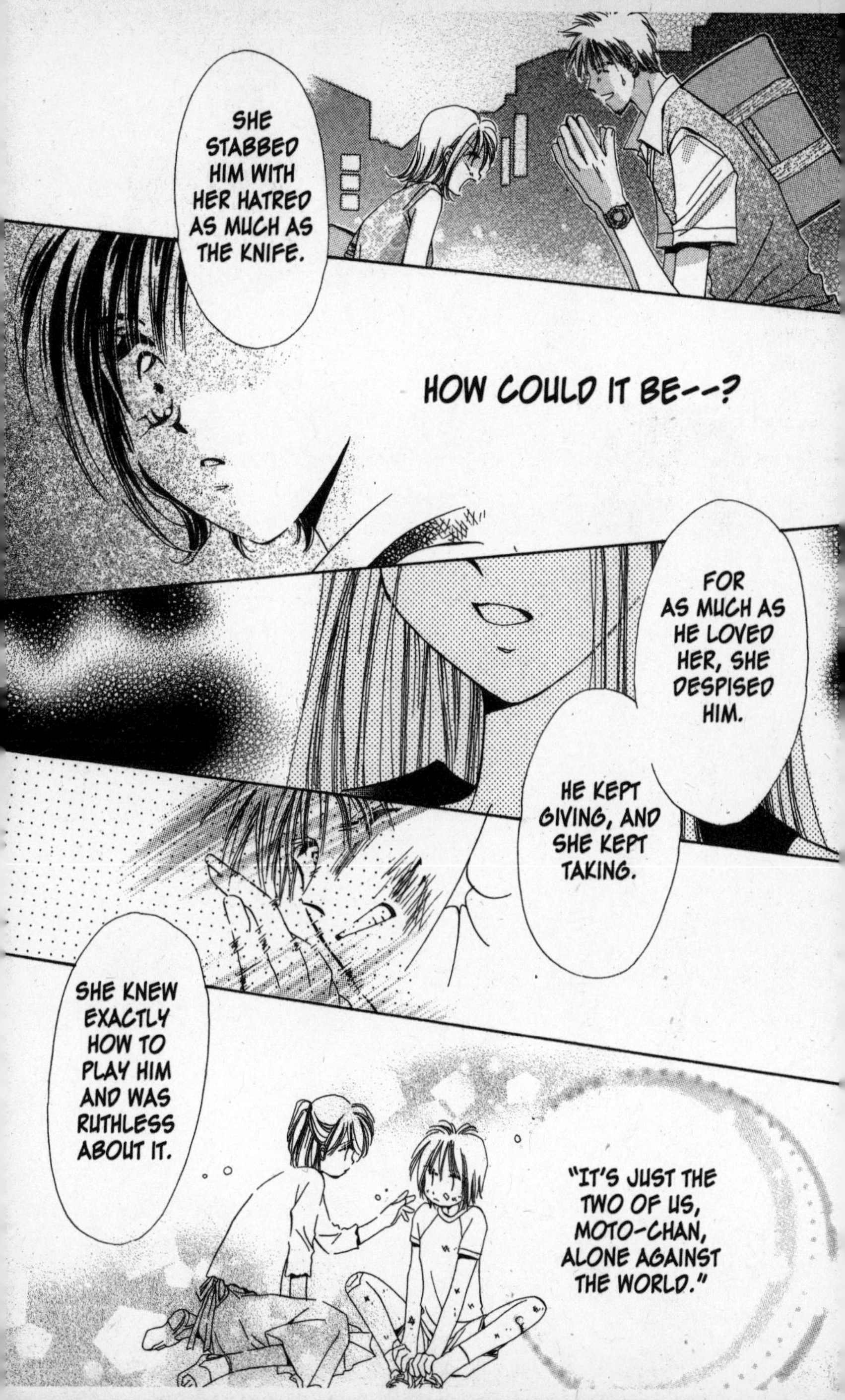
SHE STABBED HIM WITH HER HATRED AS MUCH AS THE KNIFE.
HOW COULD IT BE--?
FOR AS MUCH AS HE LOVED HER, SHE DESPISED HIM.
HE KEPT GIVING, AND SHE KEPT TAKING.
SHE KNEW EXACTLY HOW TO PLAY HIM AND WAS RUTHLESS ABOUT IT.
"IT'S JUST THE TWO OF US, MOTO-CHAN, ALONE AGAINST THE WORLD."

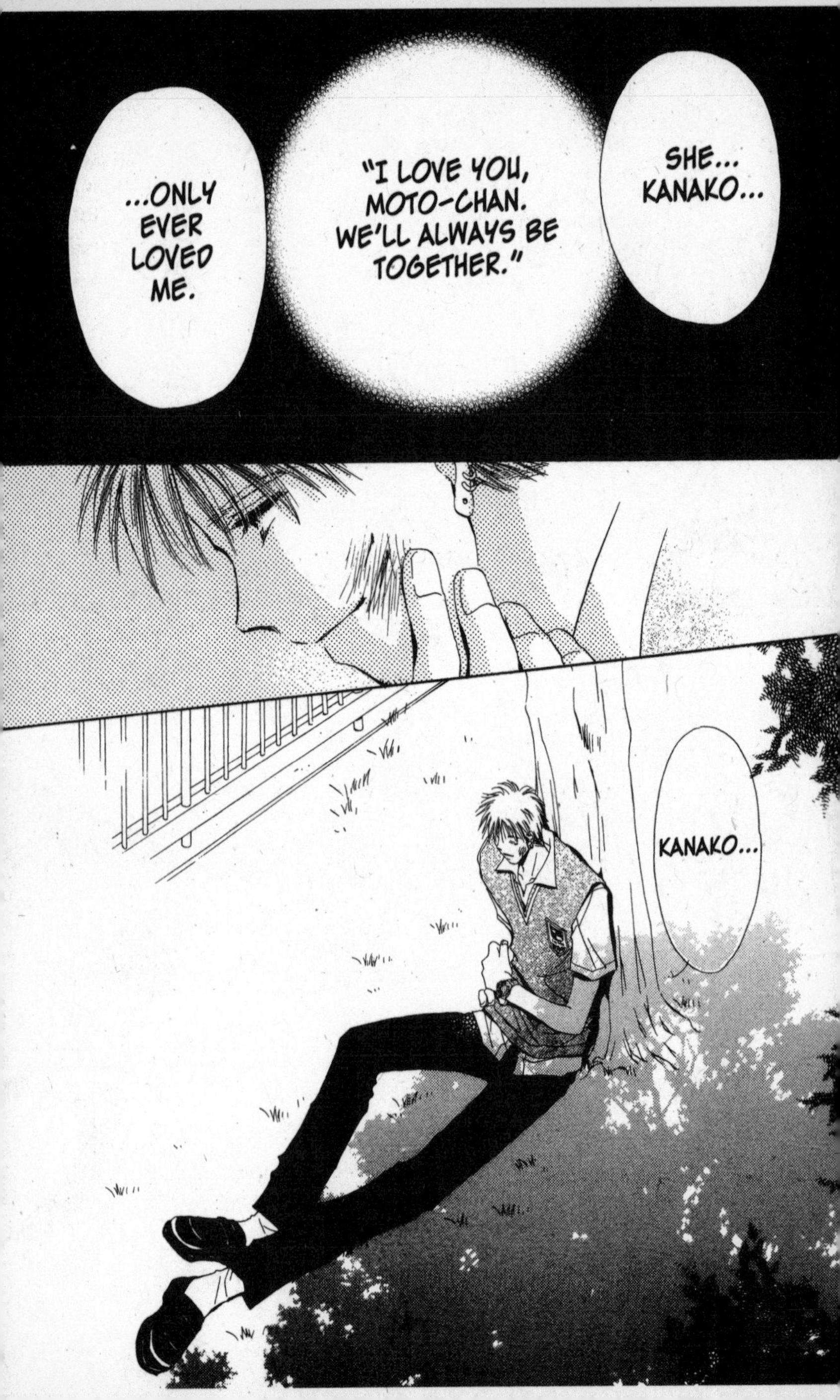
SHE... KANAKO...
"I LOVE YOU, MOTO-CHAN. WE'LL ALWAYS BE TOGETHER."
...ONLY EVER LOVED ME.
KANAKO...

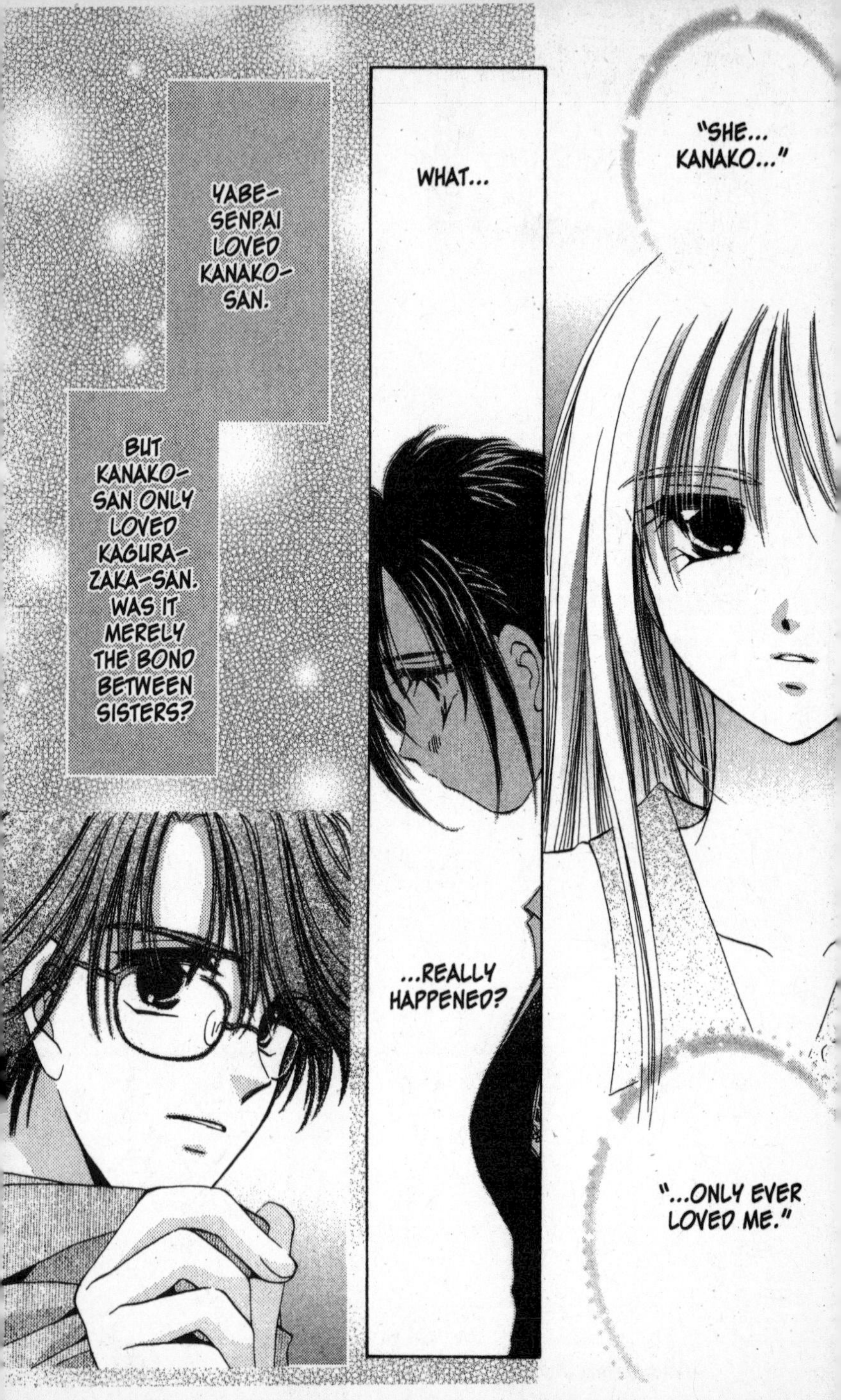
"SHE... KANAKO..."
"...ONLY EVER LOVED ME."
WHAT...
...REALLY HAPPENED?
YABE-SENPAI LOVED KANAKO-SAN.
BUT KANAKO-SAN ONLY LOVED KAGURA-ZAKA-SAN. WAS IT MERELY THE BOND BETWEEN SISTERS?

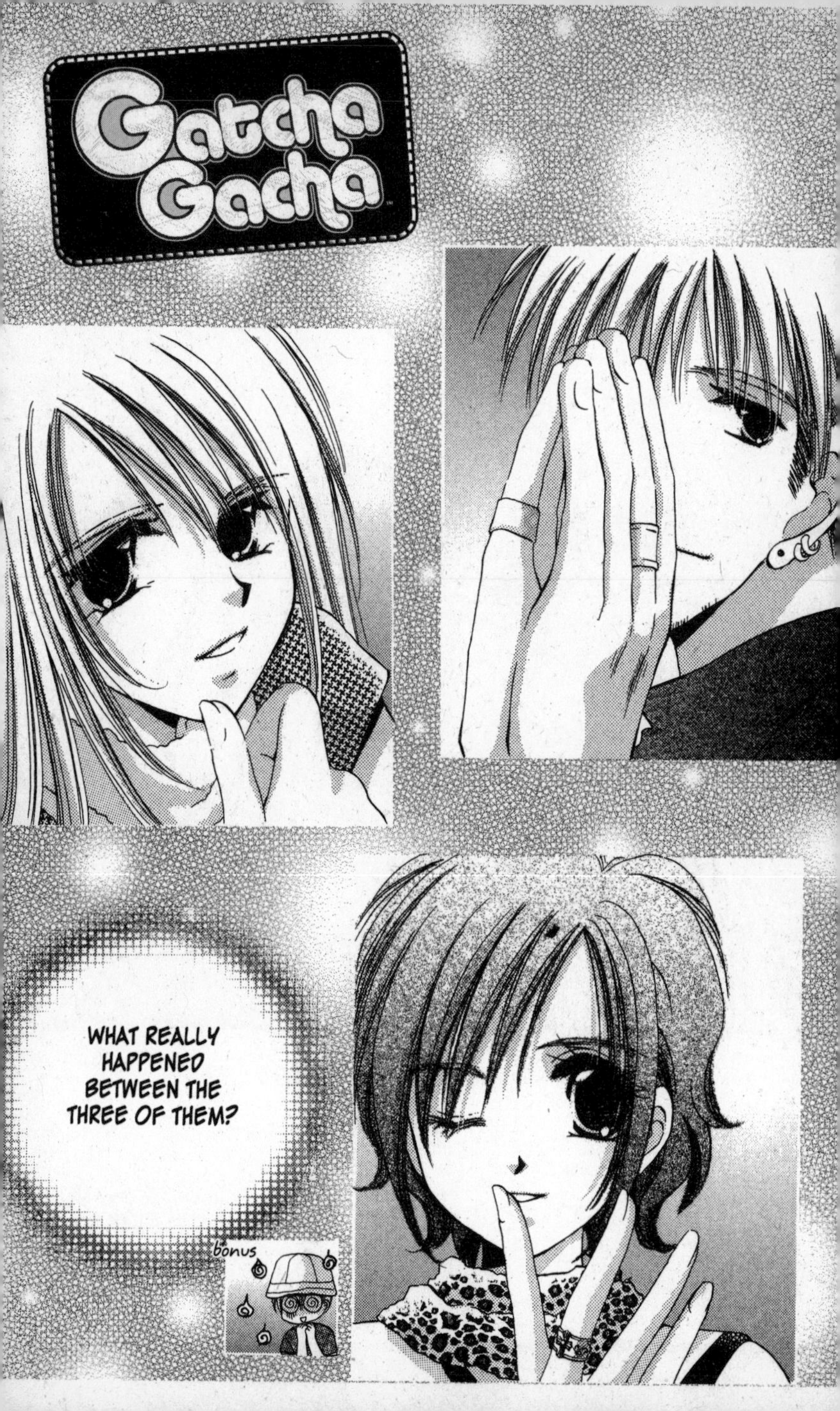
Gatcha Gacha
WHAT REALLY HAPPENED BETWEEN THE THREE OF THEM?
bonus

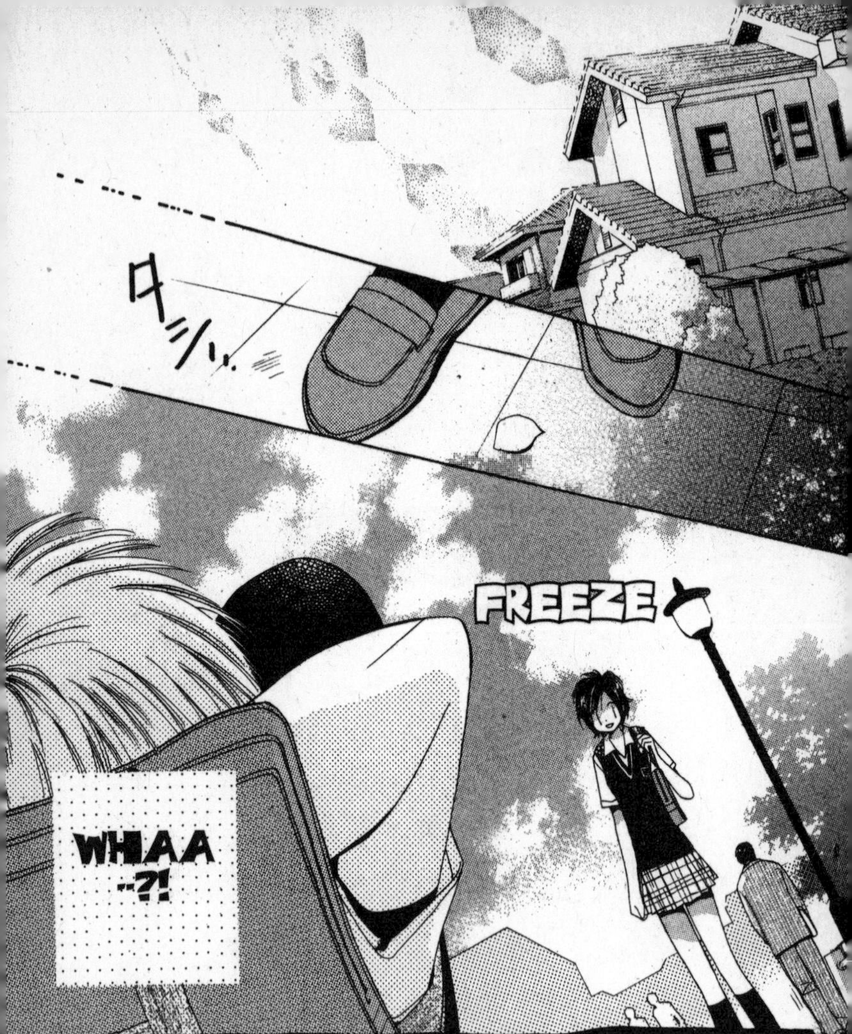
FREEZE
WHAA--?!

Please direct fan letters of love and adoration for Tachibana to:

Yutaka Tachibana
Hakusensha, *Melody* Editorial Department
2-2-2 Shinda Awaji-cho
Chiyoda-ku, Tokyo-to 101-0063 JAPAN

Crap! I only got to do two movie recommendations this time!

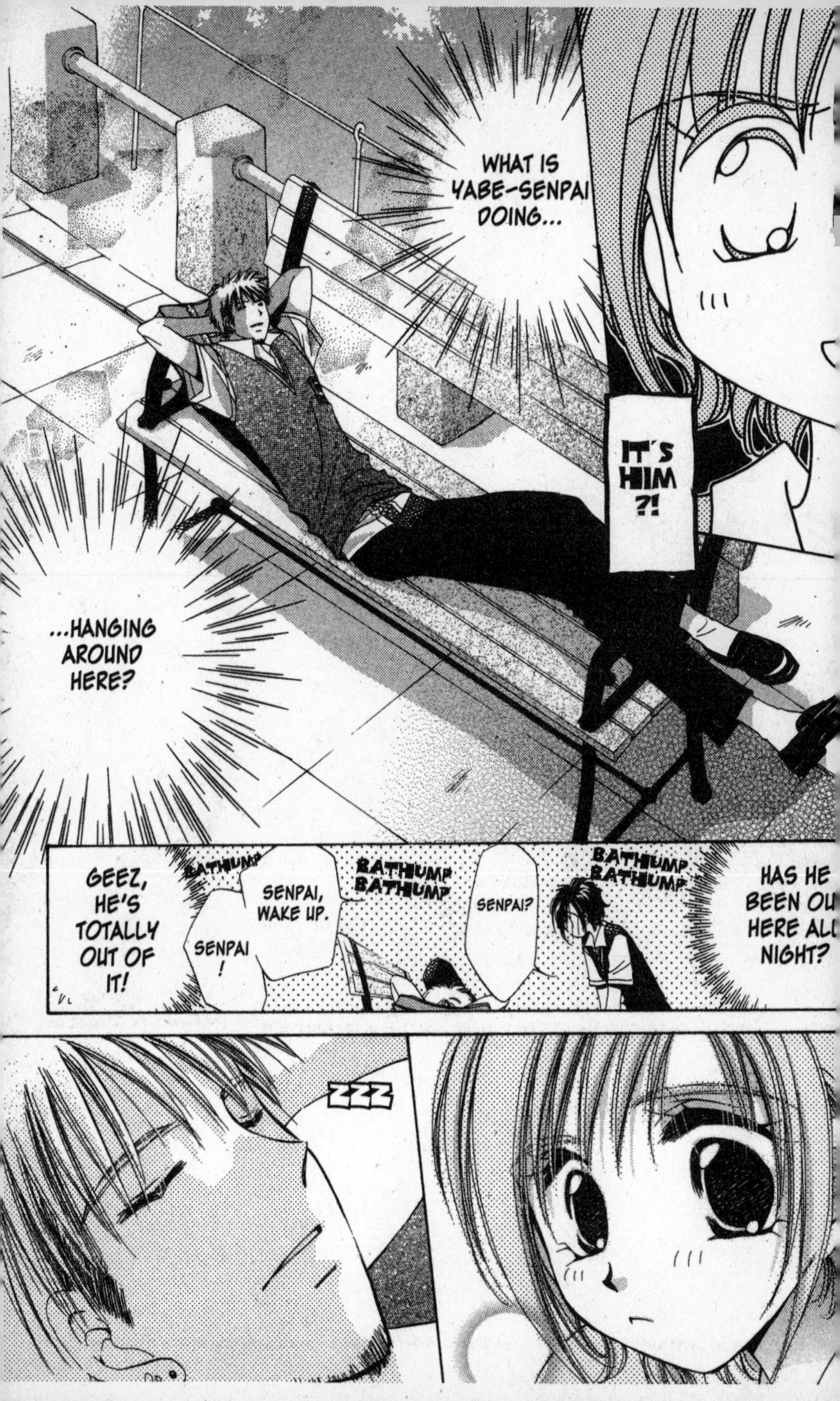
IT'S HIM ?!
WHAT IS YABE-SENPAI DOING...
...HANGING AROUND HERE?
HAS HE BEEN OU HERE ALL NIGHT?
BATHUMP BATHUMP
SENPAI?
BATHUMP BATHUMP
SENPAI, WAKE UP.
BATHUMP
SENPAI !
GEEZ, HE'S TOTALLY OUT OF IT!
ZZZ

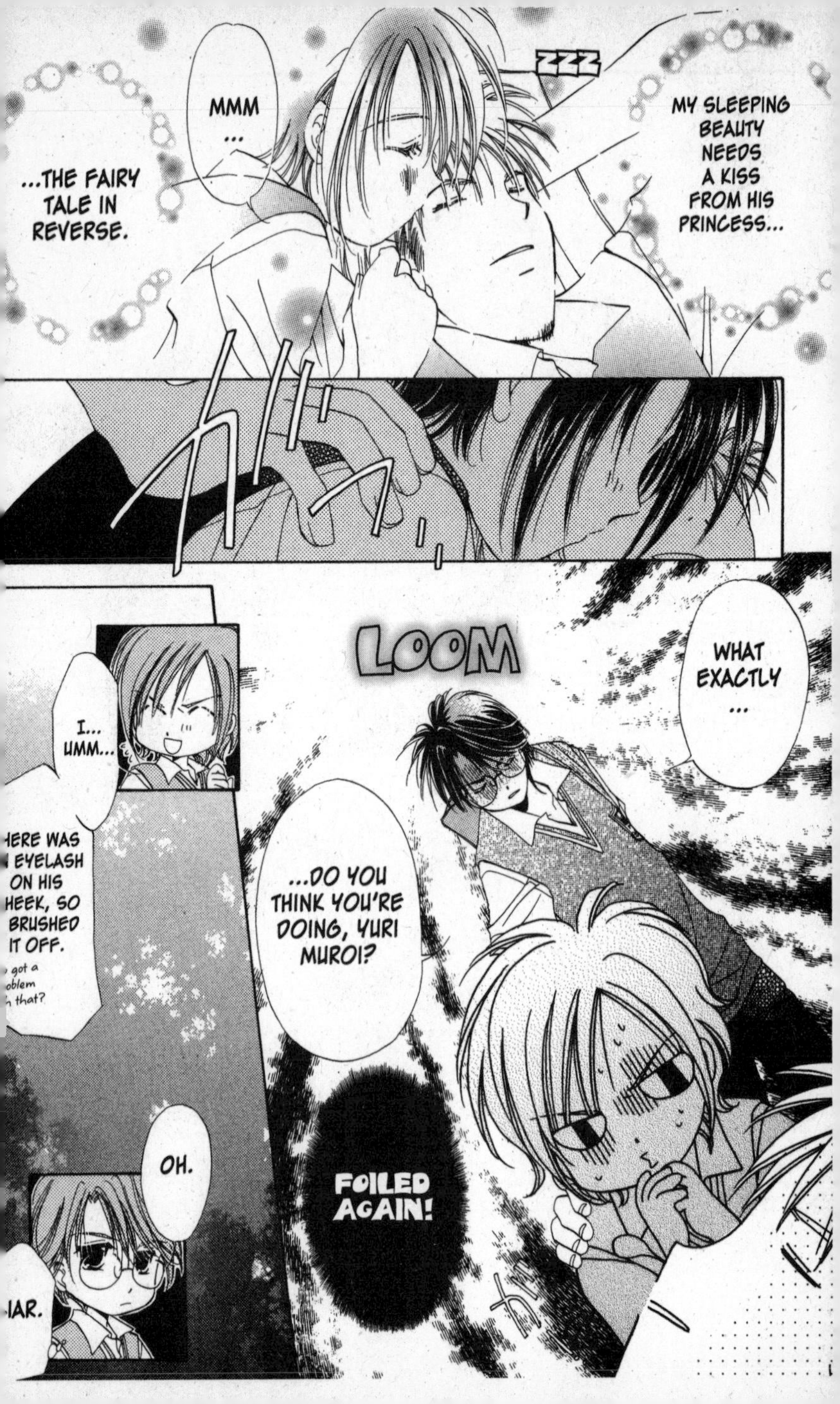
MY SLEEPING BEAUTY NEEDS A KISS FROM HIS PRINCESS...
ZZZ
MMM ...
...THE FAIRY TALE IN REVERSE.
LOOM
WHAT EXACTLY ...
...DO YOU THINK YOU'RE DOING, YURI MUROI?
FOILED AGAIN!
I... UMM...
HERE WAS EYELASH ON HIS HEEK, SO BRUSHED IT OFF.
got a oblem that?
OH.
IAR.

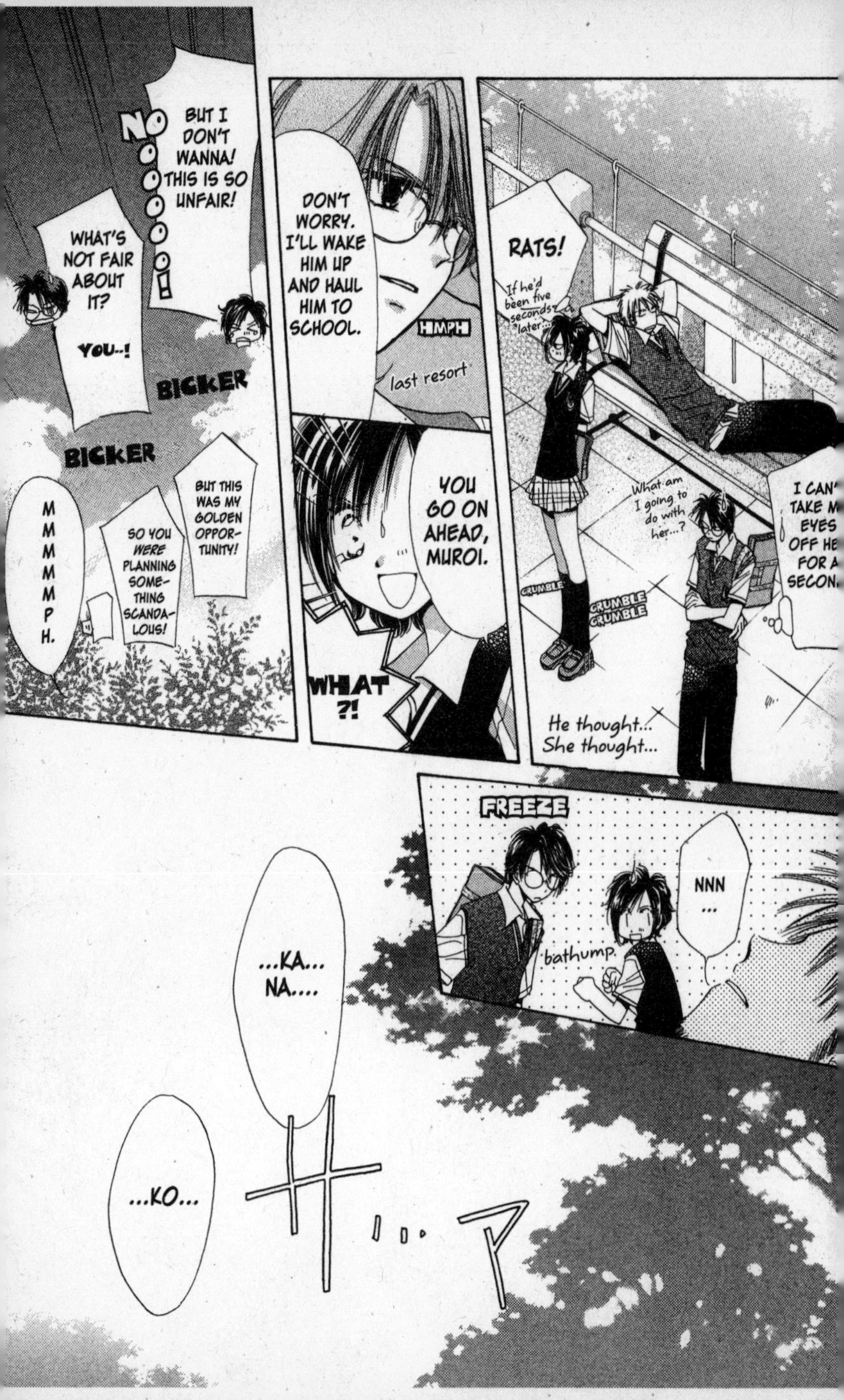
RATS!
If he'd been five seconds later...
What am I going to do with her...?
I CAN' TAKE M EYES OFF HE FOR A SECON
CRUMBLE
CRUMBLE CRUMBLE
He thought... She thought...
DON'T WORRY. I'LL WAKE HIM UP AND HAUL HIM TO SCHOOL.
HMPH
last resort
YOU GO ON AHEAD, MUROI.
WHAT ?!
NOOOOOOO!
BUT I DON'T WANNA! THIS IS SO UNFAIR!
WHAT'S NOT FAIR ABOUT IT?
YOU..!
BICKER
BICKER
BUT THIS WAS MY GOLDEN OPPORTUNITY!
SO YOU WERE PLANNING SOMETHING SCANDALOUS!
MMMMMMPH.
FREEZE
NNN ...
bathump
...KA... NA....
...KO...

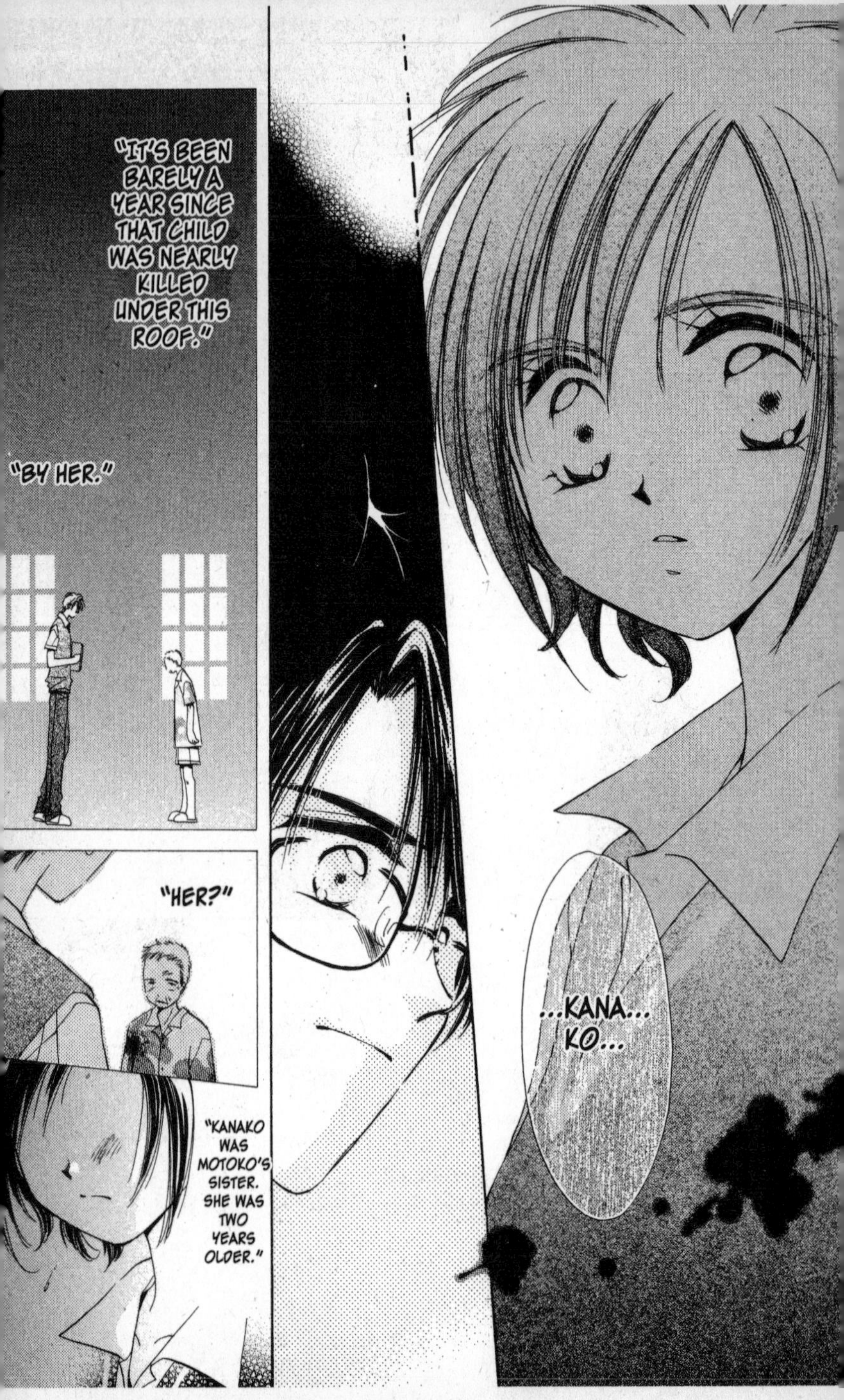
...KANA... KO...
"IT'S BEEN BARELY A YEAR SINCE THAT CHILD WAS NEARLY KILLED UNDER THIS ROOF."
"BY HER."
"HER?"
"KANAKO WAS MOTOKO'S SISTER. SHE WAS TWO YEARS OLDER."

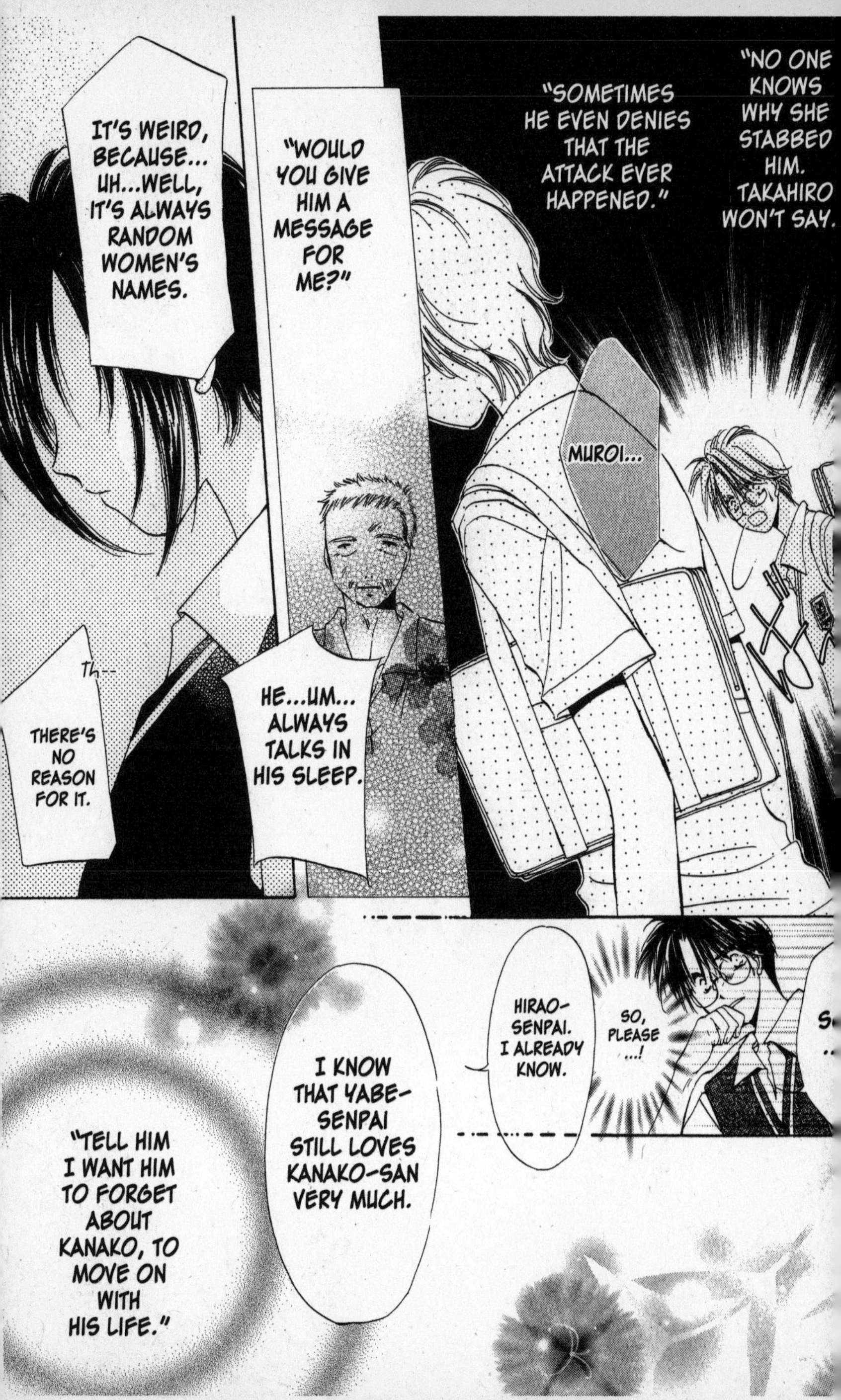
"NO ONE KNOWS WHY SHE STABBED HIM. TAKAHIRO WON'T SAY.
"SOMETIMES HE EVEN DENIES THAT THE ATTACK EVER HAPPENED."
MUROI...
"WOULD YOU GIVE HIM A MESSAGE FOR ME?"
HE...UM... ALWAYS TALKS IN HIS SLEEP.
IT'S WEIRD, BECAUSE... UH...WELL, IT'S ALWAYS RANDOM WOMEN'S NAMES.
Th--
THERE'S NO REASON FOR IT.
SO, PLEASE ...!
HIRAO-SENPAI. I ALREADY KNOW.
I KNOW THAT YABE-SENPAI STILL LOVES KANAKO-SAN VERY MUCH.
"TELL HIM I WANT HIM TO FORGET ABOUT KANAKO, TO MOVE ON WITH HIS LIFE."

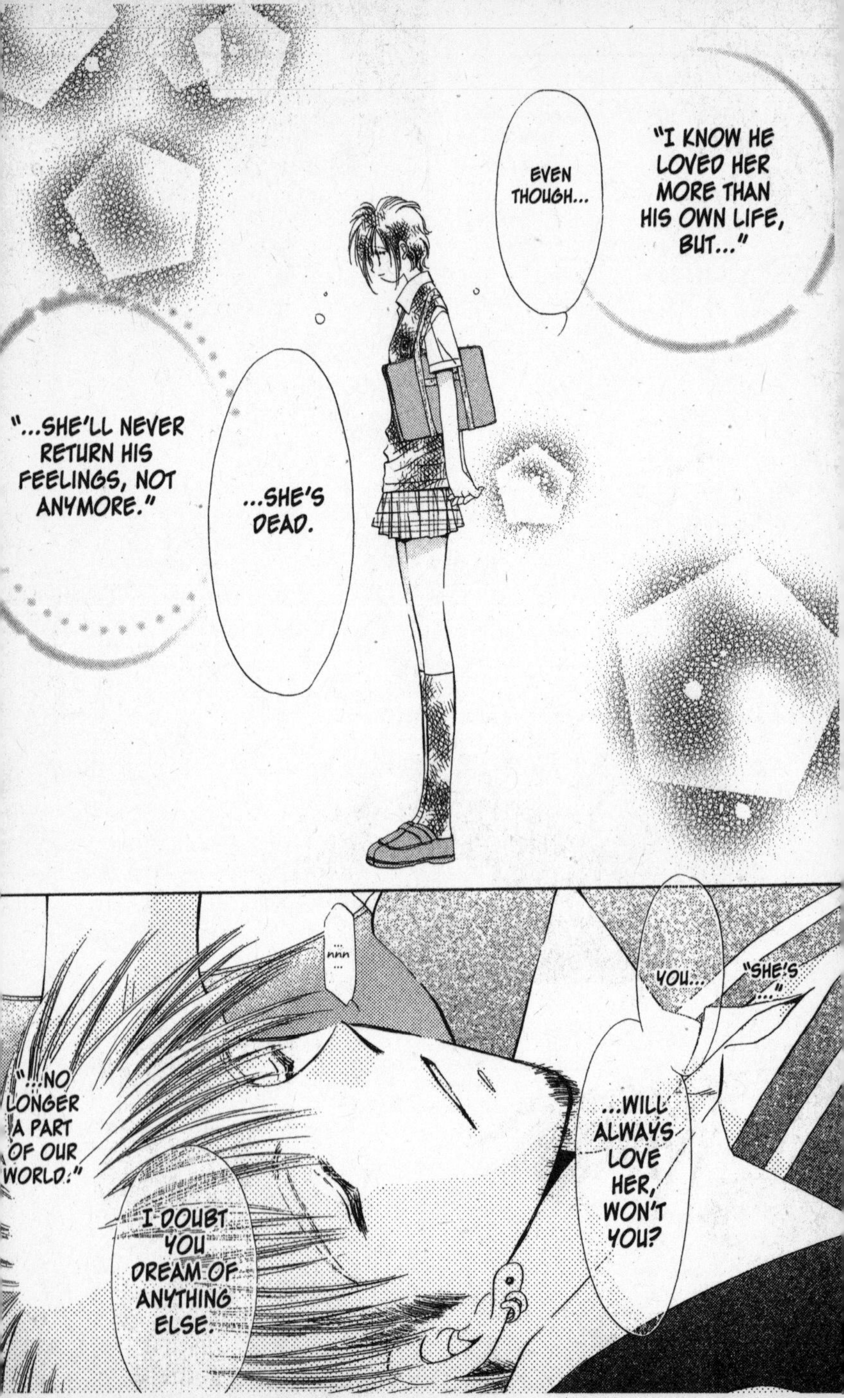
"I KNOW HE LOVED HER MORE THAN HIS OWN LIFE, BUT..."
EVEN THOUGH...
...SHE'S DEAD.
"...SHE'LL NEVER RETURN HIS FEELINGS, NOT ANYMORE."
"SHE'S ...."
YOU...
...WILL ALWAYS LOVE HER, WON'T YOU?
...nnn...
"...NO LONGER A PART OF OUR WORLD."
I DOUBT YOU DREAM OF ANYTHING ELSE.

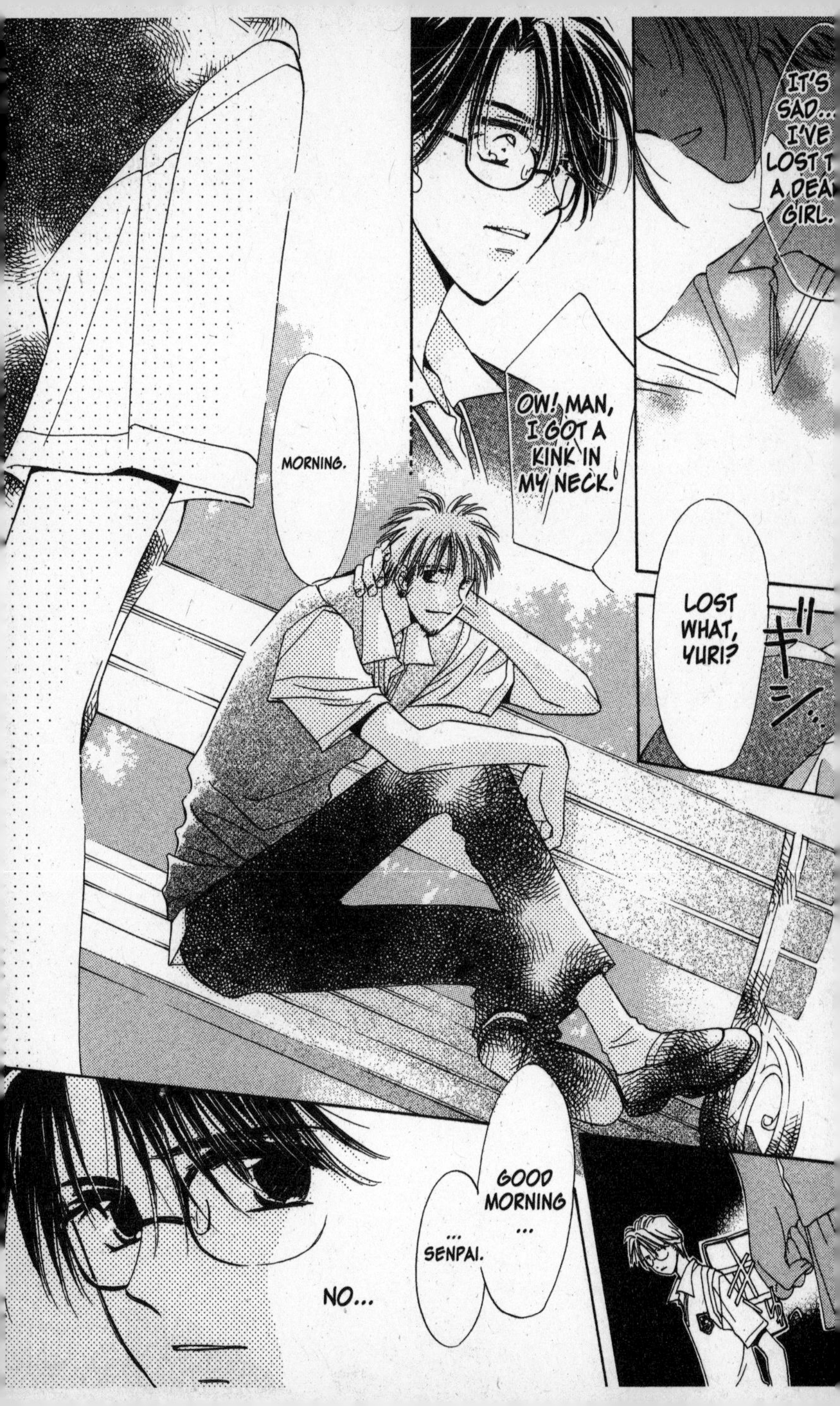
IT'S SAD... I'VE LOST T A DEA GIRL.
LOST WHAT, YURI?
ギシ…
OW! MAN, I GOT A KINK IN MY NECK.
MORNING.
GOOD MORNING ... ... SENPAI.
NO...

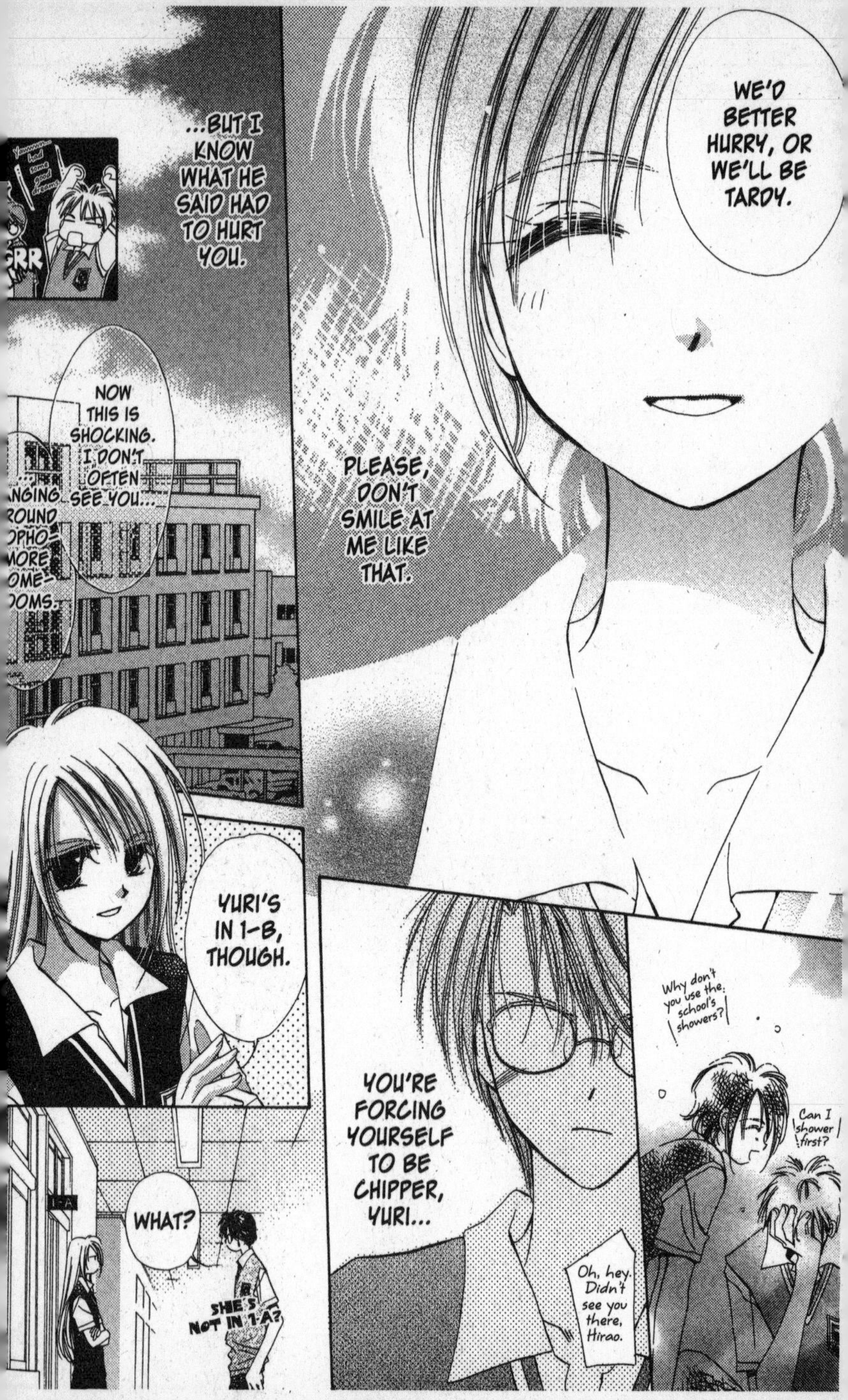
WE'D BETTER HURRY, OR WE'LL BE TARDY.
PLEASE, DON'T SMILE AT ME LIKE THAT.
...BUT I KNOW WHAT HE SAID HAD TO HURT YOU.
Yawwwn... had some good dreams
GRR
NOW THIS IS SHOCKING. I DON'T OFTEN SEE YOU...
...ANGING ROUND OPHO-MORE OME-OOMS.
YURI'S IN 1-B, THOUGH.
WHAT?
1-A
SHE'S NOT IN 1-A?
Can I shower first?
Why don't you use the school's showers?
Oh, hey. Didn't see you there, Hirao.
YOU'RE FORCING YOURSELF TO BE CHIPPER, YURI...

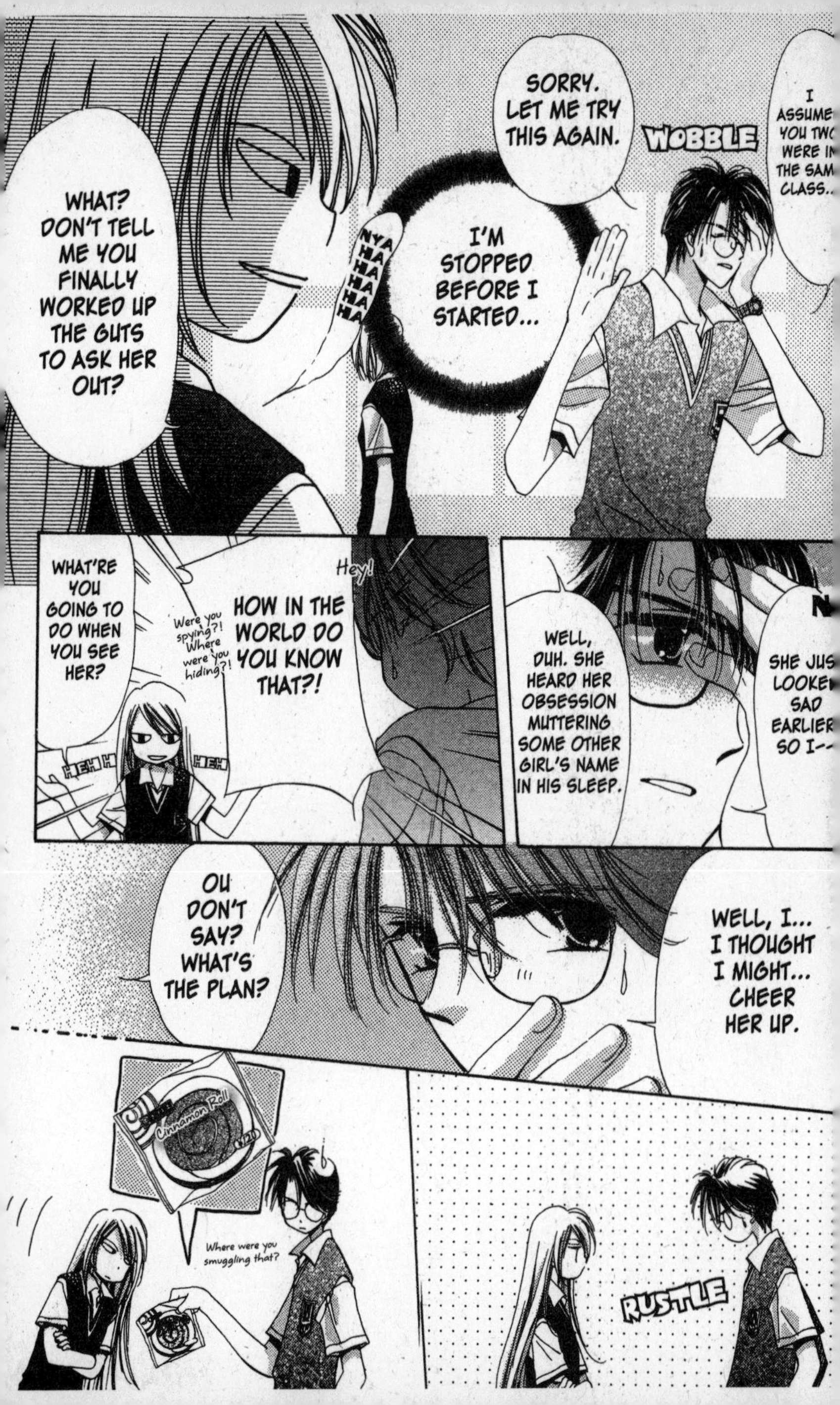
I ASSUME YOU TWO WERE IN THE SAM CLASS..
WOBBLE
SORRY. LET ME TRY THIS AGAIN.
I'M STOPPED BEFORE I STARTED...
NYA HA HA HA HA HA HA
WHAT? DON'T TELL ME YOU FINALLY WORKED UP THE GUTS TO ASK HER OUT?
SHE JUS LOOKE SAD EARLIER SO I--
WELL, DUH. SHE HEARD HER OBSESSION MUTTERING SOME OTHER GIRL'S NAME IN HIS SLEEP.
Hey!
HOW IN THE WORLD DO YOU KNOW THAT?!
Were you spying?! Where were you hiding?!
WHAT'RE YOU GOING TO DO WHEN YOU SEE HER?
HEH HEH
WELL, I... I THOUGHT I MIGHT... CHEER HER UP.
OU DON'T SAY? WHAT'S THE PLAN?
RUSTLE
Cinnamon Roll
Where were you smuggling that?

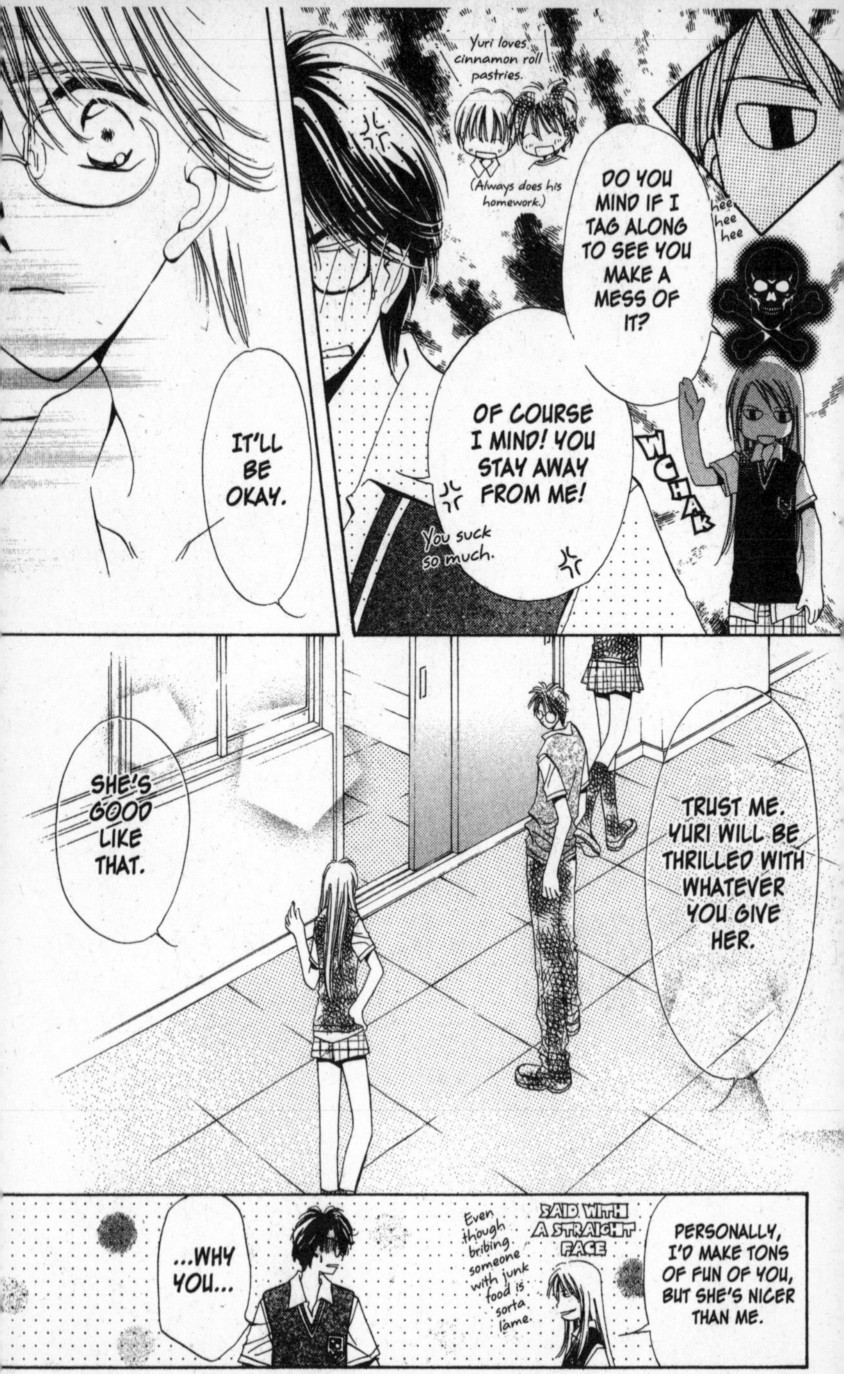
DO YOU MIND IF I TAG ALONG TO SEE YOU MAKE A MESS OF IT?
hee hee hee
Yuri loves cinnamon roll pastries.
(Always does his homework.)
WCHAK
OF COURSE I MIND! YOU STAY AWAY FROM ME!
You suck so much.
IT'LL BE OKAY.
TRUST ME. YURI WILL BE THRILLED WITH WHATEVER YOU GIVE HER.
SHE'S GOOD LIKE THAT.
PERSONALLY, I'D MAKE TONS OF FUN OF YOU, BUT SHE'S NICER THAN ME.
SAID WITH A STRAIGHT FACE
Even though bribing someone with junk food is sorta lame.
...WHY YOU...

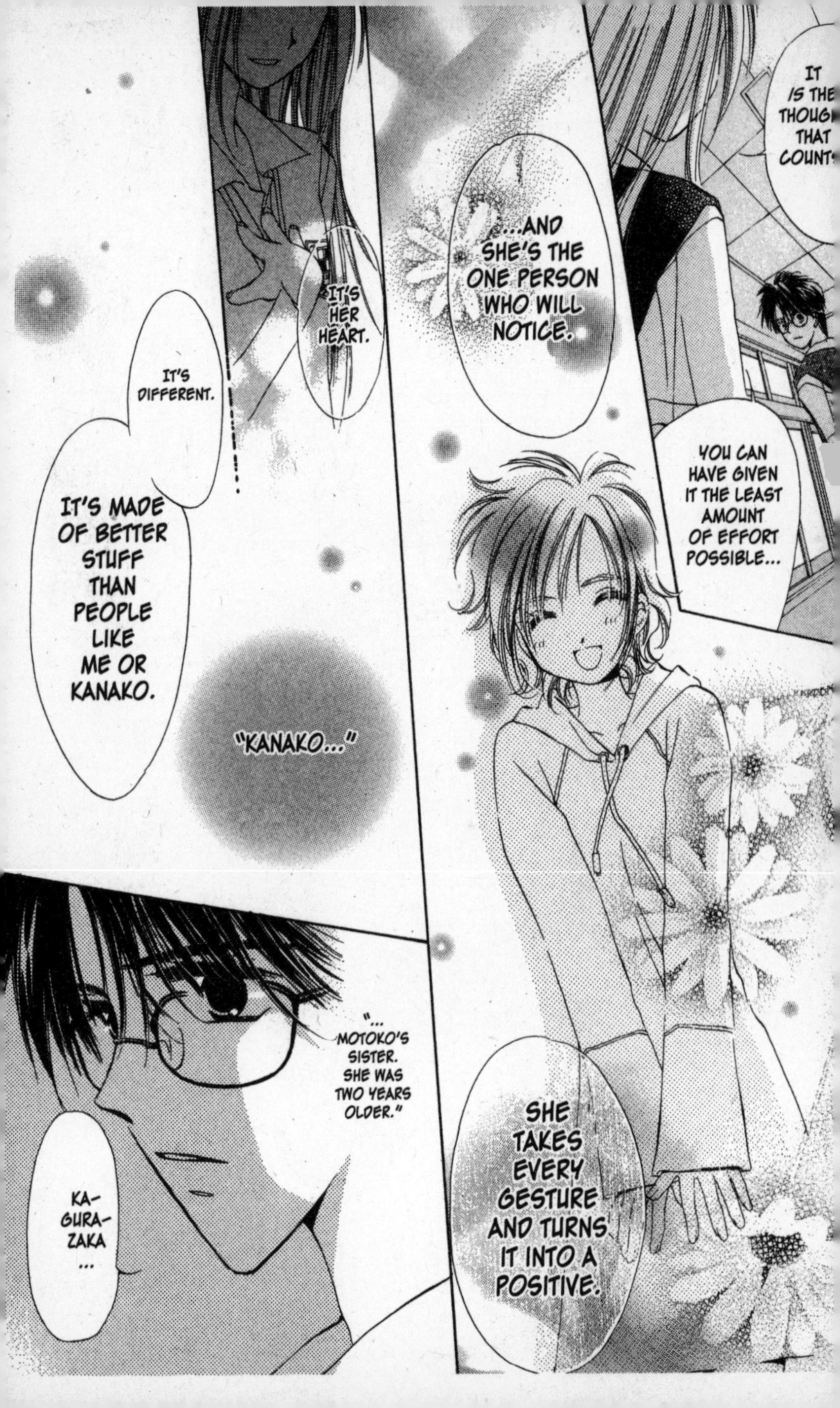
IT IS THE THOUG THAT COUNT
YOU CAN HAVE GIVEN IT THE LEAST AMOUNT OF EFFORT POSSIBLE...
...AND SHE'S THE ONE PERSON WHO WILL NOTICE.
SHE TAKES EVERY GESTURE AND TURNS IT INTO A POSITIVE.
IT'S HER HEART.
IT'S DIFFERENT.
IT'S MADE OF BETTER STUFF THAN PEOPLE LIKE ME OR KANAKO.
"KANAKO..."
"...MOTOKO'S SISTER. SHE WAS TWO YEARS OLDER."
KA-GURA-ZAKA ...

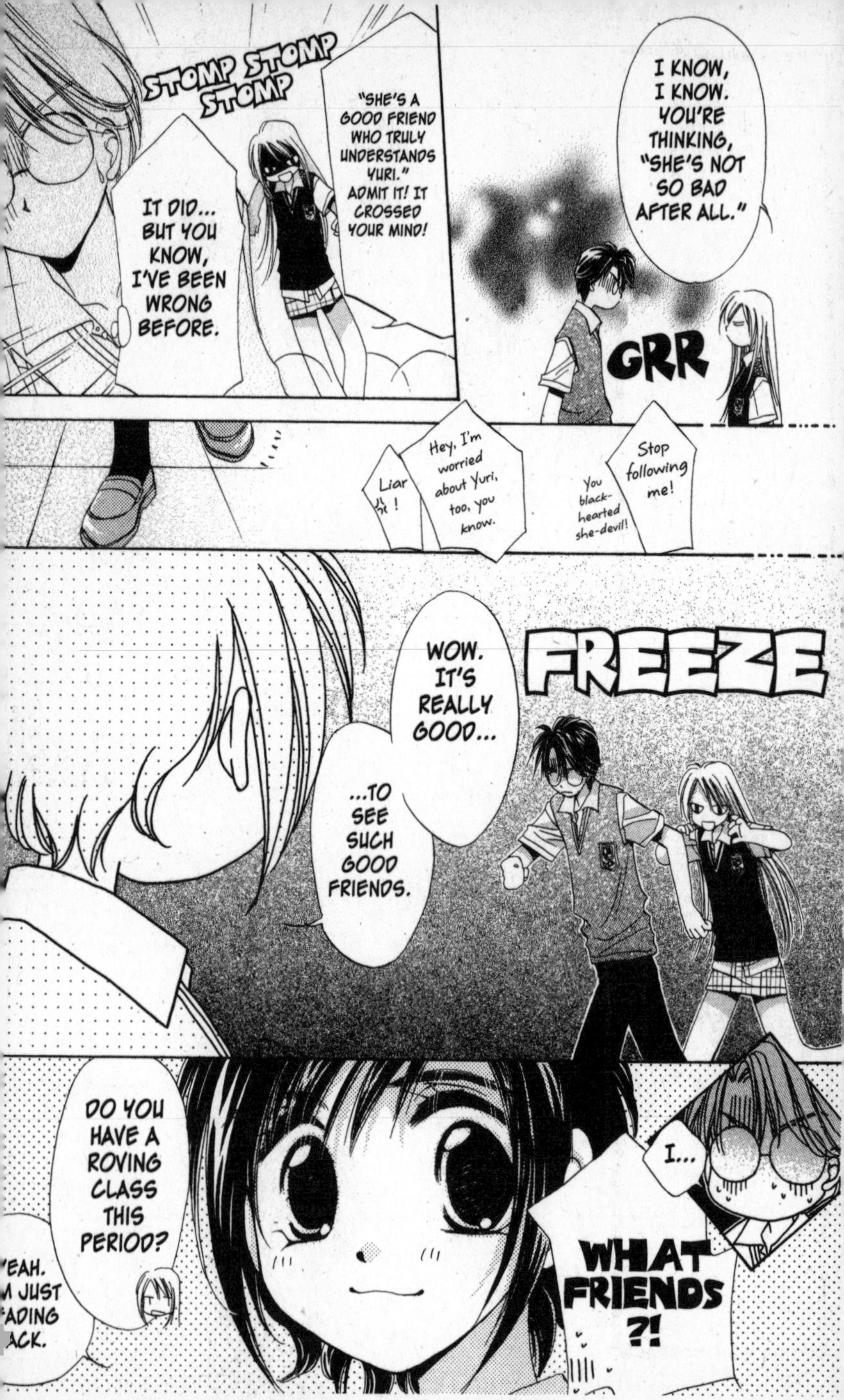

I KNOW, I KNOW. YOU'RE THINKING, "SHE'S NOT SO BAD AFTER ALL."
GRR
STOMP STOMP STOMP
"SHE'S A GOOD FRIEND WHO TRULY UNDERSTANDS YURI." ADMIT IT! IT CROSSED YOUR MIND!
IT DID... BUT YOU KNOW, I'VE BEEN WRONG BEFORE.
Stop following me!
You black-hearted she-devil!
Hey, I'm worried about Yuri, too, you know.
Liar!
FREEZE
WOW. IT'S REALLY GOOD...
...TO SEE SUCH GOOD FRIENDS.
I...
WHAT FRIENDS?!
DO YOU HAVE A ROVING CLASS THIS PERIOD?
EAH. M JUST EADING ACK.

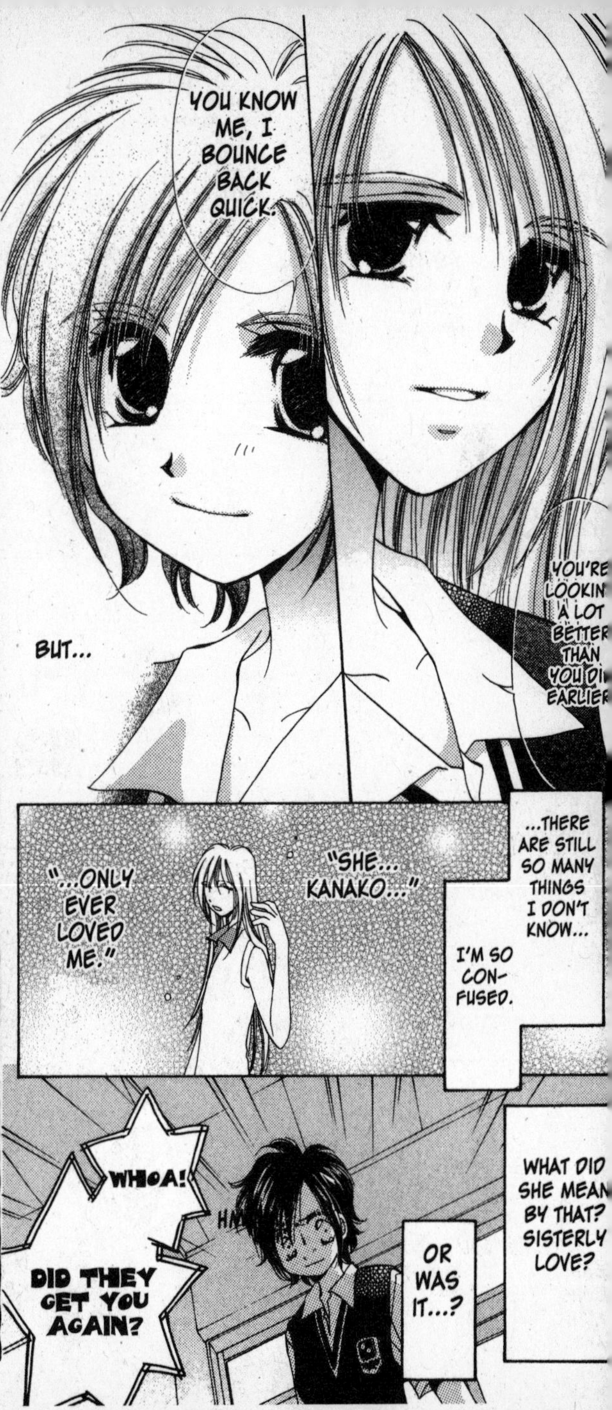
YOU'RE LOOKIN' A LOT BETTER THAN YOU DID EARLIER
YOU KNOW ME, I BOUNCE BACK QUICK.
BUT...
...THERE ARE STILL SO MANY THINGS I DON'T KNOW...
I'M SO CONFUSED.
"SHE... KANAKO..."
"...ONLY EVER LOVED ME."
WHAT DID SHE MEAN BY THAT? SISTERLY LOVE?
OR WAS IT...?
HM
WHOA!
DID THEY GET YOU AGAIN?

Not that this really bothers me or anything, but some people have pointed out that my characters' names are often pretty ugly or strangely similar to those of other characters in my other comics. "You have no affection for your own creations!" they say.

(My Evil Assistant is especially fond of this.)

That's not true...I don't think so. No, wait, it isn't! Really! It's not that I have bad taste, or that I don't really care about names or using pretty kanji to make them. I think the main reason I give them bad names is because I'm stupid.

Sekine Tomoharu

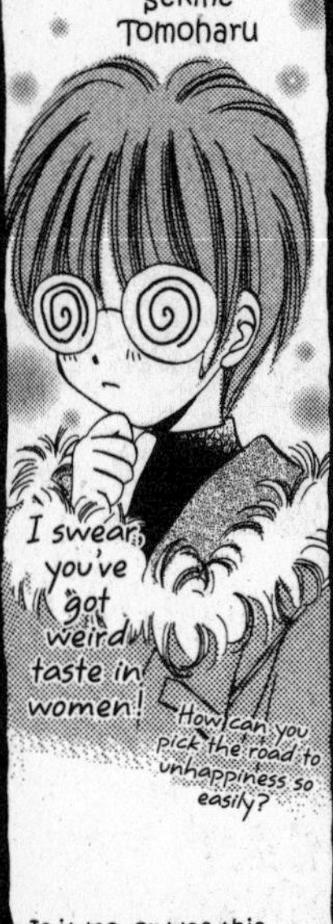
I swear, you've got weird taste in women!
How can you pick the road to unhappiness so easily?

Is it me, or was this FreeTalk kinda bland...?

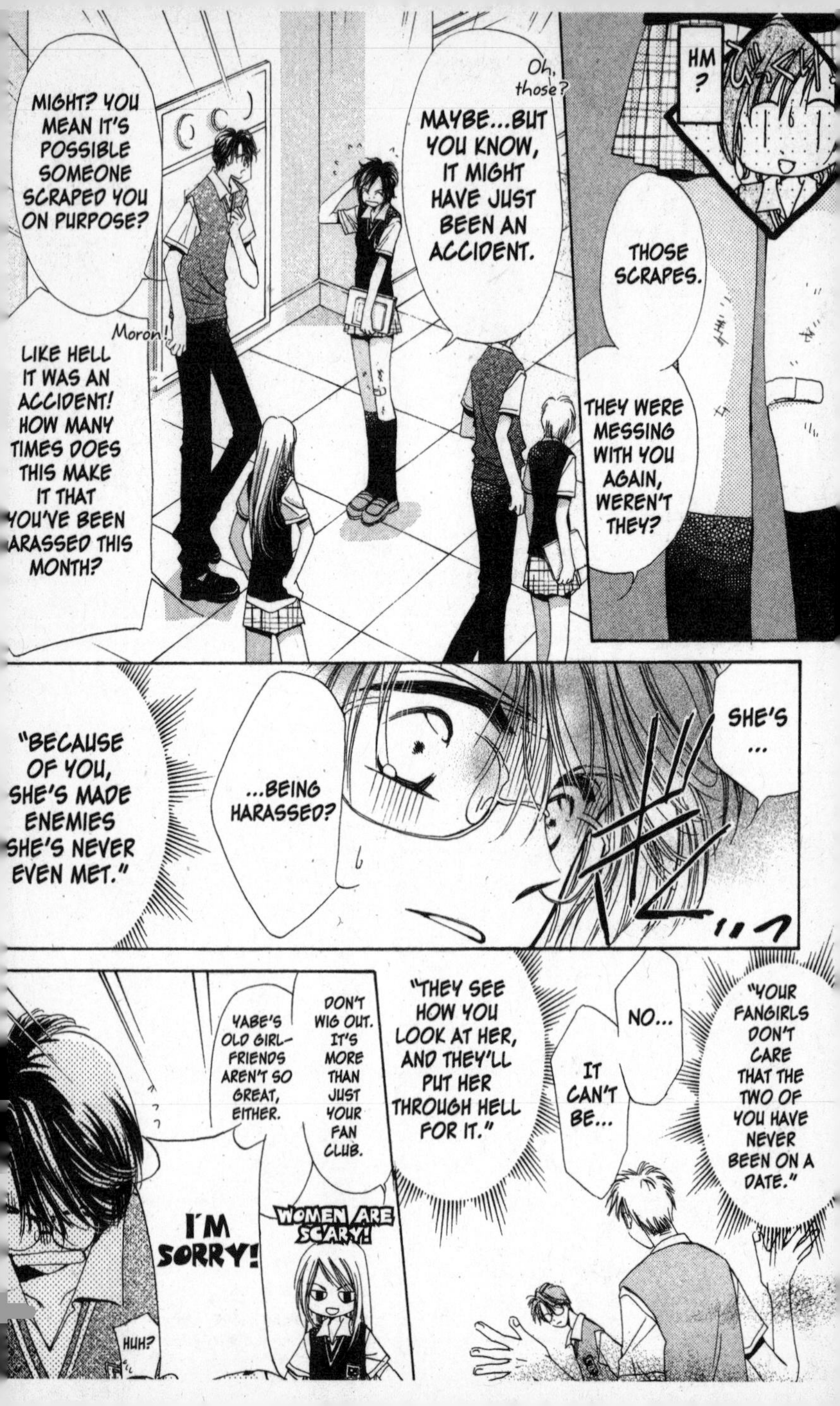
HM?
THOSE SCRAPES.
THEY WERE MESSING WITH YOU AGAIN, WEREN'T THEY?
Oh, those?
MAYBE...BUT YOU KNOW, IT MIGHT HAVE JUST BEEN AN ACCIDENT.
MIGHT? YOU MEAN IT'S POSSIBLE SOMEONE SCRAPED YOU ON PURPOSE?
Moron!
LIKE HELL IT WAS AN ACCIDENT! HOW MANY TIMES DOES THIS MAKE IT THAT YOU'VE BEEN ARASSED THIS MONTH?
SHE'S...
...BEING HARASSED?
"BECAUSE OF YOU, SHE'S MADE ENEMIES SHE'S NEVER EVEN MET."
"YOUR FANGIRLS DON'T CARE THAT THE TWO OF YOU HAVE NEVER BEEN ON A DATE."
NO...
IT CAN'T BE...
"THEY SEE HOW YOU LOOK AT HER, AND THEY'LL PUT HER THROUGH HELL FOR IT."
DON'T WIG OUT. IT'S MORE THAN JUST YOUR FAN CLUB.
YABE'S OLD GIRL-FRIENDS AREN'T SO GREAT, EITHER.
WOMEN ARE SCARY!
I'M SORRY!
HUH?

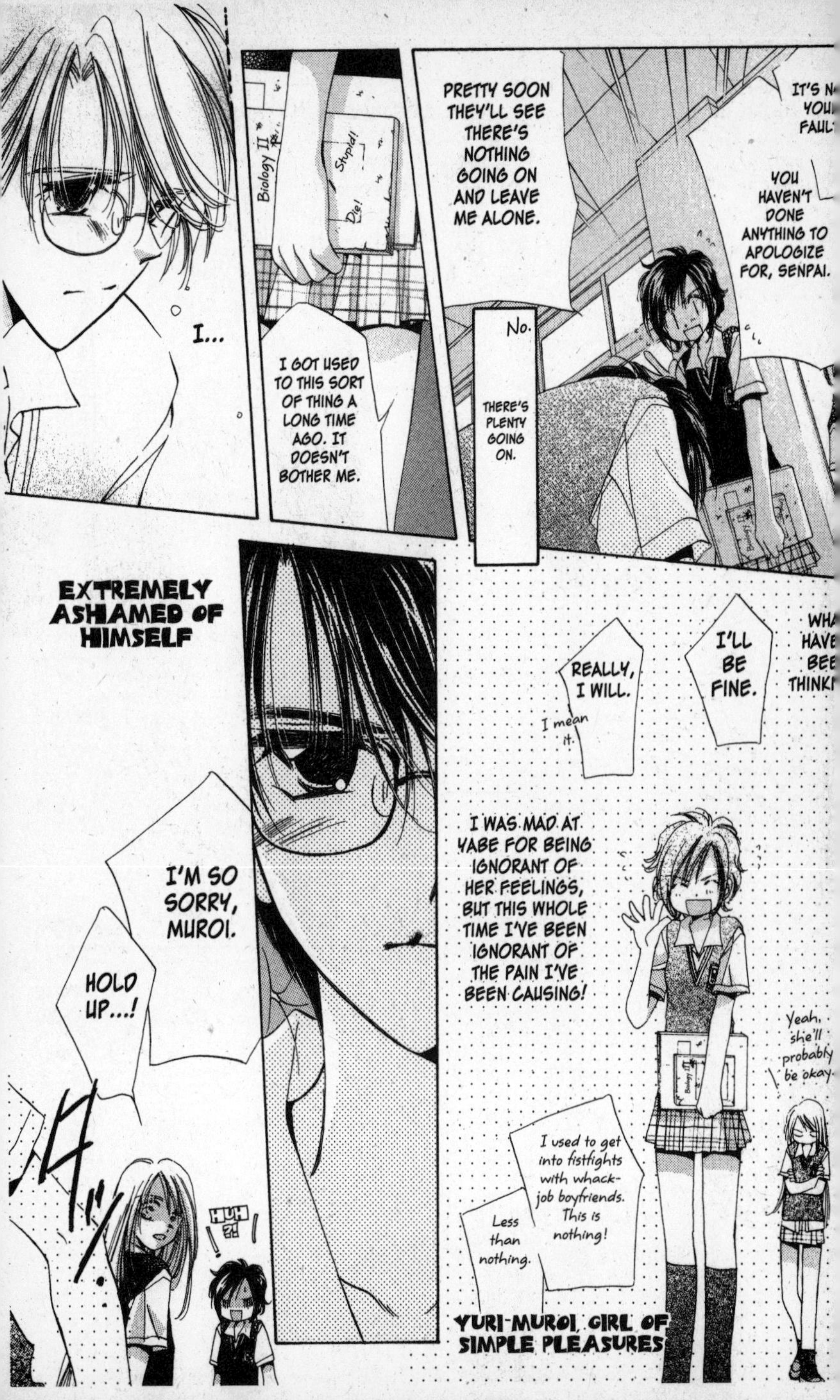
IT'S N YOU FAUL
YOU HAVEN'T DONE ANYTHING TO APOLOGIZE FOR, SENPAI.
PRETTY SOON THEY'LL SEE THERE'S NOTHING GOING ON AND LEAVE ME ALONE.
No.
THERE'S PLENTY GOING ON.
Biology II
Stupid!
Die!
I GOT USED TO THIS SORT OF THING A LONG TIME AGO. IT DOESN'T BOTHER ME.
I...
WHA HAVE BEE THINKI
I'LL BE FINE.
REALLY, I WILL.
I mean it.
I WAS MAD AT YABE FOR BEING IGNORANT OF HER FEELINGS, BUT THIS WHOLE TIME I'VE BEEN IGNORANT OF THE PAIN I'VE BEEN CAUSING!
Yeah, she'll probably be okay.
I used to get into fistfights with whack-job boyfriends. This is nothing!
Less than nothing.
YURI MUROI, GIRL OF SIMPLE PLEASURES
EXTREMELY ASHAMED OF HIMSELF
I'M SO SORRY, MUROI.
HOLD UP...!
HUH ?!

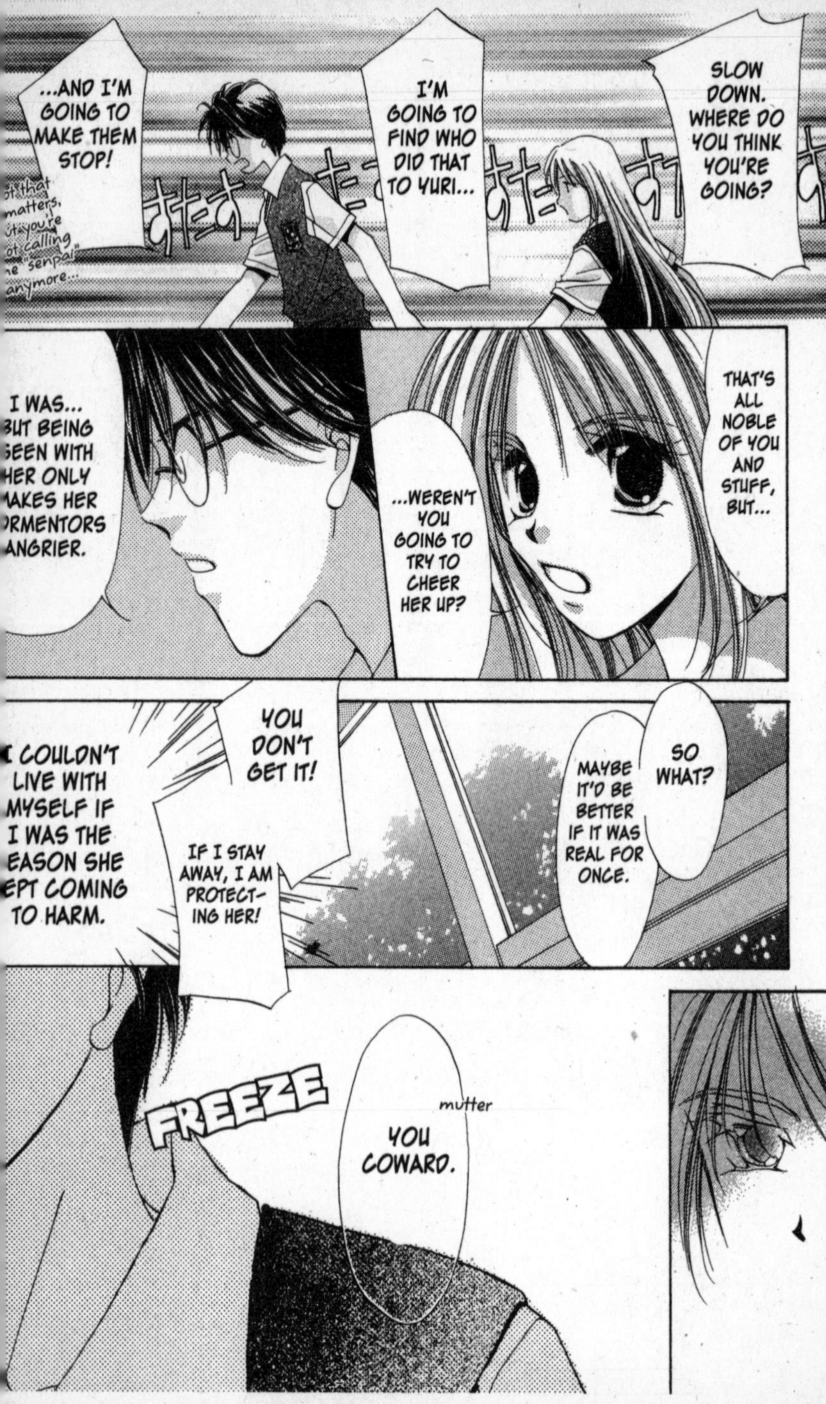
SLOW DOWN. WHERE DO YOU THINK YOU'RE GOING?
I'M GOING TO FIND WHO DID THAT TO YURI...
...AND I'M GOING TO MAKE THEM STOP!
matters, you're calling "senpai" anymore...
THAT'S ALL NOBLE OF YOU AND STUFF, BUT...
...WEREN'T YOU GOING TO TRY TO CHEER HER UP?
I WAS... HER ONLY ANGRIER.
SO WHAT?
MAYBE IT'D BE BETTER IF IT WAS REAL FOR ONCE.
YOU DON'T GET IT!
IF I STAY AWAY, I AM PROTECT-ING HER!
LIVE WITH MYSELF IF I WAS THE TO HARM.
FREEZE
mutter
YOU COWARD.

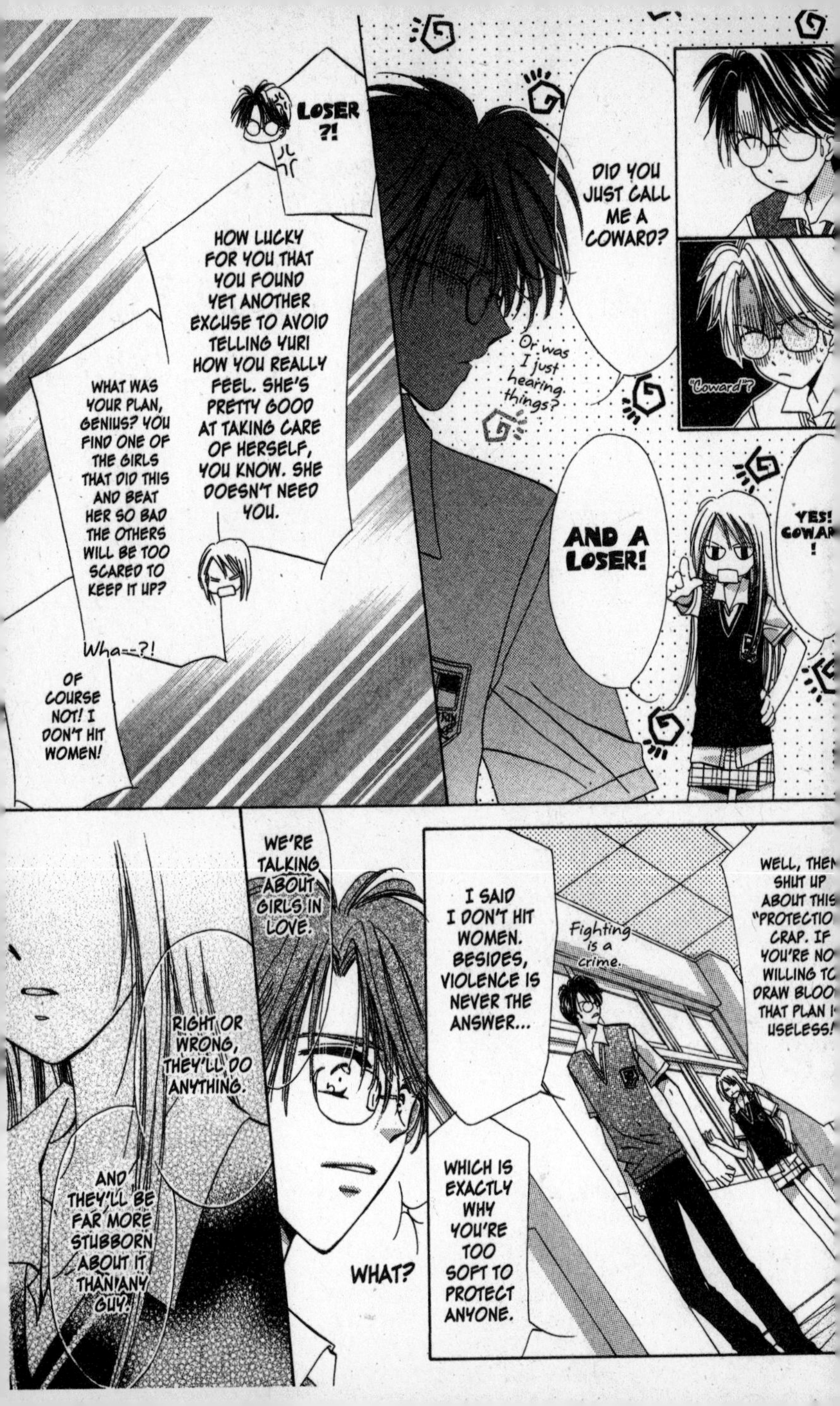
DID YOU JUST CALL ME A COWARD?
Or was I just hearing things?
"Coward"?
YES! COWAR !
AND A LOSER!
LOSER ?!
HOW LUCKY FOR YOU THAT YOU FOUND YET ANOTHER EXCUSE TO AVOID TELLING YURI HOW YOU REALLY FEEL. SHE'S PRETTY GOOD AT TAKING CARE OF HERSELF, YOU KNOW. SHE DOESN'T NEED YOU.
WHAT WAS YOUR PLAN, GENIUS? YOU FIND ONE OF THE GIRLS THAT DID THIS AND BEAT HER SO BAD THE OTHERS WILL BE TOO SCARED TO KEEP IT UP?
Wha--?!
OF COURSE NOT! I DON'T HIT WOMEN!
WELL, THEN SHUT UP ABOUT THIS "PROTECTIO CRAP. IF YOU'RE NO WILLING TO DRAW BLOO THAT PLAN I USELESS!
I SAID I DON'T HIT WOMEN. BESIDES, VIOLENCE IS NEVER THE ANSWER...
Fighting is a crime.
WHICH IS EXACTLY WHY YOU'RE TOO SOFT TO PROTECT ANYONE.
WHAT?
WE'RE TALKING ABOUT GIRLS IN LOVE.
RIGHT OR WRONG, THEY'LL DO ANYTHING.
AND THEY'LL BE FAR MORE STUBBORN ABOUT IT THAN ANY GUY!

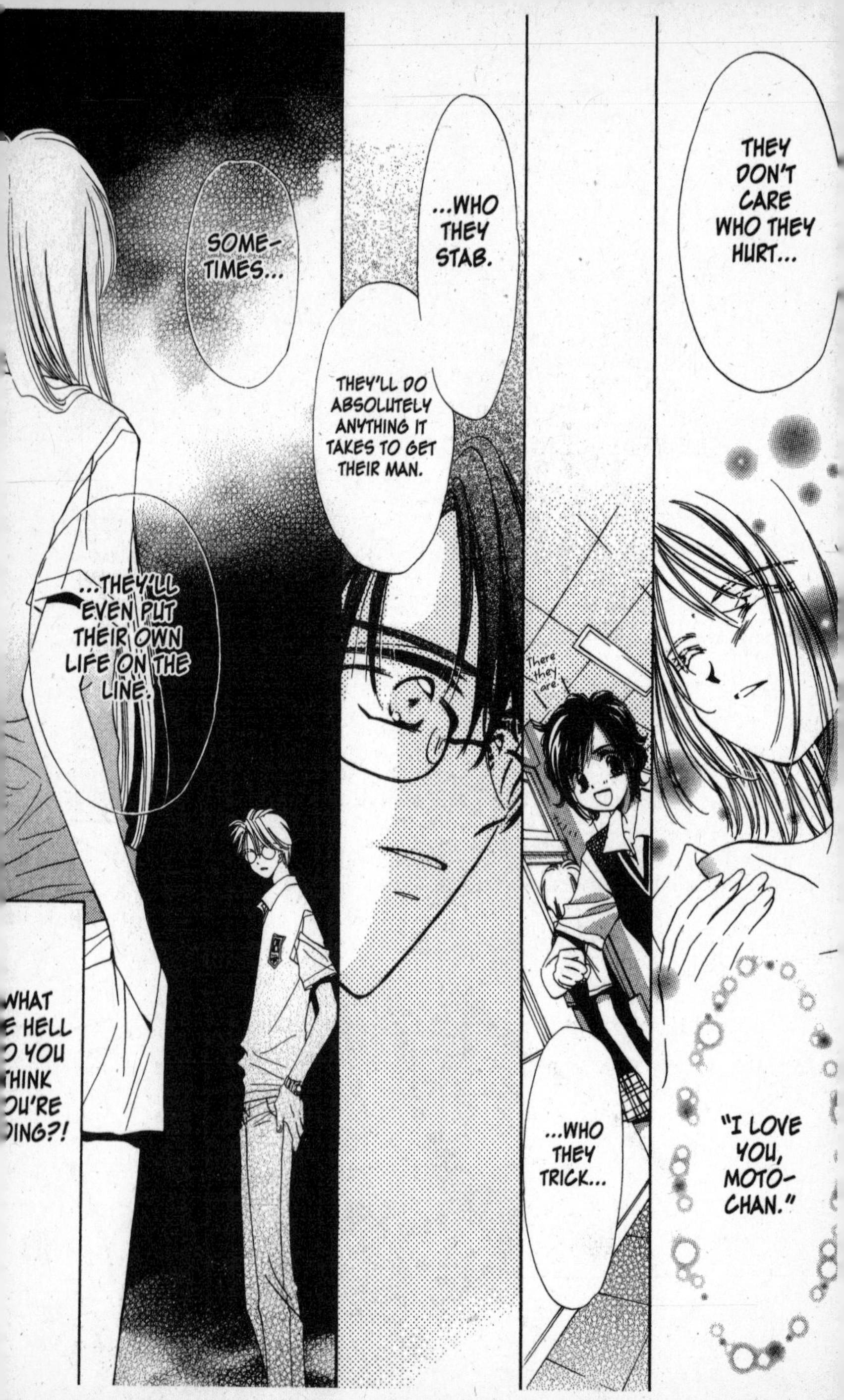

THEY DON'T CARE WHO THEY HURT...
"I LOVE YOU, MOTO-CHAN."
There they are
...WHO THEY TRICK...
...WHO THEY STAB.
THEY'LL DO ABSOLUTELY ANYTHING IT TAKES TO GET THEIR MAN.
SOME-TIMES...
...THEY'LL EVEN PUT THEIR OWN LIFE ON THE LINE.
WHAT E HELL O YOU THINK OU'RE OING?!

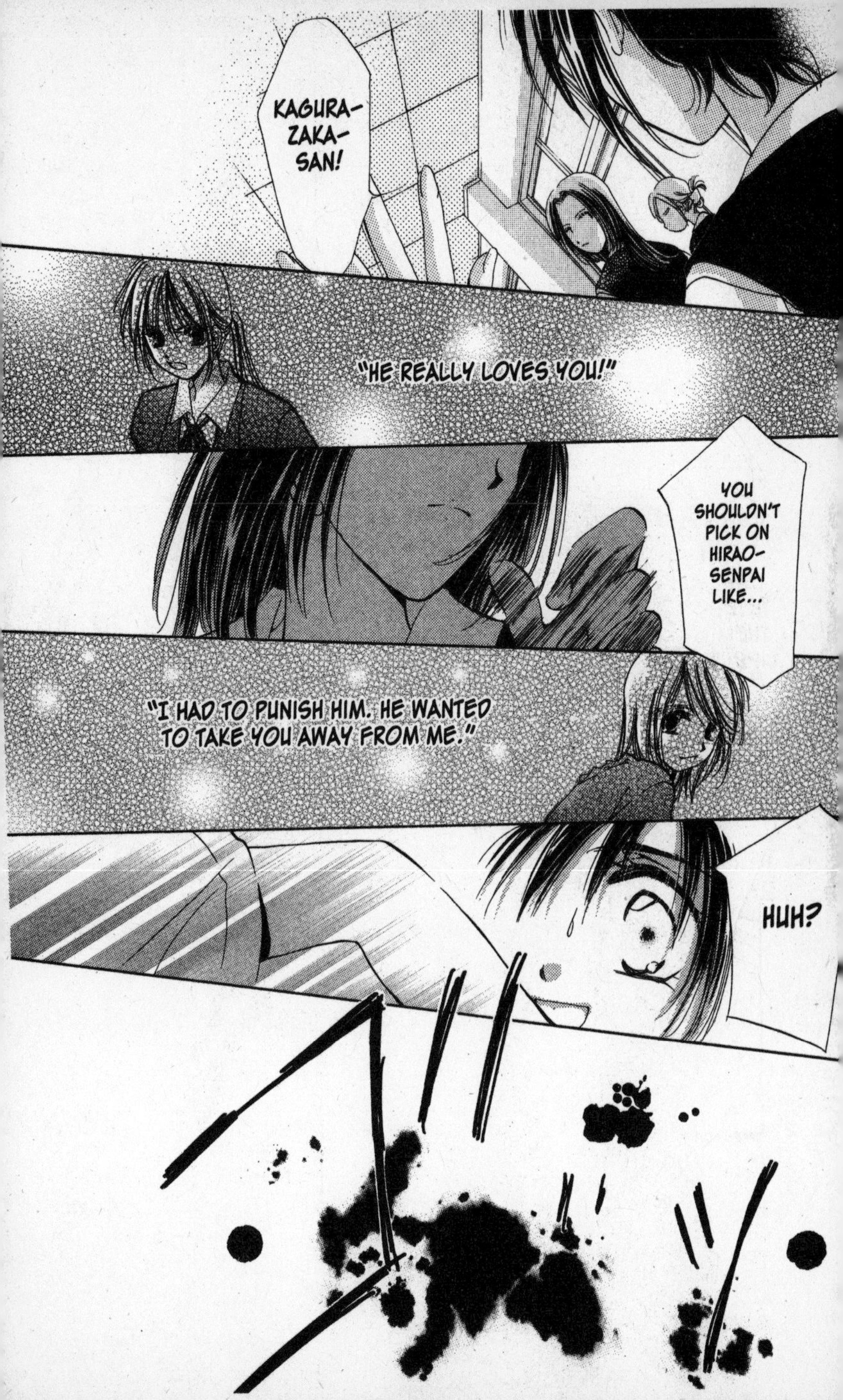
KAGURA-ZAKA-SAN!
"HE REALLY LOVES YOU!"
YOU SHOULDN'T PICK ON HIRAO-SENPAI LIKE...
"I HAD TO PUNISH HIM. HE WANTED TO TAKE YOU AWAY FROM ME."
HUH?

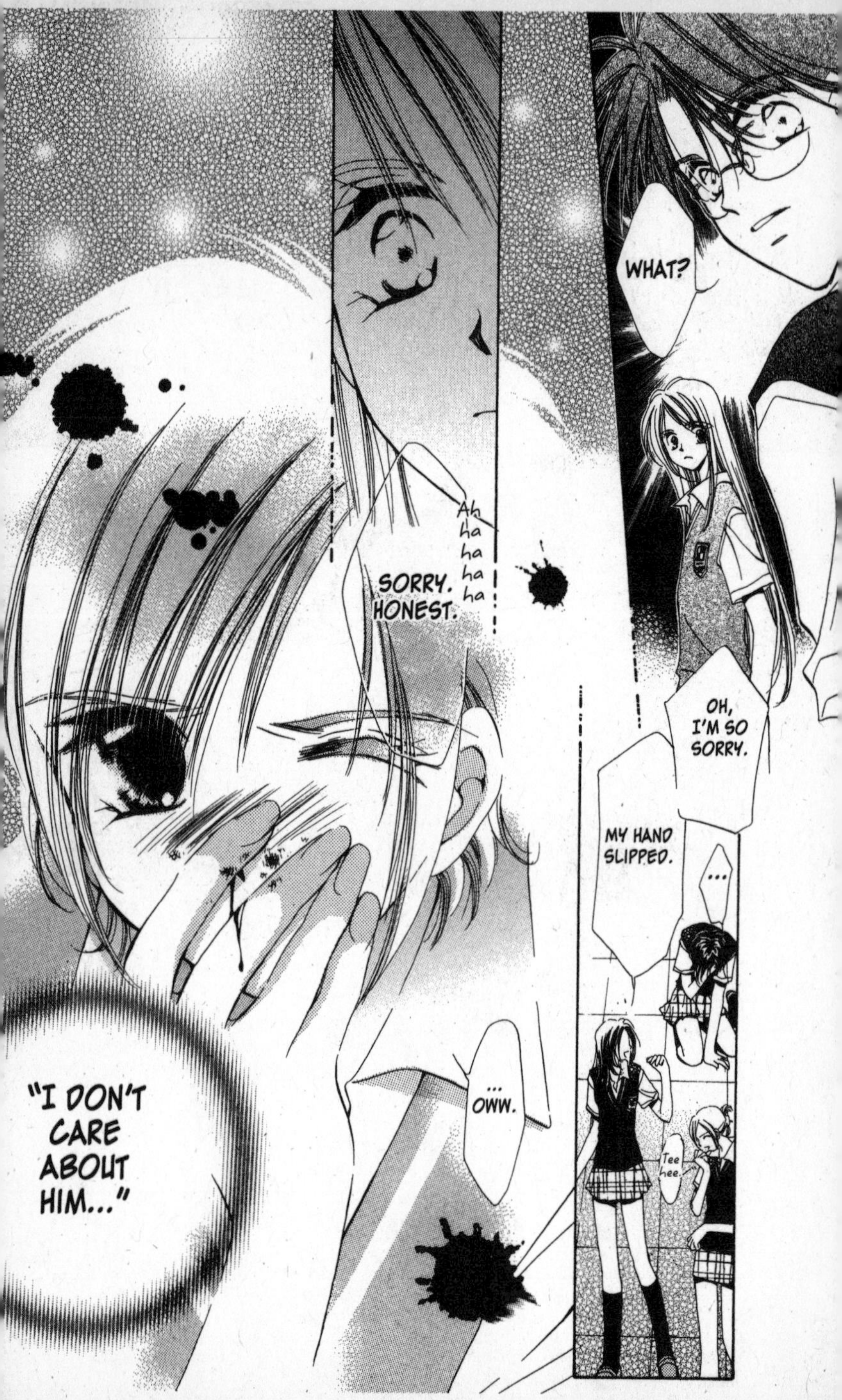
WHAT?
OH, I'M SO SORRY.
MY HAND SLIPPED.
...
Tee hee.
Ah ha ha ha ha
SORRY. HONEST.
... OWW.
"I DON'T CARE ABOUT HIM..."

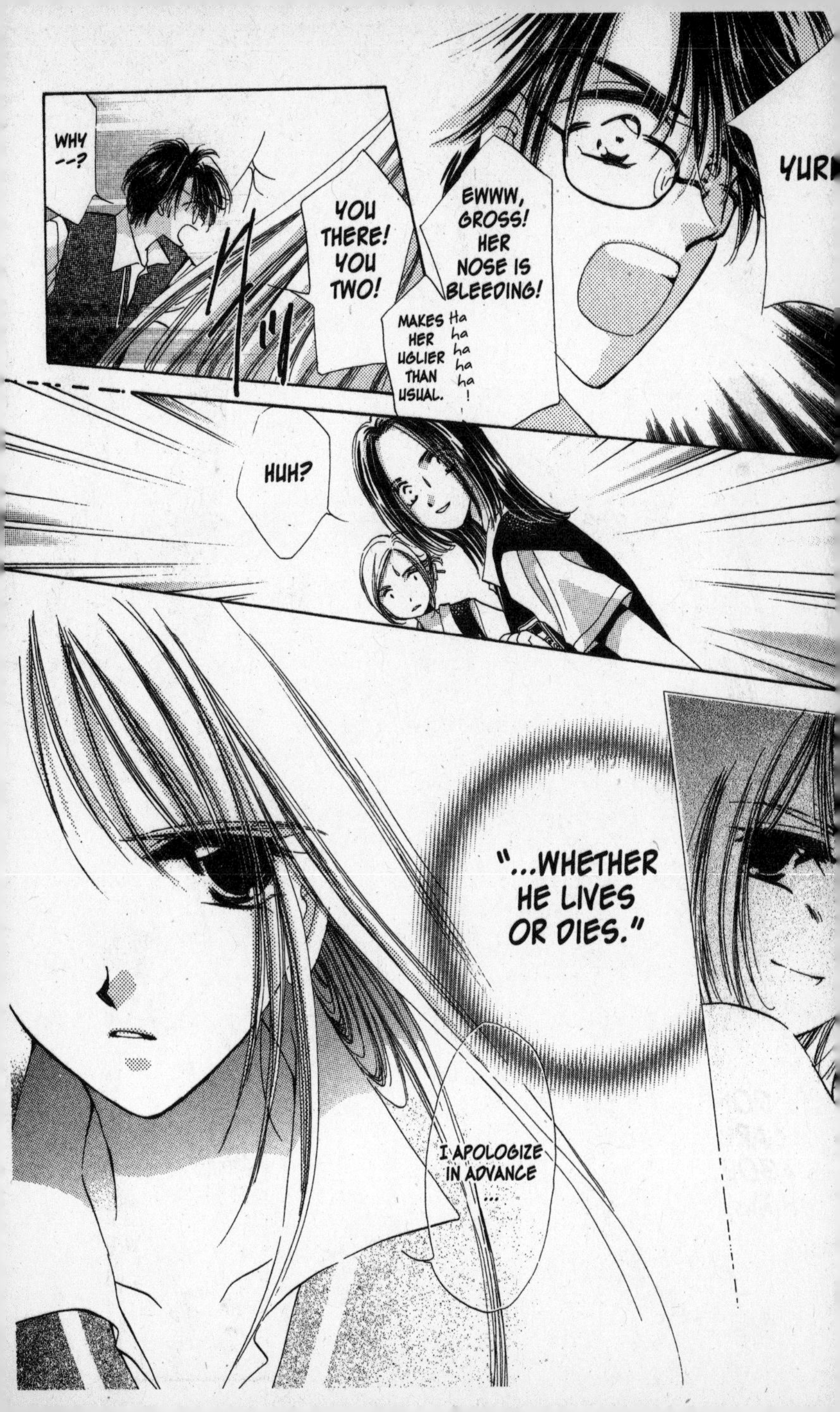
YURI
EWWW, GROSS! HER NOSE IS BLEEDING!
MAKES HER UGLIER THAN USUAL.
Ha ha ha ha ha!
YOU THERE! YOU TWO!
WHY --?
HUH?
"...WHETHER HE LIVES OR DIES."
I APOLOGIZE IN ADVANCE ...

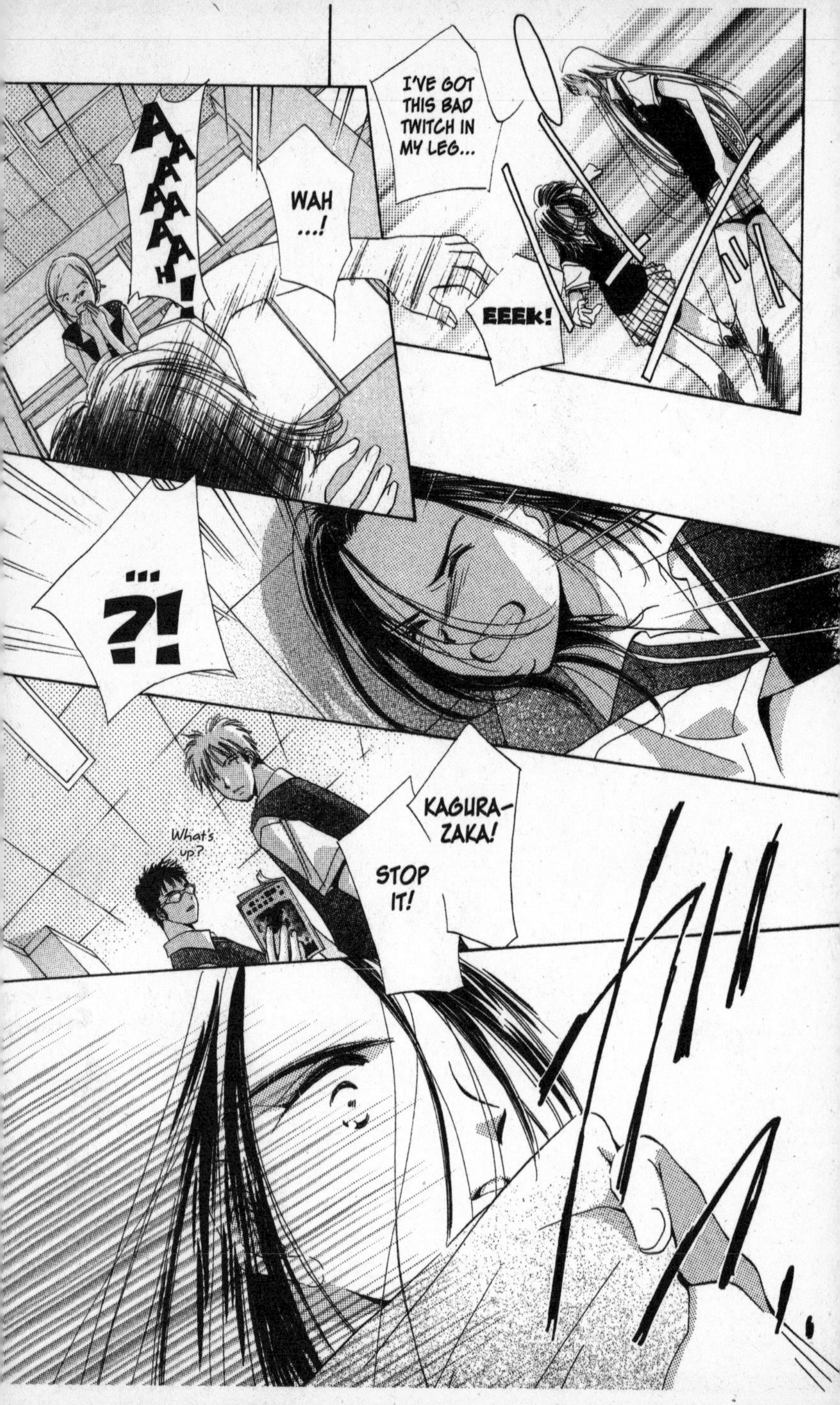
I'VE GOT THIS BAD TWITCH IN MY LEG...
EEEK!
WAH ...!
AAAAAAH!
...?!
KAGURA-ZAKA!
STOP IT!
What's up?

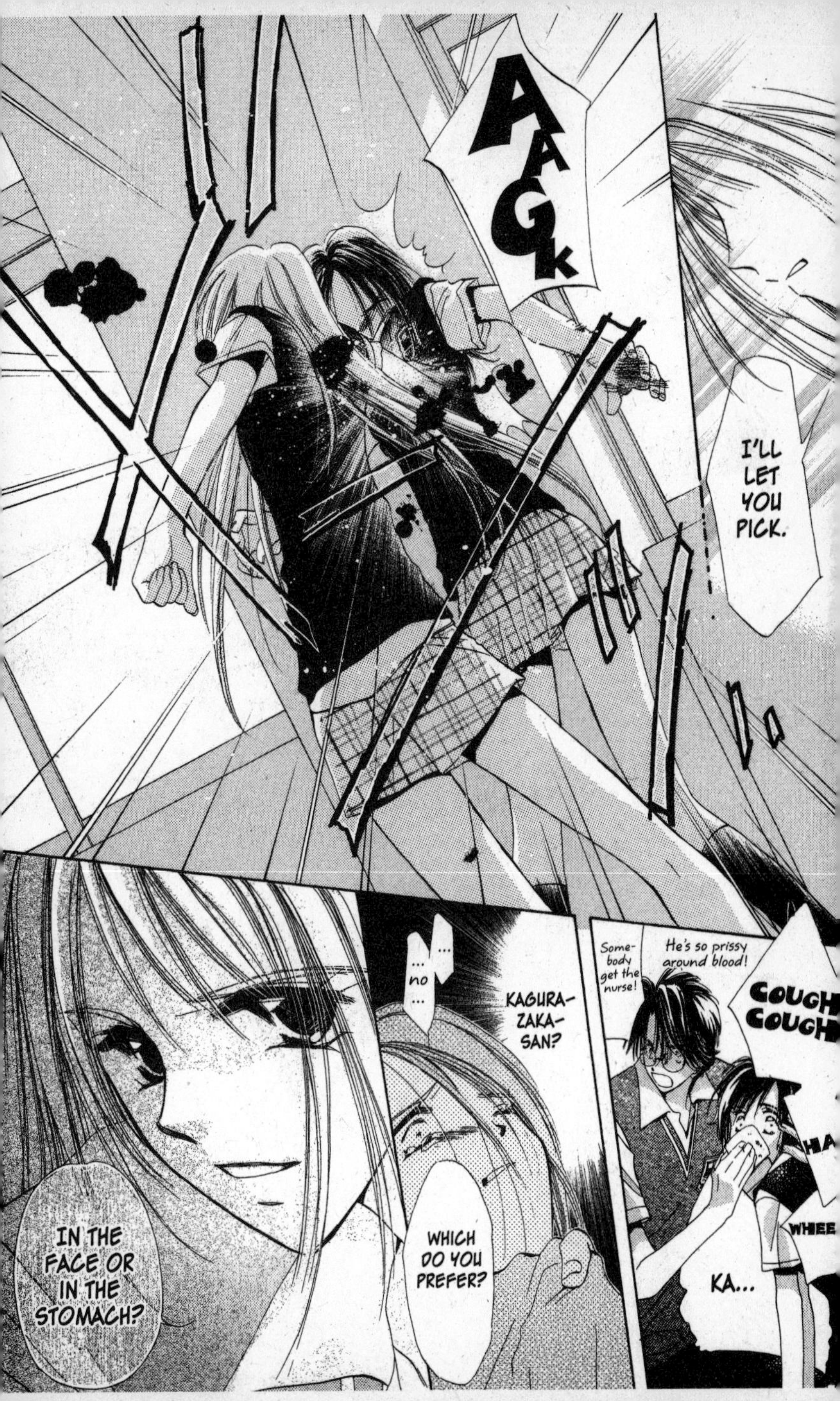
AAGK
I'LL LET YOU PICK.
COUGH COUGH
He's so prissy around blood!
Some-body get the nurse!
HA
WHEE
KA...
... ... no ...
KAGURA-ZAKA-SAN?
WHICH DO YOU PREFER?
IN THE FACE OR IN THE STOMACH?

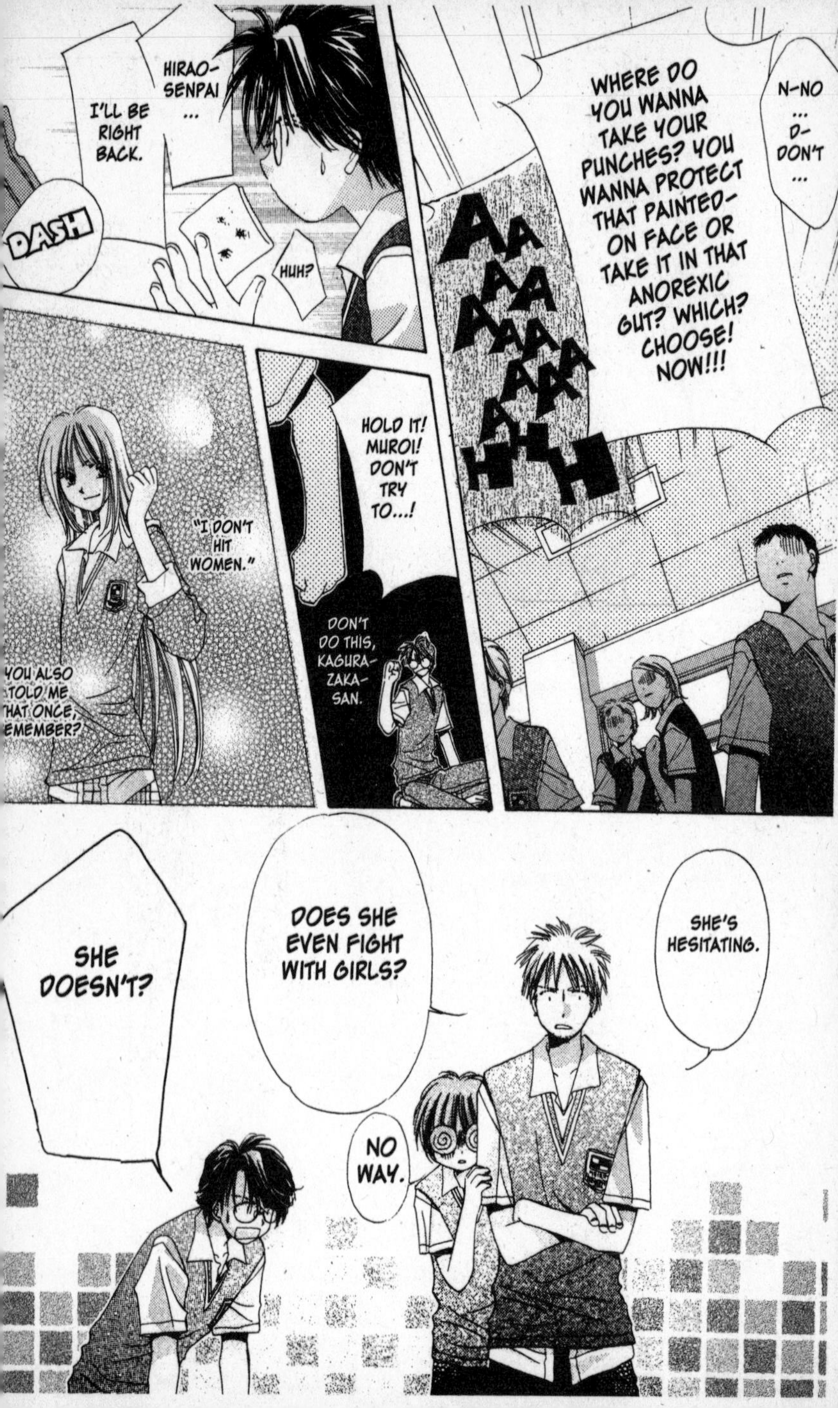
N-NO ... D-DON'T ...
WHERE DO YOU WANNA TAKE YOUR PUNCHES? YOU WANNA PROTECT THAT PAINTED-ON FACE OR TAKE IT IN THAT ANOREXIC GUT? WHICH? CHOOSE! NOW!!!
AAAAAAAAAHHH
HIRAO-SENPAI ...
I'LL BE RIGHT BACK.
HUH?
DASH
HOLD IT! MUROI! DON'T TRY TO...!
DON'T DO THIS, KAGURAZAKA-SAN.
"I DON'T HIT WOMEN."
YOU ALSO TOLD ME THAT ONCE, EMEMBER?
SHE'S HESITATING.
NO WAY.
DOES SHE EVEN FIGHT WITH GIRLS?
SHE DOESN'T?

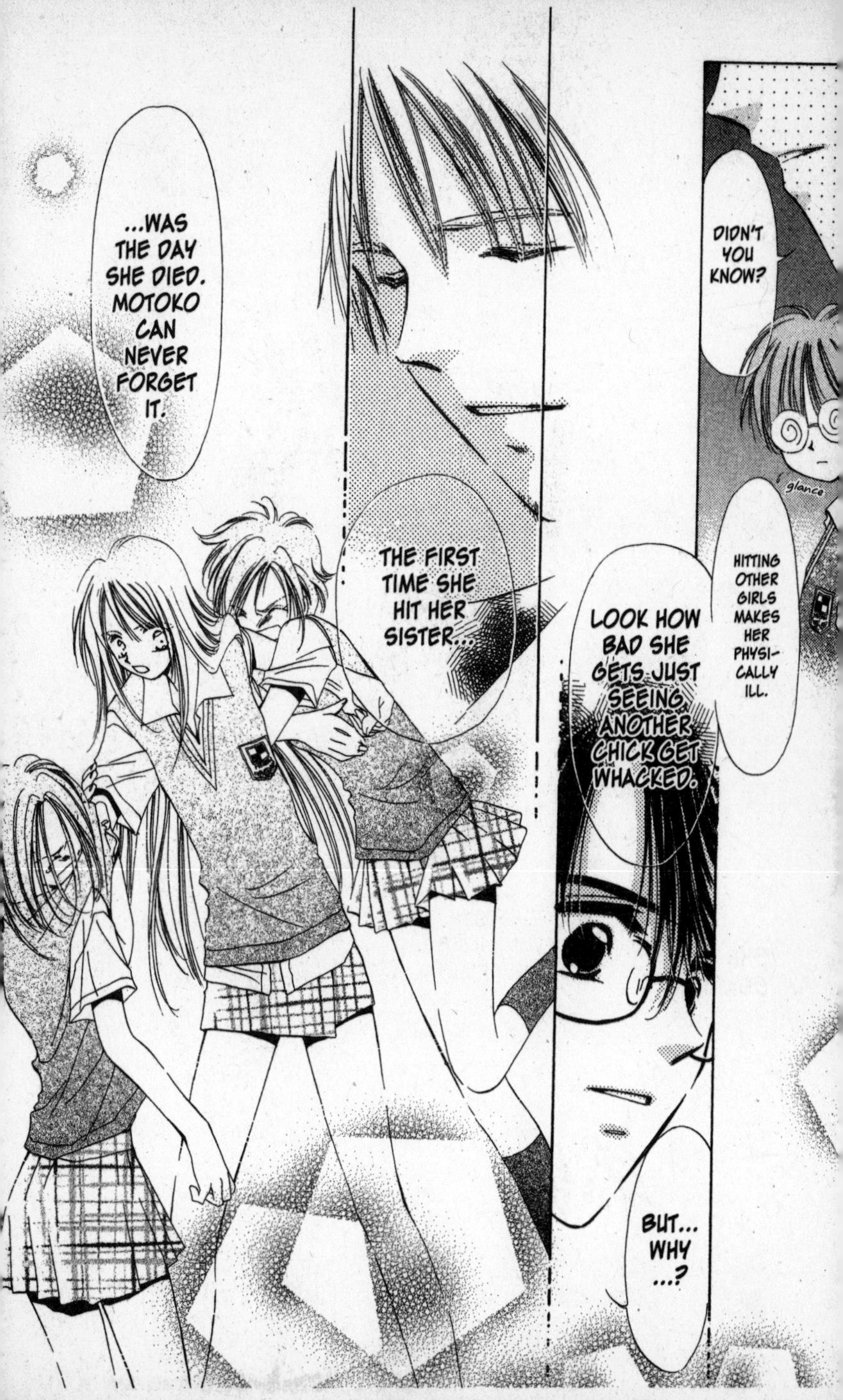
DIDN'T YOU KNOW?
glance
HITTING OTHER GIRLS MAKES HER PHYSICALLY ILL.
LOOK HOW BAD SHE GETS JUST SEEING ANOTHER CHICK GET WHACKED.
BUT... WHY ...?
THE FIRST TIME SHE HIT HER SISTER...
...WAS THE DAY SHE DIED. MOTOKO CAN NEVER FORGET IT.

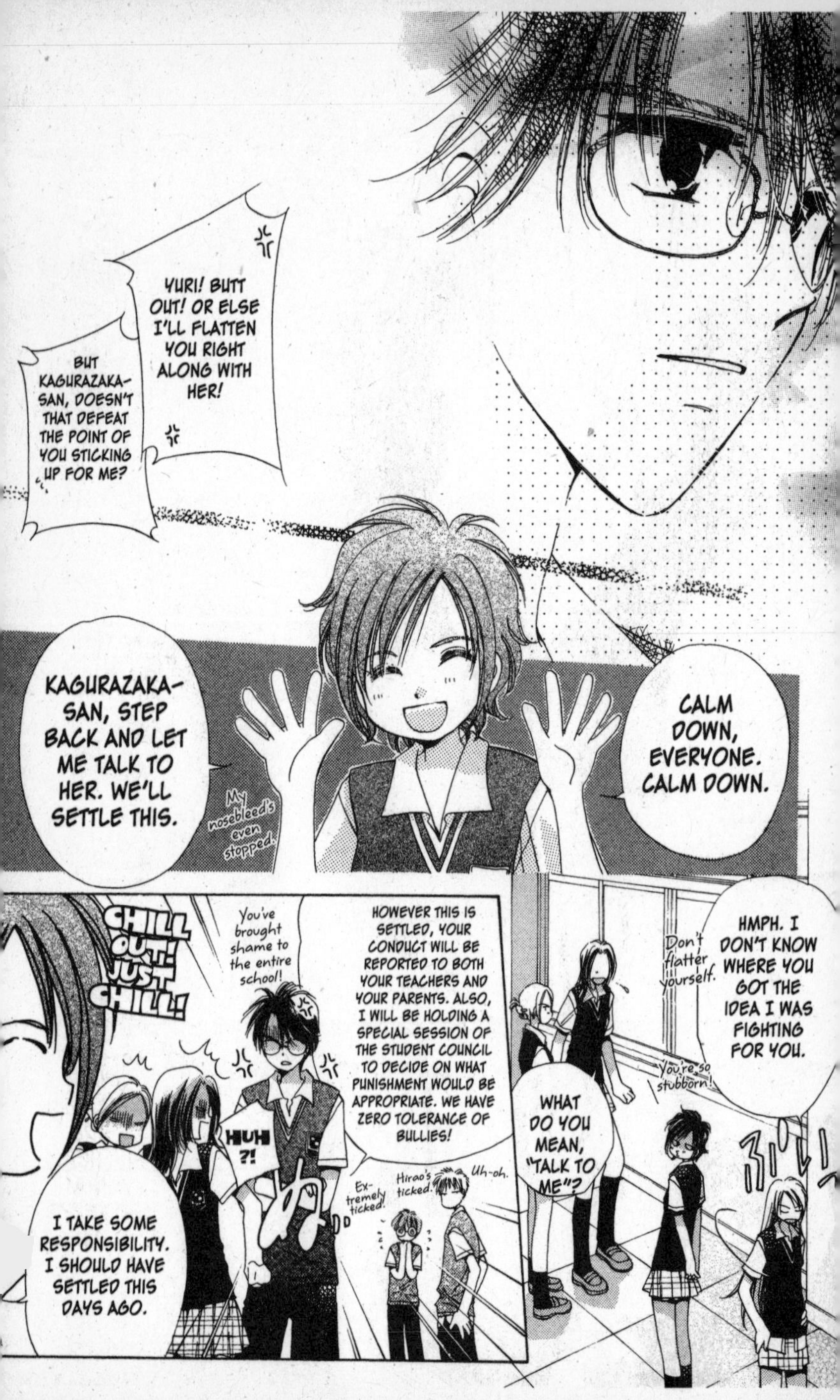

YURI! BUTT OUT! OR ELSE I'LL FLATTEN YOU RIGHT ALONG WITH HER!
BUT KAGURAZAKA-SAN, DOESN'T THAT DEFEAT THE POINT OF YOU STICKING UP FOR ME?
CALM DOWN, EVERYONE. CALM DOWN.
My nosebleed's even stopped.
KAGURAZAKA-SAN, STEP BACK AND LET ME TALK TO HER. WE'LL SETTLE THIS.
HMPH. I DON'T KNOW WHERE YOU GOT THE IDEA I WAS FIGHTING FOR YOU.
Don't flatter yourself.
You're so stubborn!
WHAT DO YOU MEAN, "TALK TO ME"?
HOWEVER THIS IS SETTLED, YOUR CONDUCT WILL BE REPORTED TO BOTH YOUR TEACHERS AND YOUR PARENTS. ALSO, I WILL BE HOLDING A SPECIAL SESSION OF THE STUDENT COUNCIL TO DECIDE ON WHAT PUNISHMENT WOULD BE APPROPRIATE. WE HAVE ZERO TOLERANCE OF BULLIES!
You've brought shame to the entire school!
CHILL OUT! JUST CHILL!
Uh-oh.
Hirao's ticked.
Ex-tremely ticked!
HUH?!
I TAKE SOME RESPONSIBILITY. I SHOULD HAVE SETTLED THIS DAYS AGO.

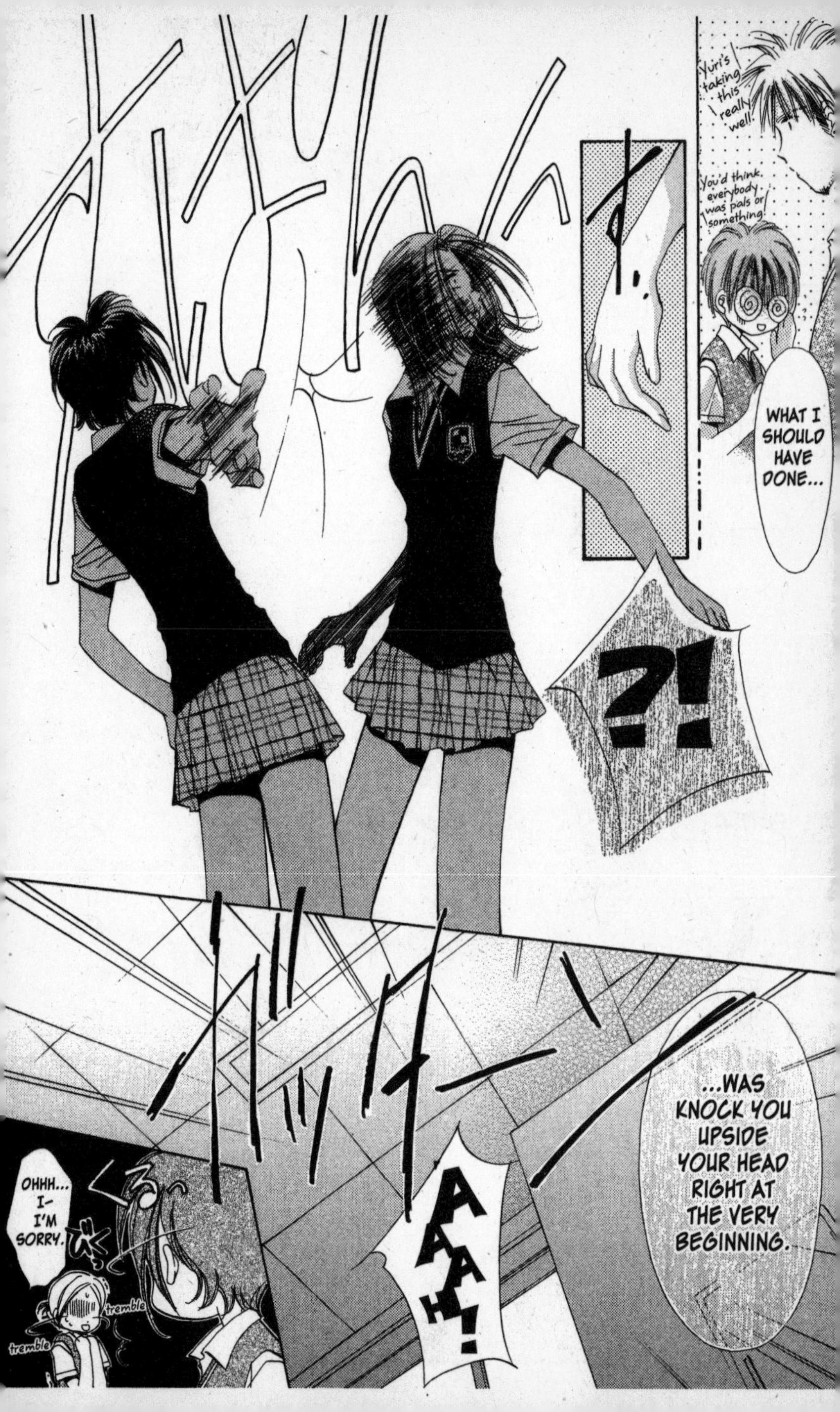
Yuri's taking this really well.
You'd think everybody was pals or something.
WHAT I SHOULD HAVE DONE...
?!
...WAS KNOCK YOU UPSIDE YOUR HEAD RIGHT AT THE VERY BEGINNING.
AAAH!
OHHH... I-I'M SORRY.
tremble
tremble

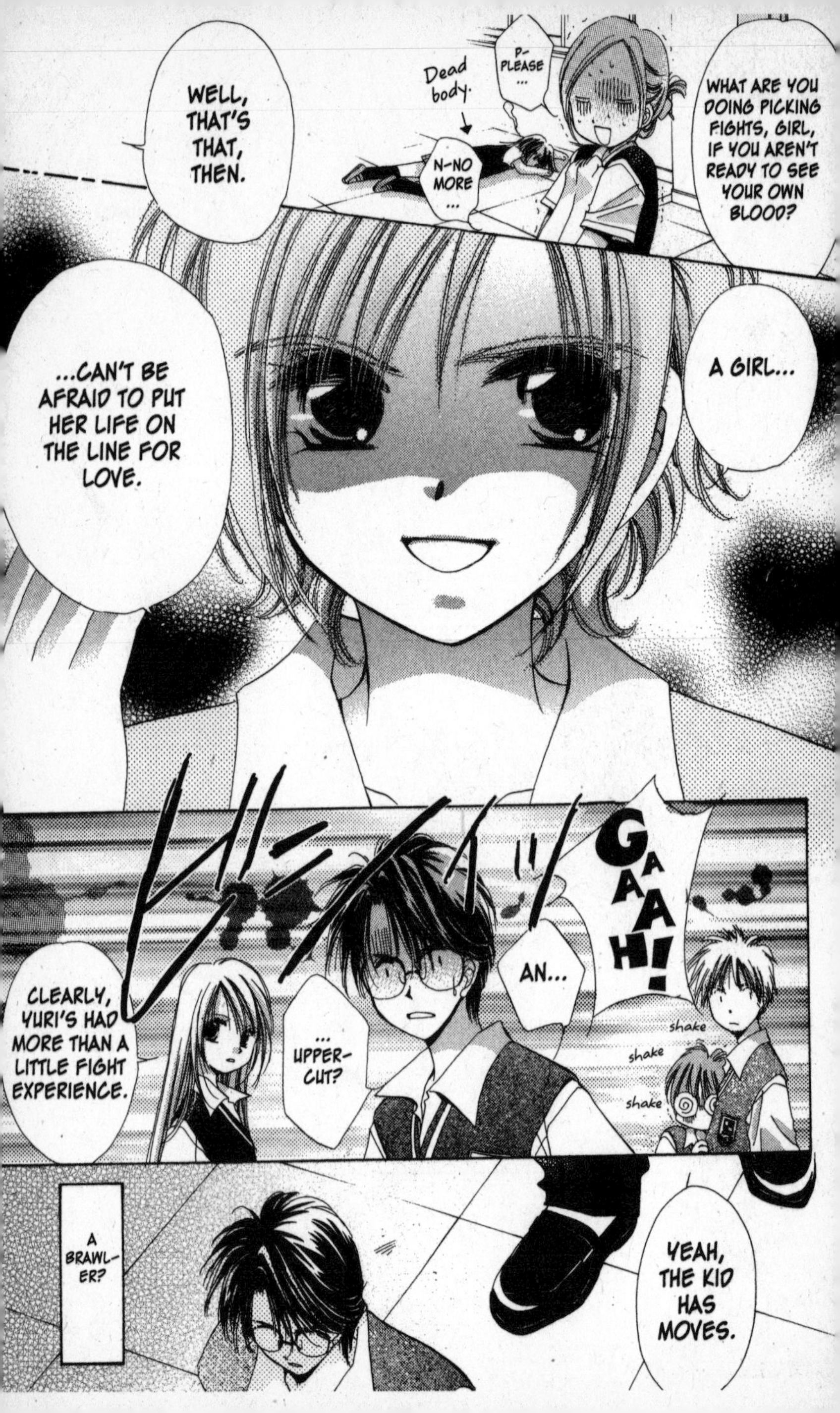

WHAT ARE YOU DOING PICKING FIGHTS, GIRL, IF YOU AREN'T READY TO SEE YOUR OWN BLOOD?
P-PLEASE...
Dead body.
N-NO MORE...
WELL, THAT'S THAT, THEN.
A GIRL...
...CAN'T BE AFRAID TO PUT HER LIFE ON THE LINE FOR LOVE.
GAAAH!
AN...
shake
shake
shake
...UPPERCUT?
CLEARLY, YURI'S HAD MORE THAN A LITTLE FIGHT EXPERIENCE.
YEAH, THE KID HAS MOVES.
A BRAWLER?

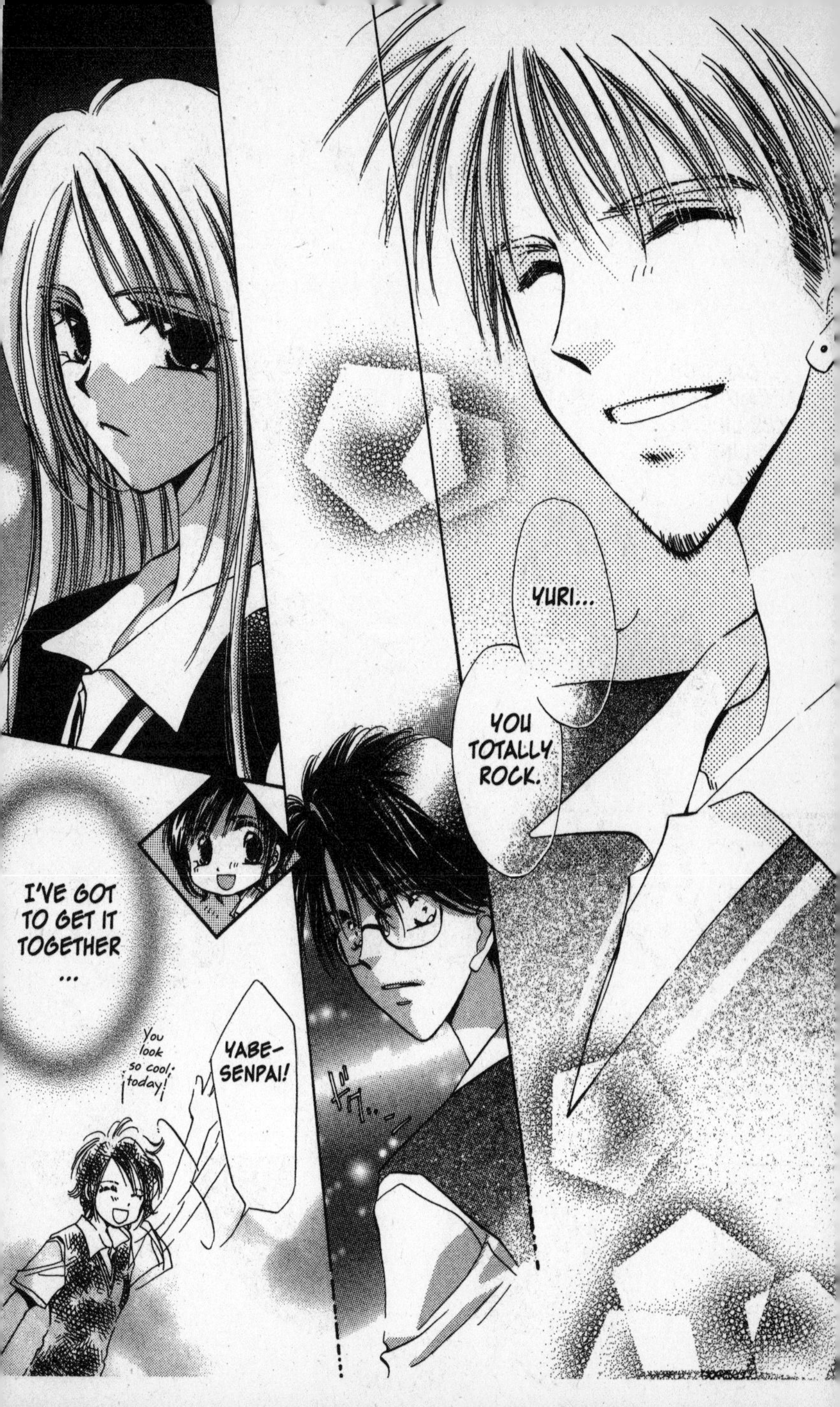
YURI...
YOU TOTALLY ROCK.
I'VE GOT TO GET IT TOGETHER ...
YABE-SENPAI!
You look so cool today!

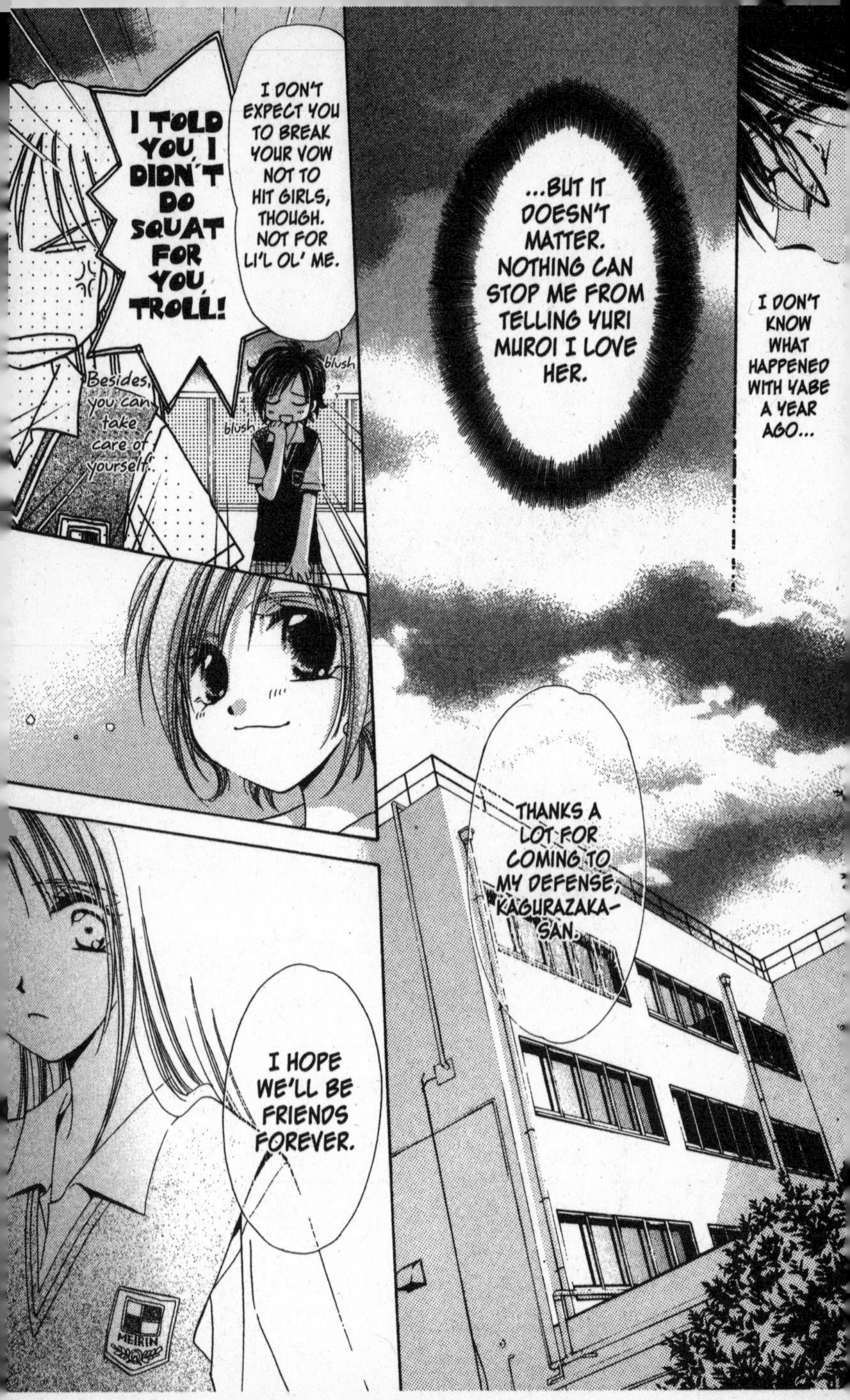
I DON'T KNOW WHAT HAPPENED WITH YABE A YEAR AGO...
...BUT IT DOESN'T MATTER. NOTHING CAN STOP ME FROM TELLING YURI MUROI I LOVE HER.
THANKS A LOT FOR COMING TO MY DEFENSE, KAGURAZAKA-SAN.
I DON'T EXPECT YOU TO BREAK YOUR VOW NOT TO HIT GIRLS, THOUGH. NOT FOR LI'L OL' ME.
blush
blush
I TOLD YOU, I DIDN'T DO SQUAT FOR YOU, TROLL!
Besides, you can take care of yourself.
I HOPE WE'LL BE FRIENDS FOREVER.
MEIRIN

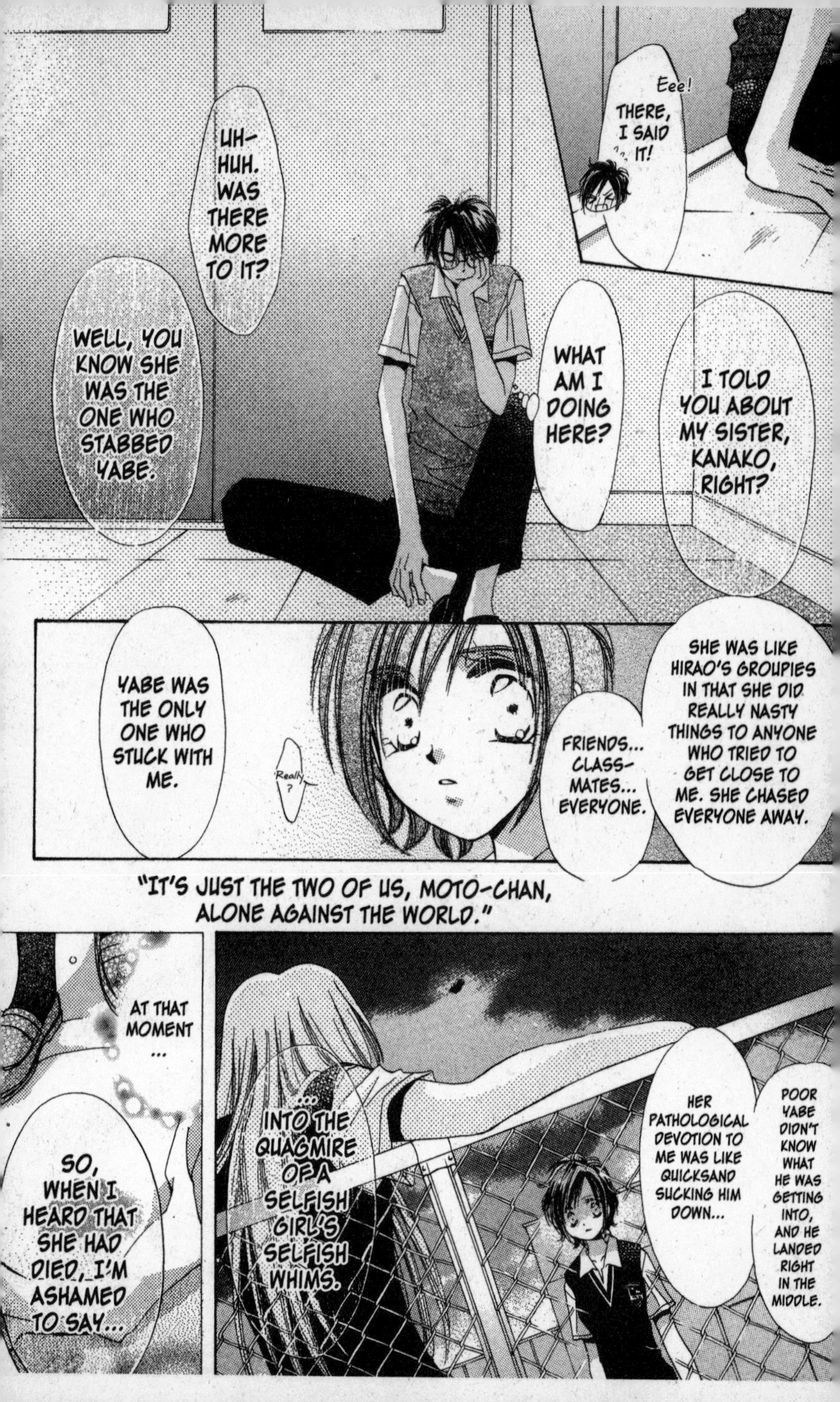
Eee!
THERE, I SAID IT!
I TOLD YOU ABOUT MY SISTER, KANAKO, RIGHT?
WHAT AM I DOING HERE?
UH-HUH. WAS THERE MORE TO IT?
WELL, YOU KNOW SHE WAS THE ONE WHO STABBED YABE.
SHE WAS LIKE HIRAO'S GROUPIES IN THAT SHE DID REALLY NASTY THINGS TO ANYONE WHO TRIED TO GET CLOSE TO ME. SHE CHASED EVERYONE AWAY.
FRIENDS... CLASSMATES... EVERYONE.
Really?
YABE WAS THE ONLY ONE WHO STUCK WITH ME.
"IT'S JUST THE TWO OF US, MOTO-CHAN, ALONE AGAINST THE WORLD."
POOR YABE DIDN'T KNOW WHAT HE WAS GETTING INTO, AND HE LANDED RIGHT IN THE MIDDLE.
HER PATHOLOGICAL DEVOTION TO ME WAS LIKE QUICKSAND SUCKING HIM DOWN...
...INTO THE QUAGMIRE OF A SELFISH GIRL'S SELFISH WHIMS.
AT THAT MOMENT...
SO, WHEN I HEARD THAT SHE HAD DIED, I'M ASHAMED TO SAY...

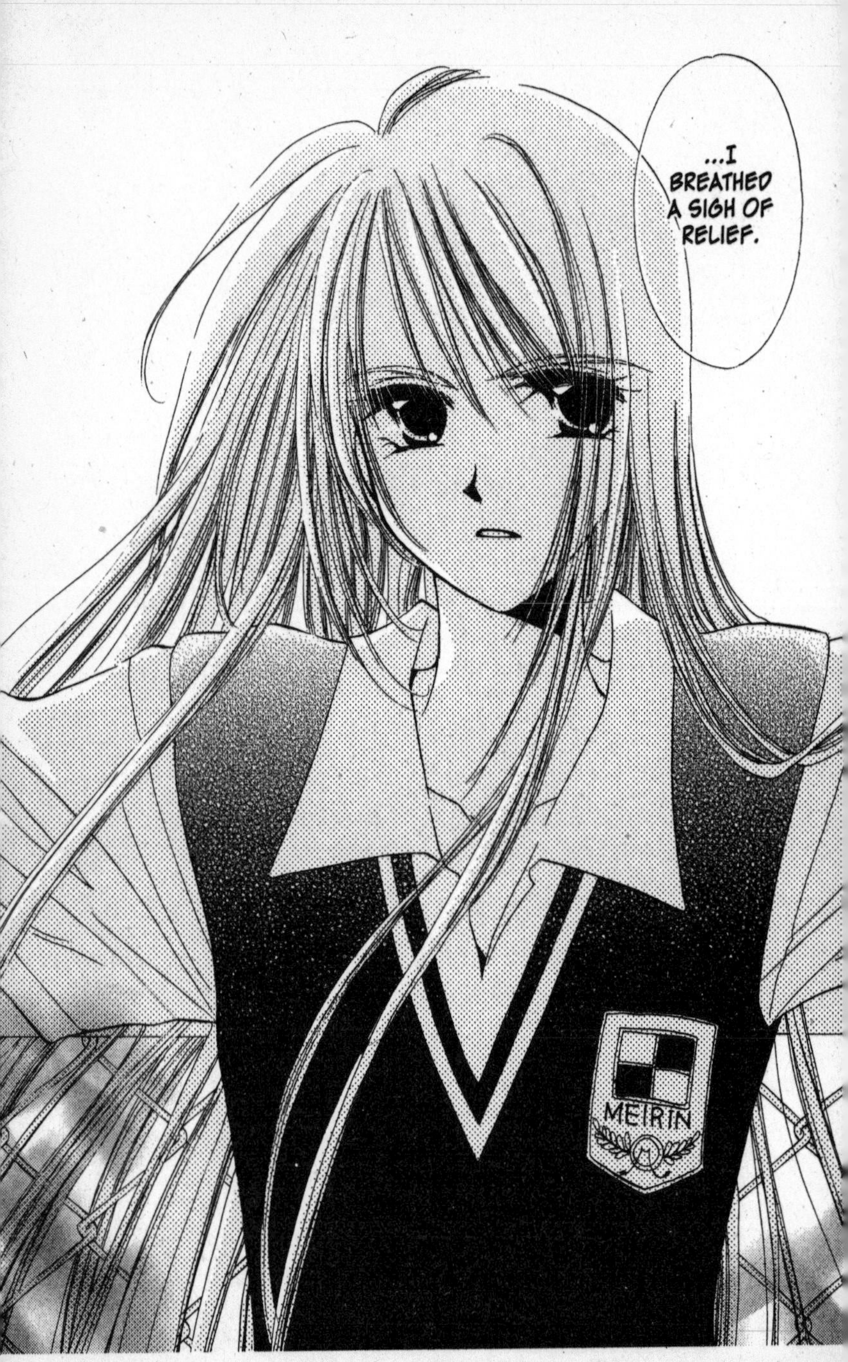
...I BREATHED A SIGH OF RELIEF.
MEIRIN

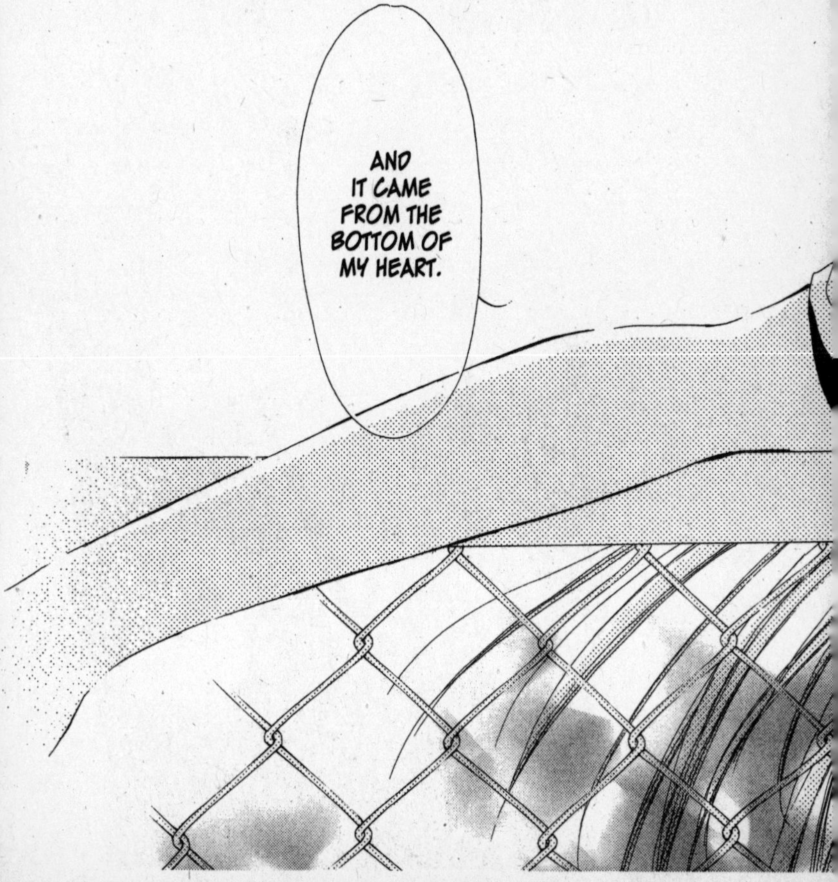
AND IT CAME FROM THE BOTTOM OF MY HEART.

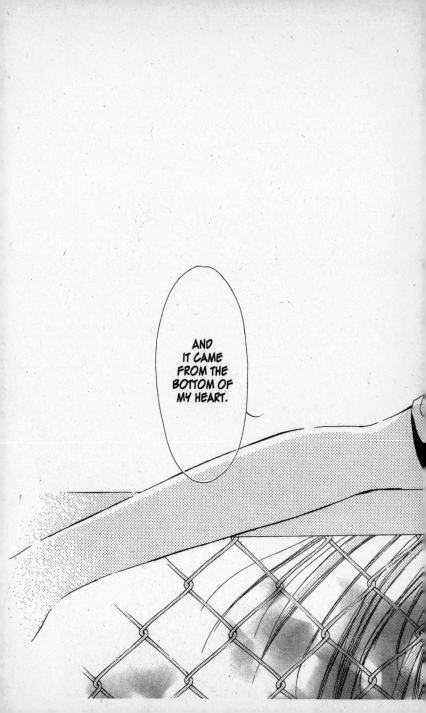

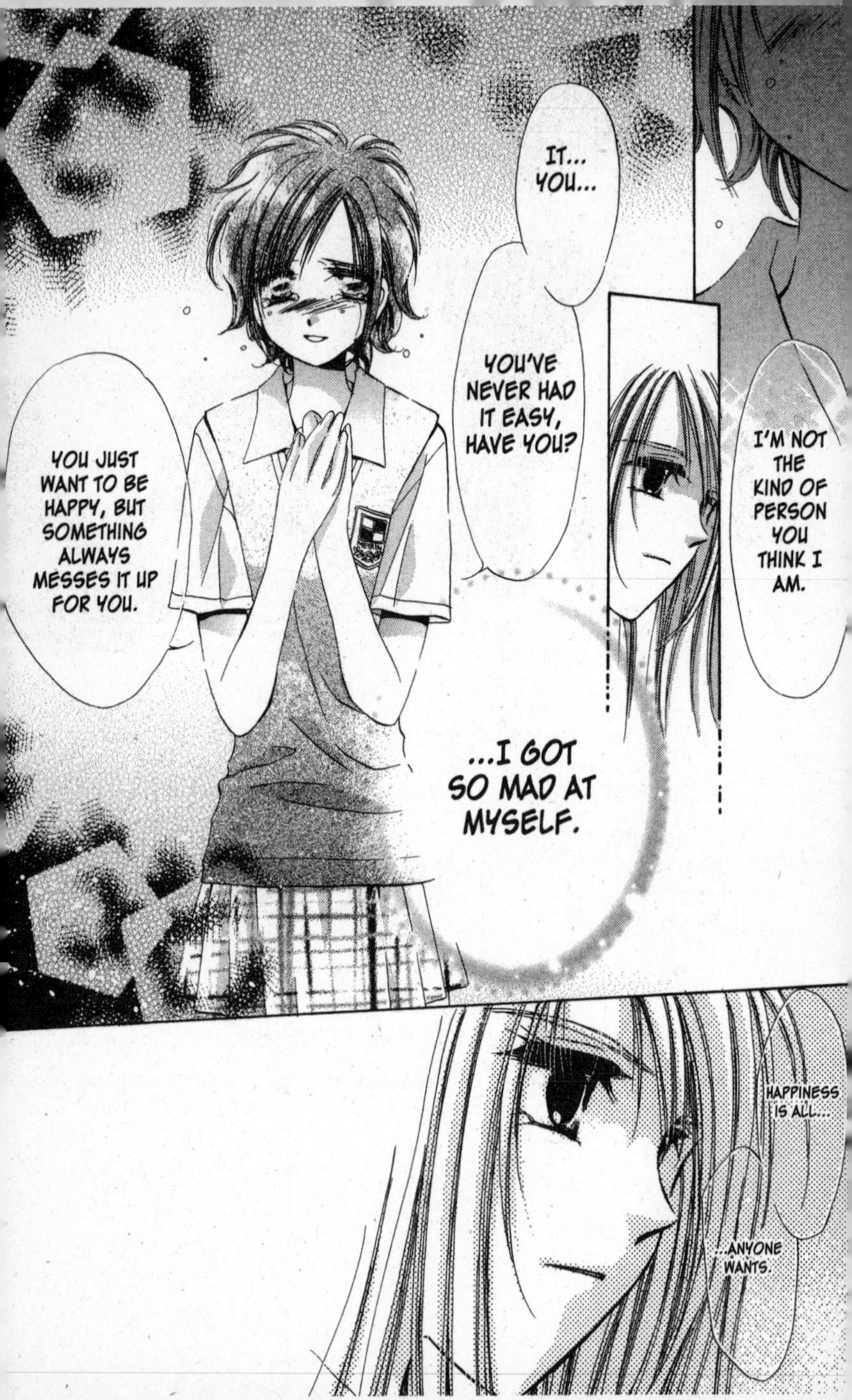
I'M NOT THE KIND OF PERSON YOU THINK I AM.
IT... YOU...
YOU'VE NEVER HAD IT EASY, HAVE YOU?
YOU JUST WANT TO BE HAPPY, BUT SOMETHING ALWAYS MESSES IT UP FOR YOU.
...I GOT SO MAD AT MYSELF.
HAPPINESS IS ALL...
...ANYONE WANTS.

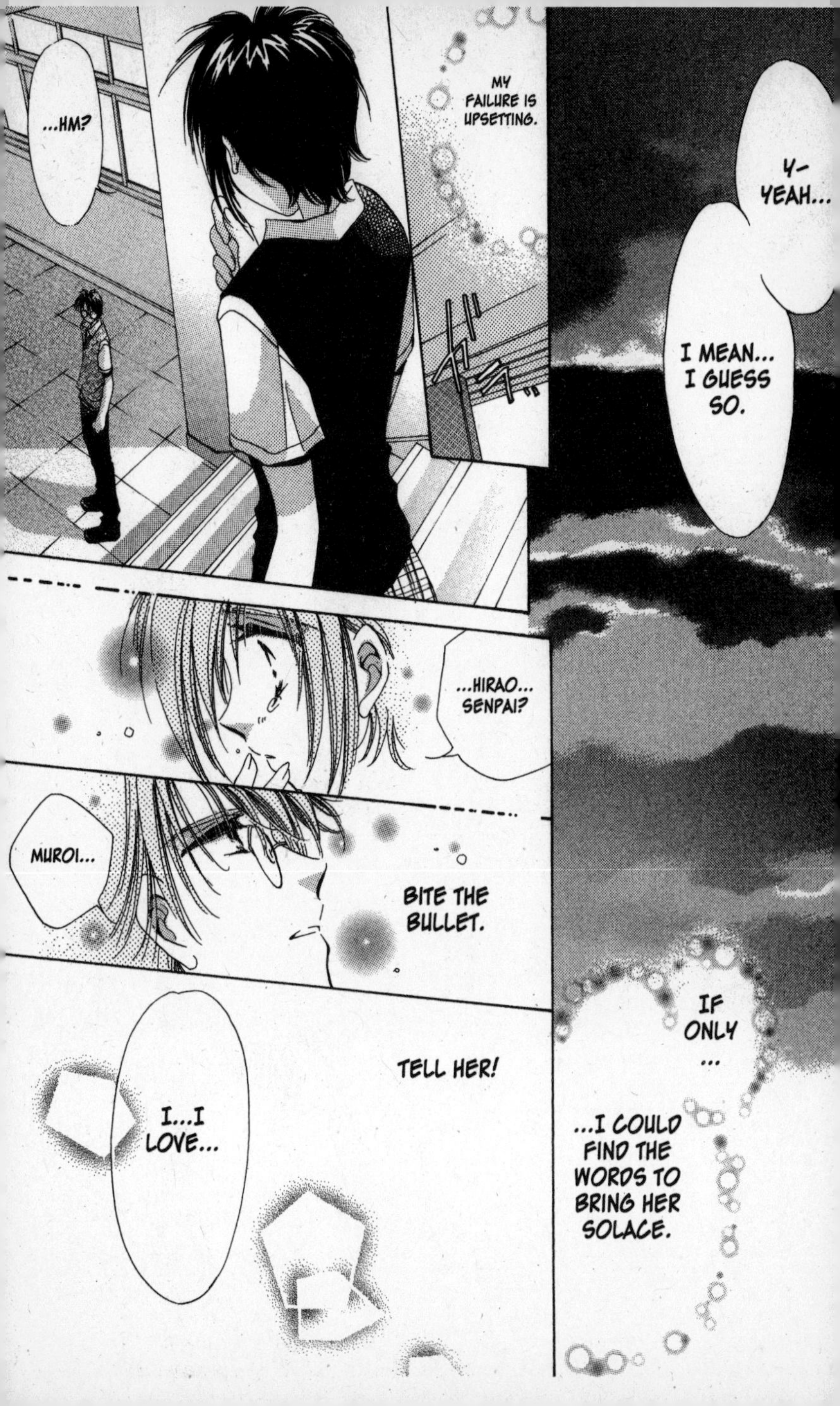
Y-YEAH...
I MEAN... I GUESS SO.
IF ONLY ...
...I COULD FIND THE WORDS TO BRING HER SOLACE.
MY FAILURE IS UPSETTING.
...HM?
...HIRAO... SENPAI?
MUROI...
BITE THE BULLET.
TELL HER!
I...I LOVE...

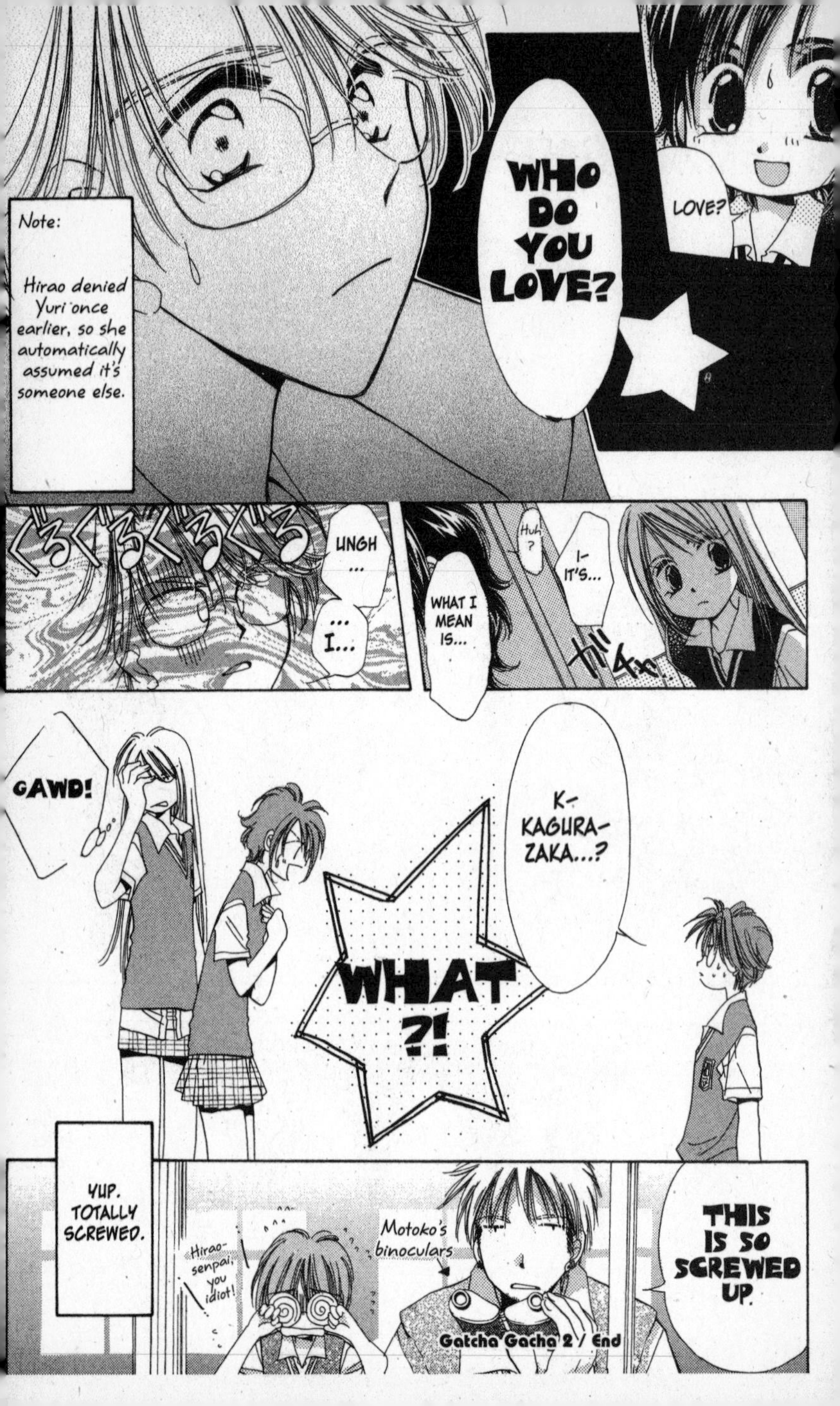
LOVE?
WHO DO YOU LOVE?
Note: Hirao denied Yuri once earlier, so she automatically assumed it's someone else.
Huh ?
I- IT'S...
WHAT I MEAN IS...
UNGH ...
... I...
ぐるぐるぐるぐる
K- KAGURA-ZAKA...?
WHAT ?!
GAWD!
THIS IS SO SCREWED UP.
Motoko's binoculars
Hirao-senpai, you idiot!
YUP. TOTALLY SCREWED.
Gatcha Gacha 2 / End

P.S
TACHIBANA TELLS IT LIKE IT IS

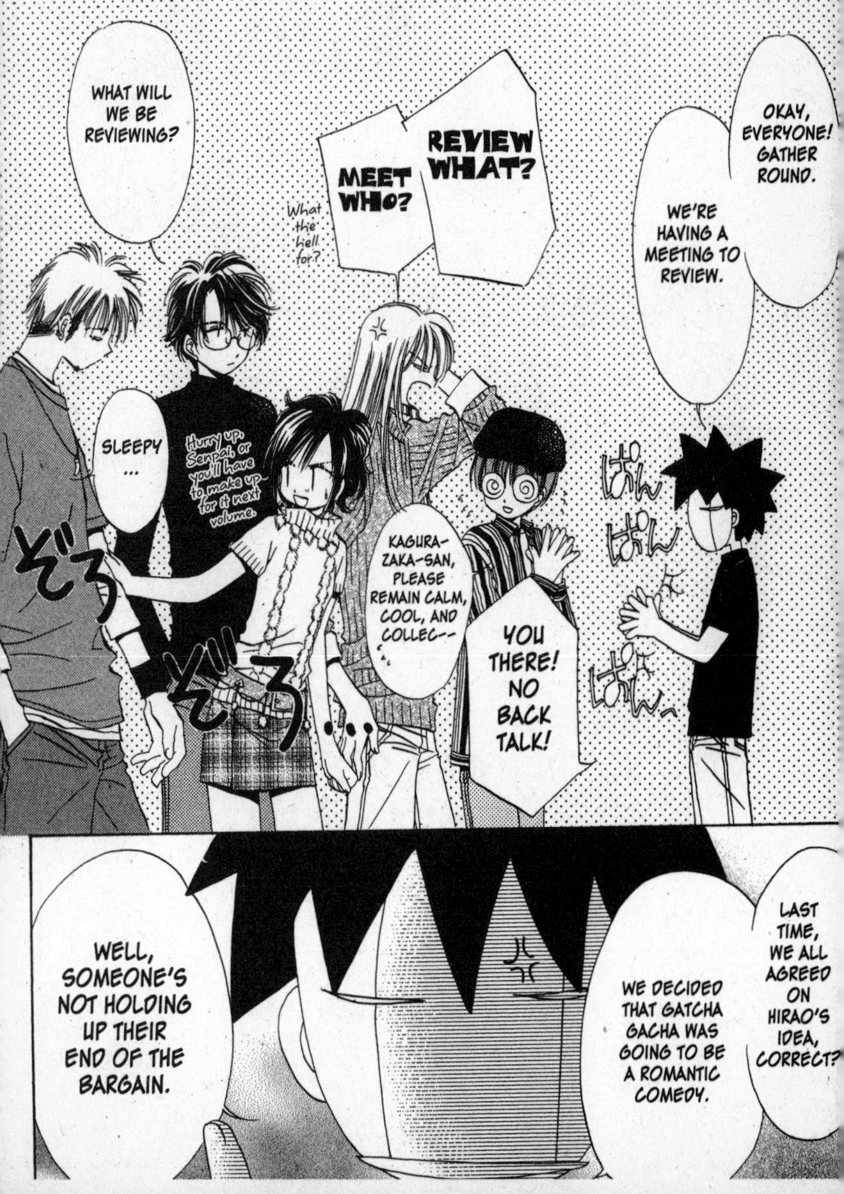
OKAY, EVERYONE! GATHER ROUND.
WE'RE HAVING A MEETING TO REVIEW.
ぱん
ぱん
ぱん
REVIEW WHAT?
MEET WHO?
What the hell for?
WHAT WILL WE BE REVIEWING?
YOU THERE! NO BACK TALK!
KAGURAZAKA-SAN, PLEASE REMAIN CALM, COOL, AND COLLEC--
...
Hurry up, Senpai, or you'll have to make up for it next volume.
SLEEPY ...
ぞろ
ぞろ
LAST TIME, WE ALL AGREED ON HIRAO'S IDEA, CORRECT?
WE DECIDED THAT GATCHA GACHA WAS GOING TO BE A ROMANTIC COMEDY.
WELL, SOMEONE'S NOT HOLDING UP THEIR END OF THE BARGAIN.

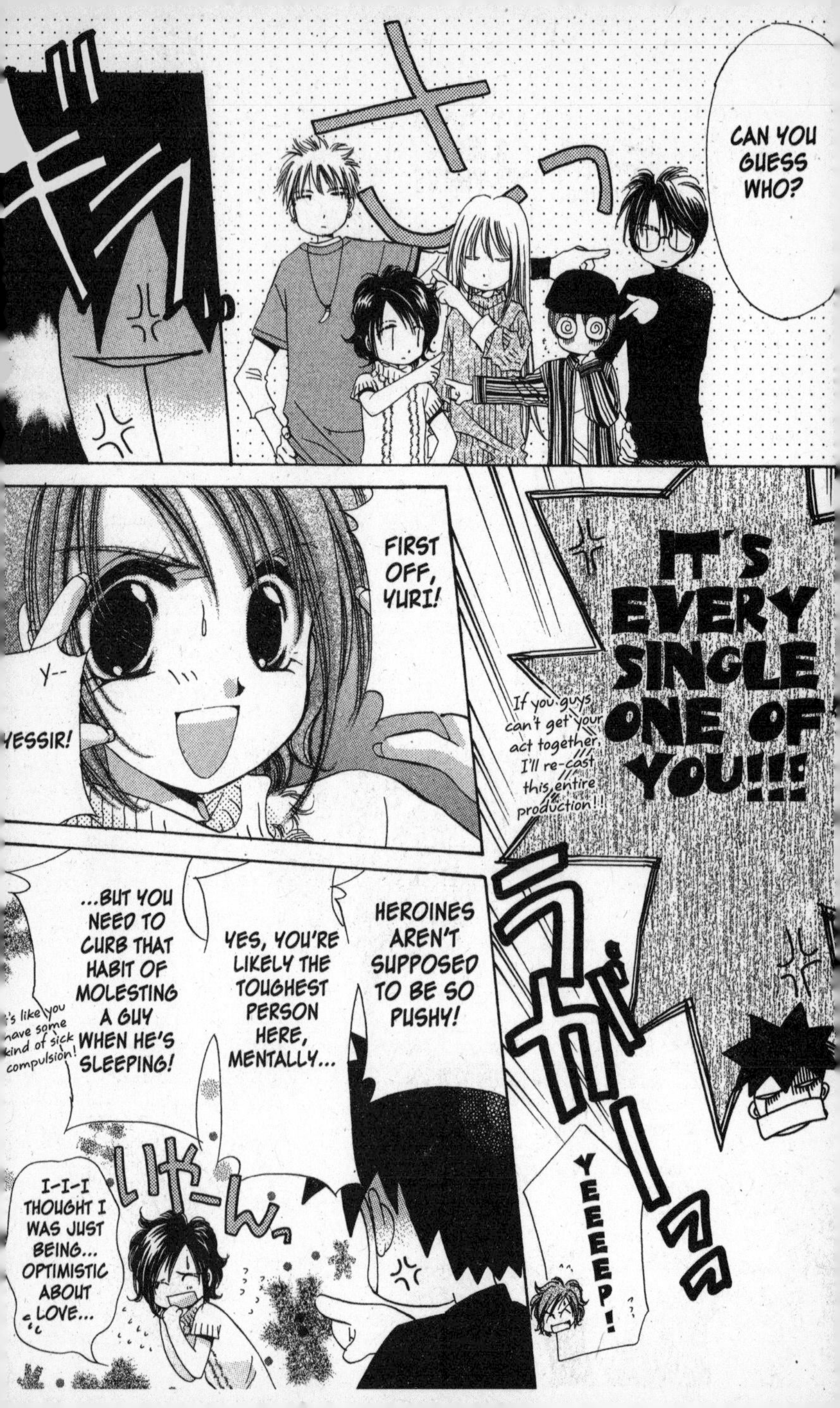
CAN YOU GUESS WHO?
IT'S EVERY SINGLE ONE OF YOU!!!
If you guys can't get your act together, I'll re-cast this entire production!
FIRST OFF, YURI!
Y--
YESSIR!
YEEEEP!
HEROINES AREN'T SUPPOSED TO BE SO PUSHY!
YES, YOU'RE LIKELY THE TOUGHEST PERSON HERE, MENTALLY...
...BUT YOU NEED TO CURB THAT HABIT OF MOLESTING A GUY WHEN HE'S SLEEPING!
's like you have some kind of sick compulsion!
I-I-I THOUGHT I WAS JUST BEING... OPTIMISTIC ABOUT LOVE...

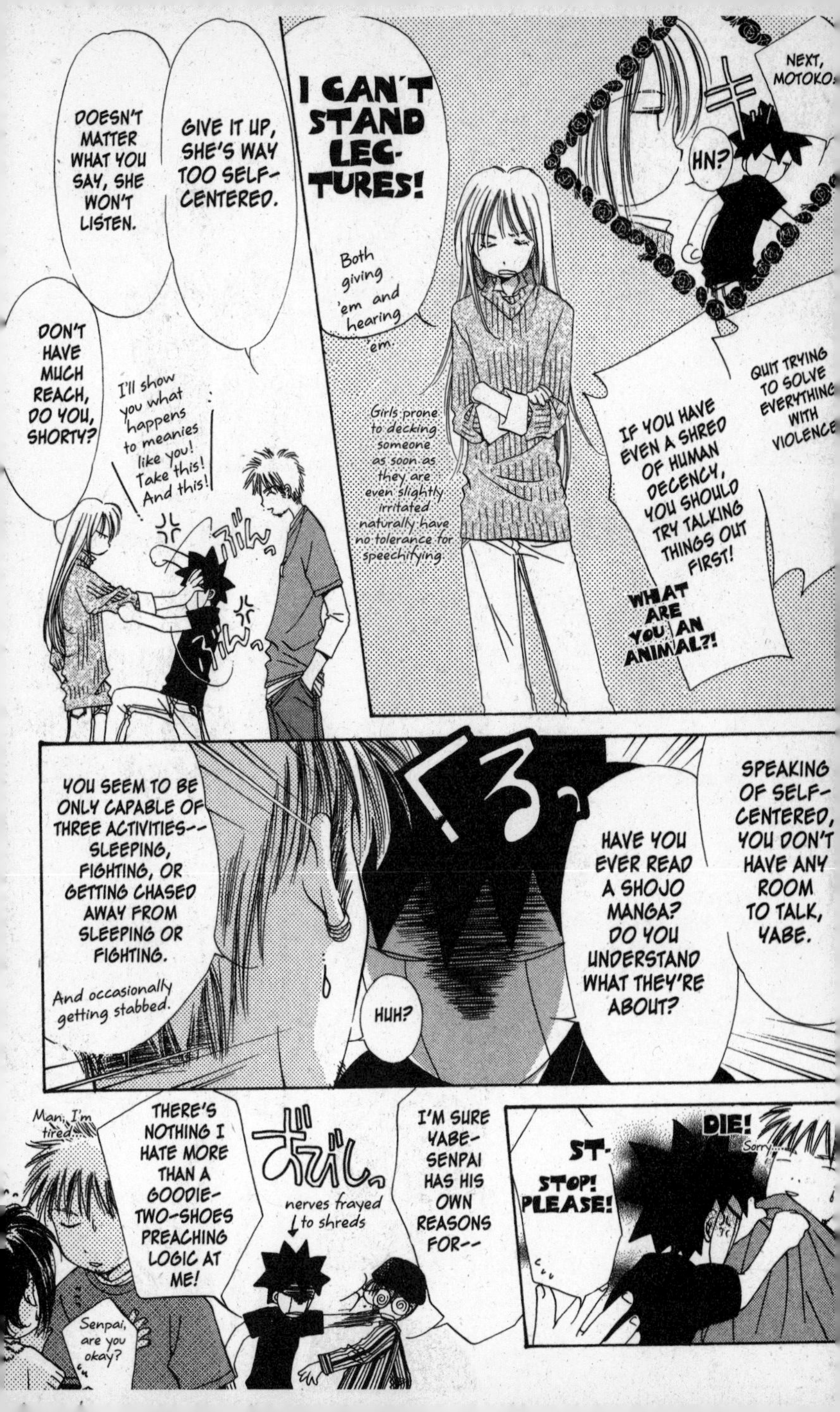
NEXT, MOTOKO:
HN?
QUIT TRYING TO SOLVE EVERYTHING WITH VIOLENCE
IF YOU HAVE EVEN A SHRED OF HUMAN DECENCY, YOU SHOULD TRY TALKING THINGS OUT FIRST!
WHAT ARE YOU AN ANIMAL?!
I CAN'T STAND LEC-TURES!
Both giving 'em and hearing 'em.
Girls prone to decking someone as soon as they are even slightly irritated naturally have no tolerance for speechifying.
GIVE IT UP, SHE'S WAY TOO SELF-CENTERED.
DOESN'T MATTER WHAT YOU SAY, SHE WON'T LISTEN.
DON'T HAVE MUCH REACH, DO YOU, SHORTY?
I'll show you what happens to meanies like you! Take this! And this!
SPEAKING OF SELF-CENTERED, YOU DON'T HAVE ANY ROOM TO TALK, YABE.
HAVE YOU EVER READ A SHOJO MANGA? DO YOU UNDERSTAND WHAT THEY'RE ABOUT?
HUH?
YOU SEEM TO BE ONLY CAPABLE OF THREE ACTIVITIES-- SLEEPING, FIGHTING, OR GETTING CHASED AWAY FROM SLEEPING OR FIGHTING.
And occasionally getting stabbed.
DIE!
Sorry...
ST- STOP! PLEASE!
I'M SURE YABE-SENPAI HAS HIS OWN REASONS FOR--
nerves frayed to shreds
THERE'S NOTHING I HATE MORE THAN A GOODIE-TWO-SHOES PREACHING LOGIC AT ME!
Man, I'm tired...
Senpai, are you okay?

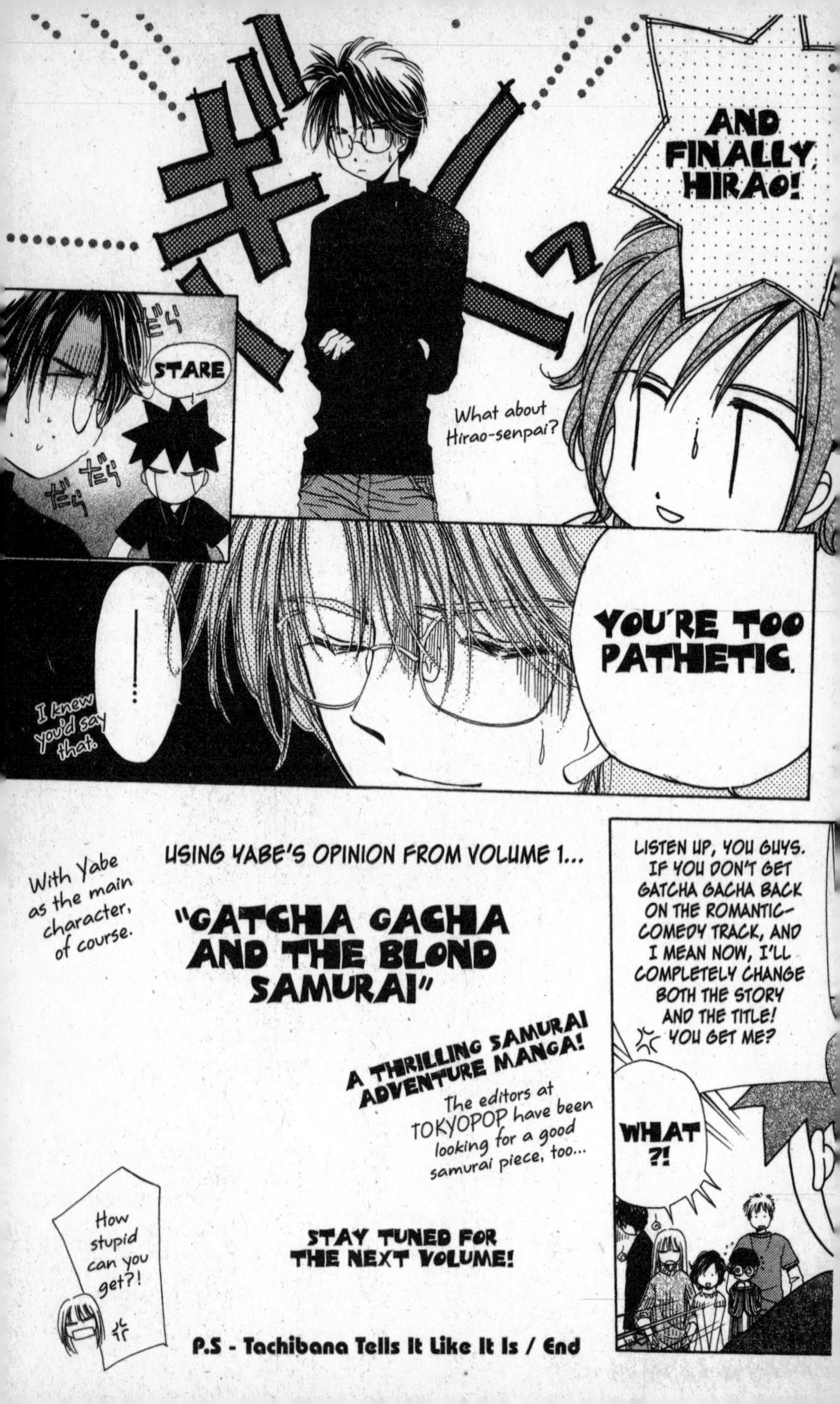
AND FINALLY, HIRAO!
What about Hirao-senpai?
STARE
YOU'RE TOO PATHETIC.
...!
I knew you'd say that.
LISTEN UP, YOU GUYS. IF YOU DON'T GET GATCHA GACHA BACK ON THE ROMANTIC-COMEDY TRACK, AND I MEAN NOW, I'LL COMPLETELY CHANGE BOTH THE STORY AND THE TITLE! YOU GET ME?
WHAT?!
USING YABE'S OPINION FROM VOLUME 1...
With Yabe as the main character, of course.
"GATCHA GACHA AND THE BLOND SAMURAI"
A THRILLING SAMURAI ADVENTURE MANGA!
The editors at TOKYOPOP have been looking for a good samurai piece, too...
How stupid can you get?!
STAY TUNED FOR THE NEXT VOLUME!
P.S - Tachibana Tells It Like It Is / End

Volume 3 is coming in just a few short months!

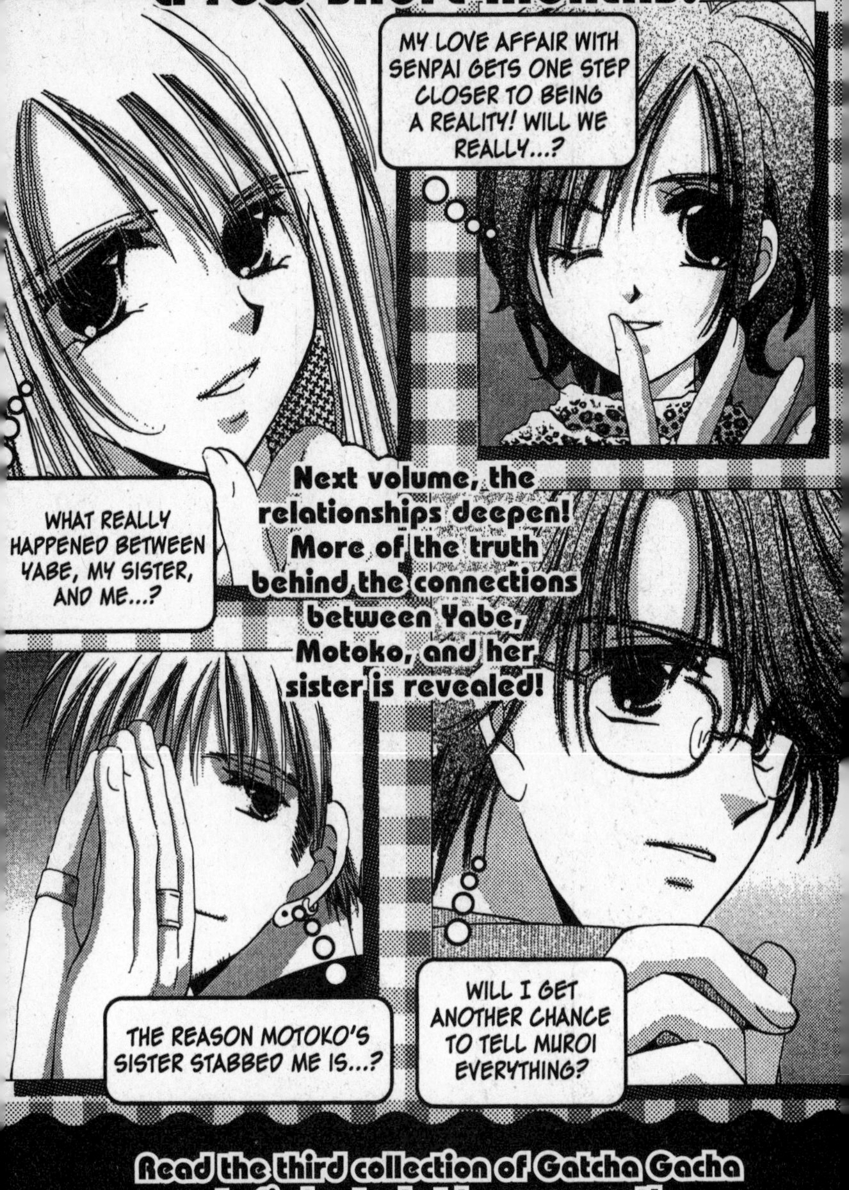
MY LOVE AFFAIR WITH SENPAI GETS ONE STEP CLOSER TO BEING A REALITY! WILL WE REALLY...?
WHAT REALLY HAPPENED BETWEEN YABE, MY SISTER, AND ME...?
Next volume, the relationships deepen! More of the truth behind the connections between Yabe, Motoko, and her sister is revealed!
WILL I GET ANOTHER CHANCE TO TELL MUROI EVERYTHING?
THE REASON MOTOKO'S SISTER STABBED ME IS...?

Read the third collection of Gatcha Gacha to find out what happens next!

TOKYOPOP MANGA SUPPLEMENT

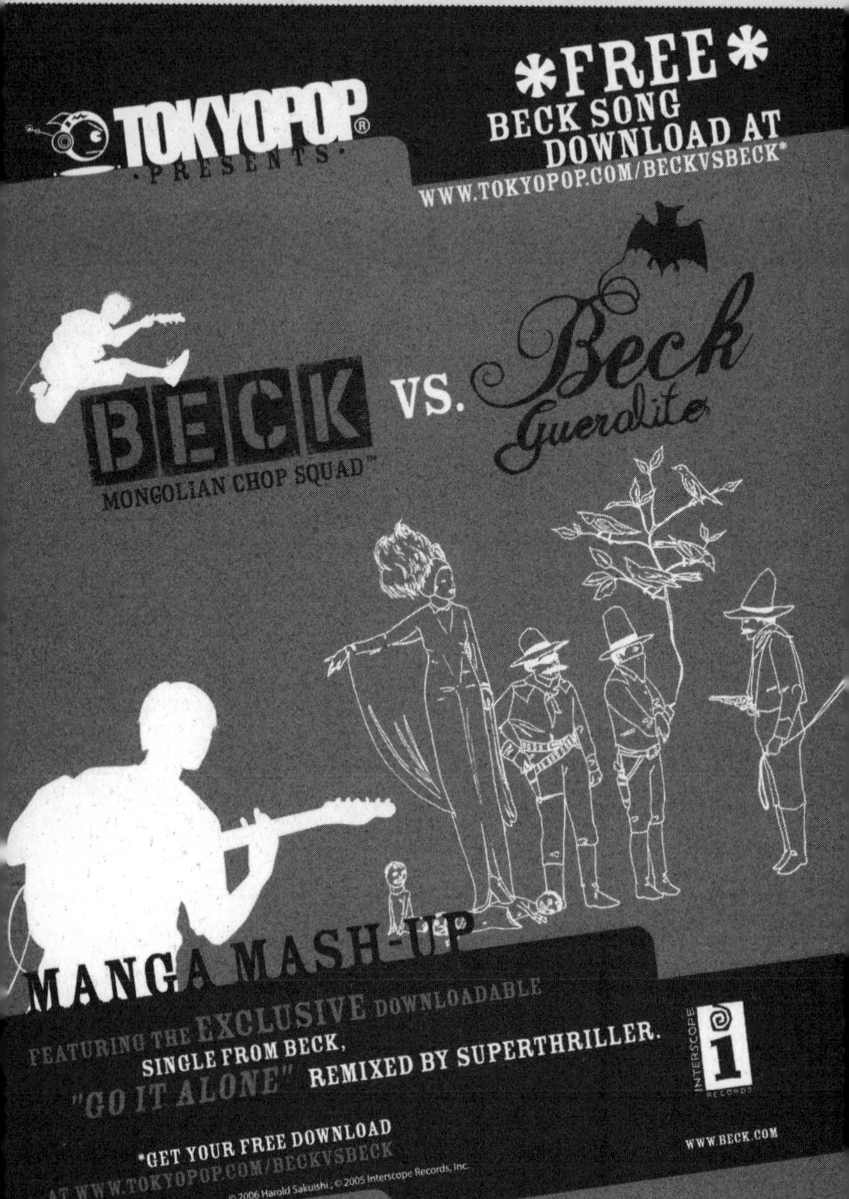
TOKYOPOP® PRESENTS
FREE
BECK SONG
DOWNLOAD AT
WWW.TOKYOPOP.COM/BECKVSBECK*
BECK
MONGOLIAN CHOP SQUAD™
VS.
Beck
Guerolito
MANGA MASH-UP
FEATURING THE EXCLUSIVE DOWNLOADABLE
SINGLE FROM BECK,
"GO IT ALONE" REMIXED BY SUPERTHRILLER.
INTERSCOPE
RECORDS
*GET YOUR FREE DOWNLOAD
AT WWW.TOKYOPOP.COM/BECKVSBECK
© 2006 Harold Sakuishi., © 2005 Interscope Records, Inc.
WWW.BECK.COM

FOR MORE INFORMATION VISIT: WWW.TOKYOPOP.COM

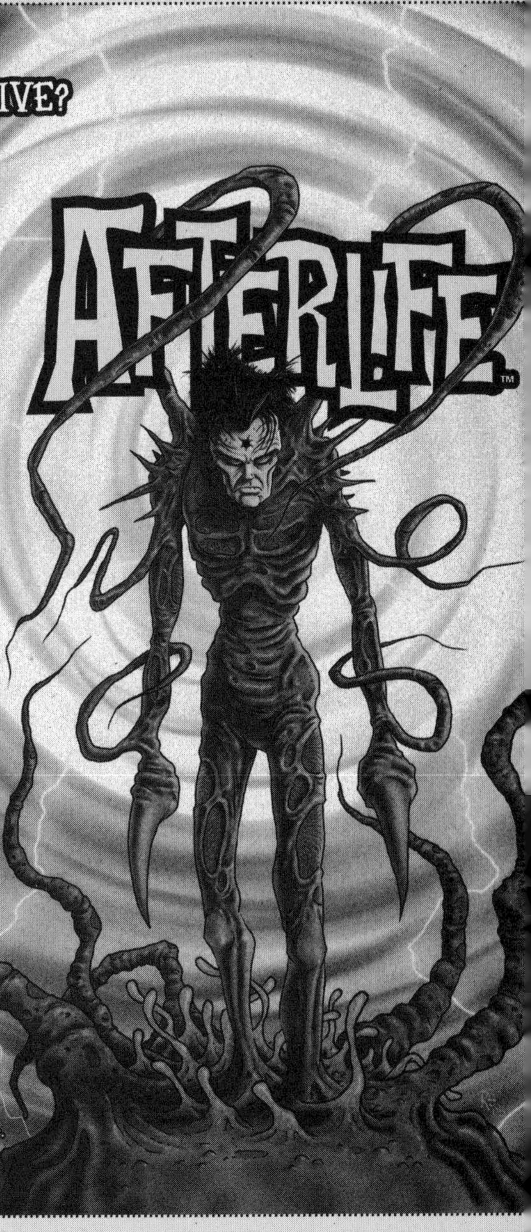
AFTERLIFE™

STOP!

This is the back of the book.
You wouldn't want to spoil a great ending!

This book is printed "manga-style," in the authentic Japanese right-to-left format. Since none of the artwork has been flipped or altered, readers get to experience the story just as the creator intended. You've been asking for it, so TOKYOPOP® delivered: authentic, hot-off-the-press, and far more fun!

DIRECTIONS

If this is your first time reading manga-style, here's a quick guide to help you understand how it works.

It's easy... just start in the top right panel and follow the numbers. Have fun, and look for more 100% authentic manga from TOKYOPOP®!